SELinux System Administration
Third Edition

Implement mandatory access control to secure
applications, users, and information flows on Linux

Sven Vermeulen

BIRMINGHAM—MUMBAI

SELinux System Administration
Third Edition

Commissioning Editor: Vijin Boricha
Acquisition Editor: Shrilekha Inani
Senior Editor: Arun Nadar
Content Development Editor: Romy Dias
Technical Editor: Soham Amburle
Copy Editor: Safis Editing
Project Coordinator: Neil Dmello
Proofreader: Safis Editing
Indexer: Pratik Shirodkar
Production Designer: Vijay Kamble

First published: September 2013
Second edition: December 2016
Third edition: November 2020

Production reference: 1041120

Published by Packt Publishing Ltd.
Livery Place
35 Livery Street
Birmingham
B3 2PB, UK.

ISBN 978-1-80020-147-7

www.packt.com

To the doctors, nurses, public health officials, and first responders who are protecting us from COVID-19.

`Packt.com`

Subscribe to our online digital library for full access to over 7,000 books and videos, as well as industry leading tools to help you plan your personal development and advance your career. For more information, please visit our website.

Why subscribe?

- Spend less time learning and more time coding with practical eBooks and Videos from over 4,000 industry professionals

- Improve your learning with Skill Plans built especially for you

- Get a free eBook or video every month

- Fully searchable for easy access to vital information

- Copy and paste, print, and bookmark content

Did you know that Packt offers eBook versions of every book published, with PDF and ePub files available? You can upgrade to the eBook version at `packt.com` and as a print book customer, you are entitled to a discount on the eBook copy. Get in touch with us at `customercare@packtpub.com` for more details.

At `www.packt.com`, you can also read a collection of free technical articles, sign up for a range of free newsletters, and receive exclusive discounts and offers on Packt books and eBooks.

Contributors

About the author

Sven Vermeulen (`sjvermeu` on Twitter) is a long-term contributor to various free software projects and the author of several online guides and resources, including the Gentoo Handbook. He got his first taste of free software in 1997 and never looked back.

Within SELinux, Sven contributed several policies to the Reference Policy project, and actively participated in policy development and user space development projects.

In his daily job, Sven is an enterprise architect in a European financial institution as well as a self-employed solution engineer and consultant. Prior to this, he graduated with an MSE in computer engineering from Ghent University and an MSc in ICT enterprise architecture from IC Institute.

I want to thank the SELinux community at large for being who they are, mature in their answers, and knowledgeable in all areas.

Closer to my heart, I would like to thank my daughter for giving me the time to work on this book, despite being locked in with me during the COVID-19 lockdown measures.

About the reviewers

David Windsor is a free software hacker who fell in love with Linux when he received his first Slackware installation disc at a Linux Users' Group in the late 1990s. He initially started contributing to Linux security as a hobbyist but has since been fortunate enough to be able to get paid to do what he loves.

David currently works at FireEye, Inc., where he does operating system security research. Previously, David has worked at Red Hat and The Linux Foundation and has contributed code to the **Kernel Self-Protection Project** (**KSPP**).

I'd like to thank Drew and Liz, loyal party members who have been there from the start. Rock on London, rock on Chicago!

Jimmy Savage is a certified Linux system administrator, DevOps tools engineer, network engineer, and security researcher. He focuses on supporting mission-critical devices and infrastructure, including everything from flight simulators, embedded systems, data centers, and beyond.

Packt is searching for authors like you

If you're interested in becoming an author for Packt, please visit `authors.packtpub.com` and apply today. We have worked with thousands of developers and tech professionals, just like you, to help them share their insight with the global tech community. You can make a general application, apply for a specific hot topic that we are recruiting an author for, or submit your own idea.

Table of Contents

2

Understanding SELinux Decisions and Logging

3

Managing User Logins

4

Using File Contexts and Process Domains

5
Controlling Network Communications

6
Configuring SELinux through Infrastructure-as-Code Orchestration

Section 2:
SELinux-Aware Platforms

7

Configuring Application-Specific SELinux Controls

8
SEPostgreSQL – Extending PostgreSQL with SELinux

9
Secure Virtualization

10

Using Xen Security Modules with FLASK

11

Enhancing the Security of Containerized Workloads

Section 3:
Policy Management

12
Tuning SELinux Policies

13
Analyzing Policy Behavior

14
Dealing with New Applications

15
Using the Reference Policy

16
Developing Policies with SELinux CIL

Preface

Security-Enhanced Linux (**SELinux**) is one of the most complete security solutions for Linux and is available by default in most major Linux distributions, such as Red Hat Enterprise Linux, CentOS, Fedora, and Gentoo, as well as being easily enabled in others, such as SUSE, Debian, and Ubuntu.

SELinux enables administrators to further harden their Linux systems and applications, making it much harder for intruders and malicious actors to abuse the system.

SELinux System Administration – Third Edition provides end-to-end coverage of SELinux on Linux systems, ranging from understanding what SELinux is and how it acts to tuning SELinux controls and its integrations within Linux and application platforms, up to the definition and maintenance of custom policies.

Who this book is for

This book is for Linux administrators who want to control the secure state of their systems. It's packed with the latest information on SELinux operations and administrative procedures so you'll be able to further harden your system through **mandatory access control** (**MAC**) – a security strategy that has been shaping Linux security for years.

The book can also be enlightening for IT architects to understand how SELinux can be positioned to enhance the security of Linux systems and Linux-hosted services within their organization.

Readers should have reasonable experience with maintaining Linux systems, covering user management, software installation and maintenance, regular Linux security controls, and network configuration.

What this book covers

Chapter 1, Fundamental SELinux Concepts, provides fundamental insights into the SELinux technology and allows you to understand the differences between SELinux implementations.

Chapter 2, Understanding SELinux Decisions and Logging, teaches you how to analyze SELinux events, and how to configure system logging to facilitate SELinux troubleshooting.

Chapter 3, Managing User Logins, allows you to manage Linux users and associate them with the right SELinux context.

Chapter 4, Using File Contexts and Process Domains, explains how SELinux labels are exposed on the system, and how to change the SELinux context of files and resources.

Chapter 5, Controlling Network Communications, introduces SELinux access control protections on a network level, ranging from socket-based protection measures to packet filtering with SELinux.

Chapter 6, Configuring SELinux through Infrastructure-as-Code Orchestration, shows you how to configure SELinux settings across large-scale environments using automation and orchestration tooling.

Chapter 7, Configuring Application-Specific SELinux Controls, explains how SELinux is adopted by several applications to augment their security posture further.

Chapter 8, SEPostgreSQL – Extending PostgreSQL with SELinux, helps you learn how to enable SEPostgreSQL in a regular PostgreSQL deployment, and how to use the SELinux controls within the database engine.

Chapter 9, Secure Virtualization, uses libvirt and other virtualization technologies together with SELinux to further protect and isolate virtual guests from each other.

Chapter 10, Using Xen Security Modules with FLASK, teaches you how Xen uses an SELinux-like approach to isolate its guests using Xen Security Modules, and how administrators can tweak and tune isolation further.

Chapter 11, Enhancing the Security of Containerized Workloads, shows how container platforms such as Docker, podman, and Kubernetes use SELinux as a means to secure the host system from potentially untrusted containers and provide isolation between containers.

Chapter 12, Tuning SELinux Policies, expands on SELinux booleans and their effect on the system and shows how to deal with different SELinux policy modules.

Chapter 13, Analyzing Policy Behavior, explains how administrators and analysts can interpret the SELinux policy and use policy analysis tooling to learn what a policy will allow.

Chapter 14, Dealing with New Applications, informs you how to apply SELinux on new applications that are not yet supported by the current SELinux policies.

Chapter 15, Using the Reference Policy, explains how to use the reference policy to create and adjust SELinux policies.

Chapter 16, Developing Policies with SELinux CIL, introduces you to the Common Intermediate Language and how to apply it to develop custom policies.

To get the most out of this book

This book focuses on the SELinux technology, which is enabled by default on many Linux distributions. While the book uses CentOS version 8 for most of its examples, any Linux distribution that has an SELinux implementation based upon the reference policy (which is the case for all major Linux distributions out there) suffices to follow this book.

In *Chapter 5, Controlling Network Communications*, one section covers using SELinux for InfiniBand infrastructure, which requires specialized hardware if you want to follow the examples to the letter. However, most of the chapter can be followed without additional requirements.

If you are using the digital version of this book, we advise you to type the code yourself or access the code via the GitHub repository (link available in the next section). Doing so will help you avoid any potential errors related to the copying and pasting of code.

Download the example code files

You can download the example code files for this book from GitHub at `https://github.com/PacktPublishing/SELinux-System-Administration-Third-Edition`.

In case there's an update to the code, it will be updated on the existing GitHub repository.

We also have other code bundles from our rich catalog of books and videos available at `https://github.com/PacktPublishing/`. Check them out!

Code in Action

Code in Action videos for this book can be viewed at `https://bit.ly/3o4paOb`.

Download the color images

We also provide a PDF file that has color images of the screenshots/diagrams used in this book. You can download it here: `https://static.packt-cdn.com/downloads/9781800201477_ColorImages.pdf`.

Conventions used

There are a number of text conventions used throughout this book.

`Code in text`: Indicates code words in text, database table names, folder names, filenames, file extensions, pathnames, dummy URLs, user input, and Twitter handles. Here is an example: "When activating a module, the `semodule` command will copy those modules into a dedicated directory."

A block of code is set as follows:

```
chain input {
  type filter hook input priority 0;
  ct state new meta secmark set tcp dport map @secmapping_in
  ct state new ct secmark set meta secmark
  ct state established,related meta secmark set ct secmark
}
```

When we wish to draw your attention to a particular part of a code block, the relevant lines or items are set in bold:

```
(roleattributeset cil_gen_require system_r)
(block pgpool
  (type domain)
  (roletype .system_r domain)
)
```

Any command-line input or output is written as follows:

```
$ cat /etc/passwd
cat: /etc/passwd: Permission denied
```

Bold: Indicates a new term, an important word, or words that you see onscreen. For example, words in menus or dialog boxes appear in the text like this. Here is an example: "This can be accomplished through the **Open Policy** button, or by navigating to **File | Open Policy**."

> Tips or important notes
> Appear like this.

Get in touch

Feedback from our readers is always welcome.

General feedback: If you have questions about any aspect of this book, mention the book title in the subject of your message and email us at customercare@packtpub.com.

Errata: Although we have taken every care to ensure the accuracy of our content, mistakes do happen. If you have found a mistake in this book, we would be grateful if you would report this to us. Please visit www.packtpub.com/support/errata, selecting your book, clicking on the Errata Submission Form link, and entering the details.

Piracy: If you come across any illegal copies of our works in any form on the Internet, we would be grateful if you would provide us with the location address or website name. Please contact us at copyright@packt.com with a link to the material.

If you are interested in becoming an author: If there is a topic that you have expertise in and you are interested in either writing or contributing to a book, please visit authors.packtpub.com.

Reviews

Please leave a review. Once you have read and used this book, why not leave a review on the site that you purchased it from? Potential readers can then see and use your unbiased opinion to make purchase decisions, we at Packt can understand what you think about our products, and our authors can see your feedback on their book. Thank you!

For more information about Packt, please visit packt.com.

Section 1:
Using SELinux

In this part, you will learn what SELinux is and how it acts on systems, as well as how to configure and manipulate SELinux essentials during system administration.

This section comprises the following chapters:

1
Fundamental SELinux Concepts

Security-Enhanced Linux (SELinux) brings additional security measures to your Linux system to further protect its resources. As part of the Linux kernel, it is a mandatory access control system supported by major Linux distributions. In this book, we cover all aspects of SELinux, from basic fundamentals to resolving SELinux issues, configuring applications to deal with SELinux, and even writing our own policies.

Before we embark on the details of SELinux, let's first cover the concepts of this technology: why SELinux uses labels to identify resources, how SELinux differs from traditional Linux access controls, how SELinux enforces security rules, and other mandatory access control systems that are supported in the Linux kernel. We will also see how the access control rules enforced by SELinux are provided through policy files. At the end of the chapter, we will cover an overview of the differences between SELinux implementations across Linux distributions.

In this chapter, we're going to cover the following main topics:

- Providing more security for Linux
- Labeling all resources and objects
- Defining and distributing policies
- Distinguishing between policies

Technical requirements

Check out the following video to see the Code in Action: `https://bit.ly/2FFaUdm`

Providing more security for Linux

Seasoned Linux administrators and security engineers already know that they need to put some trust in the users and processes of their system in order for the system to remain secure. This is partly because users can attempt to exploit vulnerabilities found in the software running on the system, but a large contribution to this trust level is because the secure state of the system depends on the behavior of the users. A Linux user with access to sensitive information could easily leak that out to the public, manipulate the behavior of the applications they launch, and do many other things that affect the security of the system. The default access controls active on a regular Linux system are **discretionary**; it is up to the users how the access controls should behave.

The Linux **discretionary access control (DAC)** mechanism is based on the user and/or group information of the process and is matched against the user and/or group information of the file, directory, or other resource being manipulated. Consider the /etc/shadow file, which contains the password and account information of the local Linux accounts:

```
$ ls -l /etc/shadow
-rw-r-----. 1 root root 1019 Nov 28 20:44 /etc/shadow
```

Without additional access control mechanisms in place, this file is readable and writable by any process owned by the root user, regardless of the purpose of the process on the system. The shadow file is a typical example of a sensitive file that we don't want to see leaked or abused in any other fashion. Yet the moment someone has access to the file, that user can copy it elsewhere, for example to a home directory, or even mail it to another computer and attempt to attack the password hashes stored within.

Another example of how Linux DAC requires trust from its users is the configuration of a database server. Database files themselves are (hopefully) only accessible to the runtime account of the **database management system (DBMS)** itself, and the Linux root user. Properly secured systems will only grant trusted users access to these files (for instance, through sudo) by allowing them to change their effective user ID from their personal user to the database runtime user or even the root account, but only for a well-defined set of commands that the system administrator has configured up front. These users too, can analyze the database files and gain access to potentially confidential information in the database without going through the DBMS. Administrators often have to put significant trust in these users to provide a secure system, rather than being able to enforce this.

However, regular users are not the only reason for securing a system. Lots of software daemons run as the Linux root user or have significant privileges on the system. Errors within those daemons can easily lead to information leakage or might even lead to remotely exploitable vulnerabilities. Backup software, monitoring software, change management software, scheduling software, and so on: they all often run with the highest privileged account possible on a regular Linux system. Even when the administrator does not allow privileged users, their interaction with daemons introduces a potential security risk. So, the users are still trusted to correctly interact with these applications in order for the system to function properly. Through this, the administrator leaves the security of the system to the *discretion* of its (many) users.

Enter SELinux, which provides an additional access control layer *on top of* the standard Linux DAC mechanism. SELinux provides a **mandatory access control (MAC)** system that, unlike its DAC counterpart, gives the administrator full control over what is allowed on the system and what isn't. It accomplishes this by supporting a policy-driven approach over what processes are and aren't allowed to do and by enforcing this policy through the Linux kernel.

Mandatory means that the operating system enforces the access control, defined solely by the policy rules that the system administrator (or security administrator) has enabled. Users and processes do not have permission to change the security rules, so they cannot work around the access controls; security is not left to their discretion anymore.

Considering the relational database example, a mandatory access control system would no longer require the administration to trust certain users, as it has full control over what these users can and cannot do. PostgreSQL, as we will see in *Chapter 8, SEPostgreSQL – Extending PostgreSQL with SELinux*, can interact with the SELinux subsystem to allow the administrator full coverage over the data access involved, even inside the database.

The word *mandatory* here, just like the word *discretionary* before, was not chosen accidentally to describe the abilities of the access control system: both are known terms in the security research field. Many security publications use these terms, including the **Trusted Computer System Evaluation Criteria** (**TSEC**) (`http://csrc.nist.gov/ publications/history/dod85.pdf`) standard (also known as the **Orange Book**) published by the Department of Defense in the United States of America in 1985. This publication has led to the Common Criteria standard for computer security certification (ISO/IEC 15408), available at `http://www.commoncriteriaportal.org/cc/`.

Next, we'll describe how the Linux kernel is responsible for the SELinux implementation.

Introducing Linux Security Modules (LSM)

Consider the example of the `shadow` file again. A MAC system can be configured to only allow a limited number of processes to read from and write to the file. On such specifically configured systems, a user logged on as `root` cannot directly access the file or even move it around. They can't even change the attributes of the file:

```
# id
uid=0(root) gid=0(root) groups=0(root),1(bin),2(daemon),3(sys),
4(adm),6(disk),10(wheel),11(floppy),26(tape),27(video) context=
sysadm_u:sysadm_r:sysadm_t:s0-s0:c0.c1023
# cat /etc/shadow
cat: /etc/shadow: Permission denied
# chmod a+r /etc/shadow
chmod: changing permissions of '/etc/shadow': Permission denied
```

The system enforces this through rules that describe when the contents of this file can be read, or when its attributes can be changed. With SELinux, these rules are defined in the SELinux policy and are loaded when the system boots. It is the Linux kernel itself that is responsible for enforcing the rules.

Mandatory access control systems such as SELinux are supported in the Linux kernel through **Linux Security Modules** (**LSM**), a Linux subsystem called before processing a user space request. Such requests are called **system calls**, and Linux supports over 100 of them.

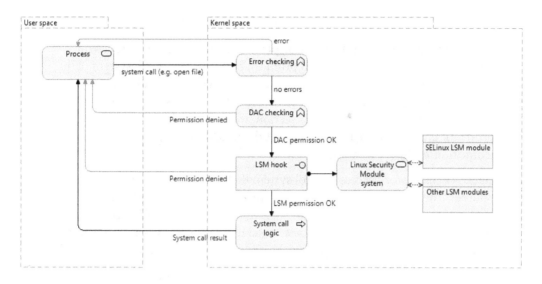

Figure 1.1 – High-level overview of how LSM integrates into the Linux kernel

LSM has been available in the Linux kernel since version 2.6, released in December 2003. It is a framework that provides hooks inside the Linux kernel at various locations, including the system call entry points. When these hooks trigger, registered security implementations such as SELinux have their functions executed automatically. In SELinux, these functions check the policy and other information before returning a go/no-go. LSM by itself does not provide any security functionality; instead, it relies on security implementations that do the heavy lifting: the framework is *modular*.

Within the LSM framework, two types of security modules exist: exclusive and non-exclusive modules. Two exclusive modules cannot be active simultaneously: each exclusive LSM module needs exclusive control over some kernel objects (generally those related to a security context) and is not able to deal with other LSM modules that need these objects as well. Non-exclusive modules don't have this need and can be combined (also known as *stacking*) at will, regardless of whether an exclusive LSM module is active or not.

A major use case for stacking LSM modules is to enable different security models within containers running on the system. Right now, it is not possible to implement a different security module within a Linux container, and the security within the container falls back to the security module of the host. To support this, more and more exclusive LSM implementations (like SELinux) are working to make their implementation non-exclusive, and we can expect improvements in this area within the next year.

SELinux is one implementation that uses LSM. Several other implementations exist:

- **AppArmor** is a mandatory access control system that has a strong focus on application-level protections (called profiles), based largely on filesystem paths. This makes AppArmor easy to understand and implement for administrators, as it does not have the complexity of abstracting rules to labels (as SELinux does). In the *Labeling all resources and objects* section, we explain why SELinux uses labels. AppArmor is an exclusive LSM module at the time of writing, but will most likely become non-exclusive very soon.

- **Smack** is a mandatory access control system that uses labels on processes and resources. The labels contain security identifiers interpreted by Smack to enforce access control, requiring fewer access rules in Smack (unlike SELinux, which does not perform an interpretation of labels – excluding sensitivity – and thus requires a higher number of policy rules). Smack is an exclusive LSM module.

- **TOMOYO Linux** is a mandatory access control system, but its access control mechanism is also easy to use for system analysis. It automatically builds up policies based on application behavior, and like AppArmor, its policies primarily use paths rather than labels. TOMOYO Linux (and its fork, **AKARI**) is a non-exclusive LSM module.

- **LoadPin** is an LSM module that ensures that the Linux kernel resources (such as kernel modules and firmware) are all loaded from a single non-writable filesystem. LoadPin is a non-exclusive LSM module.

- **Yama** is an LSM module that adds additional access controls on activities that are not sufficiently fine-grained by Linux, such as by attaching them to the memory of another process (using `ptrace`). Yama is a non-exclusive LSM module.

- **SafeSetId** is an LSM module that allows finer control over which users can use `setuid` (switching to another user) toward another user. Rather than granting the use of `setuid`, SafeSetId can limit for which users this is allowed. This ensures that vulnerabilities or misconfigurations in tools such as `sudo` are still contained. SafeSetId is a non-exclusive LSM module.

- **Lockdown** is an LSM module that protects the Linux kernel memory. It has two modes: in integrity mode, it prevents modifying kernel objects from user space (such as direct memory access or PCI access); in confidentiality mode, it additionally prevents extracting potentially confidential information from kernel objects. Lockdown is a non-exclusive LSM module.

- The **capability** LSM module is, by default, enabled on systems and provides support for Linux capabilities (a set of permissions granted to a user when the user is assigned a certain capability). It is a non-exclusive LSM module.

To query the list of active LSM modules on a system, read /sys/kernel/security/lsm:

```
$ cat /sys/kernel/security/lsm
capability,selinux
```

Next, we'll explain how SELinux works on top of regular Linux access controls.

Extending regular DAC with SELinux

SELinux does not change the Linux DAC implementation, nor can it override denials made by the Linux DAC permissions. If a regular system (without SELinux) prevents a particular access, there is nothing SELinux can do to override this decision. This is because the LSM hooks are triggered *after* the regular DAC permission checks execute, a conscious design decision from the LSM project.

For instance, if you need to allow an additional user access to a file, you cannot add an SELinux policy to do that for you. Instead, you will need to look into other features of Linux, such as the use of POSIX access control lists. Through the setfacl and getfacl commands, the user can set additional permissions on files and directories, opening up the selected resource to additional users or groups.

As an example, let's grant a user admin read-write access to a file using setfacl:

```
$ setfacl -m u:admin:rw /srv/backup/setup.conf
```

Similarly, to view the current POSIX ACLs applied to the file, use this command:

```
$ getfacl /srv/backup/setup.conf
getfacl: Removing leading '/' from absolute path names
# file: srv/backup/setup.conf
# owner: root
# group: root
user::rw-
user::admin:rw-
group::r--
mask::rw-
other::r—
```

This shows that the file is writable not only by its owner but also by the admin user.

Restricting root privileges

The regular Linux DAC allows an all-powerful user: `root`. Unlike most other users on the system, the logged-on `root` user has all the rights needed to fully manage the entire system, ranging from overriding access controls to controlling audits, changing user IDs, managing the network, and much more. This is supported through a security concept called **capabilities** (for an overview of Linux capabilities, check out the capabilities manual page: `man capabilities`). SELinux is also able to restrict access to these capabilities in a fine-grained manner.

Due to this fine-grained authorization aspect of SELinux, even the `root` user can be confined without impacting the operations on the system. The previous example of accessing `/etc/shadow` is just one example of an activity that a powerful user such as `root` still might not be able to perform due to the SELinux access controls in place.

Reducing the impact of vulnerabilities

If one benefit of SELinux needs to be stressed, then it is its ability to reduce the impact of vulnerabilities. But this vulnerability reduction is also often misunderstood.

A properly written SELinux policy confines applications so that their allowed activities are reduced to a minimum set. This **least-privilege model** ensures that abnormal application behavior is not only detected and audited but also prevented. Many application vulnerabilities can be exploited to execute tasks that an application is not meant to do. When this happens, SELinux will prevent this.

However, there are two misconceptions about SELinux's ability to thwart exploits, namely, the impact of the policy and the exploitation itself.

If the policy is not written in a least-privilege model, then SELinux might consider this non-standard behavior as normal and allow the actions to continue. For policy writers, this means that their policy rules have to be very fine-grained. Sadly, that makes writing policies very time-consuming: with more than 130 classes and over 250 permissions known to SELinux, policy rules need to take all these classes and permissions into account for each interaction.

As a result, policies tend to become convoluted and harder to maintain. Some policy writers make policies more permissive than is absolutely necessary, which might result in exploits becoming successful even though the action is not expected behavior from an application's point of view. Some application policies are explicitly marked as unconfined (which we discuss in *Chapter 14, Dealing with New Applications*), showing that they are very liberal in their allowed permissions. Fedora, CentOS, and Red Hat Enterprise Linux even start application policies as permissive and only start enforcing access controls for those applications after a few releases (and additional testing).

The second misconception is the exploit itself. If an application's vulnerability allows an unauthenticated user to use the application services as if the user were a regular, authorized user, then SELinux will not play a role in reducing the impact of the vulnerability; it will only notice the behavior of the application itself and not of the sessions internal to the application. As long as the application itself behaves as expected (such as accessing its own files and not poking around in other filesystems), SELinux will happily allow the actions to take place.

It is only when the application starts behaving erratically that SELinux stops the exploit from continuing. SELinux will prevent exploits such as **remote command execution (RCE)** against applications that should not be executing random commands (such as database management systems or web servers, excluding CGI-like functionality), whereas session hijacking or SQL injection attacks are not controllable through SELinux policies.

Enabling SELinux support

Enabling SELinux on a Linux system is not just a matter of enabling the SELinux LSM module within the Linux kernel.

An SELinux implementation contains the following:

- The SELinux kernel subsystem, implemented in the Linux kernel through LSM
- Libraries, used by applications that need to interact with SELinux
- Utilities, used by administrators to interact with SELinux
- Policies, which define the access controls themselves

The libraries and utilities are bundled by the SELinux user space project (`https://github.com/SELinuxProject/selinux`). Next to the applications and libraries provided by the SELinux user space project, various components on a Linux system are updated with SELinux-specific code, including the `init` system and several core utilities.

Because SELinux isn't just a switch that needs to be toggled, Linux distributions that support it usually come with SELinux predefined and loaded: Fedora, CentOS, and Red Hat Enterprise Linux (with its derivatives, such as Oracle Linux) are well-known examples. Other supporting distributions might not automatically have SELinux enabled but can easily support it through the installation of additional packages (which is the case with Debian and Ubuntu), and others have a well-documented approach to how to convert a system to SELinux (for example, Gentoo and Arch Linux).

Throughout the book, we will show examples for Gentoo and CentOS 8 (which is based on the free software of the Red Hat Enterprise Linux releases and is sponsored by Red Hat). These two distributions have different implementation details, which allow us to demonstrate the full potential of SELinux. To ensure the commands used within this book are available, some SELinux support tools might need to be installed.

On Gentoo Linux, install at least the following packages:

```
# emerge app-admin/setools sys-apps/policycoreutils
```

On CentOS Linux, install at least the following packages:

```
# yum install setools-console policycoreutils-python-utils
```

As packages can change over time, it is sensible to look up which package provides a particular command.

> **Important note**
>
> If the mentioned packages no longer exist or do not cover all commands, please consult your distribution's documentation on which software packages to install. Most distributions allow searching for the most appropriate package as well, such as with `e-file` in Gentoo, or `yum whatprovides` on CentOS or related distributions.

With the SELinux main functionality described, let's look at how SELinux knows what is on the system, and which abstraction it uses to allow policies to be developed for a wide set of users.

Labeling all resources and objects

When SELinux has to decide whether it has to allow or deny a particular action, it makes a decision based on the context of both the **subject** (who is initiating the action) and the **object** (which is the target of the action). These contexts (or parts of the context) are mentioned in the policy rules that SELinux enforces.

The **context** of a process is what identifies the process to SELinux. SELinux has no notion of Linux process ownership and does not care how the process is called, which process ID it has, and what account the process runs as. All it wants to know is what the context of that process is, represented to users and administrators as a **label**. *Label* and *context* are often used interchangeably, and although there is a technical distinction (one is a representation of the other), we will not dwell on that much.

Let's look at an example label – the context of the current user:

```
$ id -Z
sysadm_u:sysadm_r:sysadm_t:s0-s0:c0.c1023
```

The id command, which returns information about the current user, is shown executing with the -Z switch (a commonly agreed upon switch for displaying additional security information obtained from the LSM-based security subsystem). It shows us the context of the current user (actually the context of the id process itself when it was executing). As we can see, the context has a string representation and looks as if it has five fields (it doesn't; it has four fields – the last field just happens to contain a colon character).

SELinux developers decided to use labels instead of real process and file (or other resource) metadata for its access controls. This is different from MAC systems such as AppArmor, which uses the path of the binary (and thus the process name) and the paths of the resources to handle permission checks. The following reasons inspired the decision to make SELinux a label-based mandatory access control:

- Using paths might be easier to comprehend for administrators, but this doesn't allow us to keep the context information close to the resource. If a file or directory moves or remounts, or if a process has a different namespace view on the files, then the access controls might behave differently as they look at the path instead of the file. With label-based contexts, the system retains this information and keeps controlling the resource's access properly.

- Contexts reveal the purpose of the process very well. The same binary application can be launched in different contexts depending on how it got started. The context value (such as the one shown in the id -Z output earlier) is exactly what the administrator needs. With it, they know what the rights are of each of the running instances, but they can also deduce from it how the process was launched and what its purpose is.

- Contexts also make abstractions of the object itself. We are used to talking about processes and files, but contexts are also applicable to less tangible resources such as pipes (inter-process communication) or database objects. Path-based identification only works as long as you can write a path.

As an example, consider the following policy statements:

- Allow the httpd processes to bind to TCP port 80.

- Allow the processes labeled with httpd_t to bind to TCP ports labeled with http_port_t.

In the first example, we cannot easily reuse this policy when the web server process isn't using the `httpd` binary (perhaps because it was renamed or it isn't Apache but another web server) or when we want to have HTTP access on a different port. With the labeled approach, the binary could be called `apache2` or `MyWebServer.py`; as long as the process is labeled with `httpd_t`, the policy applies. The same happens with the port definition: you can label the port `8080` with `http_port_t` and thus allow the web servers to bind to that port as well without having to write another policy statement.

Dissecting the SELinux context

To come to a context, SELinux uses at least three, and sometimes four, values. Let's look at the context of the SSH server as an example:

```
$ ps -eZ | grep sshd
system_u:system_r:sshd_t:s0-s0:c0.c1023 2629 ? 00:00:00 sshd
```

As we can see, the process is assigned a context that contains the following fields:

- The SELinux user `system_u`
- The SELinux role `system_r`
- The SELinux type (also known as the domain when we are looking at a running process) `sshd_t`
- The sensitivity level `s0-s0:c0.c1023`

When we work with SELinux, knowing the contexts is extremely important. In most cases, it is the third field (called the **domain** or **type**) that is most important since the majority of SELinux policy rules (over 99 percent) consist of rules related to the interaction between two types (without mentioning roles, users, or sensitivity levels).

SELinux contexts are aligned with LSM security attributes and exposed to the user space in a standardized manner (compatible with multiple LSM implementations), allowing end users and applications to easily query the contexts. An easily accessible location where these attributes are presented is within the `/proc` pseudo filesystem.

Inside each process's `/proc/<pid>` location, we find a subdirectory called `attr`, inside of which the following files can be found:

```
$ ls /proc/$$/attr
current  exec  fscreate  keycreate  prev  sockcreate
```

All these files, if read, display either nothing or an SELinux context. If it is empty, then that means the application has not explicitly set a context for that particular purpose, and the SELinux context will be deduced either from the policy or inherited from its parent.

The meaning of the files are as follows:

- The `current` file displays the current SELinux context of the process.
- The `exec` file displays the SELinux context that will be assigned by the next application execution done through this application. It is usually empty.
- The `fscreate` file displays the SELinux context that will be assigned to the next file written by the application. It is usually empty.
- The `keycreate` file displays the SELinux context that will be assigned to the keys cached in the kernel by this application. It is usually empty.
- The `prev` file displays the previous SELinux context for this particular process. This is usually the context of its parent application.
- The `sockcreate` file displays the SELinux context that will be assigned to the next socket created by the application. It is usually empty.

If an application has multiple subtasks, then the same information is available in each subtask directory at `/proc/<pid>/task/<taskid>/attr`.

Enforcing access through types

The SELinux type (the third part of an SELinux context) of a process (called the **domain**) is the basis of the fine-grained access controls of that process with respect to itself and other types (which can be processes, files, sockets, network interfaces, and more). In most SELinux literature, SELinux's label-based access control mechanism is fine-tuned to say that SELinux is a **type enforcement** mandatory access control system: when some actions are denied, the (absence of the) fine-grained access controls on the type level are most likely to blame.

With type enforcement, SELinux can control an application's behavior based on how it got executed in the first place: a web server launched by a user will run with a different type than a web server executed through the `init` system, even though the process binary and path are the same. The web server launched from the `init` system is most likely trusted (and thus allowed to do whatever web servers are supposed to do), whereas a manually launched web server is less likely to be considered *normal behavior* and as such will have different privileges.

> **Important note**
>
> The majority of SELinux's online resources focus on types. Even though the SELinux type is just the third part of an SELinux context, it is the most important one for most administrators. Most documentation will even just talk about a type such as `sshd_t` rather than a full SELinux context.

Take a look at the following `dbus-daemon` processes:

```
# ps -eZ | grep dbus-daemon
swift_u:swift_r:swift_dbusd_t:s0-s0:c0.c512 571 ? 00:00:01
dbus-daemon
swift_u:swift_r:swift_dbusd_t:s0-s0:c0.c512 649 ? 00:00:00
dbus-daemon
system_u:system_r:system_dbusd_t:s0-s0:c0.c1023 2498 ? 00:00:00
dbus-daemon
```

In this example, one `dbus-daemon` process is the system D-Bus daemon running with the aptly named `system_dbusd_t` type, whereas two other ones are running with the `swift_dbusd_t` type assigned to it. Even though their binaries are the same, they both serve a different purpose on the system and as such have a different type assigned. SELinux then uses this type to govern the actions allowed by the process toward other types, including how `system_dbusd_t` can interact with `swift_dbusd_t`.

SELinux types are by convention suffixed with `_t`, although this is not mandatory.

Granting domain access through roles

SELinux roles (the second part of an SELinux context) allow SELinux to support role-based access controls. Although type enforcement is the most used (and known) part of SELinux, role-based access control is an important method to keep a system secure, especially from malicious user attempts. SELinux roles define which types (domains) can be accessed from the current context. These types (domains) on their part define the permissions. As such, SELinux roles help define what a user (who has access to one or more roles) can and cannot do.

By convention, SELinux roles are defined with an _r suffix. On most SELinux-enabled systems, the administrator can assign the following SELinux roles to users:

- The user_r role is meant for restricted users. This role is only allowed to have processes with types specific to end-user applications. Privileged types, including those used to switch to another Linux user, are not allowed for this role.

- The staff_r role is meant for non-critical operations. This role is generally restricted to the same applications as the restricted user, but it has the ability to switch roles. It is the default role for operators to have (so as to keep those users in their least privileged role as long as possible).

- The sysadm_r role is meant for system administrators. This role is very privileged, enabling various system administration tasks. However, certain end-user application types might not be supported (especially if those types are used for potentially vulnerable or untrusted software) to keep the system free from infections.

- The secadm_r role is meant for security administrators. This role allows changing the SELinux policy and manipulating the SELinux controls. It is generally used when a separation of duties is needed between system administrators and system policy management.

- The system_r role is meant for daemons and background processes. This role is quite privileged, supporting the various daemon and system process types. However, end-user application types and other administrative types are not allowed in this role.

- The unconfined_r role is meant for end users. This role allows a limited number of types, but those types are very privileged as they allow running any application launched by a user (or another unconfined process) in a more or less unconfined manner (not restricted by SELinux rules). This role, as such, is only available if the system administrator wants to protect certain processes (mostly daemons) while keeping the rest of the system operations almost untouched by SELinux.

Other roles might exist, such as `guest_r` and `xguest_r`, depending on the distribution. It is wise to consult the distribution documentation for more information about the supported roles. The `seinfo` command is the most common method to obtain an overview of available roles:

```
# seinfo --role
Roles: 9
    auditadm_r
    object_r
    secadm_r
    ...
    user_r
```

With the SELinux roles identified, let's look at how we assign roles to users.

Limiting roles through users

An SELinux user (the first part of an SELinux context) is not the same as a Linux (account) user. Unlike Linux user information, which can change while the user is working on the system (through tools such as `sudo` or `su`), the SELinux policy can (and generally will) enforce that the SELinux user remains the same even when the Linux user itself has changed. Because of the immutable state of the SELinux user, we can implement specific access controls to ensure that users cannot work around the set of permissions granted to them, even when they get privileged access.

An example of such an access control is the **user-based access control** (**UBAC**) feature that some Linux distributions (optionally) enable, which prevents users from accessing files of different SELinux users even when those users try to use the Linux DAC controls to grant access to each other's files.

The most important feature of SELinux users, however, is that SELinux user definitions restrict which roles the (Linux) user can assume. A Linux user is first assigned to an SELinux user, which does not need to be unique: multiple Linux users can be assigned to the same SELinux user. Once set, that user cannot switch to an SELinux role not associated with that SELinux user.

The following diagram shows the role-based access control implementation of SELinux:

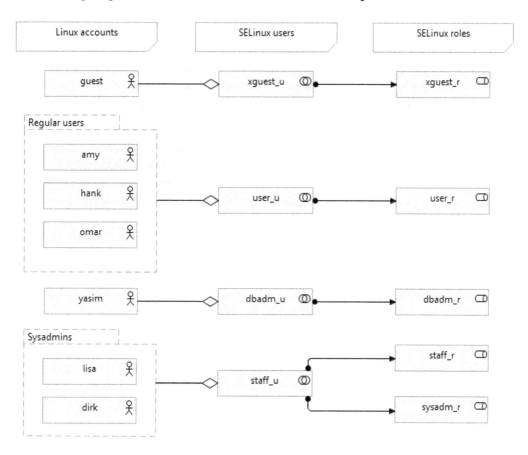

Figure 1.2 – Mapping Linux accounts to SELinux users

SELinux users are, by convention, defined with an _u suffix, although this is not mandatory. The SELinux users that most distributions have available are named after the role they represent, but instead of ending with _r, they end with _u. For instance, for the sysadm_r role, we have the sysadm_u SELinux user.

Controlling information flow through sensitivities

The fourth part of an SELinux context, the sensitivity, is not always present (some Linux distributions, by default, do not enable sensitivity labels, but most do). This part of the label is needed for the **multilevel security (MLS)** support within SELinux, which is an optional setting. Sensitivity labels allow the classification of resources and the restriction of access to those resources based on a security clearance. These labels consist of two parts: a confidentiality value (prefixed with s) and a category value (prefixed with c).

In many larger organizations and companies, documents are labeled internal, confidential, or strictly confidential. SELinux can assign processes certain clearance levels for these resources. With MLS, we can configure SELinux to follow the **Bell-LaPadula** model, a security model characterized by *no read up, no write down*: based on a process's clearance level, that process cannot read anything with a higher confidentiality level nor write to (or communicate otherwise with) any resource with a lower confidentiality level. SELinux does not use internal, confidential, and other labels. Instead, it uses numbers from zero (the lowest confidentiality) to whatever the system administrator has defined as the highest value (this is configurable and set when the SELinux policy is built).

Categories allow us to assign resources with one or more categories, and to define access controls across categories. One of the functionalities resulting from using categories is to support multitenancy (for example, systems hosting applications for multiple customers) within a Linux system. Multitenancy is provided by assigning a set of categories to the processes and resources of one tenant, whereas the processes and resources of another tenant get a different set of categories. When a process does not have the proper categories assigned, it cannot touch the resources (or other processes) that have other categories assigned.

> **Important note**
>
> An unwritten convention in the SELinux world is that (at least) two categories are used to differentiate between tenants. By having services randomly pick two categories for a tenant out of a predefined set of categories, while ensuring each tenant has a unique combination, these services receive proper isolation. The use of two categories is not mandatory, but services such as sVirt and Docker successfully implement this methodology.

In that sense, categories are like tags, allowing us to grant access only when the tags of the process and the target resource match. As multilevel security is not often used, the benefits of only using categories are persisted in what is called **multi-category security (MCS)**. This is a special MLS case, which only supports a single confidentiality level (s0).

Now that we know how labels are used by SELinux policies, let's look at how SELinux policies are defined and distributed.

Defining and distributing policies

Enabling SELinux does not automatically start the enforcement of access. If SELinux is enabled and it cannot find a policy, it will refuse to start because the policy defines the behavior of the system (what SELinux should allow). SELinux policies are generally distributed in a compiled form (just like with software) as policy modules. These modules are then aggregated into a single policy store and loaded in memory to allow SELinux to enforce the policy rules on the system.

> **Important note**
>
> Gentoo, a source-based meta-distribution, distributes SELinux policies as (source) code, compiled and built at install time, just like it does with other software.

The following diagram shows the relationship between **policy rules (policy code)**, **policy modules**, and a **policy package** (which is often a one-to-one mapping toward a **policy store**):

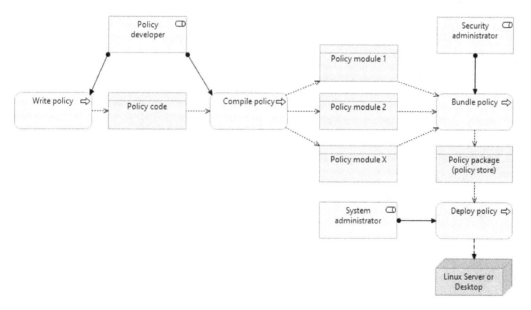

Figure 1.3 – Relationship between policy rules (code), policy modules, and policy store

As we can see, policies are first written, then compiled in modules, after which they are bundled and distributed. The next few sections describe each of these phases in detail.

Writing SELinux policies

An SELinux policy writer can write down the policy rules in three possible languages:

- In standard SELinux source format – a human-readable and well-established language for writing SELinux policies

- In reference policy style, which extends the standard SELinux source format with M4 macros to facilitate the development of policies

- In the SELinux **common intermediate language** (**CIL**) – a computer-readable (and with some effort, human-readable) format for SELinux policies

Most SELinux supporting distributions base their policy on the reference policy (`https://github.com/SELinuxProject/refpolicy/`), a fully functional SELinux policy set managed as a free software project. This allows distributions to ship with a functional policy set rather than having to write one themselves. Many project contributors are distribution developers, trying to push changes of their distribution to the reference policy project itself, where the changes are peer-reviewed to ensure no rules are brought into the project that might jeopardize the security of any platform. Writing policies without the extensive set of M4 macros offered by the reference policy project is hard, which is why the reference policy has become the de facto source for policies.

The SELinux CIL format is reasonably recent, and although it is very much in use already (the SELinux user space converts everything to CIL in the background), it is not that common yet for policy writers to use it directly.

To show the differences between these three languages, consider the web server rule we discussed earlier, repeated here for your convenience: allow the processes labeled with `httpd_t` to bind to TCP ports labeled with `http_port_t`.

In the standard SELinux source format, we write this down as follows:

```
allow httpd_t http_port_t : tcp_socket { name_bind };
```

Using reference policy style, this rule is part of the following macro call:

```
corenet_tcp_bind_http_port(httpd_t)
```

In the CIL language, the rule expression is like so:

```
(allow httpd_t http_port_t (tcp_socket (name_bind)))
```

In most representations, we can see what the rule is about:

- The subject (who is taking the action); in this case, this is the set of processes labeled with the `httpd_t` type.

- The target resource or object (the target for the action); in this case, it is the set of TCP sockets (`tcp_socket`) labeled with the `http_port_t` type. In reference policy style, this is implied by the function name.

- The action or permission; in this case, it is the action of binding to a port (`name_bind`). In reference policy style, this is implied by the function name.

- The result that the policy will enforce; in this case, it is that the action is allowed (`allow`). In reference policy style, this is implied by the function name.

A policy is generally written for an application or set of applications. So, the preceding example will be part of the policy written for web servers.

Policy writers will generally create three files per application or application set:

- A `.te` file, which contains the type enforcement rules.

- A `.if` file, which contains interface and template definitions, allowing policy writers to easily use the newly-generated policy rules to enhance other policies. You can compare this to header files in other programming languages.

- A `.fc` file, which contains file context expressions. These are rules that assign labels to resources on the filesystem.

A finished policy is then packaged into an SELinux policy module.

Distributing policies through modules

Initially, SELinux used a single, monolithic policy approach: all possible access control rules were maintained in a single policy file. It quickly became clear that this is not manageable in the long term, and the idea of developing a modular policy approach was born.

Within the modular approach, policy developers can write isolated policy sets for a particular application (or set of applications), roles, and so on. These policies then get built and distributed as policy modules. Platforms that need access controls for a particular application load the SELinux policy module that defines the access rules for that application.

The following diagram shows the building of policy modules. It also shows where CIL comes into play, even when the policy rules themselves are not written in CIL:

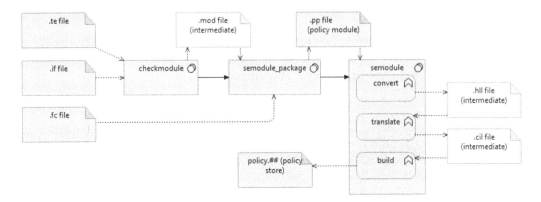

Figure 1.4 – Build process from policy rule to policy store

The binary *.pp files (which are the SELinux policy modules) are considered to be written in a **high-level language (HLL)**. Do not assume that this means they are human-readable: these files are binary files. The consideration here is that SELinux wants to support writing SELinux policies in a number of formats, which it calls high-level languages, as long as it has a parser that can convert the files into CIL. Marking the binary module formats (which in previous SELinux versions were the binary blobs loaded in memory) as high-level allows the SELinux project to introduce the distinction between high-level languages and CIL in a backward-compatible manner.

When distributing SELinux policy modules, most Linux distributions place the *.pp SELinux policy modules inside /usr/share/selinux, usually within a subdirectory named after the policy store (such as targeted). There, these modules are ready for administrators to activate them.

When activating a module, the semodule command will copy those modules into a dedicated directory (/var/lib/selinux/mcs/active/modules). When all modules are aggregated in a single location, the final policy binary is compiled, resulting in /etc/selinux/targeted/policy/policy.32 (or some other number) and loaded in memory.

On CentOS, the SELinux policies are provided by the selinux-policy-targeted (or -minimum or -mls) package. On Gentoo, they are provided by the various sec-policy/selinux-* packages (Gentoo uses separate packages for each module, reducing the number of SELinux policies loaded on an average system).

Bundling modules in a policy store

A **policy store** contains a single comprehensive policy, and only a single policy can be active on a system at any point in time. Administrators can switch policy stores, although this often requires rebooting the system and might even require relabeling the entire system (relabeling is the act of resetting the contexts on all files and resources available on that system).

The active policy on the system can be queried using `sestatus` (an SELinux status) as follows:

```
# sestatus | grep "Loaded policy name"
Loaded policy name:      mcs
```

In this example, `mcs` is the currently loaded policy (store). The policy name that SELinux will use upon its next reboot is defined in the `/etc/selinux/config` configuration file as the `SELINUXTYPE` parameter.

The system's `init` system (be it a `SysV`-compatible `init` system or `systemd`) is generally responsible for loading the SELinux policy, effectively activating SELinux support on the system. The `init` system reads the configuration, locates the policy store, and loads the policy file in memory. If the `init` system does not support this (in other words, it is not SELinux-aware) then the policy should be loaded through the `load_policy` command.

As we now have a better view of the flow used in policy development and distribution, let's see how Linux distributions can differentiate their SELinux offering.

Distinguishing between policies

The most common SELinux policy store names are `strict`, `targeted`, `mcs`, and `mls`. None of the names assigned to policy stores are fixed though, so it is a matter of convention. Hence, we recommend consulting the distribution documentation to verify what the proper name of the policy should be. Still, the name often provides some information about the SELinux options enabled through the policy.

Supporting MLS

One of the options that can be enabled is MLS support. The SELinux context will not have a fourth field with sensitivity information in it if this option is disabled, making the contexts of processes and files look as follows:

```
staff_u:sysadm_r:sysadm_t
```

To check whether MLS is enabled, it is sufficient to see whether a process context doesn't contain such a fourth field. Another way is to check the `Policy MLS Status` line in the output of `sestatus`:

```
# sestatus | grep MLS
Policy MLS status:        enabled
```

Yet another method would be to look into the pseudo file, `/sys/fs/selinux/mls`. A value of `0` means disabled, whereas a value of `1` means enabled:

```
# cat /sys/fs/selinux/mls
1
```

Policy stores that have MLS enabled are generally `targeted`, `mcs`, and `mls`, whereas `strict` generally has MLS disabled.

Dealing with unknown permissions

Permissions (such as read, open, and lock) are defined both in the Linux kernel and in the policy itself. However, sometimes, newer Linux kernels support permissions that the current policy does not yet understand.

Take the `block_suspend` permission (to be able to block system suspension) as an example. If the Linux kernel supports (and checks) this permission but the loaded SELinux policy does not understand that permission yet, then SELinux has to decide how it should deal with the permission. We can configure SELinux to perform one of the following actions:

- Allow every action related to an unknown permission (`allow`).
- Deny every action related to an unknown permission (`deny`).
- Stop and halt the system when an unknown permission is checked (`reject`).

We configure this through the `deny_unknown` value. To see the state for unknown permissions, look for the `Policy deny_unknown status` line in `sestatus`:

```
# sestatus | grep deny_unknown
Policy deny_unknown status:       allowed
```

Administrators can set this for themselves in the `/etc/selinux/semanage.conf` file through the `handle-unknown` variable (with `allow`, `deny`, or `reject`).

Supporting unconfined domains

An SELinux policy can be very strict, limiting applications as close as possible to their actual behavior, but it can also be very liberal in what applications are allowed to do. One of the concepts available in many SELinux policies is the idea of unconfined domains. When enabled, it means that certain SELinux domains (process contexts) are allowed to do almost anything they want (of course, within the boundaries of the regular Linux DAC permissions, which still hold) and only a select number of domains are truly confined (restricted) in their actions.

Unconfined domains are introduced to allow SELinux to be active on desktops and servers where administrators do not want to fully restrict the entire system, but only a few of the applications running on it. Generally, these implementations focus on constraining network-facing services (such as web servers and database management systems) while allowing end users and administrators to roam around unrestricted.

With other MAC systems, such as AppArmor, *unconfinement* is inherently part of the design of the system as they only restrict actions for well-defined applications or users. However, SELinux is designed to be a full mandatory access control system and thus needs to provide access control rules even for those applications that aren't the security administrator's primary focus. By marking these applications as unconfined, almost no restrictions are imposed by SELinux.

We can see whether unconfined domains are enabled on the system using `seinfo`, by querying the policy and asking it whether the `unconfined_t` SELinux type is defined. On a system where unconfined domains are supported, this type will be available:

```
# seinfo -t unconfined_t
Types: 1
  unconfined_t
```

For a system where unconfined domains are not supported, the type will not be part of the policy:

```
# seinfo -t unconfined_t
Types: 0
```

Most distributions that enable unconfined domains call their policy `targeted`, but this convention is not always followed. Hence, it is always best to consult the policy using `seinfo`. CentOS enables unconfined domains, whereas with Gentoo, this is a configurable setting through the `unconfined USE` flag.

Limiting cross-user sharing

When UBAC is enabled, certain SELinux types will be protected by additional constraints. This will ensure that one SELinux user cannot access the files (or other specific resources) of another user, even when those users are sharing their data through the regular Linux permissions. UBAC provides some additional control over information flow between resources, but it is far from perfect. Essentially, it is made to isolate SELinux users from one another.

> **Important note**
>
> A constraint in SELinux is an access control rule that uses all parts of a context to make its decision. Unlike type enforcement rules, which are purely based on the type, constraints can take the SELinux user, SELinux role, or sensitivity label into account. Constraints are generally developed once and left untouched – most policy writers will not touch constraints during their development efforts.

Many Linux distributions, including CentOS, disable UBAC. Gentoo allows users to decide whether they want UBAC through the Gentoo `ubac USE` flag (which is enabled by default).

Incrementing policy versions

While checking the output of `sestatus`, we see that there is also a reference to a policy version:

```
# sestatus | grep version
Max kernel policy version:        32
```

This version has nothing to do with the versioning of policy rules but with the SELinux features that the currently running kernel supports. In the preceding output, 32 is the highest policy version that the running kernel supports. Every time a new feature is added to SELinux, the version number is increased. We can find the policy file itself (which contains all the SELinux rules loaded at boot time by the system) in `/etc/selinux/targeted/policy` (where targeted refers to the policy store used, so if the system uses a policy store named `mcs`, then the path will be `/etc/selinux/mcs/policy`).

If multiple policy files exist, use `seinfo` to discover which policy version file is used:

```
# seinfo | grep Version
Policy version:                   31 (MLS enabled)
```

A list of policy feature enhancements and the Linux kernel version in which that given feature is introduced is provided next. Many of the features are only of concern to policy developers, but knowing the evolution of the features gives us a good idea about the evolution of SELinux:

- Version 12 represents the "old API" for SELinux, which is now deprecated.

- Version 15, introduced in Linux 2.6.0, provided the new API for SELinux.

- Version 16, introduced in Linux 2.6.5, added support for conditional policy extensions.

- Version 17, introduced in Linux 2.6.6, added support for IPv6.

- Version 18, introduced in Linux 2.6.8, added support for fine-grained netlink socket permissions.

- Version 19, introduced in Linux 2.6.12, added support for MLS.

- Version 20, introduced in Linux 2.6.14, reduced the size of the access vector table.

- Version 21, introduced in Linux 2.6.19, added support for MLS range transitions.

- Version 22, introduced in Linux 2.6.25, added policy capabilities.

- Version 23, introduced in Linux 2.6.26, added support for per-domain permissive mode.

- Version 24, introduced in Linux 2.6.28, added support for explicit hierarchy (type bounds).

- Version 25, introduced in Linux 2.6.39, added support for filename-based transitions.

- Version 26, introduced in Linux 3.0, added support for role-transitions for non-process classes, as well as support for role attributes.

- Version 27, introduced in Linux 3.5, added support for the flexible inheritance of the SELinux user and SELinux role for newly-created objects.

- Version 28, introduced in Linux 3.5, added support for the flexible inheritance of the SELinux type for newly-created objects.

- Version 29, introduced in Linux 3.14, added support for attributes within SELinux constraints.

- Version 30, introduced in Linux 4.3, added support for extended permissions, implemented first on ioctl controls. It also introduced enhanced SELinux Xen support.

- Version 31, introduced in Linux 4.13, added support for InfiniBand access controls.

- Version 32, introduced in Linux 5.5, added support for automatically deducing the intersection in sensitivity labels, called **greatest lower bound, largest upper bound (glblub)**.

By default, when an SELinux policy is built, the highest supported version as defined by the Linux kernel and `libsepol` (the library responsible for building the SELinux policy binary) is used. Administrators can force a version to be lower using the `policy-version` parameter in `/etc/selinux/semanage.conf`.

Different policy content

Besides the policy capabilities described in the previous section, the main difference between policies (and distributions) is the policy content itself. We already covered that most distributions base their policy on the reference policy project. Although the reference policy project is considered the *master* for most distributions, each distribution has its own set of deviations from this main policy set.

Many distributions make extensive additions to the policy without directly passing the policies to the upstream reference policy project. There are several possible reasons why this is not directly done:

- The policy enhancements or additions are still immature: Fedora, CentOS, and Red Hat initially start with active, permissive policies, meaning the policies are not enforced. Instead, SELinux logs what it would have prevented and, based on those logs, the policies are then enhanced. This means that a policy is only ready after a few releases.

- The policy enhancements or additions are too specific to the distribution: If a policy set is not reusable for other distributions, then some distributions will opt to keep those policies to themselves as the act of pushing changes to *upstream* projects takes quite some effort.

- The policy enhancements or additions haven't followed the upstream rules and guidelines: The reference policy has a set of guidelines that policies need to adhere to. If a policy set does not comply with these rules, then the reference policy will not accept the contribution.

- The policy enhancements or additions are not implementing the same security model as the reference policy project wants: As SELinux is a very extensive mandatory access control system, it is possible to write completely different policies.

- The distribution does not have the time or resources to push changes upstream.

This means that SELinux policies can differ between distributions (and even releases of the same distribution).

With this, we can conclude on some of the differentiation that distributions can put into their SELinux policies: they can opt to enable or disable MLS support, allow or deny unknown permissions, add distribution-provided unconfined domains, support user-based access controls, and/or deviate from the reference policy project to suit the distribution's principles.

Summary

In this chapter, we saw that SELinux offers a more fine-grained access control mechanism on top of the Linux access controls. SELinux is implemented through Linux Security Modules and uses labels to identify its resources and processes based on ownership (user), role, type, and even the security sensitivity and categorization of the resource. We covered how SELinux policies are handled within an SELinux-enabled system and briefly touched upon how policy writers structure policies.

Linux distributions implement SELinux policies, which can differ between distributions based on supported features, such as sensitivity labels, the default behavior for unknown permissions, support for confinement levels, or specific constraints put in place, such as UBAC. However, most of the policy rules themselves are similar and are even based on the same upstream reference policy project.

Switching between SELinux enforcement modes and understanding the log events that SELinux creates when it prohibits certain access is the subject of our next chapter. In it, we will also cover how to approach the often-heard requirement of disabling SELinux, and why doing so is the wrong way forward.

Questions

1. What is the most important difference between a DAC and a MAC system?

2. How does Linux support the different MAC technologies?

3. What four fields constitute an SELinux context?

4. How does SELinux support role-based access controls?

5. Why isn't there a single SELinux policy for all Linux distributions?

2
Understanding SELinux Decisions and Logging

Once we enable SELinux on the system, it starts its access control functionality, as described in the previous chapter. Once it starts, administrators need to keep a close eye on its actions, and often need to deal with unexpected behavior if one or more applications are not acting according to the SELinux policy. Through SELinux logging, we learn how SELinux enforces its policies toward the applications on the system.

Administrators have to know how to switch between SELinux in full-enforcement mode (resembling a host-based intrusion prevention system) versus its permissive, logging-only mode, and use its various methods to toggle the SELinux state (enabled or disabled; permissive or enforcing). Furthermore, we should know how to disable SELinux's enforcement for a single domain rather than an entire system, and learn to interpret the SELinux log events that describe which activities SELinux has prevented. We will finish with an overview of common methods for analyzing these logging events in day-to-day operations.

In this chapter, we're going to cover the following main topics:

- Switching SELinux on and off
- SELinux logging and auditing
- Getting help with denials

Technical requirements

Check out the following video to see the Code in Action: `https://bit.ly/3dFaUXm`

Switching SELinux on and off

This is perhaps a weird section to begin with, but disabling SELinux is a commonly requested activity. Some vendors do not support their application running on a platform that has SELinux enabled, as those vendors do not have the expertise to develop SELinux policies for their own applications, or are not able to educate their own support lines to deal with SELinux.

Furthermore, system administrators are generally reluctant to use security controls they do not understand or find too complex to maintain. Luckily, SELinux is becoming a de facto standard technology in several Linux distributions, which is increasing its exposure and understanding among administrators. SELinux is also capable of selectively disabling its access controls for a part of a system rather than requiring us to disable it for a complete system.

Setting the global SELinux state

SELinux supports three major states that it can be in: `disabled`, `permissive`, and `enforcing`. These states are set in the `/etc/selinux/config` file, through the `SELINUX` variable, as illustrated in the following code snippet:

```
$ grep ^SELINUX= /etc/selinux/config
SELINUX=enforcing
```

When the `init` system process loads the SELinux policy, the SELinux code checks the state that the administrator has configured. The states are described as follows:

- If the state is `disabled`, then the SELinux code disables further support, booting the system further without activating SELinux.

- If the state is `permissive`, then SELinux is active but will not enforce its policy on the system. Instead, SELinux will report any violation against the policy, but will not prevent the action itself. This is sometimes called **host intrusion detection** as it works in reporting-only mode.

- If the state is `enforcing`, then SELinux is active and will enforce its policy on the system. Violations are reported and denied. This is sometimes called **host intrusion prevention**, as it enforces the rules while logging the actions it takes.

We can use the `getenforce` command or the `sestatus` command to get information about the current state of SELinux, like so:

```
$ sestatus | grep mode
Current mode:    enforcing
$ getenforce
Enforcing
```

It is also possible to query the `/sys/fs/selinux/enforce` pseudo-file to get similar information. If the file returns 1, then SELinux is in enforcing mode. If it returns 0, then it is in permissive mode. The following code snippet shows SELinux in enforcing mode:

```
$ cat /sys/fs/selinux/enforce
1
```

When we change the `/etc/selinux/config` file, then we need to reboot the system for the changes to take effect. However, if we boot a system without SELinux support (`disabled`), re-enabling SELinux support alone will not suffice: the administrator will need to make sure that all files on the system are relabeled (the context of all files needs to be set). Without SELinux support, Linux will create and update files without updating or setting the SELinux labels on those files. When the system is later rebooted with SELinux support, SELinux will not have any knowledge of the context of a file unless the labels are reset.

Relabeling the filesystem is covered in *Chapter 4, Using File Contexts and Process Domains*.

In many situations, administrators often want to disable SELinux when it starts preventing certain tasks. This is careless to say the least, and here's why:

- SELinux is a security component—part of the operating system. Disabling SELinux is like disabling a firewall because it is blocking some communication. It might help because it's a faster way of getting something to work again, but you're removing measures that were enabled to protect you.

- Just as with a firewall, SELinux is configurable by rules. If an application is prevented from working correctly, we need to update the rules for that application, just as with additional firewall rules that enable a particular network flow. We will start updating SELinux policy rules from *Chapter 5, Controlling Network Communications,* onward.

- In the worst case, when we want to allow every action an application performs unconditionally, we can still leave SELinux on and just run this application in an unrestricted SELinux domain, called a *permissive* domain.

Distributions put significant effort in the integration of SELinux within their products, and they have awesome support channels to help you out if all things fail.

Switching to permissive or enforcing mode

Most distribution-provided Linux kernels allow switching between enforcing and permissive mode through a simple administrative command. This feature is called the **SELinux development mode** and is supported by the CONFIG_SECURITY_SELINUX_ DEVELOP kernel configuration parameter. This kernel parameter, if set, also has the Linux kernel boot in permissive mode first, unless a specific boot option (enforcing=1) is set.

Although we could consider this development mode a risk (all a malicious person would need to do is switch SELinux to permissive mode to disable its access controls), switching the mode requires strong administrative privileges (like the root user has), which most application domains don't have.

The command to switch between permissive mode and enforcing mode is the setenforce command. It takes a single argument: 0 (permissive) or 1 (enforcing). The permissive and enforcing strings are allowed by the command as well.

The change takes effect immediately. For instance, we can use the following command to switch to permissive mode:

```
# setenforce 0
```

The effect of `setenforce` is the same as writing the right integer value into the `/sys/fs/selinux/enforce` pseudo-file, as illustrated in the following code snippet:

```
# echo 0 > /sys/fs/selinux/enforce
```

Switching between permissive and enforcing mode can be of interest for policy developers or system administrators who are modifying the system to use SELinux properly. We can also use it to quickly verify whether an application warning or error is due to SELinux access controls or not—assuming the application is not SELinux-aware, which we will talk about in the *Understanding SELinux-aware applications* section.

On production systems, it might be of interest to disable the ability to switch to permissive mode. Disabling this feature usually requires the Linux kernel to be rebuilt, but SELinux policy developers have also thought of a different way to disallow users from toggling the SELinux state. The privileges that users need to switch to permissive mode are conditional, and system administrators can easily toggle this to disable switching back from enforcing mode to permissive mode. The condition is implemented through an SELinux Boolean called `secure_mode_policyload` whose default value is `off` (meaning switching SELinux state is allowed).

SELinux Booleans are configurable options that take on a single value (`on` or `off`, although `true`/`false` and `1`/`0` are valid values as well) and manipulate parts of the active SELinux policy. The value of the conditionals can be persisted (meaning they survive reboots) or be kept only during the current boot session. We can persist the value across reboots by adding `-P` to the `setsebool` command, as follows:

```
# setsebool -P secure_mode_policyload on
```

SELinux Booleans are covered in more depth in *Chapter 12, Tuning SELinux Policies*.

The use of the `secure_mode_policyload` SELinux Boolean allows administrators to restrict switching from enforcing mode back to permissive mode. This does not disable SELinux completely, but only toggles whether it will act upon its policies or not.

Switching from a disabled state to a running state is not supported. However, the reverse is possible, but only under the following condition: if the Linux kernel is built with the `SECURITY_SELINUX_DISABLE` kernel configuration parameter, then services such as `init` can effectively disable SELinux at runtime, but only if no SELinux policy is loaded yet. This functionality, however, is not recommended to be actively used, and was only introduced for platforms where boot options are hard to use. The feature is marked as deprecated in recent kernels as such platforms are few in number.

Using kernel boot parameters

Using the `setenforce` command makes sense when we want to switch to permissive or enforcing mode at a point in time when we have interactive access to the system. But what if we need this on system boot? If the system refuses to boot properly due to SELinux access controls, we cannot edit the `/etc/selinux/config` file. Luckily, we can change the SELinux state through other means as well.

The solution is to use kernel boot parameters. We can boot a Linux system with one or two parameters that take precedence over the `/etc/selinux/config` setting, as follows:

- `selinux=0`: This informs the system to disable SELinux completely, and has the same effect as setting `SELINUX=disabled` in the configuration file. When set, the other parameter (`enforcing`) is not consulted. Please remember that booting a system with SELinux disabled means that to enable it again, we need to relabel all files and resources on the filesystem. The `selinux=` parameter is supported through the `CONFIG_SECURITY_SELINUX_BOOTPARAM` kernel configuration.

- `enforcing=0`: This informs the system to run SELinux in permissive mode, and has the same effect as setting `SELINUX=permissive` in the configuration file.

- `enforcing=1`: This informs the system to run SELinux in enforcing mode, and has the same effect as setting `SELINUX=enforcing` in the configuration file.

Consider a Linux system that uses GRUB2 as its boot loader, and we want to add `enforcing=0` to the boot entry. To accomplish this, we execute the following steps:

1. Reboot the system until the GRUB2 boot screen comes up.

2. Navigate with the arrow keys to the boot entry for which the SELinux state must be altered. This is usually the default boot entry and should be already selected.

3. Press the *E* key to edit the boot entry line. Do this before the GRUB2 timer reaches zero; otherwise, the system will continue to boot.

4. Use the arrow keys to go to the end of the line that starts with `options`. If no such line exists, go to the end of the line that starts with `linux`, `linux16`, or `linuxefi`.

5. Add `enforcing=0` to the end of this line.

6. Press *Ctrl + X* or *F10* to boot the entry.

Other boot loaders have similar approaches to changing the boot line without persisting it for every reboot. Consult your distribution documentation for more details.

Alongside the SELinux-specific parameters, there are a few **Linux Security Module** (**LSM**)-related boot parameters that can be useful to know, especially when you are combining multiple LSM modules on the same system. These are detailed as follows:

- The `lsm.debug` boot parameter enables LSM initialization debugging output, showing which LSM modules it effectively enables or ignores, and which LSM modules are considered as exclusive.

- The `lsm=lsm1,…,lsmN` option chooses the order of LSM initialization. For instance, to initialize SELinux before lockdown, use `lsm=selinux,lockdown`.

- The `security=` boot parameter enables selection of the active, major/exclusive LSM module. This parameter, however, is deprecated, favoring the `lsm=` parameter.

When using SELinux in production, it might be wise to properly protect the boot menu— for instance, by password-protecting the menu and regularly verifying the integrity of the boot menu files.

Disabling SELinux protections for a single service

Since policy version 23 (which came with Linux 2.6.26), SELinux also supports a more granular approach to switching between permissive and enforcing mode: the use of permissive domains. As mentioned before, a domain is a term that SELinux uses for types (labels) assigned to processes. With **permissive domains**, we can mark one or more domains as permissive (and, as such, not enforced by SELinux rules), even though the rest of the system is still running in enforcing mode.

To make a domain permissive, we use the `semanage` command, as follows:

```
# semanage permissive -a minidlna_t
```

With the same `semanage` command, we can list the currently defined permissive domains, like this:

```
# semanage permissive -l
Builtin Permissive Types

Customized Permissive Types

minidlna_t
```

In the previous example, you will notice that there is also room for *built-in* permissive types. These are domains that have been marked as permissive by the policy developers of the Linux distribution itself. Some distributions opt to introduce new application policies in permissive mode first, allowing users to test out the policies before enforcing them. When that is the case, you can find these permissive domains under `Builtin Permissive Types`.

Another method for listing the custom permissive types (those not marked as permissive through the distribution) is to use the `semodule` command. In the previous chapter, we briefly touched on this command when talking about SELinux policy modules. We can use it to list the SELinux policy modules that have `permissive_` in their name because the `semanage permissive` command generates a small SELinux policy module to mark the domain as permissive, as illustrated in the following code snippet:

```
# semodule -l | grep permissive_
permissive_minidlna_t
```

To remove the permissive mode from the domain, pass the `-d` argument to the `semanage` command. This is only possible for domains that the system administrator marked as permissive, though—distribution-provided permissive domains cannot be switched to enforcing mode through this approach. This is illustrated in the following code snippet:

```
# semanage permissive -d minidlna_t
```

When a domain is marked as permissive, the application should behave as if SELinux is not enabled on the system (SELinux will not be enforcing anything that particular application/domain does), making it easier for us to discover whether SELinux is really causing a permission issue. Note, though, that other domains (including those that interact with a permissive domain) are themselves still governed and enforced through the SELinux access controls.

Understanding SELinux-aware applications

Most applications themselves do not have knowledge that they are running on an SELinux-enabled system. Without this knowledge, permissive mode truly means that the application behaves as if SELinux were not enabled to begin with. However, some applications actively rely on the SELinux policy to make access control decisions, or interact with SELinux for further information gathering. We call these applications **SELinux-aware** because they change their behavior based on the SELinux-related information available.

Sadly, many of these SELinux-aware applications do not properly validate whether they are running in permissive mode or not. As a result, running these applications in a permissive domain (or the entire system in permissive mode) will generally not result in the application running as if SELinux were not active.

Examples of such applications are the **Secure Shell** (**SSH**) daemon, the system login service, the `init` system, and some cron daemons, as well as several core Linux utilities (such as `ls` and `id`). They might show permission failures or different behavior based on the SELinux policy, even if SELinux is not in enforcing mode.

We can find out whether an application is SELinux-aware by checking whether the application is dynamically linked with the `libselinux` library. Such checks are possible with `readelf`, `ldd`, or `objdump`, as follows:

```
$ readelf -d /bin/ls | grep selinux
0x0000000000000001 (NEEDED)          Shared library: [libselinux.
so.1]
$ ldd /bin/ls | grep selinux
libselinux.so.1 => /lib64/libselinux.so.1 (0x00005d415f3f03f0)

$ objdump -x /bin/ls | grep selinux
NEEDED      libselinux.so.1
```

Knowing whether an application is SELinux-aware or not can help in troubleshooting failures, as the application's behavior might still be different between a disabled SELinux state and a permissive SELinux state.

Up until now, we've focused on enabling or disabling SELinux, and thus on a granular or coarse-grained matter. Once it is enabled though, its interaction with the administrator will be through policy enforcement and logging. So, let's look at how SELinux handles logging.

SELinux logging and auditing

SELinux developers understand that a security-oriented subsystem such as SELinux can only succeed if it is capable of enhanced logging and—even—debugging. Every action that SELinux takes, as part of the LSM hooks that it implements, should be auditable. Denials (actions that SELinux prevents) should always be logged so that administrators can take due action. SELinux tuning and changes, such as loading new policies or altering SELinux Booleans, should always result in an audit event.

Following audit events

By default, SELinux will send its messages to the Linux audit subsystem (assuming the Linux kernel is configured with the audit subsystem enabled through the CONFIG_AUDIT kernel configuration). There, the messages are picked up by the Linux audit daemon (auditd) and logged in the /var/log/audit/audit.log file. Distributions and administrators can define additional handling rules by configuring the audit dispatcher process (audisp), which picks up audit events and dispatches them to one or more separate processes. The SELinux troubleshooting daemon (setroubleshootd), an optional service to provide help with troubleshooting SELinux events, uses this to get access to audit events.

The audit event flow is shown in this diagram:

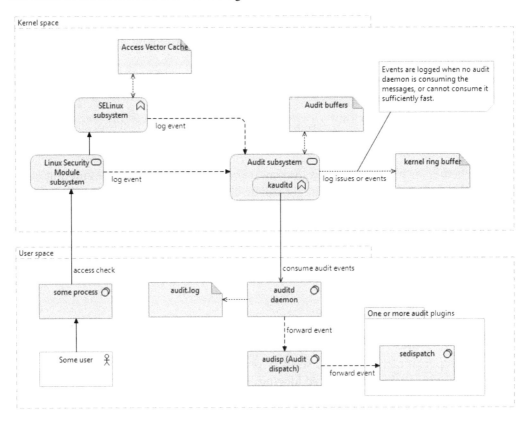

Figure 2.1 – Flow of audit events generated by SELinux

With SELinux enabled, (almost) every permission check that results in a denial is logged. When Linux auditing is enabled, these denials are logged by the audit daemon in the audit.log file by default. If the audit daemon is unavailable, the events are stored in the Linux kernel message buffer, which we can consult using the dmesg command. The events in the kernel message buffer are also often captured through the system logger.

If the SELinux troubleshooting daemon is installed, then the audit daemon will, alongside its logging, also dispatch the events through the audit dispatch system toward the sedispatch command. This command will further handle the event and send it through D-Bus (a system bus implementation popular on Linux systems) to the SELinux troubleshooting daemon. This daemon will analyze the event and might suggest one or more fixes to the administrator. We will cover the SELinux troubleshooting daemon in the *Getting help with denials* section.

Whenever SELinux verifies a particular access, it does not always go over the entire policy. Instead, it has an **access vector cache** (**AVC**), in which it stores the results of previous access attempts. This cache ensures that SELinux can quickly react to activities without having a huge impact on performance. We notice the abbreviation of this cache as the message type for most SELinux events, as shown at the beginning of the following example:

```
type=AVC msg=audit(03/22/2020 12:15:38.557:2331): avc: denied
{ read } for pid=12569 comm="dmesg" name="xterm-256color"
dev="sdb2" ino=131523 scontext=sysadm_u:sysadm_r:dmesg_t:s0-
s0:c0.c1023 tcontext=system_u:object_r:etc_t:s0 tclass=file
permissive=0
```

When the Linux kernel checks a permission request, this request is represented as an *access vector*, and the cache is then consulted to quickly find the appropriate response. If the cache has the right access vector, then the decision is taken from the cache; otherwise, the SELinux subsystem consults the policy itself and updates the cache. Of course, SELinux invalidates the cache when a new policy is loaded or the policy is dynamically adjusted. This ensures that all permission checks are in line with the active policy.

This inner working of SELinux is less relevant to most administrators, but at least now we know where the term *AVC* comes from.

Tuning the AVC

The AVC can be slightly tuned, by setting the size of the cache or its related tables.

We can configure the cache size itself through the /sys/fs/selinux/avc/cache_ threshold pseudo-file (available if the CONFIG_SECURITY_SELINUX_AVC_STATS kernel configuration is set). For instance, to increase the cache size to 768 entries (the default is 512), the following command would be used:

```
# echo 768 > /sys/fs/selinux/avc/cache_threshold
```

To confirm the cache threshold, read the file, as follows:

```
# cat /sys/fs/selinux/avc/cache_threshold
768
```

The AVC hash statistics are available through the hash_stats pseudo-file, as illustrated in the following code snippet:

```
$ cat /sys/fs/selinux/avc/hash_stats
entries: 506
buckets used: 233/512
longest chain: 5
```

If you suspect that lower system performance is due to SELinux, then we advise you to look at the longest chain output in hash_stats. If it is longer than 10, then some performance impact can be expected, and updating the cache size might help.

The avcstat command shows the evolution of the cache over time (the first number is the total since boot). When the number of cache misses is high or volatile, or the number of reclaims (obsoleting oldest cache entries and reusing them for new ones) is volatile, then the cache size might need to be increased. The command is illustrated in the following code snippet:

```
$ avcstat 5
lookups    hits         misses       allocs       reclaims
frees
58396334   58382324     14010        14010        10736
13511
591        591          0            0            0          0
1657       1653         4            4            0          0
```

Recent kernels also allow the number of buckets used through a kernel configuration parameter to be set (CONFIG_SECURITY_SELINUX_SIDTAB_HASH_BITS), and its cache statistics can be viewed through the /sys/fs/selinux/ss/sidtab_hash_stats pseudo-file, as illustrated in the following code snippet:

```
$ cat /sys/fs/selinux/ss/sidtab_hash_stats
entries: 285
buckets use: 55/512
longest chain: 3
```

Another performance parameter is the size of the internal **session ID (SID)** (the internal identifier used to represent contexts) to the string cache. Sadly, we can only configure this parameter at kernel build time, using the CONFIG_SECURITY_SELINUX_SID2STR_CACHE_SIZE setting.

Uncovering more logging

There is an important SELinux policy directive that provides control over what is (not) audited, and that is dontaudit. A dontaudit rule in the SELinux policy tells SELinux that an access denial should not be logged. This is the only example where SELinux won't log a denial—the SELinux policy writer has explicitly disabled the auditing of events. This is usually done to remove clutter from the logs and hide cosmetic denials that have no influence on the security of the system.

The seinfo utility can tell us how many of these rules, as well as its sibling rule auditallow (log events, even though they are allowed by the policy), are currently active, as illustrated in the following code snippet:

```
$ seinfo | grep -i audit
Auditallow:      1      Dontaudit:      5559
Auditallowxperm: 0      Dontauditxperm:    0
```

Luckily, we can disable these dontaudit rules at will. Through the following semodule command, these rules are removed from the active policy:

```
# semodule --disable_dontaudit --build
```

The arguments can also be abbreviated to -D and -B, respectively. To re-enable the dontaudit rules, just rebuild the policy like so:

```
# semodule -B
```

Disabling the dontaudit rules can sometimes help in troubleshooting failures that do not result in any useful audit event. Generally speaking, though, audit events that policy writers mark as cosmetic are not the cause of a failure.

Configuring Linux auditing

SELinux will try to use the audit subsystem when available and will fall back to regular system logging when it isn't. This can either be because the Linux kernel audit subsystem is not configured or because the Linux audit daemon itself is not running.

For a Linux audit, we usually do not need to configure anything as SELinux AVC denials are logged by default. You will find the denials in the audit log file (/var/log/audit/audit.log), usually together with the system call and other event messages related to the same action, as illustrated in the following code snippet:

```
type=PROCTITLE msg=audit(...) : proctitle=ping 8.8.8.8
type=SYSCALL msg=audit(...) : arch=x86_64 syscall=socket
success=no exit=EACCES(Permission denied) a0=inet a1=SOCK_
DGRAM a2=icmp a3=0x7fffac013050 items=0 ppid=2685 pid=17292
auid=admin uid=root gid=root euid=root suid=root fsuid=root
egid=root sgid=root fsgid=root tty=tty1 ses=1 comm=ping
exe=/bin/ping subj=sysadm_u:sysadm_r:ping_t:s0-s0:c0.c1023
key=(null)
  type=AVC msg=audit(...) : avc:  denied  { create } for
pid=17292 comm=ping scontext=sysadm_u:sysadm_r:ping_t:s0-
s0:c0.c1023 tcontext=sysadm_u:sysadm_r:ping_t:s0-s0:c0.c1023
tclass=icmp_socket permissive=0
```

To configure the target log file for the audit system, use the log_file parameter in /etc/audit/auditd.conf.

To enable remote audit logging (to centralize audit events from multiple hosts on a single system), you have the option of either enabling syslog forwarding or enabling the audisp-remote plugin.

With syslog forwarding, the audit dispatch daemon is configured to send audit events to the local system logger as well. It is then up to the administrator to configure the local system logger to pass on events toward a remote system.

> **Informational note**
>
> The use of syslog forwarding has the advantage that no additional software deployments and daemons are needed on the servers to centralize their log events. The setup is hence also reusable in case hardened appliances are introduced to the environment. Of course, other log management solutions exist that can watch for log events and send those to the central server. These, however, require more configuration, and introduce an additional software agent to install.

Edit the `/etc/audit/plugins.d/syslog.conf` file and set `active` to `yes`, as follows:

```
# vi /etc/audit/plugins.d/syslog.conf
active = yes
direction = out
path = /sbin/audisp-syslog
type = always
args = LOG_INFO
format = string
```

Using the system logger to centralize audit events might not be the best option though, as system loggers generally use unencrypted—and often not even guaranteed—data delivery. With the `audisp-remote` plugin, we can even use an encrypted channel to send the audit events, and provide guaranteed delivery to a remote `auditd` server.

First, configure the audit daemon on the target (log) server to accept audit logs from remote hosts by enabling the audit daemon to listen on port 60. We also change the event formatting to an enriched value and add hostnames to the events so that we can distinguish events from multiple hosts, as follows:

```
# vi /etc/audit/auditd.conf
tcp_listen_port = 60
log_format = ENRICHED
name_format = HOSTNAME
```

Next, on the source systems, configure `auditd.conf` as shown in the previous code snippet, but without the port setting. Then, configure the `audisp-remote` plugin to connect to the target server's audit daemon, as follows:

```
# vi /etc/audit/audisp-remote.conf
remote_server = <targethostname>
port = 60
```

Finally, enable the `audisp-remote` plugin, as follows:

```
# vi /etc/audit/plugins.d/au-remote.conf
active = yes
```

Don't forget to restart the audit daemon so that the changes take effect.

We can only recommend you always use the Linux audit subsystem. Not only does it integrate nicely with troubleshooting utilities; it also allows administrators to use the audit tools to query the audit logs or even generate reports, such as with `aureport`, as illustrated in the following code snippet:

```
# aureport --avc --start recent
AVC Report
==================================================================
# date time comm subj syscall class permission obj result event
==================================================================
...
7. 03/21/2020 19:40:55 sudo sysadm_u:sysadm_r:sysadm_sudo_t:s0-
s0:c0.c1023 257 dir search sysadm_u:sysadm_r:sysadm_t:s0-s0:c0.
c1023 denied 1067
...
10. 03/21/2020 19:48:19 dmesg sysadm_u:sysadm_r:dmesg_t:s0-
s0:c0.c1023 21 file read system_u:object_r:etc_t:s0 denied 1080
```

The Linux audit system is an important aide for Linux administrators, and not just for SELinux troubleshooting. But next to the Linux audit system, events can also be directed toward the local system logger, as explained next.

Configuring the local system logger

When auditing is not enabled, or the Linux audit daemon is not running, then the system logger is responsible for capturing SELinux events. The system logger will log these events through the kernel logging facility (`kern.*`). Most system loggers will save these kernel log events in a general log file, such as `/var/log/messages`.

We can configure the system logger to direct SELinux AVC messages into its own log file, such as `/var/log/avc.log`. For instance, for the `rsyslog` system logger, we can add in a configuration entry under `/etc/rsyslog.d` named `99-selinux.conf`, with the following content:

```
# vi /etc/rsyslog.d/99-selinux.conf
:msg, contains, "avc: "        -/var/log/avc.log
```

After restarting the system logger, the AVC-related messages will show up in the `/var/log/avc.log` file.

When the local system logger handles SELinux logging, an easy method to quickly obtain the latest AVC denials (or other messages) is through the `dmesg` command, as illustrated in the following code snippet:

```
# dmesg | grep avc | tail
```

Be aware, though, that unlike the audit logs, many systems allow the `dmesg` content to be read by regular users. This might result in some information leakage to untrusted users. For this reason, some SELinux policies do not allow regular users to access the kernel ring buffer (and, as such, use `dmesg`) unless the `user_dmesg` SELinux Boolean is set to `on`, as illustrated in the following code snippet:

```
# setsebool user_dmesg on
```

The `user_dmesg` SELinux Boolean is not available on CentOS, though. There, only the standard unconfined user type and the administrative user type have access to the kernel ring buffer. To prevent other users from reading this information, you need to map these users to non-administrative SELinux users, such as `user_u` or `(x)guest_u`, which is something described further on in this book.

Reading SELinux denials

The one thing every one of us will have to do several times with SELinux systems is to read and interpret SELinux denial information. When SELinux prohibits access and there is no `dontaudit` rule in place to hide it, SELinux will log it. If nothing is logged, it was probably not SELinux that was responsible for the failure. Remember: SELinux comes after Linux **discretionary access control (DAC)** checks, so if a regular permission doesn't allow a certain activity then SELinux is never consulted.

SELinux denial messages are logged the moment SELinux prevents some access from occurring. When SELinux is in enforcing mode, the application usually returns a **Permission denied** error, although sometimes it might be a bit more obscure. An example of this can be seen in the following code snippet:

```
$ ls /proc/1
ls: cannot access '/proc/1': Permission denied
# ls -ldZ /proc/1
dr-xr-xr-x. 9 root system_u:system_r:init_t:s0 0 Mar 21 10:54 /
proc/1
```

So, what does a denial message look like? The following command output shows a denial from the audit subsystem, which we can query through the `ausearch` command:

```
# ausearch -m avc -ts recent -i
type=AVC msg=audit(03/22/2020 12:15:38.557:2331): avc: denied
{ read } for pid=12569 comm="dmesg" name="xterm-256color"
dev="sdb2" ino=131523 scontext=sysadm_u:sysadm_r:dmesg_t:s0-
s0:c0.c1023 tcontext=system_u:object_r:etc_t:s0 tclass=file
permissive=0
```

Let's break up this denial into its individual components. The following list gives more information about each part of the preceding denials. As an administrator, knowing how to read denials is extremely important, so take enough time for this:

- **SELinux action**: The action that SELinux took or would take if run in `enforcing` mode. This is usually `denied`, although some actions are explicitly marked to be audited as well and would result in `granted`. Example: `denied`

- **Permissions**: The checked permissions (action initiated by the process). This is usually a single permission, although it can sometimes be a set of permissions. Example: `{ read }`

- **Process ID (PID)**: The ID of the process that was performing the action. Example: `pid=12569`

- **Process name**: The process name (command). It doesn't display any arguments to the command, though. Example: `comm="dmesg"`

- **Target name**: The name of the target (resource) that the process is performing an action on. If the target is a file, then the name is usually the filename or directory. Example: `name="xterm-256color"`

- **Target device**: The device on which the target resource resides. Together with the next field (inode number) this allows us to uniquely identify the resource on a system. Example: `dev="sdb2"`

- **Target file inode number**: The inode number of the target file or directory. Together with the device, this allows us to find the file on the filesystem. Example: `ino=131523`

- **Source context**: The context in which the process resides (the domain of the process). Example: `scontext=sysadm_u:sysadm_r:dmesg_t:s0-s0:c0.c1023`

- **Target context**: The context of the target resources. Example: `tcontext=system_u:object_r:etc_t:s0`

- **Object class**: The class of the target object—for instance, a directory, file, socket, node, pipe, file descriptor, filesystem, or capability. Example: `tclass=file`

- **Permissive mode**: The mode the domain was in when the action was executed. If set to `0`, then SELinux was in enforcing mode; otherwise, it was permissive (either for the system or for the given domain). Example: `permissive=0`

We can interpret the previous denial like so: SELinux has denied the `dmesg` command to read a file named "`xterm-256color`". The file has inode number `131523` on device `/dev/sdb2` and is labeled as `etc_t`. The `dmesg` command has PID `12569` and is labeled as `dmesg_t`. The `dmesg_t` domain was not in permissive mode.

Depending on the action and the target class, SELinux uses different fields to give all the information we need to troubleshoot a problem. Consider the following denial:

```
type=AVC msg=audit(03/22/20 18:12:52.177:2326): avc:
denied  { name_bind } for  pid=15983 comm="nginx"
src=89 scontext=system_u:system_r:httpd_t:s0
tcontext=system_u:object_r:reserved_port_t:s0 tclass=tcp_socket
permissive=0
```

The preceding denial came up because the nginx web server was configured to listen on a non-default port (89 instead of the default 80).

Identifying the problem is a matter of understanding how the operations work and properly reading the denials. The denial logs give us enough to get us started, giving a clear idea of what was denied.

Administrators might want to update the SELinux policy to allow a specific action (by adding an `allow` rule to the SELinux policy, as described further on in this book). This is, however, not always the right approach because other options exist and are usually better, such as these:

- Providing the right label on the target resource (usually the case when the target is a non-default port, non-default location, and so on)

- Switching Booleans (flags that manipulate the SELinux policy) to allow additional privileges

- Providing the right label on the source process (often the case when the acting application is not installed by the distribution package manager)

- Using the application as intended instead of through other means (as SELinux only allows expected behavior), such as starting a daemon through a service (`init` script or systemd unit) instead of through a command-line operation

If the preceding nginx example were a wanted configuration (using a non-default port), then we should label this port as a **HyperText Transfer Protocol** (**HTTP**) port and not allow the `httpd_t` domain to bind on (many) other ports.

Other SELinux-related event types

Although most SELinux log events are AVC-related, they aren't the sole event types an administrator will have to deal with. Most audit events will show SELinux information as part of the event, even though SELinux has little to do with the event itself, but a few audit event types are directly concerned with SELinux.

> **Tip**
> A full list of all possible audit events is available in the `linux/audit.h` header file, located in `/usr/include`.

USER_AVC

A `USER_AVC` event resembles regular AVC audit events, but now the source is a user space object manager. These are applications that use SELinux policy rules, but they enforce these rules themselves rather than through the kernel.

The following example is such an event, generated by D-Bus:

```
type=USER_AVC msg=audit(03/22/2020 11:25:56.123:154)
: pid=540 uid=dbus auid=unset ses=unset
subj=system_u:system_r:system_dbusd_t:s0-s0:c0.c1023
msg='avc:  denied  { acquire_svc } for service=com.redhat.
tuned spid=1460 scontext=system_u:system_r:tuned_t:s0
tcontext=system_u:system_r:tunned_t:s0 tclass=dbus permissive=0
exe=/usr/bin/dbus-daemon sauid=dbus hostname=? addr=?
terminal=?'
```

The event has two parts. Everything up to the `msg=` string is information about the user space object manager that generated the event, and is the first part of the event. The true event itself (which is the second part) is stored within the `msg=` part and includes similar fields, as we already know from regular AVCs.

SELINUX_ERR

An `SELINUX_ERR` event comes up when SELinux detects a general policy violation rather than an access control violation. It cannot be resolved by SELinux policy writers by just allowing the operation. These events usually point to a misuse of applications and services that the policy is not tailored to accomplish, and an example is shown in the following code snippet:

```
type=PATH msg=audit(03/22/2020 12:25:53.104:2364) : item=0
name=/usr/sbin/rpc.nfsd inode=3019958 dev=08:12 mode=file,755
ouid=root ogid=root rdev=00:00 obj=system_u:object_r:nfsd_
exec_t:s0 nametype=NORMAL cap_fp=none cap_fi=none cap_fe=0 cap_
fver=0 cap_frootid=0
type=SELINUX_ERR msg=audit(03/22/2020 12:25:53.104:2364) :
op=security_compute_sid invalid_context=sysadm_u:sysadm_r:nfsd_
t:s0-s0:c0.c1023 scontext=sysadm_u:sysadm_r:sysadm_t:s0-s0:c0.
c1023 tcontext=system_u:object_r:nfsd_exec_t:s0 tclass=process
```

In the preceding example, a user (running in the `sysadm_t` domain) was executing `rpc.nfsd` (with `nfsd_exec_t` as the label), and the policy wanted to transition to the `nfsd_t` domain. However, that resulted in a full context of `sysadm_u:sysadm_r:nfsd_t:s0-s0:c0.c1023`, which is not a valid context. The `sysadm_r` SELinux role does not support the `nfsd_t` domain.

MAC_POLICY_LOAD

A `MAC_POLICY_LOAD` event occurs whenever the system loads a new SELinux policy in memory. This occurs when the administrator loads a new or updated SELinux policy module, rebuilds the policy with the `dontaudit` rules disabled, or toggles an SELinux Boolean that the administrator wants to persist across reboots. Such an event is illustrated in the following code snippet:

```
type=MAC_POLICY_LOAD msg=audit(03/22/2020 12:28:17.077:2368) :
auid=admin ses=1 lsm=selinux res=yes
```

When a `MAC_POLICY_LOAD` event occurs, you might notice a subsequent `USER_MAC_POLICY_LOAD` event. This occurs when a user space object manager detects an update on the SELinux policy and takes action. Note that not all user space object managers will send out this event: some object managers will query the live policy and, as such, do not need to act when a new policy loads.

MAC_CONFIG_CHANGE

When an SELinux Boolean changes but doesn't persist, then a `MAC_CONFIG_CHANGE` event will be dispatched. This tells the administrator that the active policy has been instructed to change its behavior slightly, but within the bounds of the existing loaded policy. Such an event is illustrated in the following code snippet:

```
type=MAC_CONFIG_CHANGE msg=audit(03/22/2020 12:29:49.564:2370)
: bool=virt_use_nfs val=0 old_val=1 auid=admin ses=1
```

In the preceding example, the `virt_use_nfs` SELinux Boolean was changed from the value 1 (on) to 0 (off).

MAC_STATUS

A `MAC_STATUS` event shows up when the SELinux enforcement state has been changed. For instance, when an administrator uses `setenforce 0` to put SELinux in permissive mode, then the following event occurs:

```
type=MAC_STATUS msg=audit(03/22/2020 12:30:45.200:2372) :
enforcing=0 old_enforcing=1 auid=admin ses=1 enabled=1 old-
enabled=1 lsm=selinux res=yes
```

`MAC_STATUS` is also used to inform administrators when the SELinux state itself (enabled or disabled) is altered.

NetLabel events

NetLabel is a Linux kernel project to support labeled network packets, allowing security contexts such as SELinux contexts to be passed on between hosts. One of the protocols that the NetLabel implementation supports in Linux is **Common IP Security Option** (**CIPSO**) labeling, which we will cover in *Chapter 5*, *Controlling Network Communications*.

The following audit events are related to the NetLabel capability:

- `MAC_UNLBL_STCADD` and `MAC_UNLBL_STCDEL` events are triggered when a static label is added or removed. Static labeling means that if a packet is received or sent and it does not have a label, then this "default" static label is assigned.

- `MAC_MAP_ADD` and `MAC_MAP_DEL` events are triggered when a mapping between a labeling protocol (such as CIPSO) and its parameters against an LSM (SELinux) domain is added or removed from the configuration.

- `MAC_CIPSOV4_ADD` and `MAC_CIPSOV4_DEL` events are triggered when a CIPSO (IPv4) configuration is added or removed.

Labeled IPsec events

Another labeled network protocol that Linux supports is **labeled IPsec**, where **IPsec** is short for **Information Protocol Security**. Through this, the SELinux context of the source process (which is communicating over the IPsec tunnel toward a target resource) is known by the IPsec daemons at both ends of the tunnel. Furthermore, SELinux will contain rules about which domains can communicate over an IPsec tunnel and which domains can communicate with each other network-wise.

The following audit events are related to IPsec:

- `MAC_IPSEC_ADDSA` and `MAC_IPSEC_DELSA` events are used when a security association is added or removed (new IPsec tunnels are defined or deleted).

- `MAC_IPSEC_ADDSPD` and `MAC_IPSEC_DELSPD` events are used when a security policy definition is added or removed. Security policies generally describe whether network packets need to be handled by IPsec and, if so, through which security association.

- A `MAC_IPSEC_EVENT` event is a generic event for IPsec audit messages.

SELinux support for labeled IPsec is described further on in this book.

Using ausearch

The `ausearch` command, part of the Linux audit framework, is a frequently used command for querying audit events stored on the system. We already briefly covered it when taking a first look at an AVC denial, but only briefly mentioning it won't do it justice.

With `ausearch`, we can search for events that originated during or after a selected time period. We used the `-ts recent` (time start) option in the past, which displays events that occurred during the past 10 minutes. The argument can also be a timestamp. Other supported shorthand values are listed as follows:

- `today`, meaning starting at 1 second past midnight on the current day

- `yesterday`, meaning starting at 1 second past midnight the previous day

- `this-week`, `this-month`, or `this-year`, meaning starting at 1 second past midnight on the first day of the current week, current month, or current year

- `checkpoint`, which uses the timestamp mentioned in a checkpoint file created in a previous run

- `boot`, which implies only events since the system booted should be shown

- `week-ago`, meaning starting at 1 second after midnight exactly 7 days ago

The use of `checkpoint` is particularly useful when troubleshooting SELinux issues as it allows us to show denials (and other SELinux events) since the last invocation of the `ausearch` command. This is illustrated in the following code snippet:

```
# ausearch --checkpoint /root/ausearch-checkpoint.txt -ts
checkpoint
```

This allows administrators to perform minor tweaks and reproduce the problem and only see the events since then, instead of going through all events over and over again.

By default, the `ausearch` command displays all events stored in the audit log. On busy systems, this can be very verbose and may result in unwanted events being displayed as well. Luckily, users can limit the type of events queried through the `ausearch` command.

For SELinux troubleshooting, using `avc`, `user_avc`, `selinux_err` limits the events nicely to those needed for the job, as illustrated in the following code snippet:

```
# ausearch -m avc,user_avc,selinux_err -ts recent
```

If the numeric display of fields such as user IDs and timestamps is too confusing, then it is possible for `ausearch` to look up and translate user IDs to usernames and timestamps to formatted time fields. Add the `-i` option to `ausearch` to have it interpret these fields and display the interpreted values instead.

In this section, we've seen how SELinux notifies the system about its actions through log events, and where these log events are stored. In the next section, we'll look at how to act upon these events.

Getting help with denials

On some distributions, additional support tools are available that help us identify the cause of a denial. These tools have some knowledge of common mistakes (for instance, setting the right context on files to allow the web server to read them). Other distributions require us to use our experience to make proper decisions, supporting us through the distribution mailing lists, bug tracking sites, and other cooperation locations—for example, **Internet Relay Chat** (**IRC**).

Troubleshooting with setroubleshoot

In CentOS (and other **Red Hat Enterprise Linux** (RHEL)-related distributions such as Fedora), additional tools are present that help us troubleshoot denials. The tools work together to catch a denial, look for a plausible solution, and inform the administrator about the denial and its suggested resolutions.

When used on a graphical workstation, denials can even result in popups that ask the administrator to review them immediately. Install the setroubleshoot package to get this support. On servers without a graphical environment, administrators can see the information in the system logs or can even configure the system to send out SELinux denial messages via email. Install the setroubleshoot-server package to get this support.

Under the hood, it is the audit daemon that triggers its audit event dispatcher application (audispd). This application supports plugins, something the SELinux folks gratefully implemented. They built an application called sedispatch that will act as a plugin for audispd. The sedispatch application checks whether the audit event is an SELinux denial and, if so, forwards the events to D-Bus. D-Bus then forwards the events to the setroubleshootd application (or launches the application if it isn't running yet), which analyzes the denial and prepares feedback for the administrator.

When running on a workstation, seapplet is triggered to show a popup on the administrator workstation. The administrator can then select **Show** to view more details. Administrators don't need a graphical user interface to be informed about SELinux issues, though. You can find analyzed feedback on the filesystem, and in the system logs you can read how to easily reach this information, as illustrated in the following code snippet:

```
Mar 22 11:40:35 ppubssa3ed setroubleshoot[1544]: SELinux is
preventing /usr/sbin/nginx from name_bind access on the tcp_
socket port 89. For complete SELinux messages run: sealert -l
f2914dba-04ef-44ca-9a0b-0f5e62ec72e4
```

We can look at a complete explanation through the sealert command (as mentioned in the log), as follows:

```
# sealert -l f2914dba-04ef-44ca-9a0b-0f5e62ec72e4
SELinux is preventing /usr/sbin/nginx from name_bind access on
the tcp_socket port 89.
*****  Plugin bind_ports (99.5 confidence) suggests
************************
If you want to allow /usr/sbin/nginx to bind to network port 89
Then you need to modify the port type.
Do
```

```
# semanage port -a -t PORT_TYPE -p tcp 89
    where PORT_TYPE is one of the following: http_cache_port_t,
http_port_t, jboss_management_port_t, jboss_messaging_port_t,
ntop_port_t, puppet_port_t.

*****  Plugin catchall (1.49 confidence) suggests
***************************

. . .
```

The `sealert` application is a command-line application that parses the information stored by the `setroubleshoot` daemon (in `/var/lib/setroubleshoot`).

This will provide us with a set of options to resolve the denial. In the case of the Apache-related denial shown earlier, `sealert` gives us one option with a certain confidence score. Depending on the problem, this tool might show multiple options, each with its own confidence figure (that is, how certain `sealert` is that this is the right resolution).

As we can see from this example, the `setroubleshoot` application itself uses plugins to analyze denials. These plugins (offered through the `setroubleshoot-plugins` package) look at a denial to check whether they match a particular, well-known use case (for example, when to change an SELinux Boolean or when a target resource has a wrong context) and give feedback to `setroubleshoot` about how certain the plugin is so that this denial can be resolved through its recommended method.

Sending emails when SELinux denials occur

Once a system is fine-tuned and denials no longer occur regularly, administrators can opt to have `setroubleshootd` send emails whenever a new denial comes up. This truly brings SELinux's host intrusion detection/prevention capabilities on top, as administrators do not need to constantly watch their logs for information. However, keep in mind that this could lead to a sudden burst in emails, which might result in **Denial of Service (DoS)**-like behavior, if many denials are triggered. Administrators should only implement this if their email infrastructure has rate limiting or other **Quality of Service (QoS)** controls in place.

Open /etc/setroubleshoot/setroubleshoot.conf in a text editor and locate the [email] section. Update the parameters to match the local mailing infrastructure, as follows:

```
# vi /etc/setroubleshoot/setroubleshoot.conf
[email]
recipients_filepath = /var/lib/setroubleshoot/email_alert_
recipients
smtp_port = 25
smtp_host = localhost
from_address = selinux@infra.example.com
subject = [infra] SELinux Alert for host infra.example.com
```

Next, edit the email_alert_recipients file (as referenced through the recipients_filepath variable), and add the email addresses that need to be notified when an SELinux alert comes up.

Finally, restart the D-Bus daemon, as follows:

```
# systemctl restart dbus
```

When working on a non-systemd system, use the following command instead:

```
# service dbus restart
```

The D-Bus restart is needed as D-Bus manages the setroubleshootd daemon.

Using audit2why

If setroubleshoot and sealert are not available in the Linux distribution, we can still get some information about a denial. Although it isn't as extensive as the plugins offered by setroubleshoot, the audit2why utility (which is short for audit2allow -w) does provide some feedback on a denial. Sadly, it isn't always right in its deduction.

Let's try it out against the same denial for which we used sealert, as follows:

```
# ausearch -m avc -ts recent | audit2why
type=AVC msg=audit(1584880436.644:385): avc:
denied  { name_bind } for  pid=5119 comm="nginx"
src=89 scontext=system_u:system_r:httpd_t:s0
tcontext=system_u:object_r:reserved_port_t:s0 tclass=tcp_socket
permissive=0

  Was caused by:
```

```
    Missing type enforcement (TE) allow rule.

    You can use audit2allow to generate a loadable module to
allow this access.
```

The `audit2why` utility here didn't consider that the context of the target location was wrong, and it suggests that the policy be updated to allow the web server to bind to the `unreserved_port_t` type, unlike the information provided by `setroubleshoot`, which was more accurate, recommending that the target port be relabeled instead.

As the output of the command mentions, another tool exists called `audit2allow`, which can convert a denial into an SELinux policy. We will cover `audit2allow` in *Chapter 12, Tuning SELinux Policies*.

Interacting with systemd-journal

Alongside the Linux audit system, which is used for most SELinux logging and events, we can also gather information through other logging systems. systemd's journal, for instance, captures SELinux context information with the events and allows administrators to use this information while querying the journal.

For instance, to see the events in `systemd-journal` that are generated by an application associated with the `system_u:system_r:sssd_t:s0` context, the following command can be used:

```
# journalctl _SELINUX_CONTEXT="system_u:system_r:sssd_t:s0"
-- Logs begin at Sun 2020-03-22 10:43:48 UTC, end at Sun 2020-
03-22 12:40:12 UTC. --
Mar 22 10:43:51 ppubssa3ed sssd[545]: Starting up
Mar 22 10:43:51 ppubssa3ed sssd[be[implicit_files]][623]:
Starting up
Mar 22 10:43:51 ppubssa3ed sssd[nss][630]: Starting up
```

Because `systemd-journal` adds the SELinux context of the originating application, it is harder for malicious applications to generate fake events. Whereas regular system loggers just capture string events, `systemd-journal` retrieves the SELinux context from the system. Using the SELinux context, it is easy to group events across different but strongly related applications and have a higher guarantee that events come from a particular application.

When the `bash-completion` package is installed, we can even use it to see which
SELinux contexts are present in the `systemd-journal` logs, which makes querying the
journal logs much easier, as follows:

```
# journalctl _SELINUX_CONTEXT=<tab><tab>
kernel
system_u:system_r:auditd_t:s0
system_u:system_r:chronyd_t:s0
...
```

To find messages related to nginx, use the embedded `grep` filter, as follows:

```
# journalctl -g nginx
-- Logs begin at Sun 2020-03-22 10:43:48 UTC, end at Sun 2020-
03-22 12:52:26 UTC. --
Mar 22 11:40:32 ppubssa3ed systemd[1]: Starting The nginx HTTP
and reverse proxy server...
Mar 22 11:40:32 ppubssa3ed nginx[1538]: nginx: the
configuration file /etc/nginx/nginx.conf syntax is ok
Mar 22 11:40:32 ppubssa3ed nginx[1538]: nginx: [emerg] bind()
to 0.0.0.0:89 failed (13: Permission denied)
...
Mar 22 11:40:35 ppubssa3ed setroubleshoot[1544]: SELinux is
preventing /usr/sbin/nginx from name_bind access on the tcp_
socket port 89. For complete SELinux messages run: sealert -l
f2914dba-04ef-44ca-9a0b-0f5e62ec72e4
```

The benefit of the embedded `grep` filter is that `journalctl` will still show the multiline
messages, whereas actually redirecting the `journalctl` output through `grep` would
only show the individual lines that match the expression.

Using common sense

Common sense is not easy to document, but reading a denial often leads to the right
solution when we have some experience with file labels (and what they are used for).
If we get a denial about a web server failing to read its files, and the context of the file
is (for instance) `user_home_t`, then that should ring a bell. End user home files, for
instance, use the `user_home_t` context, which is not suitable for system files that the
web server reads.

One way to make sure that the context of the target resource is correct is to verify it with `matchpathcon`. This utility returns the context as it should be according to the SELinux policy, as follows:

```
$ matchpathcon /srv/www/html/index.html
/srv/www/html/index.html      system_u:object_r:httpd_sys_
content_t:s0
```

Performing this for denials related to files and directories might help in finding a proper solution quickly.

Furthermore, many domains have specific manual pages that inform the reader about types commonly used for each domain, as well as how to deal with the domain in more detail (for example, the available booleans, common mistakes made, and so on). These manual pages start with the main service and are suffixed with `_selinux`, as illustrated here:

```
$ man ftpd_selinux
```

In most cases, the approach to handling denials can be best described as follows:

- Is the target resource label (such as the file label) the right one? Verify this with `matchpathcon`, or compare with labels of working (accessible) resources.

- Is the source label (the domain) the expected one? An SSH daemon should run in the `sshd_t` domain, not the `init_t` domain. If this is not the case, make sure that the labels of the application itself (such as its executable binary) are correct (again, use `matchpathcon` for this).

- Is the denial one that might be covered by an SELinux boolean? In that case, the policy might already have the appropriate rules in place, only requiring a change in an SELinux boolean value. `setroubleshootd` will report this if it is the case. Usually, the manual page of the domain (such as `httpd_selinux`) will also cover the available SELinux Booleans. We explain how to query and adjust SELinux Booleans in *Chapter 12, Tuning SELinux Policies*.

Changing file labels will be discussed in *Chapter 4, Using File Contexts and Process Domains*.

To close off this section, common sense will be your most prolific approach to managing SELinux denials, but the aforementioned tools will be of assistance to begin with.

Summary

In this chapter, we saw how to enable and disable SELinux, both on a complete system level as well as a per-service level using various methods: kernel boot options, an SELinux configuration file, or plain commands. One such command is `semanage permissive`, which can disable SELinux protections for a single service.

Next, we saw where SELinux logs its events and how to interpret them, which is one of the most common tasks an administrator has to undertake when dealing with SELinux. To assist us with this interpretation, we can use tools such as `setroubleshoot`, `sealert`, and `audit2why`. We also touched upon several utilities related to Linux auditing to help us sift through various events.

In the next chapter, we will look at the first administrative task on SELinux systems: managing user accounts, their associated SELinux roles, and security clearances for the resources on the system.

Questions

1. What should administrators try before disabling SELinux?

2. Where can administrators find SELinux logs by default?

3. How do we know whether an application is SELinux-aware?

4. What is the purpose of the AVC?

5. Are AVC events the only type of events for SELinux?

3
Managing User Logins

When we log in to an SELinux-enabled system, we receive an SELinux context to work in. This context contains an SELinux user, an SELinux role, a domain, and optionally, a sensitivity range. As the SELinux user defines the roles and types that can be accessed, managing user logins and SELinux users is the first step in configuring end users on the system.

To enable properly configured users, we will learn to define users that have sufficient rights to do their jobs, ranging from regular users with strict SELinux protections to fully privileged administrative users with few SELinux protections. We will create and assign categories and sensitivities, as well as assign roles to users and use various tools to switch roles. At the end of the chapter, we will see how SELinux integrates with the Linux authentication process.

In this chapter, we're going to cover the following main topics:

- User-oriented SELinux contexts
- SELinux users and roles
- Handling SELinux roles
- SELinux and PAM

Technical requirements

Check out the following video to see the Code in Action: `https://bit.ly/3jbASmr`

User-oriented SELinux contexts

Once logged in to a system, our user will run inside a certain context. This user context defines the rights and privileges that we, as a user, have on the system. The command to obtain current user information, `id`, also supports displaying the current SELinux context information:

```
$ id -Z
unconfined_u:unconfined_r:unconfined_t:s0-s0:c0.c1023
```

On SELinux systems with a targeted policy type, chances are very high that all users are logged in as `unconfined_u` (the first part of the context). On more restricted systems, the user can be `user_u` (regular restricted users), `staff_u` (operators), `sysadm_u` (system administrators), or any of the other SELinux users.

The SELinux user defines the roles that the user can switch to. SELinux roles themselves define the application domains that the user can use. By default, a fixed number of SELinux users are available on the system, but administrators can create additional SELinux users. It is also the administrator's task to assign Linux logins to SELinux users.

SELinux roles, on the other hand, cannot be created through administrative commands, as SELinux roles are part of the SELinux policy. For this, the SELinux policy needs to be enhanced with additional rules that create the role. We will touch upon that in *Chapter 15, Using the Reference Policy*.

To view the currently available roles, use `seinfo`:

```
# seinfo --role
Roles: 14
   auditadm_r
   dbadm_r
   ...
   xguest_r
```

SELinux roles can be coarse-grained (such as `sysadm_r`) or more functionality-oriented (such as `dbadm_r`). Custom SELinux roles can even be very fine-grained, only granting the ability to transition into limited domains.

Let's see how to create and manage SELinux users.

SELinux users and roles

In SELinux-enabled environments, the login binary calls the libselinux API to establish the initial mapping between SELinux users and local users. Then, after finding the right SELinux user, the system looks up the role and domain that the user should be in and sets that as the user's context.

Listing SELinux user mappings

When logged in to the system, we can use id -Z to obtain the current SELinux context. For many users, this context will be defined by the unconfined user (unconfined_u), regardless of their username. If not that, it will generally be a context based on one of sysadm_u, staff_u, or user_u. This is because most Linux distributions will only provide a limited set of SELinux users by default, aligned with the SELinux roles that they support.

During login, the service process through which the login is handled will check a local definition file to find the appropriate mapping between the Linux account and the SELinux user. Let's look at the existing login mappings using semanage login -l. The following output is the default output on a CentOS system:

```
# semanage login -l
Login Name          SELinux User        MLS/MCS Range        Service

__default__         unconfined_u        s0-s0:c0.c1023       *
root                unconfined_u        s0-s0:c0.c1023       *
```

The output of the command shows one login mapping per line. Each mapping consists of the following:

- The Login Name for which the mapping is applicable (that is, the username)
- The SELinux User to which the login is mapped
- The MLS/MCS Range to which the login is mapped
- The Service for which the mapping applies (this is used for local customizations, which we will tackle in the *Customizing logins for services* section)

The login name can contain a few special values that do not map directly to a single Linux account:

- `__default__` is a catch-all rule. If none of the other rules match, then the users are mapped to the SELinux user identified through this line. In the given example, all users are mapped to the `unconfined_u` SELinux user, meaning regular Linux users are hardly confined in their actions. When this isn't meant to happen, administrators usually map regular logins to restricted SELinux users, while administrative logins are mapped to the `staff_u` or `sysadm_u` SELinux users.

- Login names starting with `%` will map to groups. This allows administrators to map a group of people directly to an SELinux user rather than having to manage the mappings individually.

When both an individual user mapping and group mapping match, then the individual user mapping takes precedence. When multiple group definitions exist, then SELinux will use the first matching group mapping (in the order listed in the underlying `seusers` configuration file).

> **Important note**
> System processes (non-interactively logged-in Linux accounts) are mapped to the `system_u` SELinux user. This SELinux user should never be assigned to end user logins.

In the case of an MLS- or MCS-enabled system, the mapping contains information about the user's allowed sensitivity range (MLS/MCS range). This way, we can map multiple users to the same restricted SELinux user, while differentiating between these users through the allowed sensitivities. For instance, one user might only be allowed to access low-sensitivity areas (`s0`), whereas another user might also have access to higher sensitivities (for example, `s1`) or different categories.

Mapping logins to SELinux users

Let's use a few examples to show how we make these mappings work. For more intricate details on this, see the *SELinux and PAM* section. We'll assume we have a Linux user called `lisa`, and we want her account to be mapped to the `staff_u` SELinux user, whereas all other users in the `users` group are mapped to the `user_u` SELinux user.

We can accomplish this through the `semanage login` command, using the `-a` (add) option:

```
# semanage login -a -s staff_u lisa
# semanage login -a -s user_u %users
```

The `-s` parameter assigns the SELinux user to the given login, whereas the `-r` parameter handles the sensitivity (and categories) for that user. For instance, let's modify (using `-m` instead of `-a`) the recently created group-based definition by mapping to the `staff_u` user instead, and limiting these users to the `s0-s0` sensitivity range and categories `c0` to `c4`:

```
# semanage login -m -s staff_u -r "s0-s0:c0.c4" %users
```

The sensitivity range of a login mapping may not exceed the range assigned to the SELinux user. For example, if the `staff_u` SELinux user itself is only granted access to `s0-s0:c0.c3`, then the previous command will fail as it is trying to assign a broader access range. We'll discuss how to define SELinux users and their range in the *Creating SELinux users* section.

The `semanage login` command updates the `seusers` file located inside `/etc/selinux/targeted`. If multiple group mappings are defined, then the order of mappings within this file defines which mapping applies to a given user. Users that belong to multiple mapped groups will be assigned an SELinux user based on the first match.

While it is possible to update the order of the entries in the `seusers` file, this is not recommended. Every time `semanage login` modifies the `seusers` file, it will reorder the mappings. Instead, when a user belongs to multiple mapped groups, we advise you to create an individual (user-based) mapping. This is also shown whenever we create a group mapping for a group that contains users for which active mappings already exist:

```
# semanage login -a -s guest_u %nginx
libsemanage.add_user: User taylor is already mapped to group
users, but also belongs to group nginx. Add an explicit mapping
for this user to override group mappings.
```

The changes take effect when a new login occurs, so we should force a logout for these users. The following command kills all the processes of the `lisa` user, forcing a logout for that user:

```
# pkill -KILL -u lisa
```

Also, when we modify a user's settings, we should also reset the contexts of that user's home directory (while that user is not logged in). To accomplish this, use `restorecon` as follows:

```
# restorecon -RF /home/lisa
```

The `-F` option in the preceding command forces a reset, while `-R` does this recursively.

> **Important note**
>
> Running the `restorecon -RF` command will also reset file contexts that the user has manually set using tools such as `chcon`. We recommend defining SELinux user mappings up front, or recursively changing only the SELinux user of the files using `chcon -R -u`. The `chcon` application and file contexts are discussed in the next chapter.

To remove a login mapping, use the `-d` (delete) option. Don't forget to run the `restorecon` command afterward:

```
# semanage login -d lisa
# restorecon -RF /home/lisa
```

Don't forget to force a user logout again if this user is active on the system.

Customizing logins for services

When login mappings are added using `semanage login`, they apply to all services. There is no option in `semanage` to allow customizing the mappings based on the service. However, that does not mean it is not possible.

The SELinux user space tools and libraries will consult the following two configuration files to know what the mappings are:

- The `/etc/selinux/targeted/seusers` file contains the standard, service-agnostic mappings. This file is managed by `semanage login` and should not be updated through any other means.
- The `/etc/selinux/targeted/logins` directory contains customized mappings, one file per Linux account. So, the custom mapping for the root user will be in `/etc/selinux/targeted/logins/root`.

Inside the files for customized mappings, administrators can define, per service, a different SELinux user to map to. The services are the **Pluggable Authentication Modules (PAM)** services through which a user can log in, and more information on this can be found in the *SELinux and PAM* section.

For instance, to have the `root` user – when logged in through SSH – be mapped to the `user_u` SELinux user rather than their default `unconfined_u` user, the `root` file would need to contain the following:

```
sshd:user_u:s0
```

When querying the current mapping, `semanage login` will show this customization as follows:

```
# semanage login -l
...
Local customization in /etc/selinux/targeted/logins
root          user_u              s0              sshd
```

Of course, this customization does not need to be so drastic. It can also be used to limit the user's default MLS/MCS range. For instance, to limit the categories to `c0.c8` (rather than the default `c0.c1023` range) you would use the following:

```
sshd:unconfined_u:s0-s0:c0.c8
```

Such customizations allow us to flexibly change the access control policies based on the PAM service used.

Creating SELinux users

By default, only a small number of SELinux users are available for mapping to logins. If we want more control over the Linux accounts and their mappings, we need to create additional SELinux users.

First, list the currently known SELinux users using the `semanage user -l` command, as follows:

```
# semanage user -l
SELinux    Labeling    MLS/         MLS/
User       Prefix      MCS Level    MCS Range         SELinux
Roles

guest_u    user        s0           s0                guest_r
root       user        s0           s0-s0:c0.c1023    staff_r
```

```
...
...
xguest_u    user           s0             s0                    xguest_r
```

Next, create a new SELinux user with `semanage user`, using the `-a` (add) option. We need to give SELinux additional information about this SELinux user, such as the following:

- The default sensitivity (using the `-L` option) for the SELinux user. This is the sensitivity that the user starts with.

- The security clearance (using the `-r` option) applicable to the SELinux user. This range cannot be extended when defining login mappings. It is, however, possible to give a user a more limited range, as long as it is bounded by the current range.

- The allowed role or roles (using the `-R` option) for the SELinux user.

> **Tip**
>
> The labeling prefix shown in the previous example is used to dynamically create SELinux policies with specific prefixes, such as `<prefix>_home_t` for user's home files. Most distributions leave this to the default *user* setting, and changing it is done through the (undocumented) `-P` parameter to `semanage user`.

In the following example, we're configuring the SELinux user `finance_u`:

```
# semanage user -a -L s0 -r "s0-s0:c0.c127" -R user_r finance_u
```

When the command creates the SELinux user, its information becomes part of the SELinux policy. From this point onward, administrators can map Linux accounts to this SELinux user.

> **Important note**
>
> SELinux roles are enabled through the SELinux user that a Linux account is mapped to. When an administrator wants to allow additional existing roles to a Linux account, the administrator either updates existing SELinux mappings to include the new role(s) or creates a new SELinux user that has access to the new role(s) and then maps this SELinux user to the Linux account.

Just like with login mappings, `semanage user` also accepts the `-m` option to modify an existing entry, or `-d` to delete one. For instance, the following command deletes the `finance_u` SELinux user:

```
# semanage user -d finance_u
```

Separate SELinux users enhance the audit information since SELinux users generally do not change during a user's session, whereas the effective Linux user ID can. If the user creates files or other resources, these resources also inherit the SELinux user part in their security context.

Listing accessible domains

When creating SELinux users, one of the parameters that needs to be provided is the role or roles for an SELinux user. Most of the roles are self-explanatory: the `dbadm_r` role is for DBAs, whereas the `webadm_r` role is for web application infrastructure administrators. If a role is not clear, or an administrator is not certain which accesses are part of a given role, the administrator can still query the SELinux policy for more information.

Informational note

This book will mostly focus on the command-line utilities used to query and interact with the active SELinux policy. In *Chapter 13, Analyzing Policy Behavior*, we will also cover the graphical utility `apol`.

As documented earlier, roles define which domains are accessible for the users associated with the role. We saw that `seinfo` can show us the available roles, but it can do more. It can list the domains accessible for a role as well, using the `-x` option:

```
# seinfo -r dbadm_r -x
Roles: 1
  role dbadm_r types { ... qmail_inject_t user_mail_t ... };
```

In this example, users running with the `dbadm_r` role as part of their security context will be able to transition to, for instance, the `qmail_inject_t` (the domain used to read email messages and pass those on to the `qmail` queue) and `user_mail_t` (the domain used for generic email-sending command-line applications) domains.

The information provided through the **dominated roles** is usually not of concern to the administrators. Role dominance, although supported in SELinux core, is not used by Linux distribution policies. It signifies the inheritance of (other) roles, but it will always just show the queried role.

Managing categories

Sensitivity labels and their associated categories are identified through numeric values, which is great for computers but not that obvious for users. Luckily, the SELinux utilities support translating the levels and categories to human-readable values, even though they are still stored as numbers. As a result, almost all tools that can show contexts will show them translated rather than presented as numerical values.

The translations are managed through the `setrans.conf` file, located in `/etc/selinux/targeted`. Inside this file, we can name specific values (for example, `s0:c102`) or ranges (such as `s0-s0:c1.c127`) with a string that is much easier for administrators to use. However, for translations to be performed, **mcstransd** – the MCS translation daemon – needs to be running.

Consider our example of the `finance_u` SELinux user who was allowed access to the `c0.c127` category range. Two of the categories within that range are `c102`, which we will tag as `Contracts`, and `c103`, which we will tag as `Salaries`. The `c1.c127` range will be labeled as `FinanceData`. The following diagram shows the relationship between these various categories:

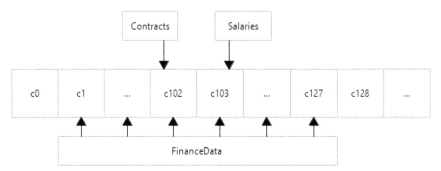

Figure 3.1 – Relationship of the example categories and category range

To accomplish this, the following should be placed in the `setrans.conf` file:

```
s0:c102=Contracts
s0:c103=Salaries
s0-s0:c1.c127=FinanceData
```

After editing the `setrans.conf` file, the `mcstransd` application needs to be restarted.

These translations are handled by the SELinux utilities, which connect to the `mcstransd` daemon through the `.setrans-unix` socket located in `/var/run/setrans` to query the `setrans.conf` file. If the daemon is not running or the communication with the daemon fails, the numeric sensitivity and category values are displayed.

For instance, with the daemon running, the output of id -Z is now as follows:

```
# id -Z
unconfined_u:unconfined_r:unconfined_t:SystemLow-SystemHigh
```

We can view the available sensitivities and their human-readable counterparts using the chcat tool. The following example displays the translations after adding the finance-related ones:

```
$ chcat -L
s0            SystemLow
s0-s0:c0.c1023    SystemLow-SystemHigh
s0:c0.c1023       SystemHigh
s0:c102           Contracts
s0:c103           Salaries
s0-s0:c1.c127     FinanceData
```

The same chcat utility can be used to assign categories to users. For instance, to grant the Salaries category to the lisa Linux user, we'd use the following command:

```
# chcat -l -- +Salaries lisa
```

The previous command grants the Salaries category (c103) to the Linux user lisa. The user mapping is immediately updated with this information. Again, we need to make sure that the lisa user is logged out for the changes to take effect.

With this, we end our section on managing SELinux users and logins. We've learned how to align users with SELinux users so that they log in to the system with the correct context. In the next section, we will look at the SELinux roles and how to apply those to SELinux users.

Handling SELinux roles

We saw how SELinux users define the role(s) that a user can hold. But how does SELinux enforce which role a user logs in through? And when logged in, how can a user switch their active role?

Defining allowed SELinux contexts

To select the context assigned to a successfully authenticated user, SELinux introduces the notion of a default context. Based on the context of the service through which a user logs in (or through which the user executes commands), the system selects the right user context.

Inside the `/etc/selinux/targeted/contexts` directory, a file called `default_contexts` exists. Each line in this file starts with the SELinux context information of the parent process and is then followed by an ordered list of all the contexts that could be picked based on the user's allowed SELinux role(s).

Consider the following line of code for the `sshd_t` context:

```
system_r:sshd_t:s0      user_r:user_t:s0 \
                        staff_r:staff_t:s0 \
                        sysadm_r:sysadm_t:s0 \
                        unconfined_r:unconfined_t:s0
```

This line of code mentions that when a user logs in through a process running in the `sshd_t` domain, the listed roles are checked against the roles of the user. The user will transition to the first context listed that matches the roles the user can use.

For instance, assume we are mapped to an SELinux user that has access to both the `staff_r` and `sysadm_r` roles. In that case, we will log in as `staff_r:staff_t` since that is the first match.

However, like the `seusers` file for the Linux account mappings, the `default_contexts` file is a default file that can be overruled through specific customizations. These customizations are stored in the `/etc/selinux/targeted/contexts/users` subdirectory. These files are named after the SELinux user for which they take effect. This allows us to assign different contexts for particular SELinux users even if they share the same roles with other SELinux users. Because SELinux checks the entries per line, we do not need to copy the entire content of the `default_contexts` file. Only the configuration lines that we want to see a different configuration for need to be listed; SELinux will automatically use the `default_contexts` file for the rest.

Let's modify the default contexts so that the `staff_u` SELinux user logs in with the `sysadm_r` role (and with the `sysadm_t` type) when logged in through SSH. To do so, use the `sshd_t` line, modify it, and save the result as `/etc/selinux/targeted/contexts/users/staff_u`:

```
system_r:sshd_t:s0      sysadm_r:sysadm_t:s0
```

Specifically, for the SSH daemon, we also need to enable the `ssh_sysadm_login` boolean, which is a special precaution SELinux policy developers have made to prevent users from immediately logging in with highly privileged accounts:

```
# setsebool ssh_sysadm_login on
```

With these settings in place, we've set `sysadm_r:sysadm_t:s0` as the only possible context, ensuring that the target context is `staff_u:sysadm_r:sysadm_t`.

Validating contexts with getseuser

To validate whether our change succeeded, we can ask SELinux what the result of a context choice will be without having to parse the files ourselves. We can accomplish this through the `getseuser` command, which takes two arguments: the Linux user account and the context of the process that switches the user context.

> **Important note**
>
> The `getseuser` command is a helper utility offered by the SELinux user space project, but is not made available on all distributions. You will find it on Debian and Gentoo, but not on CentOS or other Red Hat Enterprise Linux-derived distributions.

Here's an example that checks what the context would be for the `sven` user when they log in through a process running in the `sshd_t` domain:

```
# getseuser sven system_u:system_r:sshd_t
seuser: user_u, level s0-s0
Context 0  user_u:user_r:user_t:s0
```

One of the advantages of the `getseuser` command is that it asks the SELinux code what the context should be, which not only looks through the `default_contexts` and customized files, but also checks whether the target context can be reached or not, and that there are no other constraints that prohibit the change to this context.

Switching roles with newrole

After having successfully authenticated and logged in, users will be assigned the context through the configuration mentioned in the *SELinux users and roles* section. If the SELinux user has access to multiple roles, however, then the Linux user can use the `newrole` application to transition from one role to another.

Consider an SELinux system without unconfined domains and where we are, by default, logged in as the `staff_r` role. To perform administrative tasks, we need to switch to the `sysadm_r` administrative role, which we can do with the `newrole` command. This command only works when working through a secure terminal listed in `/etc/securetty`:

```
$ id -Z
staff_u:staff_r:staff_t:s0
$ newrole -r sysadm_r
Password: (Enter user password)
$ id -Z
staff_u:sysadm_r:sysadm_t:s0
```

Notice how the SELinux user remains constant but the role and domain have changed.

The `newrole` command can also be used to transition to a specific sensitivity, as follows:

```
$ newrole -l s0-s0:c0.c100
```

When we *switch* to another role or sensitivity, what we actually do is create a new session (with a new shell) that has this new role or sensitivity. The command does not change the context of the current session, nor does it exit from the current session.

We can return from our assigned role and go back to the first session by exiting (through `exit`, `logout`, or *Ctrl + D*).

Managing role access through sudo

Most administrators use `sudo` for privilege delegation: allowing users to run certain commands in a more privileged context than the user is otherwise allowed. The `sudo` application is also capable of switching SELinux roles and types.

We can pass the target role and type to `sudo` directly. For instance, we can tell `sudo` to switch to the administrative role when we edit a PostgreSQL configuration file:

```
$ sudo -r sysadm_r -t sysadm_t vim /var/lib/pgsql/data/pg_hba.conf
```

However, we can also configure sudo through the /etc/sudoers file to allow users to run commands within a certain role and/or type, or get a shell within a certain context. Consider a user that has access to both the user_r and dbadm_r roles (with the dbadm_r role being a role designated for database administrators). Within the sudoers file, the following line allows the myuser user to run any command through sudo, which, when triggered, will run with the dbadm_r role and within the dbadm_t domain:

```
myuser ALL=(ALL) TYPE=sysadm_t ROLE=sysadm_r ALL
```

Often, administrators will prefer sudo over newrole as the latter does not change the effective user ID, which is often required for end users when they want to invoke a more privileged command (concerning the root user or a service-specific runtime account) anyway. The sudo application also has great logging capabilities, and we can even have commands switching roles without requiring the end user to explicitly mention the target role and type. Sadly, it does not support changing sensitivities.

Reaching other domains using runcon

Another application that can switch roles and sensitivities is the runcon application. The runcon command is available for all users and is used to launch a specific command as a different role, type, and/or sensitivity. It even supports changing the SELinux user – assuming the SELinux policy lets you.

The runcon command does not have its own domain – it runs in the context of the user executing the command. As such, the privileges of the user domain itself govern the ability to change the role, type, sensitivity, or even SELinux user.

Most of the time, we will use runcon to launch applications with a particular category. This allows us to take advantage of the MCS approach in SELinux without requiring applications to be MCS-enabled:

```
$ runcon -l Salaries bash
$ id -Z
unconfined_u:unconfined_r:unconfined_t:Salaries
```

For instance, in the previous example, we run a shell session with the Salaries category (prohibiting it from accessing resources that do not have the same or fewer categories set).

Switching to the system role

Sometimes, administrators will need to invoke applications that should not run under their current SELinux user context but instead as the `system_u` SELinux user with the `system_r` SELinux role. SELinux policy administrators acknowledge this need, and allow a *very* limited set of domains to switch the SELinux user to a different user – perhaps contrary to the purpose of the immutability of SELinux users mentioned earlier. Yet, as there are cases where this is needed, SELinux needs to accommodate this. One of the applications allowed to switch the SELinux user is `run_init` (through its `run_init_t` domain).

The `run_init` application is mainly (almost exclusively) used to start background system services on a Linux system. Using this application, the daemons do not run under the user's SELinux context but the system's, as required by SELinux policies.

As this is only needed on systems where launching additional services is done through service scripts, distributions that use `systemd` do not require the use of `run_init`. `systemd` already runs with the `system_r` role and is responsible for starting additional services. As such, no role transition is needed. Other `init` systems, such as Gentoo's OpenRC, integrate `run_init` so that administrators do not generally need to invoke `run_init` manually.

Most SELinux policies enable role-managed support for selective service management (for non `systemd` distributions). This allows users that do not have complete system administration rights to still manipulate a select number of services on a Linux system, allowed by the SELinux policy. These users are to be granted the `system_r` role, but once accomplished, they do not need to call `run_init` to manipulate specific services anymore. The transitions happen automatically and only for the services assigned to the user – other services cannot be launched by these users.

This finalizes our section on handling SELinux roles. We've learned how to manage SELinux roles and switching roles and contexts, as well as how to define the target role and type in the case of privilege escalation. In the last section of this chapter, we will look at how PAM is used to configure the SELinux context setup on the system.

SELinux and PAM

With all the information about SELinux users and roles, we have not touched upon how exactly applications or services create and assign an SELinux context to a user. As mentioned earlier on, this is coordinated through the use of Linux's PAM services.

Assigning contexts through PAM

End users log in to a Linux system through either a login process (triggered through a getty process), a networked service (for example, the OpenSSH daemon), or through a graphical login manager (xdm, kdm, gdm, slim, and so on).

These services are responsible for switching our effective user ID (upon successful authentication, of course) so that we are not active on the system as the root user. For SELinux systems, these processes also need to switch the SELinux user (and role) accordingly, as otherwise, the context will be inherited from the service, which is obviously wrong for any interactive session.

In theory, all these applications can be made fully SELinux aware, linking with the SELinux user space libraries to get information about Linux mappings and SELinux users. Instead of converting all these applications, the developers decided to take the authentication route to the next level using the PAM services that Linux systems provide.

PAM offers a very flexible interface for handling different authentication methods on Linux (and Unix) systems. All applications mentioned earlier use PAM for their authentication steps. To enable SELinux support for these applications, we need to update their PAM configuration files to include the pam_selinux.so library.

The following code listing is an excerpt from CentOS's /etc/pam.d/remote file, limited to PAM's session service directives. It triggers the pam_selinux.so library code as part of the authentication process, as follows:

```
session     required     pam_selinux.so close
session     required     pam_loginuid.so
session     required     pam_selinux.so open
session     required     pam_namespace.so
session     optional     pam_keyinit.so force revoke
session     include      password-auth
session     include      postlogin
```

The arguments supported by the pam_selinux.so code are described in the pam_selinux manual page. In the preceding example, the close option clears the current context (if any), whereas the open option sets the context of the user. The pam_selinux module takes care of querying the SELinux configuration and finding the right mappings and context based on the service name used by the daemon.

Prohibiting access during permissive mode

Having SELinux active and enforcing on a system improves its resilience against successful exploits and other malicious activities, especially when the system is used as a shell server (or provides other interactive services) and the users are confined – meaning they are mapped to `user_u` or other confined SELinux users.

Some administrators might want to temporarily switch the system to permissive mode. This could be to troubleshoot issues or to support some changes made on the system. When using permissive mode, it would be a good idea to ensure that the interactive services are not usable for regular users.

With `pam_sepermit`, this can be enforced on the system. The PAM module will deny a set of defined users access to the system if the system is in permissive mode. By default, these users are mentioned in `/etc/security/sepermit.conf`, but a different file can be configured through the `conf=` option inside the PAM configuration itself.

In the `sepermit.conf` file, there are three approaches to document which users should be denied access when the system is in permissive mode:

- Regular usernames
- Group names, prefixed with the `@` sign
- SELinux usernames, prefixed with the `%` sign

Within this file, we list each user, group, or SELinux user on a single line. After each entry, we can (but don't have to) add one or two options:

- `exclusive` means that the system will allow the user to be active even when the system is in permissive mode, but only a single session can be active. When the user logs out, all active processes will be killed.
- `ignore` will return `PAM_IGNORE` as the return status if SELinux is in enforcing mode, and `PAM_AUTH_ERR` if SELinux is in permissive mode. This allows special constructs/branches for this user in PAM based on the permissive state of the system.

To enable `pam_sepermit`, it's sufficient to enable the module in the auth PAM service as follows:

```
auth required    pam_sepermit.so
```

Of course, don't forget to remove all active user sessions when switching to permissive mode, as any running session is otherwise left untouched.

Polyinstantiating directories

The last PAM module we'll look at is pam_namespace.so. Before we dive into configuring this module, let's first look at what polyinstantiation is about.

Polyinstantiation is an approach where, when a user logs in to a system, the user gets a view on filesystem resources specific to its session, while optionally hiding the resources of other users. This differs from regular access controls, where the other resources are still visible, but might just be inaccessible.

This session-specific view, however, does not just use regular mounts. The module uses the Linux kernel namespace technology to force a (potentially more limited) view on the filesystem, isolated and specific to the user session. Other users have a different view on the filesystem.

Let's use a common example. Assume that all users, except root, should not have access to the temporary files generated by other users. With standard access controls, these resources would still be visible (perhaps not readable, but their existence or the directories they reside in would be visible). Instead, with polyinstantiation, a user will only see their own /tmp and /var/tmp views.

The following setting in /etc/security/namespace.conf will remap these two locations:

```
/tmp       /tmp/tmp-inst/          level root
/var/tmp   /var/tmp/tmp-inst/      level root
```

On the real filesystem, those locations will be remapped to a subdirectory inside /tmp/tmp-inst and /var/tmp/tmp-inst. The end users do not know or see the remapped locations – for them, /tmp and /var/tmp are as they would expect.

The format (and thus polyinstantiation) of the subdirectories created depends on the third option within the namespace.conf file. The supported options are as follows:

- user, which will create a subdirectory named after the user (such as lisa)
- level, which will create a subdirectory named after the user sensitivity level and username (such as system_u:object_r:tmp_t:s0-s0:c0.c1023_lisa)
- context, which will create a subdirectory named after the process context (including the sensitivity level) and username (such as system_u:object_r:user_tmp_t:s0_lisa)

For SELinux systems, the most common setting is `level`.

> **Tip**
>
> In the default `namespace.conf` file, you might notice that this also has support for home directories. When enabled with the `level` or `context` method, this will ensure that users have a sensitivity-specific home directory set. For instance, if the system configuration forces the user to have a lower sensitivity when logged in through SSH than when the user logs in through the terminal, a different home directory view will be used.

In the previous example, only the root user is exempt from these namespace changes. Additional users can be listed (comma-separated), or an explicit list of users can be given for which polyinstantiation needs to be enabled (if we prefix the user list with the ~ character). To allow the namespace changes to take place, the target locations need to be available on the system with the `000` permission:

```
# mkdir /tmp-inst && chmod 000 /tmp-inst
```

Next, enable `pam_namespace.so` in the PAM configuration files at the session service:

```
session    required    pam_namespace.so
```

Finally, make sure that SELinux allows polyinstantiated directories. On CentOS, this is governed through the `polyinstantiation_enabled` SELinux boolean:

```
# setsebool polyinstantiation_enabled on
```

Other distributions will have it through the `allow_polyinstantiation` SELinux boolean.

With the polyinstantiation support, we close off this final section of the chapter, where we learned how PAM is used to trigger SELinux context changes on the system.

Summary

SELinux maps Linux users onto SELinux users and defines the roles a user can be assigned through the SELinux user definitions. We learned how to manage those mappings and SELinux users with the `semanage` application, and how to grant the right roles to the right people.

We also saw how the same commands are used to grant the proper sensitivity to the user and how we can describe these levels in the `setrans.conf` file. We used the `chcat` tool to do most of the category-related management activities.

After assigning roles to the users, we saw how to jump from one role to another using `newrole`, `sudo`, `runcon`, and `run_init`. We ended this chapter with important insights into how SELinux is integrated into the Linux authentication process and how to tune a Linux system further using a couple of SELinux-aware PAM modules.

In the next chapter, we will learn to manage the labels on files and processes, and see how we can query the SELinux policy rules.

Questions

1. Why can't we just add an SELinux role to a Linux account?

2. Can Linux accounts be mapped to more than one SELinux user?

3. Besides associating the valid SELinux roles, what other advantages does an SELinux user have?

4. What purpose does PAM have when dealing with Linux accounts and SELinux mappings?

4
Using File Contexts and Process Domains

SELinux-enabled systems are strongly dependent on the notion of contexts (on resources) and domains (on processes). The access controls that SELinux enforces use these contexts to identify the resources, and define the enforcement rules within the policy. Because of its inherent reliance on these contexts, this chapter will go into detail on file contexts, context definitions, and process domains.

We will work with the file contexts and learn where they are stored so that you can easily adjust your system to work optimally with SELinux. We assign contexts to resources both temporarily (for testing purposes) and permanently, and learn how these contexts are used to automatically deduce the process domain. Once we know how to obtain process domain information, we will query the SELinux policy to learn about the current access controls.

In this chapter, we're going to cover the following main topics:

- Introduction to SELinux file contexts
- Keeping or ignoring contexts
- SELinux file context expressions
- Modifying file contexts
- The context of a process
- Limiting the scope of transitions
- Types, permissions, and constraints

Technical requirements

Check out the following video to see the Code in Action: `https://bit.ly/3m3JzkP`

Introduction to SELinux file contexts

SELinux file contexts are the most important configuration that a system administrator will have to work with when working with SELinux on the system. Contexts for files are generally identified through a label that is assigned to the file. Mislabeled files are a constant source of headaches for sysadmins, and most common SELinux issues are resolved by correcting the SELinux context.

Knowing where and how SELinux contexts are used is key to understanding and resolving SELinux related issues. The following diagram shows how contexts are applied on regular Linux resources, and how the LSM subsystem uses these contexts for decision making:

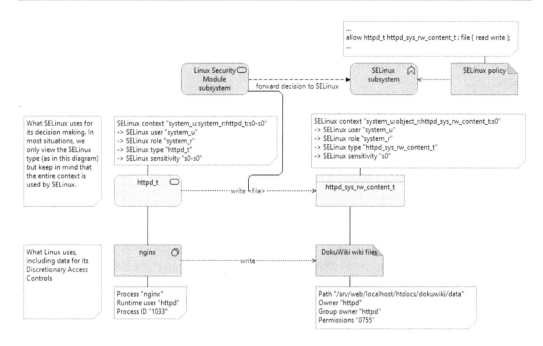

Figure 4.1 – Distinction between contexts and regular Linux info

Let's consider a web-based deployment as an example: DokuWiki. This is a popular PHP wiki that uses files rather than a database as its backend system, and is easy to install and manage. As a web hosting platform, we will use nginx.

Getting context information

Let's assume that the DokuWiki application will be hosted at /srv/web/localhost/ htdocs/dokuwiki and that it will store its wiki pages (user content) in the data/ subdirectory. We start by downloading the latest DokuWiki tarball from the project site, http://download.dokuwiki.org, and extract it to this location:

```
# mkdir -p /srv/web/localhost/htdocs/
# tar -C /srv/web/localhost/htdocs/ -xvf dokuwiki.tgz
# chown -R nginx:nginx /srv/web/localhost/htdocs/dokuwiki
```

While distributions might have prepackaged DokuWiki installations available, we will use the manual installation approach to show the various file context-related actions in this chapter.

The contexts of files can easily be acquired using the `-Z` option of the `ls` command. Most utilities that can provide feedback on contexts will try to do so using the `-Z` option, as we saw with the `id` utility in *Chapter 1*, *Fundamental SELinux Concepts*, and *Chapter 3*, *Managing User Logins*.

Let's look at the current context of the `dokuwiki` directory itself:

```
# ls -dZ /srv/web/localhost/htdocs/dokuwiki
undefined_u:object_r:var_t:s0 /srv/web/localhost/htdocs/
dokuwiki
```

The context displayed here is `var_t`. In the *Keeping or ignoring contexts* section, we will change this to the correct context (as `var_t` is too generic and not meant for hosting web content).

File and directory contexts are stored in the filesystem as extended attributes when the filesystem supports this. An **extended attribute** (often abbreviated to **xattr**) is a key/value combination associated with a resource's inode (an information block that represents a file, directory, or symbolic link on a filesystem). Each resource can have multiple extended attributes, but only one value per unique key. When we talk about assigning a **label** to a file or directory (or relabeling a file), then we imply setting or updating this extended attribute, as it is the label that SELinux will use to obtain the SELinux context for the file.

> **Important note**
>
> Filesystems that do not support extended attributes can still be used on SELinux-enabled systems. However, the entire filesystem (including all its files and directories) will then be shown with a single context, and differentiation across resources on the filesystem is not possible. We explain how to define file contexts on these filesystems in the *Using mount options to set SELinux contexts* subsection in this chapter.

By convention, extended attributes on Linux use the following syntax:

```
<namespace>.<attribute>=<value>
```

The namespace of an extended attribute allows for additional access controls or features. Of the currently supported extended attribute namespaces (`security`, `system`, `trusted`, and `user`), the `security` namespace enforces specific restrictions on manipulating the attribute: if no security module is loaded (for instance, SELinux is not enabled), then only processes with the `CAP_SYS_ADMIN` capability (basically root or similarly privileged processes) can modify this parameter.

We can query the existing extended attributes using the `getfattr` application, as shown in the following example:

```
$ getfattr -m . -d dokuwiki
# file: dokuwiki
security.selinux="unconfined_u:object_r:var_t:s0"
```

As we can see, the `security.selinux` extended attribute hosts the SELinux context. This ensures that non-administrative users cannot alter the SELinux context of a file when SELinux is disabled and that the SELinux policy controls who can manipulate contexts when SELinux is enabled.

The `stat` application can also be used to show SELinux contexts:

```
$ stat dokuwiki
  File: dokuwiki
  Size: 211            Blocks: 0         IO Block: 4096
directory
Device: fd01h/64769d   Inode: 8512888    Links: 8
Access: (0755/drwxr-xr-x)    Uid: (      0/    root) Gid: (
0/ root)
Context: unconfined_u:object_r:var_t:s0
...
```

Getting context information from a file or directory should be as common to an administrator as getting regular access control information (the read (`r`), write (`w`), and execute (`x`) flags).

Interpreting SELinux context types

After using SELinux for a while, the motive behind using file labels to assign an SELinux context to the file becomes somewhat clearer. SELinux contexts are named after their purpose, allowing administrators to more easily see whether a context is correctly assigned.

Consider the context of a user file in its home directory (`user_home_t`), a directory in `/tmp` for a Java application (`java_tmp_t`), or a socket of `rpcbind` (`rpcbind_var_run_t`). All these files or directories have considerably different purposes on the filesystem, and this reflects itself in the assigned contexts.

Policy writers will always try to name the context consistently, making it easier for us to understand the purpose of the file, but also to make the policy almost self-explanatory so that administrators can understand the purpose of the policy without additional documentation needs.

For the regular filesystem, for instance, files are labeled with a context resembling their main location as they have similar security properties. For example, we find binaries in the /bin folder (and /usr/bin) to be associated with the bin_t type, boot files in /boot associated with boot_t, and generic system resources in /usr associated with usr_t.

We can also find more application-specific contexts. For instance, for the PostgreSQL database server, we have the following:

- The postgresql_t context is meant for the application itself (process type or domain).

- The postgresql_port_t context is meant for the TCP port on which the PostgreSQL daemon listens.

- The postgresql_server_packet_t and postgresql_client_packet_t contexts are types associated with network packets received (in case of the postgresql_server_packet_t type) or sent to the PostgreSQL port.

- The postgresql_exec_t type is assigned to the postgres binary.

- The various postgresql_*_t types for specific filesystem locations related to the daemon, such as postgresql_var_run_t (to apply to resources in /var/run), postgresql_etc_t (to apply to resources in /etc), postgresql_log_t (to apply to resources in /var/log), and postgresql_tmp_t (to apply to resources in /tmp).

- The mysqld_db_t type for the database files themselves.

Based on the context of a file or resource, administrators can easily detect anomalies in the system setup. An example of an anomaly is when we move a file from the user's home directory to a web server location. When this occurs, the file retains the user_home_t context as extended attributes are moved with it. As the web server process isn't allowed to access user_home_t by default, it will not be able to serve this file to its users.

Let's see how to properly set contexts during such copy or move operations.

Keeping or ignoring contexts

Now that we are aware that file contexts are stored as extended attributes, how do we ensure that files receive the correct label when they are written or modified? To set an SELinux context on a filesystem resource, a few guidelines exist, ranging from inheritance rules to explicit commands.

Inheriting the default contexts

By default, the SELinux security subsystem uses context inheritance to identify which context should be assigned to a file (or directory, socket, and so on) when it is created. A file created in a directory with a `var_t` context will be assigned the `var_t` context as well. This means that the file inherits the context from the parent directory and not from the context of the executing process.

There are a few exceptions to this though:

- SELinux-aware applications can force the context of a file to be different (assuming the SELinux policy allows it, of course). As this is within the software code itself, this behavior cannot be generally configured.

- An application called `restorecond` can be used that enforces contexts on various paths/files based on SELinux's context rules. We will cover these rules and the `restorecond` application in the *SELinux file context expressions* and *Modifying file contexts* sections, respectively.

- The SELinux policy allows for transition rules that consider the context of the process creating new files or directories, as well as the name of the file the process is creating.

It is these transition rules we will cover next.

Querying transition rules

Type transition rules are policy rules that force the use of a different type upon certain conditions. For file contexts, such a type transition rule can be as follows: if a process running in the `httpd_t` domain creates a file in a directory labeled with the `var_log_t` SELinux type, then the type identifier of the file becomes `httpd_log_t`.

Basically, this rule assigns the `httpd_log_t` web server log context to any file placed in a log directory by web servers, rather than the default `var_log_t`, which would be the case when standard inheritance was used.

We can query these type transition rules using `sesearch`. The `sesearch` application is one of the most important tools available to query the current SELinux policy. For the previous example, we need the (source) domain and the (target) context of the directory: `httpd_t` and `var_log_t`. In the following example, we use `sesearch` to find the type transition declaration related to the `httpd_t` domain toward the `var_log_t` context:

```
$ sesearch -T -s httpd_t -t var_log_t
  type_transition httpd_t var_log_t:file httpd_log_t;
```

The `type_transition` line is an SELinux policy rule, which maps perfectly to the description. Let's look at another set of type transition rules for the `tmp_t` type (assigned to the directory used for temporary files, such as `/tmp` and `/var/tmp`):

```
$ sesearch -T -s httpd_t -t tmp_t
type_transition httpd_t tmp_t:dir httpd_tmp_t;
type_transition httpd_t tmp_t:file httpd_tmp_t;
type_transition httpd_t tmp_t:file krb5_host_rcache_t HTTP_23;
type_transition httpd_t tmp_t:file krb5_host_rcache_t HTTP_48;
type_transition httpd_t tmp_t:lnk_file httpd_tmp_t;
type_transition httpd_t tmp_t:sock_file httpd_tmp_t;
```

The policy tells us that, if a file, directory, symbolic link, or socket is created in a directory labeled `tmp_t`, then this newly created resource gets the `httpd_tmp_t` context assigned (and thus not the default, inherited `tmp_t` one). Alongside these rules, it also contains two named file transitions, which are more flexible transition rules.

With **named file transitions**, the policy can consider the name of the file (or directory) created to select a more appropriate context. In the previous example, if a file named `HTTP_23` or `HTTP_48` is created in a directory labeled `tmp_t`, then it does not get the `httpd_tmp_t` context assigned (as would be implied by the regular type transition rules), but the `krb5_host_rcache_t` type (used for Kerberos implementations) instead.

Type transitions not only give us insight into what labels (and thus also SELinux contexts) are going to be assigned, but also give us some clues as to which types are related to a particular domain. In the web server example, we found out by querying the policy that its log files are most likely labeled `httpd_log_t`, and its temporary files `httpd_tmp_t`.

Copying and moving files

File contexts can also be transferred together with the file itself during copy or move operations. By default, Linux will do the following:

- Retain the file context in case of a move (`mv`) operation on the same filesystem (as this operation does not touch extended attributes, but merely adjusts the metadata of the file).

- Ignore the current file context in case of a move operation across a filesystem boundary, as this creates a new file, including content and extended attributes. Instead, it uses the inheritance (or file transition rules) to define the target context.

- Ignore the file context in case of a copy (`cp`) operation, instead using the inheritance (or file transition rules) to define the target context.

Luckily, this is just default behavior (based on the extended attribute support of these utilities) that can be manipulated freely.

We can use the -Z option to tell mv that the context of the file should be set to the default type associated with the target location. For instance, in the next example, two files are moved from a user's home directory to the /srv directory. The first example will retain its file context (user_home_t or admin_home_t), while the second one will receive the type associated with user files placed in /srv (var_t):

```
# touch test1 test2
# mv test1 /srv
# mv -Z test2 /srv
# ls -Z /srv/test*
staff_u:object_r:admin_home_t:s0 /srv/test1
staff_u:object_r:var_t:s0 /srv/test2
```

Similarly, we can tell the cp command through the --preserve=context option to preserve the SELinux context while copying files. Using the same example, we now get the following:

```
# cp test1 /srv
# cp --preserve=context test2 /srv
# ls -Z /srv/test*
staff_u:object_r:var_t:s0 /srv/test1
staff_u:object_r:admin_home_t:s0 /srv/test2
```

Most of the utilities provided through the coreutils package support the -Z option: mkdir (to create a directory), mknod (to create a device file), mkfifo (to create a named pipe), and so on.

> **Important note**
>
> If the mv command returns failed to set the security context when using the -Z option, then it is very likely that the location either does not have a valid context associated with it, or that the filesystem does not support SELinux labels. The former is for instances applicable when moving files to /tmp as the CentOS SELinux policy does not have any default context set for files and directories inside /tmp. Newly created resources always need to have their own affiliated labels applied (such as user_tmp_t).

Even more so, many of these utilities allow the user to explicitly provide a context through the --context option. For instance, to create a directory, /srv/foo, with the context user_home_t, using mkdir by default would not work, as the target context would be set to var_t. With the --context option, we can tell the utility to set a specific context:

```
# mkdir --context=user_u:object_r:user_home_t:s0 /srv/foo
# ls -dZ /srv/foo
user_u:object_r:user_home_t:s0 /srv/foo
```

For other utilities, it is best to consult the manual page and see how the utility deals with extended attributes. For instance, the rsync command can preserve the extended attributes by using the -X or --xattrs option.

Temporarily changing file contexts

We can use the chcon tool to update the context of the file (or files) directly. In our previous example, we noticed the var_t label on the DokuWiki files. This is a generic type for variable data and is not the right context for web content. We can use chcon to put the httpd_sys_content_t label on these files, which would allow web servers to have read access on these resources:

```
# chcon -R -t httpd_sys_content_t /srv/web
```

Another feature that chcon offers is to tell it to label a file or location with the same context as a different file. In the next example, we use chcon to label /srv/web and its resources with the same context as used for the /var/www directory:

```
$ chcon -R --reference /var/www /srv/www
```

If we change the context of a file through chcon and set it to a context different from the one in the context list, then the context might be reverted later: package managers might reset the file contexts back to their intended value, or the system administrator might trigger a fill filesystem relabeling operation.

Until now, we've only focused on the type part of a context. Contexts, however, also include a role part and an SELinux user part. If UBAC is not enabled, then the SELinux user has no influence on any decisions, and resetting it has little value. If UBAC is enabled, though, it might be necessary to reset the SELinux user values on files. Utilities such as chcon can set the SELinux user as well:

```
# chcon -u system_u -R /srv/web
```

The role for a file is usually `object_r` as roles currently only make sense for users (processes).

To be able to change contexts, we do need the proper SELinux privileges, named `relabelfrom` and `relabelto`. These rights are granted on domains to indicate whether the domain can change a label from one type to another. If we find denials in the audit log related to these permissions, then this means that the policy prohibits the domain from changing the contexts.

Placing categories on files and directories

We focused primarily on changing types and briefly touched SELinux users, but another important part is to support categories and sensitivity levels. With `chcon`, we can add sensitivity levels and categories as follows:

```
# chcon -l s0:c0,c2 doku.php
```

Another tool that can be used to assign categories is the `chcat` tool. With `chcat`, we can assign additional categories rather than having to reiterate them, as would be the case with `chcon`, and even enjoy the human-readable category levels provided by the `setrans.conf` file:

```
# chcat -- +Contracts doku.php
```

To remove a category, just use the minus sign:

```
# chcat -- -Contracts doku.php
```

To remove all categories, use the `-d` option:

```
# chcat -d doku.php
```

Users and administrators should keep in mind that applications generally do not set categories themselves, so they need to be added ad hoc.

Using multilevel security on files

When the system uses an MLS policy, the `chcon` tool needs to be used. The syntax is the same as with categories. For instance, to set the sensitivity `s1` and category set `c2` and `c4` to `c10` on all files of a user's home directory, you'd do the following:

```
$ chcon -R -l s1:c2,c4.c10 /home/lisa
```

Remember that both the context of the user executing `chcon` and the context of the user who will use the data must be able to deal with the mentioned sensitivity.

Backing up and restoring extended attributes

As with the regular file operation tools (such as `mv` and `cp`), backup software, too, needs to consider SELinux contexts. Two important requirements exist for a backup tool when working with SELinux-enabled systems:

- The backup tool must run in an SELinux context capable of reading all files in scope of the backup, and, of course, of restoring those files as well. If no specific SELinux policy for the backup tool exists, then it might need to run in an unconfined or highly privileged domain to succeed.

- The backup tool must be able to back up and restore extended attributes.

A popular tool for taking backups (or archives) is the `tar` application, which supports SELinux contexts as follows:

```
# tar cjvf dokuwiki-20200405.tar.bz2 /srv/web --selinux
```

When creating a tar archive, add `--selinux` to include SELinux contexts (both during the creation of the archive and when extracting files from the archive).

Using mount options to set SELinux contexts

Not all filesystems support extended attributes. When we use a filesystem without extended attribute support, then the SELinux context of a file is either based on the filesystem type itself (each filesystem has its own associated context) or is passed on to the system using a `mount` option.

The most commonly used `mount` option in these situations is the `context=` option. When set, it will use the mentioned context as the context for all the resources in the filesystem. For instance, to mount an external USB drive that hosts a FAT filesystem while ensuring that end users can write to it, we could mount it with the `user_home_t` context:

```
# mount -o context="user_u:object_r:user_home_t:s0" /dev/sdc1 /
media/usb
```

If the filesystem supports extended attributes but doesn't have all files labeled yet, then we can use the `defcontext=` option to tell Linux that, if no SELinux context is available, then the default context provided should be used:

```
# mount -o defcontext="system_u:object_r:var_t:s0" /dev/sdc1 /
srv/backups
```

Another mount option is `fscontext=`. This assigns a context on the filesystem type rather than the context of the files on the filesystem. For instance, a CD/DVD filesystem can be ISO 9660, Joliet, or UDF. SELinux uses this type definition on a filesystem to map permissions such as mount operations and file creation. With the `fscontext=` option, the filesystem type can be set differently from what the default filesystem type would be.

The last option that can be used when mounting filesystems is the `rootcontext=` option. This will force the root inode of the filesystem to have the given context even before the filesystem is visible to the user space. Permission checks on the location during the mount operation itself can cause havoc when the location does not have the expected context (especially when filesystems are mounted outside their expected location). The `rootcontext=` option provides a reusable configuration option to set the expected context:

```
# mount -o rootcontext="system_u:object_r:tmp_t:s0" -t tmpfs
none /var/tmp
```

That's it – these are all the context-related mount options. A final note though: the `context=` option is mutually exclusive to the `defcontext=` and `fscontext=` options. So, while the `defcontext=` and `fscontext=` options can be used together, they cannot be used with the `context=` option. Assuming the target filesystem allows for extended attributes, then we can use the file context expressions, which we will cover in the next section.

SELinux file context expressions

When we think that the context of a file is wrong, we need to correct the context. SELinux offers several methods to do so, and some distributions even add in more. We can use tools such as `chcon`, `restorecon` (together with `semanage`), `setfiles`, `rlpkg` (Gentoo), and `fixfiles`. Of course, we could also use the `setfattr` command, but that would be the least user-friendly approach for setting contexts.

Let's see how we can set context expressions in a more manageable way.

Using context expressions

In the SELinux policy, a list of regular expressions is kept that informs the SELinux utilities and libraries what the context of a file (or other filesystem resource) should be. Though this expression list is not enforced on the system directly, administrators and SELinux utilities use it to see whether a context is correct, and to reset contexts to what they are supposed to be. You can find the list itself in `/etc/selinux/targeted/contexts/files` in the various `file_contexts.*` files.

As an administrator, we can query this list through `semanage fcontext` as follows:

```
# semanage fcontext -l
SELinux fcontext type          Context
/            directory    system_u:object_r:root_t:s0
...
/vmlinuz.*        symbolic link        system_u:object_r:boot_t:s0
/xen(/.*)?        all files    system_u:object_r:xen_image_t:s0
...
```

An example of a tool that queries this information is `matchpathcon`, which we introduced in *Chapter 2, Understanding SELinux Decisions and Logging*:

```
# matchpathcon /srv/web/localhost/htdocs/dokuwiki
/srv/web/localhost/htdocs/dokuwiki  system_u:object_r:var_t:s0
```

Not all the entries are visible through the `semanage` application though. Entries related to specific user home directories (such as `/home/lisa/.ssh`) are not shown as these entries depend on the Linux user (and, more importantly, its associated SELinux user).

But for all other entries, the output of the command contains the following:

- A regular expression that matches one or more paths
- The classes to which the rule is applicable, but translated into a more human-readable format
- The context to assign to the resources that match the expression and class list

The class list allows us to differentiate contexts based on the resource class. The `semanage fcontext` output uses human-readable identifiers: resource classes can be a regular file (`--`), a directory (`-d`), a socket (`-s`), a named pipe (`-p`), a block device (`-b`), a character device (`-c`), or a symbolic link (`-l`). When it says all files, the line is valid regardless of the class.

Right now, we have not defined such rules yet, but after the next section, even defining custom SELinux context expressions will no longer hold any secrets. An important property of the context list is how SELinux prioritizes its application – after all, we could easily have two expressions that both match a certain resource or path. Within SELinux, the most specific rule wins. The logic used is as follows (in order):

1. If line A has a regular expression and line B doesn't, then line B is more specific.

2. If the number of characters before the first regular expression in line A is less than the number of characters before the first regular expression in line B, then line B is more specific.

3. If the number of characters in line A is less than in line B, then line B is more specific.

4. If line A does not map to a specific SELinux type (the policy editor has explicitly told SELinux not to assign a type) and line B does, then line B is more specific.

There is a caveat with the rule order, however. When additional rules are added through semanage (which we describe in the next section), then SELinux's utilities apply the rules in the order they were added rather than their specificity. So, instead of the most specific rule, the most recently added rule that matches the path is used.

Registering file context changes

Because changing an SELinux context using chcon is often just a temporary measure, it is seriously recommended to only use chcon when testing the impact of a context change. Once the change is acceptable, we need to register it through semanage. For instance, to permanently mark /srv/web (and all its subdirectories) as httpd_sys_content_t, and the DokuWiki data/ and conf/ folders as httpd_sys_rw_content_t (to allow the web server to modify these resources), we need to execute the following:

```
# semanage fcontext -a -t httpd_sys_content_t "/srv/web(/.*)?"
# semanage fcontext -a -t httpd_sys_rw_content_t "/srv/web/
localhost/htdocs/dokuwiki/data(/.*)?"
# semanage fcontext -a -t httpd_sys_rw_content_t "/srv/web/
localhost/htdocs/dokuwiki/conf(/.*)?"
# restorecon -Rv /srv/web
```

What we do here is register /srv/web and its subdirectories as httpd_sys_
content_t and the two writable directories as httpd_sys_rw_content_t through
semanage. Then, we use restorecon to (recursively) reset the contexts of /srv/web
to the value registered in the context list. This is the recommended approach for setting
contexts on most resources.

These registrations are local (custom) context expressions and are stored in a separate
configuration file (file_contexts.local). Considering the priority of (locally
added) expressions, it is important to have the *most specific entries added last*, as otherwise
the more broadly defined rule for httpd_sys_content_t would be applied to the
entire directory. This is unlike the priority rules for (policy added) expressions that do
have the concept of *most specific rule wins*.

The semanage fcontext application can also be used to inform SELinux that a part
of the filesystem tree should be labeled similarly as a different location on the filesystem.
Such an **equivalency rule** allows us to use different paths for application installations or
file destinations and tell semanage to apply the same contexts as if the destination were
the default.

Let's make this more visible through an example, and have everything under /srv/web
be labeled in a similar manner to the files at /var/www (including subdirectories),
so /srv/web/icons gets the same context as /var/www/icons. We use the -e
option of semanage fcontext to create such an equivalency as follows:

```
# semanage fcontext -a -e /var/www /srv/web
# restorecon -Rv /srv/web
```

This will create a substitution entry so that anything under /srv/web gets the same label
as if it were at the same location under /var/www.

Most distributions already configure a few equivalency rules that we can read as follows:

```
# cat /etc/selinux/targeted/contexts/files/file_contexts.subs_
dist
/run /var/run
...
/sysroot/tmp /tmp
```

The semanage fcontext -1 command will show these equivalent locations at the
end of its output as well.

Optimizing recursive context operations

The `restorecon` application resets the SELinux context of files and other resources based on the context definitions managed through the SELinux policy and `semanage fcontext`. When applying `restorecon` in a recursive fashion against directories, this might take a while. To improve performance in this situation, the SELinux authors support the skipping of `restorecon` operations.

With the `-D` option to `restorecon`, an additional extended attribute will be written to the main directory that contains a hash of the file context definitions used when invoking the command:

```
# restorecon -RD /home
```

Subsequent invocations of `restorecon` with `-D` will check this hash to see whether any of the file context definitions that impact this directory have been modified (using `semanage fcontext`). If there aren't, then the restore operation will be skipped:

```
# restorecon -RvD /home
 Skipping restorecon as matching digest on: /home
```

Once we update a definition that influences the given location, then `restorecon` will reset the contexts appropriately:

```
# semanage fcontext -a -t httpd_user_content_t "/home/[^/]*/
cgi-bin(/.*)?"
# restorecon -RvD /home
Relabeled /home/lisa/cgi-bin from staff_u:object_r:user_
home_t:s0 to staff_u:object_r:httpd_user_content_t:s0
Updated digest for: /home
```

The `restorecon_xattr` command can be used to manage these extended attributes (view or delete) and show how the attributes are formed:

```
# restorecon_xattr -v /home
specfiles SHA1 digest: 7ed69be330ad60811481e455ca8e5ab0b1556036
calculated using the following specfile(s):
/etc/selinux/targeted/contexts/files/file_contexts.subs_dist
...
/etc/selinux/targeted/contexts/files/file_contexts.local.bin

/home Digest: 7ed69be330ad60811481e455ca8e5ab0b1556036 Match
```

The `digest` referenced is the `security.restorecon_last` or `security.sehash` extended attributes. More recent user space tools use the latter, and apply their logic to each subdirectory, whereas older user space utilities use the former and only apply their logic on the selected directory.

The disadvantage of the `security.restorecon_last` usage is that it does not work with subdirectories: if we apply a recursive `restorecon` operation against /, then this tool will ignore the digest on /home. With the `security.sehash` usage, a recursive operation against / will check the digest for /home as well.

Using customizable types

Some SELinux types are meant for files whose paths cannot be accurately defined by administrators or where the administrator does not want the context to be reset when a relabeling operation is triggered. For these purposes, SELinux supports what it calls **customizable types**. When tools that manage file contexts (such as `restorecon`) encounter a file with a customizable type set, they will not revert its context to the registered context definition.

The customizable types are declared in the `customizable_types` file inside /etc/selinux/targeted/contexts. To have `restorecon` relabel such files, administrators need to pass the force reset option (-F) before the tool resets the contexts.

Let's look at the contents of this `customizable_types` file:

```
$ cat /etc/selinux/targeted/contexts/customizable_types
container_file_t
sandbox_file_t
...
httpd_user_content_t
git_session_content_t
home_bin_t
user_tty_device_t
```

As an example, we can mark a file in a home directory as home_bin_t, which is a customizable type, and as such, this file will not be relabeled back to user_home_t when a filesystem relabeling operation is done:

```
$ chcon -t home_bin_t ~/convert.sh
```

Marking other types as customizable requires updating the `customizable_types` file, as there is no user command that adds or removes type definitions from this list. Because this file can be overwritten when the distribution or administrator pushes out a new policy package, it needs to be governed carefully.

That said, the use of customizable types has its advantages. As an administrator, we might want to create and support specific types as usable by end users who can use `chcon` to set the contexts of individual files in their home directory. By having those types marked as customizable types, a relabeling operation against `/home` will not reset those contexts.

When the target type is not a customizable type, administrators generally prefer to use `semanage fcontext` to add an expression and `restorecon` to fix the context of the files. Most administrators will use directory-based labeling: this is much easier to maintain, and much easier to explain to end users. Many will even use this approach for customizable types:

```
# semanage fcontext -a -t home_bin_t "/home/[^/]*/bin(/.*)?"
```

With this command, user binaries and scripts located in the `~/bin` directory will be labeled as `home_bin_t`.

Compiling the different file_contexts files

Inside the `/etc/selinux/targeted/contexts/files` directory, five different `file_contexts` files can be found:

- The `file_contexts` file itself (without any suffix) is the basic expression file provided by the SELinux policy offered through the Linux distribution.

- The `file_contexts.local` file contains the locally added rules (through the `semanage fcontext` command, which we covered earlier in this chapter).

- The `file_contexts.homedirs` file contains the expressions for the user home directories. When new user mappings are created and managed through `semanage login` and `semanage user`, this file is adjusted to reflect the new situation.

- The `file_contexts.subs_dist` file contains equivalency rules, provided by the distribution's SELinux policy, which tell SELinux to consider one part of the filesystem as having the same labeling rules as another location.

- The `file_contexts.subs` file contains locally managed equivalency rules (through the `semanage fcontext` command, covered earlier in this chapter).

Alongside those files, you will find associated `*.bin` files (so `file_contexts.bin` for the `file_contexts` file, `file_contexts.local.bin` for the `file_contexts.local` file, and so on). These `*.bin` files are automatically created, but in case of a discrepancy, administrators can rebuild the files themselves as well using the `sefcontext_compile` command:

```
# cd /etc/selinux/targeted/contexts/files
# sefcontext_compile file_contexts.local
```

These files contain the same information as the main file, but are precompiled to make lookups faster. Unless the tools detect that the `*.bin` files are older than their source files, the SELinux utilities will use the compiled versions of these files.

Exchanging local modifications

When local modifications are registered through `semanage fcontext`, they only apply to a single system. If local definitions need to be reapplied on various systems, administrators can extract the local modifications and import them on another system.

To export the local modifications, use `semanage export`:

```
# semanage export -f local-mods.conf
```

The file that contains the local modifications (`local-mods.conf` in the example) can be adjusted at will. This allows administrators to remove all lines except those they want to apply on other systems.

With the local modifications stored in the file, transport the file to the other system(s) and import the settings:

```
# semanage import -f ./local-mods.conf
```

The imported settings are immediately registered. Of course, in case of filesystem changes (`semanage fcontext`), don't forget to run `restorecon` against the target directories.

Modifying file contexts

We now know how to set SELinux contexts, both directly through tools such as `chcon` as well as through the `restorecon` application, which queries the SELinux context list to know what context a file should have. Yet `restorecon` is not the only application that considers this context list.

Using setfiles, rlpkg, and fixfiles

The `setfiles` application is an older one, which requires the path to the context list file itself to reset contexts. It is often used under the hood of other applications, so most administrators do not need to call `setfiles` directly anymore:

```
# setfiles /etc/selinux/targeted/contexts/files/file_contexts /
srv/web
```

Another set of tools are the `rlpkg` (Gentoo) and `fixfiles` (CentOS and related distributions) applications. Both these applications have a nice feature: they can be used to reset the contexts of the files of an application rather than having to iterate over the files manually and run `restorecon` against them.

In the next example, we're using these tools to restore the contexts of the files provided by the `nginx` package:

```
# rlpkg nginx
# fixfiles -R nginx restore
```

Another feature of both applications is that they can be used to relabel the entire filesystem without the need to perform a system reboot, like so:

```
# rlpkg -a -r
# fixfiles -f -F relabel
```

Of course, this is not as fine-grained as the commands before.

Relabeling the entire filesystem

The `rlpkg` and `fixfiles` commands as listed in the previous section are not the only available approaches for relabeling the entire filesystem when working with a CentOS (or related) distribution. SELinux offers two other methods to ask the system to perform a full filesystem relabeling operation during (re)boot: placing a touch file (which the system reads at boot time) or configuring a boot parameter.

The touch file is called `.autorelabel` and should be placed in the root filesystem. Once set, the system needs to be rebooted:

```
# touch /.autorelabel
# reboot
```

We trigger the same behavior if we add the `autorelabel=1` parameter to the boot parameter list (like where we can set the `selinux=` and `enforcing=` parameters as discussed earlier).

Asking the system to perform a full filesystem relabeling operation will take a while. When finished, the system will reboot again. Touch files will be removed automatically after the relabeling operation has finished.

Automatically setting context with restorecond

Contexts can also be applied by the `restorecond` daemon. The purpose of this daemon is to enforce the expression list rules onto a configurable set of locations, defined in the `/etc/selinux/restorecond.conf` file.

The following set of files and directories is an example list of locations configured in the `restorecond.conf` file so that `restorecond` automatically applies the SELinux contexts on these files and directories whenever it detects a context change in them:

```
/etc/services
/etc/resolv.conf
/etc/samba/secrets.tdb
...
/root/.ssh/*
```

In this case, if a process creates a file that matches any of the previously created paths, the Linux inotify subsystem will notify `restorecond` of it. `restorecond` will then relabel the file according to the expression list, applying the correct label regardless of the process (and context) that created the file.

The use of `restorecond` is primarily for historical reasons, when SELinux didn't support named file transitions. At that time, writing `resolv.conf` in `/etc` could not be differentiated from writing to the `passwd` file in `/etc`. The introduction of named file transitions has considerably reduced the need for `restorecond`.

Setting SELinux context at boot with tmpfiles

If the Linux distribution uses `systemd`, then you can use `systemd-tmpfiles` to automatically set SELinux context at boot. `systemd` uses the `tmpfiles` application to automatically create and manage volatile locations on the system, such as locations inside `/run` when `/run` is a `tmpfs`-mounted filesystem (an in-memory filesystem).

Administrators can configure `tmpfiles` to automatically create files, directories, device files, symbolic links, and others at boot, and to reset the permissions on resources. It is through this reset operation that we can use `tmpfiles` to set the right SELinux context at boot time.

In *Chapter 3*, *Managing User Logins*, we covered polyinstantiation, where users get their own private view on filesystem resources. The example we gave used a directory called `/tmp/tmp-inst`, which had to have the `000` permission set, and which will host the user-oriented `/tmp` views. Rather than having to create and set this permission each time, we can configure `tmpfiles` to do this for us, and define the right SELinux context up front:

```
# semanage fcontext -a -t tmp_t -f d "/tmp/tmp-inst"
```

In `/etc/tmpfiles.d`, we create a file called `selinux-polyinstantiation.conf` with the following content:

```
d /tmp/tmp-inst 000 root root
```

The name of the file can be chosen freely, but make sure it uses the `.conf` suffix. Every time the system boots, `systemd-tmpfiles` will ensure that the `/tmp/tmp-inst` directory is created with the appropriate permissions.

If a location does not need to be created, but only its SELinux context reset, then you can use the `z` (one resource) or `Z` (recursively) options in the `tmpfiles` configuration. This is used, for instance, by the default SELinux `tmpfiles` configuration, `selinux-policy.conf`, in `/usr/lib/tmpfiles.d`:

```
z /sys/devices/system/cpu/online - - -
```

The - used is to inform `tmpfiles` not to adjust the permissions and ownership, and only to reset the SELinux context.

The context of a process

As everything in SELinux works with contexts, even processes are assigned a context, also known as the domain. Let's see how we can obtain this information, how SELinux transitions from one domain to another, and learn how to query the SELinux policy to find more information about these transitions.

Getting a process context

We saw that the nginx web server runs in the httpd_t domain, which can be seen with
the ps -eZ command, as follows:

```
# ps -eZ | grep nginx
system_u:system_r:httpd_t:s0   3744 ?    00:00:00 nginx
```

Several other ways exist to obtain the process context. Although the method with ps
is the most obvious, these other methods can prove useful in scripted approaches
or through monitoring services.

A first approach is to read the /proc/<pid>/attr/current pseudo-file, which
we've already encountered in *Chapter 1, Fundamental SELinux Concepts*. It displays
a process's current security context:

```
# pidof nginx
3746 3745 3744
# cat /proc/3744/attr/current
system_u:system_r:httpd_t:s0
```

To receive a somewhat more human-readable output, use the secon command for the
given process ID:

```
# secon --pid 3744
user: system_u
role: system_r
type: httpd_t
sensitivity: s0
clearance: s0
mls-range: s0
```

Finally, the SELinux user space project has a helper utility called getpidcon, which the
libselinux library optionally provides. Although this utility is not available on CentOS
(or related distributions), other distributions such as Gentoo do have it. The utility
requires a single PID and returns its context:

```
# getpidcon 679
system_u:system_r:nginx_t:s0
```

Now, the Apache processes don't themselves inform SELinux that they need to run in the
httpd_t (or, for Gentoo, the nginx_t) domain. For that, transition rules exist in the
SELinux policy that govern when and how processes are executed in a specific domain.

Transitioning toward a domain

Just as we have seen with files, if a process forks and creates a new process, this process, by default, inherits the context of the parent process. For the web server, the main process is running in the `httpd_t` domain, so all the launched worker processes inherit the `httpd_t` domain from it.

To differentiate the domain of one process from another, domain transitions can be defined. A **domain transition** (also known as a process transition or type transition) is a rule in SELinux that tells SELinux another domain is to be used for a forked process (actually, it is when the parent process calls the `execve()` function, most likely after a `fork()` operation).

Like the file-based transitions, domain transitions can be queried using `sesearch`. Let's investigate the domains allowed to transition to the `httpd_t` domain:

```
$ sesearch -T -t httpd_exec_t
type_transition certwatch_t httpd_exec_t:process httpd_t;
type_transition cluster_t httpd_exec_t:process httpd_t;
type_transition initrc_t httpd_exec_t:process httpd_t;
...
type_transition system_cronjob_t httpd_exec_t:process httpd_t;
```

In this case, SELinux will switch the context of a launched web server to `httpd_t` if the parent process is running in one of the mentioned domains (such as the `initrc_t` domain) and is executing a file labeled as `httpd_exec_t` (the label assigned to the `httpd` and `nginx` binaries).

But for this to truly happen, several other permissions (next to the domain transition) need to be in place. The following list describes these various permissions:

- The source process (such as `initrc_t`) needs to be allowed to transition to the `httpd_t` domain, governed by the transition privilege on the process class:

  ```
  $ sesearch -s initrc_t -t httpd_t -c process -p
  transition -A
  ```

- The source process (such as `initrc_t`) needs to have the right of execution on the file it is launching (`httpd_exec_t`):

  ```
  $ sesearch -s initrc_t -t httpd_exec_t -c file -p execute
  -A
  ```

- The `httpd_exec_t` type must be identified as an entry point for the `httpd_t` domain. SELinux uses an **entry point** to ensure that a domain transition only occurs when using the specified file context on the executing binary or script:

```
$ sesearch -s httpd_t -t httpd_exec_t -c file -p
entrypoint -A
```

- The target domain must be allowed for the role that the parent process is in. In the case of system daemons, the role is `system_r`:

```
$ seinfo -r system_r -x | grep httpd_t
```

A graphical representation of these rights is as follows:

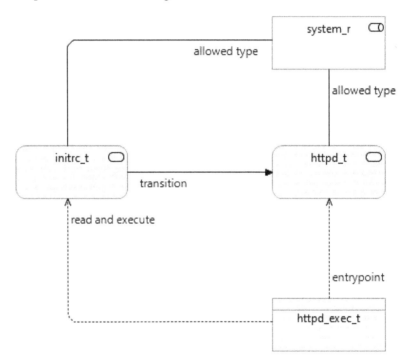

Figure 4.2 – Graphical overview of the necessary transition permissions

Only when all these privileges are allowed will a domain transition occur. If not, then either the execution of the application fails (if the domain has no `execute` or `execute_no_trans` rights on the file), or it executes but remains running in the same domain as the parent process.

Domain transitions are an important concept as they inform the administrator how an application gets into its privileged context. To analyze this, many security administrators look at how one context can transition to another. We explain policy analysis in *Chapter 13, Analyzing Policy Behavior.*

For policy writers, deciding when to create a domain transition and when to keep the processes running in the same (source) context is a matter of design. Generally, policy developers will try to keep the parent context confined so that every additional privilege is a source of consideration for switching to another domain (which has that privilege). Basically, policy developers will trigger a transition when the target application requires significantly more (or different) permissions than the source domain holds.

That is also why the `unconfined_t` domain has fewer transitions when executing user applications compared to the confined user domains, `user_t` or `guest_t`: the `unconfined_t` domain already holds many privileges, so transitioning to a different domain has little value. Note that this is a decision made by the policy writers or Linux distribution, not by the SELinux technology itself. All SELinux does is enforce the policy rules.

Verifying a target context

When executing applications, the SELinux policy might have the command run in a different domain. Although we could start querying all rules with `sesearch`, a simpler command exists that tells us what the target context is when we execute a command or script: `selinuxexeccon`.

This command requires at least one argument (the path of the binary or script that would be executed) and an optional second (the source context). If we omit the second argument, the tool will use the current context as the source context.

For instance, to find out in which domain the `passwd` command would run when executed from the current context, we'd use this command:

```
# selinuxexeccon /usr/bin/passwd
unconfined_u:unconfined_r:passwd_t:s0-s0:c0.c1023
```

The following example shows the target context when the `init_t` domain executes the `nginx` binary:

```
# selinuxexeccon /usr/sbin/nginx system_u:system_r:init_t:s0
system_u:system_r:httpd_t:s0
```

Using `selinuxexeccon` is much faster than querying all appropriate permissions separately.

Other supported transitions

Regular domain transitions are the most common transitions in SELinux, but other transitions are possible as well. For instance, some applications (such as `cron` or `login`) are SELinux-aware and will specify which domain to transition to. These applications call the `setexeccon()` method (set execution context) to specify the target domain and do not use a type transition rule. The other privilege requirements, however, still hold.

Some SELinux-aware applications are even able to change their *current* context (and not just the context of the application they execute). To accomplish this, the application domain needs the `dyntransition` privilege (one of the privileges supported for process-level activities). One example of such an application is OpenSSH, which, by default, runs in the `sshd_t` domain but can transition to the `sftpd_t` type.

Querying initial contexts

When SELinux does not have a label yet for a resource, it will assign an initial context (or initial **security ID (SID)**) to the resource. For a few classes, the SELinux policy will have a default initial context from which it can further jumpstart and assign labels.

The initial contexts for various SIDs can be queried using `seinfo`:

```
# seinfo --initalsid -x
Initial SIDs: 27
   sid any_socket system_u:object_r:unlabeled_t:s0
   sid devnull system_u:object_r:null_device_t:s0
...
   sid unlabeled system_u:object_r:unlabeled_t:s0
```

As you can see, not all classes have a default context assigned, as other classes have their contexts derived from the contexts of the currently listed initial SIDs.

Tweaking memory protections

Legacy binaries on Linux systems might require execution permissions to be set on memory regions when these are used for reading, even when the execute permission is not actually used. This read-implies-exec is a nuisance for mandatory access controls such as SELinux because they need to document the appropriate permissions in their policy. If an application needs read access, does the policy then also have to include the implied execute rights? And if the policy does not include execute rights, should the read operation then fail because it implied execute permissions?

> **Informational note**
>
> Read-implies-exec is a legacy support for running old binaries or binaries compiled for other Unix systems where applications do not explicitly mark their executable memory as executable, assuming that every memory region that is marked as readable is executable. This creates a security risk as malicious actors can load in executable code dynamically without the system being able to prevent the application to execute this code. Many operating systems nowadays have clear memory protection routines in place, including preventing data from becoming executable. Sadly, we often need to deal with legacy situations, so all operating systems have methods in place that selectively disable these memory controls, and within Linux this is done through its **personalities** support (see man personality for more information).

SELinux developers allow administrators to select their most appropriate permission handling by introducing a memory protection check that can be tuned. The checkreqprot option can be set to 0 to check protections as handled by the kernel, or 1 to check protections as asked by the application.

On older systems, this option will be set to 1 to support these legacy binaries. Recent distributions, however, build their applications appropriately, and the more secure setting 0 is used, as displayed by the sestatus command:

```
# sestatus | grep Memory
Memory protection checking:    actual (secure)
```

You can toggle this support through /sys/fs/selinux/checkreqprot:

```
# echo 1 > /sys/fs/selinux/checkreqprot
# sestatus | grep Memory
Memory protection checking:    requested (insecure)
```

The parameter's default value is configured when building the Linux kernel, through the CONFIG_SECURITY_SELINUX_CHECKREQPROT_VALUE kernel configuration parameter. Administrators can also boot the system with the checkreqprot= boot parameter to have the specified value set.

Limiting the scope of transitions

For security reasons, Linux systems can reduce the ability of processes to gain elevated privileges under certain situations or provide additional constraints to reduce the likelihood of vulnerabilities to be exploitable. SELinux developers, too, honor these situations.

Sanitizing environments on transition

When we execute a higher-privileged command (be it a `setuid` application or one where capabilities are added to the session), the **GNU C library** (**glibc**) will sanitize the environment. This means that a set of security-sensitive environment variables are discarded to make sure that attackers, malicious persons, or malicious applications cannot negatively influence the session.

This secure execution is controlled through an **Executable and Linkable Format** (**ELF**) auxiliary vector called **AT_SECURE**. When set, environment variables such as `LD_PRELOAD`, `LD_AUDIT`, `LD_DEBUG`, `TMPDIR`, and `NLSPATH` are removed from the session.

SELinux will force this sanitation on domain transitions as well, ensuring that the newly executed domain does not have access to these sensitive environment variables. Of course, sometimes the transitioned domain requires these variables. Not all domains can deal with sanitized environments, or use these environment variables to pass along important information, so always dropping the environment variables might result in unusable application domains.

To allow transitions without sanitizing the environment, the `noatsecure` permission can be granted to domain transitions. For instance, let's consider the execution of a Firefox plugin:

```
# sesearch -t mozilla_plugin_t -p noatsecure -A
...
allow unconfined_t mozilla_plugin_t:process { ... noatsecure
...};
...
```

When an application running in the `unconfined_t` domain executes the plugin (which results in a domain transition to `mozilla_plugin_t`), the environment variables need to be kept as otherwise the plugin might not function properly. As such, the SELinux policy grants the `noatsecure` permission to the domains that invoke Firefox plugins.

Disabling unconstrained transitions

A second security constraint that Linux supports is to mount a filesystem with the `nosuid` option. When set, no `setuid` and `setgid` binaries on that filesystem will have any effect on the effective user or group ID of the executing session. Essentially, a `setuid` application on a filesystem mounted with `nosuid` will act as if no `setuid` bit is set.

To ensure that transitions triggered by applications hosted on a `nosuid`-mounted filesystem do not allow for elevated privileges, SELinux policy developers must explicitly mark a transition as allowed for `nosuid`-mounted filesystems, using the `nosuid_transition` permission. This permission is part of the `process2` class:

```
$ sesearch -s unconfined_t -p nosuid_transition -A
allow unconfined_t initrc_t:process2 { nnp_transition nosuid_
transition };
...
```

This allows policy developers to differentiate regular domain transitions from `nosuid`-constrained domain transitions.

> **Note**
>
> SELinux has a limit on the number of privileges that can be assigned to a class. When the number of privileges exceeds 32, the SELinux developers will create a different class and the permissions continue in this second class. Right now, the two classes that have more than 32 permissions are the `capability` class and the `process` class.

This permission-based approach might not be in place on all SELinux-enabled systems though. It is enabled when the `nnp_nosuid_transition` policy capability is defined and set to `1`:

```
# cat /sys/fs/selinux/policy_capabilities/nnp_nosuid_transition
1
```

If this capability value is `0`, then SELinux will use a concept called **type bounds** to support domain transitions for applications hosted on `nosuid`-mounted filesystems. Any executable with a file context that would result in a domain transition will only result in a domain transition if the target domain is bounded by the parent domain.

> **Note**
>
> **Policy capabilities** cannot be tweaked by administrators. They are used by policy developers to inform the Linux kernel which behavior it expects. For the `nnp_nosuid_transition` capability, the policy developer informs the kernel that the `nosuid_transition` and `nnp_transition` permission checks should be used rather than bounded domains, and that its policy will generally only include support for the transitions and not for the bounded domains.

If it is not bounded, then the domain transition will not occur, and the session will remain in the current context (or the command will fail to execute if the application is not allowed to run in the current context).

A **bounded domain** is not just calculated live based on the permissions though. SELinux has an explicit rule that enforces a target domain to be bounded by a parent domain. Even when permissions are later added to the bounded domain, they will be denied by the SELinux security subsystem if they aren't part of the parent domain.

With `seinfo`, these type bounds can be listed as follows:

```
# seinfo --typebounds
```

Most distributions, however, do not have bounded domains defined in their SELinux policy anymore, as the new `nosuid_transition` permission is much more flexible. The use of bounded domains required policy developers to extend the permissions of the parent domain every time the child domain needed to be extended, which was a major nuisance when the parent domain is a generic one (be it a container management platform or a system service daemon).

Using Linux's NO_NEW_PRIVS

The use of filesystems mounted with `nosuid` is a specific case of Linux's **No New Privilege** (**NNP**) support. NNP is a process-specific attribute that tells the Linux kernel that the process is no longer to be granted additional privileges. From that point onward, the constraints as mentioned before hold, and SELinux will only allow domain transitions if it has the `nnp_transition` permission, or toward a bounded domain if the `nnp_nosuid_transition` policy capability is not set.

The parameter can be set by applications themselves using the process control function `prctl()`, but the user can also influence this. The `setpriv` command can be used to launch applications with `PR_SET_NO_NEW_PRIVS` set (the parameter that applications can pass through the `prctl()` function).

As an example, create the following simple Python-based CGI script in a `cgi-bin` directory inside a regular user's home directory:

```
#!/usr/bin/env python3
import sys, time
import subprocess
import cgi, cgitb
cgitb.enable()
print('Content-Type: text/html;charset=utf-8\n')
PIPE = subprocess.PIPE
```

```
STDOUT = subprocess.STDOUT
pd = subprocess.Popen(['ping', '-c', '1', 'localhost'],
stdout=PIPE, stderr=STDOUT)
while True:
  output = pd.stdout.read(1)
  if output == '' and pd.poll() != None:
    break
  if output != '':
    sys.stdout.write(output.decode('utf-8'))
    sys.stdout.flush()
```

With this CGI script now available, first launch a simple CGI-capable web server (we will pick port 6020 as unprivileged users should be able to bind processes to this port) and connect to it:

```
$ python3 -m http.server --cgi 6020
```

In a different session, connect to the web server and call the newly created Python script (here named test.py):

```
$ curl http://localhost:6020/cgi-bin/test.py
PING localhost(localhost(::1)) 56 data bytes ...
```

Now, launch the same CGI-capable web server, but with NNP enabled:

```
$ setpriv --no-new-privs python3 -m http.server --cgi 6020
```

Again, connect to the web server and call the test.py CGI script:

```
$ curl http://localhost:6020/cgi-bin/test.py
ping: socket: Permission denied
```

Because Linux's NNP is enabled, the ping command is not able to obtain the higher privileges needed to open the socket.

Sometimes, you'll notice a denial for the execute_no_trans permission in the SELinux audit logs. This occurs when the SELinux policy does not allow an application to be executed without transitioning.

Types, permissions, and constraints

Now that we know more about types (for processes, files, and other resources), let's explore how these are used in the SELinux policy in more detail.

Understanding type attributes

We have discussed the `sesearch` application already and how it can be used to query the current SELinux policy. Let's look at a specific process transition:

```
$ sesearch -s initrc_t -t httpd_t -c process -p transition -A
allow initrc_domain daemon:process transition;
```

Even though we asked for the rules related to the `initrc_t` source domain and the `httpd_t` target, we get a rule back for the `initrc_domain` source domain and the `daemon` target. What `sesearch` did here was show us how the SELinux policy allows the requested permission, but through *attributes* assigned to the `initrc_t` and `httpd_t` types.

Type attributes in SELinux are used to group multiple types and assign privileges to those groups rather than having to assign the privileges to each type individually. For `initrc_domain`, the following types are all tagged with this attribute, as can be seen through the `seinfo` application:

```
$ seinfo -a initrc_domain -x
Type Attributes: 1
  attribute initrc_domain;
    cluster_t;
    . . .
    initrc_t;
    . . .
    piranha_pulse_t;
```

As we can see, the `initrc_t` type is indeed one of the types tagged with `initrc_domain`. Similarly, the `daemon` attribute is assigned to several types (several hundred, even). So, the single allow rule mentioned earlier consolidates more than a thousand rules into one.

Attributes are increasingly used in the policy as a way of consolidating and simplifying policy development. With `seinfo -a`, you can get an overview of all the attributes supported in the current policy.

Querying domain permissions

The most common rules in SELinux are the `allow` rules, informing the SELinux subsystem what permissions a domain has. `allow` rules use the following syntax:

```
allow <source> <destination> : <class> <permissions>;
```

The `<source>` field is almost always a domain, whereas the `<destination>` field can be any type.

The `<class>` field allows us to differentiate privileges based on the resource, whether it is for a regular file, a directory, a TCP socket, a capability, and so on. A full overview of all supported classes can be obtained from `seinfo -c`. Each class has a set of permissions assigned to it that SELinux can control. For instance, the `sem` class (used for semaphore access) has the following permissions associated with it:

```
$ seinfo -c sem -x
Classes: 1
  class sem
inherits ipc
```

The reference to `ipc` in the output informs us that the class inherits permission from the common `ipc` class, which we can query as follows:

```
$ seinfo --common=ipc -x
Commons: 1
{
  write
  destroy
  ...
  create
}
```

In the `<permissions>` field, most rules will bundle a set of permissions using curly brackets:

```
allow user_t etc_t : file { ioctl read getattr lock execute
execute_no_trans open };
```

This syntax allows policy developers to make very fine-grained permission controls. We can use the `sesearch` command to query these rules. The more options are given to the `sesearch` command, the finer-grained our search parameters become. For instance, `sesearch -A` would give us all allow rules currently in place. Adding a source (`-s`) filters the output to only show the allow rules for this domain. Adding a destination or target (`-t`) filters the output even more. Other options that can be used to filter through allow rules with `sesearch` are the class (`-c`) and permission (`-p`) options.

As you might have guessed by now, `sesearch` is an extremely versatile command for querying the active policy, showing us the SELinux policy rules that match the options given.

Learning about constraints

The `allow` statements in SELinux, however, only focus on type-related permissions. Sometimes though, we need to restrict certain actions based on the user or role information. SELinux supports this through constraints.

Constraints in SELinux are rules applied against a class and a set of its permissions that must be true for SELinux to further allow the request. Consider the following constraint on process transitions:

```
constrain process
  { transition dyntransition noatsecure siginh rlimitinh }
  (
    u1 == u2 or
    (
      t1 == can_change_process_identity and
      t2 == process_user_target
    ) or (
      t1 == cron_source_domain and
      (
        t2 == cron_job_domain or
        u2 == system_u
      )
    ) or (
      t1 == can_system_change and
      u2 == system_u
    ) or (
      t1 == process_uncond_exempt
    )
  );
```

This constraint says that at least one of the following rules must be true if a `transition`, `dyntransition`, or any of the other three mentioned process permissions is invoked:

- The SELinux user of the source (`u1`) and that of the target (`u2`) must be the same.
- The SELinux type of the source (`t1`) must have the `can_change_process_identity` attribute set, and the SELinux type of the target (`t2`) must have the `process_user_target` attribute set.
- The SELinux type of the source (`t1`) must have the `cron_source_domain` attribute set, and either the target type (`t2`) should have `cron_job_domain` as an attribute, or the target SELinux user (`u2`) should be `system_u`.
- The SELinux type of the source (`t1`) must have the `can_system_change` attribute set, and the SELinux user of the target (`u2`) must be `system_u`.
- The SELinux type of the source (`t1`) must have the `process_uncond_exempt` attribute set.

It is through constraints that UBAC is implemented as follows:

```
u1 == u2
or u1 == system_u
or u2 == system_u
or t1 != ubac_constrained_type
or t2 != ubac_constrained_type
```

You can list the currently enabled constraints using `seinfo --constrain`. Multiple constraints can be active for the same class and permission set. In that case, all the constraints need to be true for the permission to go through.

Summary

In this chapter, we learned how file contexts are stored as extended attributes on the filesystem and how we can manipulate the contexts of files and other filesystem resources. Next, we found out where SELinux keeps the definitions that describe which SELinux contexts to assign to the files.

We also learned to work with the `semanage` tool to manipulate this information and worked with a few tools that use this information to enforce contexts on resources.

On the process level, we got our first taste of SELinux policies, identifying when a process launches inside a certain SELinux domain. With it, we covered the `sesearch` and `seinfo` applications to query the SELinux policy. Finally, we looked at some of Linux's security implementations that limit the transition scope of applications, which also influences SELinux domain transitions.

In the next chapter, we will expand our knowledge of protecting the operating system through the networking-related features of SELinux.

Questions

1. What is the most common option for Linux tools to display or explicitly set SELinux contexts?

2. How is an SELinux context for a file or directory stored on the system?

3. Why is `chcon` not recommended to persist SELinux context changes?

4. Is the order of context definitions using the `semanage fcontext` command important?

5. How do you relabel files on the filesystem?

6. What privileges does a domain need before it can transition to another domain?

7. How do SELinux policies bundle multiple types together to facilitate policy development?

5
Controlling Network Communications

The SELinux mandatory access controls go much beyond its file and process access controls. One of the features provided by SELinux is its ability to control network communications. By default, general network access controls use the socket-based access control mechanism, but more detailed approaches are also possible.

In this chapter, we will learn how network access controls are governed by SELinux, cover what administrators can do to further strengthen network communications using `iptables`, and describe how SELinux policies can be used for cross-system security through labeled IPsec. We'll finish the chapter with an introduction to CIPSO labeling and its integration with SELinux.

We cover the following topics in this chapter:

- Controlling process communications
- Linux firewalling and SECMARK support
- Securing high-speed InfiniBand networks
- Understanding labeled networking
- Using labeled IPsec with SELinux
- Supporting CIPSO with NetLabel and SELinux

Technical requirements

Not all sections in this chapter apply to all environments. For InfiniBand support, for instance, InfiniBand hardware is needed, whereas for NetLabel/CIPSO support, the network in its entirety needs to support the CIPSO (or CALIPSO in the case of IPv6) protocol for the hosts to be able to communicate with each other.

Check out the following video to see the Code in Action: `https://bit.ly/34bVDdm`

Controlling process communications

Linux applications communicate with each other either directly or over a network. But the difference between direct communication and networked communication, from an application programmer's point of view, is not always that big. Let's look at the various communication methods that Linux supports and how SELinux aligns with them.

Using shared memory

The least network-like method is the use of shared memory. Applications can share certain parts of the memory with each other and use those shared segments to communicate between two (or more) processes. To govern access to the shared memory, application programmers can use **mutual exclusions** (**mutexes**) or **semaphores**. A semaphore is an atomically incremented or decremented integer (ensuring that two applications do not overwrite each other's values without knowing about the value change), whereas a mutex can be interpreted as a special semaphore that only takes the values 0 or 1.

On Linux, two implementations exist for shared memory access and control: SysV-style and POSIX-style. We will not dwell on the advantages and disadvantages of each, but rather look at how SELinux governs access to these implementations.

SELinux controls the SysV-style primitives through specific classes: `sem` for semaphores and `shm` for shared memory. The semaphores, mutexes, and shared memory segments inherit the context of the first process that creates them.

Administrators who want to control the SysV-style primitives can use the various `ipc*` commands: `ipcs` (to list), `ipcrm` (to remove), and `ipcmk` (to create).

For instance, let's first list the resources and then remove the listed shared memory:

```
# ipcs
...
------ Shared Memory Segments ------
key            shmid owner       perms bytes nattch       status
0x0052e2c1 0         postgres     600   56    6
# ipcrm -m 0
```

When POSIX-style semaphores, mutexes, and shared memory segments are used, SELinux controls those operations through the file-based access controls. The POSIX-style approach uses regular files in /dev/shm, which is simpler for administrators to control and manage.

Communicating locally through pipes

A second large family of communication methods in operating systems is the use of pipes. As the name implies, pipes are generally one-way communication tunnels, with information flowing from one (or more) senders to one receiver (there are exceptions to this, such as Solaris pipes, which act as bidirectional channels, but those are not supported on Linux). Another name for a pipe is **first-in, first-out** (**FIFO**).

We have two types of pipes in Linux: **anonymous pipes** (also known as **unnamed pipes**) and **named pipes**. The difference is that a named pipe uses a file in the regular filesystem as its identification, whereas anonymous pipes are constructed through the applications with no representation in the regular filesystem.

In both cases, SELinux will see the pipes as files of the fifo_file class. Named pipes will have their path associated with the regular filesystem and are created using the mknod or mkfifo commands (or through the mkfifo() function when handled within applications). Anonymous pipes, however, will be shown as part of the pipefs filesystem. This is a pseudo filesystem, not accessible to users, but still represented as a filesystem through Linux's **virtual file system** (**VFS**) abstraction.

From an SELinux policy point of view, the FIFO file is the target for which the access controls apply: two domains that both have the correct set of privileges toward the context of the FIFO file will be able to communicate with each other.

Administrators can find out which process is communicating over FIFOs with other processes through tools such as `lsof`, or by querying the `/proc` filesystem (as part of the `/proc/<pid>/fd` listings). The `lsof` tool supports the `-Z` option to show the SELinux context of the process, and even supports wildcards:

```
# lsof -Z *:postfix_*
```

In this example, `lsof` displays information about all processes that use a `postfix_*` label.

Conversing over UNIX domain sockets

With pipes supporting one-way communication only, any conversation between two processes would require two pipes. Also, true client/server-like communication with pipes is challenging to implement. To accomplish the more advanced communication flows, processes will use sockets.

Most administrators are aware that TCP and UDP communication occurs over sockets. Applications can bind to a socket and listen for incoming communications or use the socket to connect to other, remote services. But even on a single Linux system, sockets can be used to facilitate the communication flows. There are two socket types that can be used for process communication: UNIX domain sockets and netlink sockets. **Netlink sockets** are specific to the Linux operating system and are quite low-level, resembling the `ioctl()` system call usage. **UNIX domain sockets**, on the other hand, are higher-level and more directly accessible by administrators, which is why we explain them here in more detail.

We can distinguish between two UNIX domain socket definitions, as with pipes: unnamed sockets and named sockets. And like pipes, the distinction is in the path used to identify a socket. Named sockets are created on the regular filesystem, while unnamed sockets are part of the `sockfs` pseudo filesystem. Similarly, sockets can be queried through utilities such as `lsof` or through the `/proc/<pid>/fd` listings.

There is another distinction regarding UNIX domain sockets though, namely, the communication format that the UNIX domain socket allows. UNIX domain sockets can be created as **datagram sockets** (data sent to the socket retains its chunk size and format) or **streaming sockets** (data sent to the socket can be read in different-sized chunks). This has some repercussions for the SELinux policy rules.

For SELinux, communicating over UNIX domain sockets requires both domains to have the proper communication privileges toward the socket file type (`open`, `read`, and `write`), depending on the direction of the communication.

Additionally, the sending (client) domain requires additional privileges toward the receiving (server) domain:

- The connectto privilege in the unix_stream_socket class in the case of stream sockets
- The sendto privilege in the unix_dgram_socket class in the case of datagram sockets

As you can see, the privileges depend on the communication type used across the socket.

Understanding netlink sockets

Another socket type that can be used for process communication is netlink. **Netlink sockets** are sockets that allow user space applications to communicate and interact with kernel processes, and, in special cases (where network management is delegated to a user space process by the Linux kernel), also communicate with another user space application. Unlike the regular UNIX domain sockets, whose target context associates with the owner of that socket, netlink sockets are always local to the SELinux context.

Put differently, when a domain such as sysadm_t wants to manipulate the kernel's routing information, it will open and communicate with the kernel through a netlink route socket, identified through the netlink_route_socket class:

```
$ sesearch -s sysadm_t -t sysadm_t -c netlink_route_socket -A
allow sysadm_t domain:netlink_route_socket getattr;
allow sysadm_t sysadm_t:netlink_route_socket { append bind ...
};
```

As applications gain more features, it might be that some of these features are no longer allowed by the current SELinux policy. Administrators will then need to update the SELinux policy to allow the netlink communication.

An overview of supported netlink sockets can be devised from the netlink information on the manual page (man netlink), from which the SELinux classes can easily be derived. For instance, the NETLINK_XFRM socket is supported through the SELinux netlink_xfrm_socket class.

Dealing with TCP, UDP, and SCTP sockets

When we go further up the chain, we look at socket communication over the network. In this case, rather than communicating directly between processes (and thus in Linux terminology between SELinux domains), the flows are from, and to, TCP, UDP, and **Stream Control Transmission Protocol (SCTP)** sockets.

SELinux will assign types to these ports as well, and these types are then the types to use for socket communication. For SELinux, a client application connecting to the DNS port (TCP port 53, which receives the `dns_port_t` type in most SELinux policies) uses the `name_connect` permission within the `tcp_socket` class toward the port type. The SCTP protocol (with the `sctp_socket` class) uses the same permission. For UDP services (and thus the `udp_socket` class), `name_connect` is not used. Daemon applications use the `name_bind` privileges to bind themselves to their associated port.

> **Important note**
>
> Support for SCTP has only been recently introduced in SELinux, and not all Linux distributions have updated their policies accordingly. To see whether SCTP support is active, check the value of the `/sys/fs/selinux/policy_capabilities/extended_socket_class` file. A value of 1 means that the policy has SCTP support included, whereas a value of 0 (or an absent file) means that the system does not yet support SCTP.

Administrators can fine-tune which label to assign to which TCP, UDP, or SCTP port. For this, the `semanage port` command can be used. For instance, to list the current port definitions, you'd use this command:

```
# semanage port -l
SELinux Port Type       Proto Port Number
afs3_callback_port_t    tcp   7001
...
http_port_t             tcp   80, 81, 443, 488, 8008, 8009, ...
```

In this example, we see that the `http_port_t` label is assigned to a set of TCP ports. Web server domains that can bind to `http_port_t` are, as such, allowed to bind to any of the mentioned ports.

To allow a daemon, such as an SSH server, to bind to other (or additional) ports, we need to tell SELinux to map this port to the appropriate label. For instance, to allow the SSH server to bind to port 10122, we first check whether this port already holds a dedicated label. This can be accomplished using the `sepolicy` command:

```
$ sepolicy network -p 10122
10122: udp unreserved_port_t 1024-32767
10122: tcp unreserved_port_t 1024-32767
10122: sctp unreserved_port_t 1024-32767
```

The `unreserved_port_t` label is not a dedicated one, so we can assign the `ssh_port_t` label to it:

```
# semanage port -a -t ssh_port_t -p tcp 10122
```

Removing a port definition works similarly:

```
# semanage port -d -t ssh_port_t -p tcp 10122
```

When a specific port type is already assigned, then the utility will give the following error:

```
# semanage port -a -t ssh_port_t -p tcp 80
 ValueError: Port tcp/80 already defined
```

If this is the case and another port cannot be used, then no option exists other than to modify the SELinux policy.

Listing connection contexts

Many of the tools in an administrator's arsenal can display security context information. As with the core utilities, most of these tools use the -Z option for this. For instance, to list the running network-bound services, netstat can be used:

```
# netstat -naptZ | grep ':80'
tcp  0  0 0.0.0.0:80  0.0.0.0:* LISTEN 17655/nginx: master
system_u:system_r:httpd_t:s0
```

Even `lsof` displays the context when asked to:

```
# lsof -i :80 -Z
COMMAND PID    SECURITY-CONTEXT             USER FD TYPE DEVICE
SIZE/OFF NODE NAME
nginx   17655 system_u:system_r:httpd_t:s0 root 8u IPv4 31230
0t0       *:http (LISTEN)
```

Another advanced command for querying connections is the `ss` command. Just calling `ss` will display all the connections of the current system. When adding -Z, it adds the context information as well.

For instance, the following command queries for listening TCP services:

```
# ss -ltnZ
```

More advanced queries can be called as well — consult the `ss` manual page for more information.

> **Note**
>
> The use of the -Z option to show SELinux context information or consider
> SELinux context information in the activity that is requested by the user is
> a general but not mandatory practice amongst application developers. It is
> recommended to check the manual page of the application to confirm whether,
> and how, SELinux is supported by a tool. For instance, to get the ss manual
> page, run man ss.

All these interactions are still quite primitive in nature, with the last set (which focuses on sockets) being more network-related than the others. Once we look into interaction between systems, we might not have enough control through just the sockets though. To enable more fine-grained control, we'll look at firewall capabilities and their SECMARK support next.

Linux firewalling and SECMARK support

The approach with TCP, UDP, and SCTP ports has a few downsides. One of them is that SELinux has no knowledge of the target host, so cannot reason about its security properties. This method also offers no way of limiting daemons from binding on any interface: in a multi-homed situation, we might want to make sure that a daemon only binds on the interface facing the internal network and not the internet-facing one, or vice versa.

In the past, SELinux allowed support for this binding issue through the **interface** and **node** labels: a domain could be configured to only bind to one interface and not to any other, or even on a specific address (referred to as the node). This support had its flaws though, and has been largely deprecated in favor of SECMARK filtering.

Before explaining SECMARK and how administrators can control it, let's first take a quick look at Linux's netfilter subsystem, the de facto standard for local firewall capabilities on Linux systems.

Introducing netfilter

Like LSM, the Linux netfilter subsystem provides hooks in various stages of its networking stack processing framework, which can then be implemented by one or more modules. For instance, ip_tables (which uses the iptables command as its control application) is one of those modules, while ip6_tables and ebtables are other examples of netfilter modules. Modules implementing a netfilter hook must inform the netfilter framework of that hook's priority. This enables controllable ordering in the execution of modules (as multiple calls for the same hook can and will be used together).

The `ip_tables` framework is the one we will be looking at in more detail because it supports the SECMARK approach. This framework is commonly referred to as just `iptables`, which is the name of its control application. We will be using this term for the remainder of this book.

`iptables` offers several *tables*, functionally-oriented classifications for network processing. The common ones are as follows:

- The `filter` table enables the standard network-filtering capabilities.

- The `nat` table is intended to modify routing-related information from packets, such as the source and/or destination address.

- The `mangle` table is used to modify most of a packet's fields.

- The `raw` table is enabled when administrators want to opt out certain packets/flows from the connection-tracking capabilities of netfilter.

- The `security` table is offered to allow administrators to label packets once regular processing is complete.

Within each table, `iptables` offers a default set of chains. These default chains specify where in the processing flow (and thus which hook in the netfilter framework) rules are to be processed. Each chain has a default policy – the default return value if none of the rules in a chain match. Within the chain, administrators can add several rules to process sequentially. When a rule matches, the configured action applies. This action can be to allow the packet to flow through this hook in the netfilter framework, be denied, or perform additional processing.

Commonly provided chains (not all chains are offered for all tables) include the following:

- The PREROUTING chain, which is the first packet-processing step once a packet is received

- The INPUT chain, which is for processing packets meant for the local system

- The FORWARD chain, which is for processing packets meant to be forwarded to another remote system

- The OUTPUT chain, which is for processing packets originating from the local system

- The POSTROUTING chain, which is the last packet-processing step before a packet is sent

Overly simplified, the implementation of these tables and their chains roughly associates with the priority of the calls within the netfilter framework. The chains are easily associated with the hooks provided by the netfilter framework, whereas the table tells netfilter which chain implementations are to be executed first.

Implementing security markings

With packet labeling, we can use the filtering capabilities of `iptables` (and `ip6tables`) to assign labels to packets and connections. The idea is that the local firewall tags packets and connections and then the kernel uses SELinux to grant (or deny) application domains the right to use those tagged packets and connections.

This packet labeling is known as **SECurity MARKings** (**SECMARK**). Although we use the term SECMARK, the framework consists of two markings: one for packets (SECMARK) and one for connections, that is, **CONNection MARKings** (**CONNMARK**). The SECMARK capabilities are offered through two tables, `mangle` and `security`. Only these tables currently have the action of tagging packets and connections available in their rule set:

- The `mangle` table has a higher execution priority than most other tables. Implementing SECMARK rules on this level is generally done when all packets need to be labeled, even when many of these packets will eventually be dropped.

- The `security` table is next in execution priority after the `filter` table. This allows the regular firewall rules to be executed first, and only tag those packets allowed by the regular firewall. Using the `security` table allows the `filter` table to implement the discretionary access control rules first and have SELinux execute its mandatory access control logic only if the DAC rules are executed successfully.

Once a SECMARK action triggers, it will assign a packet type to the packet or communication. SELinux policy rules will then validate whether a domain is allowed to receive (`recv`) or send packets of a given type. For instance, the Firefox application (running in the `mozilla_t` domain) will be allowed to send and receive HTTP client packets:

```
allow mozilla_t http_client_packet_t : packet { send recv };
```

Another supported permission set for SECMARK-related packets is `forward_in` and `forward_out`. These permissions are checked when using forwarding in netfilter.

One important thing to be aware of is that once a SECMARK action is defined, then all the packets that eventually reach the operating system's applications will have a label associated with them — even if no SECMARK rule exists for the packet or connection that the kernel is inspecting. If that occurs, then the kernel applies the default `unlabeled_t` label. The default SELinux policy implemented in some distributions (such as CentOS) allows all domains to send and receive `unlabeled_t` packets, but this is not true for all Linux distributions.

Assigning labels to packets

When no SECMARK-related rules are loaded in the netfilter subsystem, then SECMARK is not enabled and none of the SELinux rules related to SECMARK permissions are checked. The network packets are not labeled, so no enforcement can be applied to them. Of course, the regular socket-related access controls still apply — SECMARK is just an additional control measure.

Once a single SECMARK rule is active, SELinux starts enforcing the packet-label mechanism on all packets. This means that all the network packets now need a label on them (as SELinux can only deal with labeled resources). The default label (the initial security context) for packets is `unlabeled_t`, which means that no marking rule matches this network packet.

Because SECMARK rules are now enforced, SELinux checks all domains that interact with network packets to see whether they are authorized to send or receive these packets. To simplify management, some distributions enable send and receive rights against the `unlabeled_t` packets for all domains. Without these rules, all network services would stop functioning properly the moment a single SECMARK rule becomes active.

To assign a label to a packet, we need to define a set of rules that match a particular network flow, and then call the SECMARK logic (to tag the packet or communication with a label). Most rules will immediately match the `ACCEPT` target as well, to allow this particular communication to reach the system.

Let's implement two rules:

- The first is to allow communication toward websites (port `80`) and tag the related network packets with the `http_client_packet_t` type (so that web browsers are allowed to send and receive these packets).

- The second is to allow communication toward the locally running web server (port `80` as well) and tag its related network packets with the `http_server_packet_t` type (so that web servers are allowed to send and receive these packets).

For each rule set, we also enable connection tracking so that related packets are automatically labeled correctly and passed.

Use the following commands for the web server traffic:

```
# iptables -t filter -A INPUT -m conntrack --ctstate
ESTABLISHED,RELATED -j ACCEPT
# iptables -t filter -A INPUT -p tcp -d 192.168.100.15 --dport
80 -j ACCEPT
# iptables -t security -A INPUT -p tcp --dport 80 -j SECMARK
--selctx "system_u:object_r:http_server_packet_t:s0"
# iptables -t security -A INPUT -p tcp --dport 80 -j
CONNSECMARK --save
```

Use these commands for the browser traffic:

```
# iptables -t filter -A OUTPUT -m conntrack --ctstate
ESTABLISHED -j ACCEPT
# iptables -t filter -A OUTPUT -p tcp --dport 80 -j ACCEPT
# iptables -t security -A OUTPUT -p tcp --dport 80 -j SECMARK
--selctx "system_u:object_r:http_client_packet_t:s0"
# iptables -t security -A OUTPUT -p tcp --dport 80 -j
CONNSECMARK --save
```

Finally, to copy connection labels to the established and related packets, use the following commands:

```
# iptables -t security -A INPUT -m state --state
ESTABLISHED,RELATED -j CONNSECMARK --restore
# iptables -t security -A OUTPUT -m state --state
ESTABLISHED,RELATED -j CONNSECMARK --restore
```

Even this simple example shows that firewall rule definitions are an art by themselves, and that the SECMARK labeling is just a small part of it. However, using the SECMARK rules makes it possible to allow certain traffic while still ensuring that only well-defined domains can interact with that traffic. For instance, it can be implemented on kiosk systems to only allow one browser to communicate with the internet while all other browsers and commands aren't. Tag all browsing-related traffic with a specific label, and only allow that browser domain the send and recv permissions on that label.

Transitioning to nftables

While `iptables` is still one of the most widely used firewall technologies on Linux, two other contenders (`nftables` and `bpfilter`) are rising rapidly in terms of popularity. The first of these, `nftables`, has a few operational benefits over `iptables`, while retaining focus on the netfilter support in the Linux kernel:

- The code base for `nftables` and its Linux kernel support is much more streamlined.

- Error reporting is much better.

- Filtering rules can be incrementally changed rather than requiring a full reload of all rules.

The `nftables` framework has recently received support for SECMARK, so let's see how to apply the `http_server_packet_t` and `http_client_packet_t` labels to the appropriate traffic.

The most common approach for applying somewhat larger `nftables` rules is to use a configuration file with the `nft` interpreter set:

```
#!/usr/sbin/nft -f
flush ruleset
table inet filter {
  secmark http_server {
    "system_u:object_r:http_server_packet_t:s0"
  }
  secmark http_client {
    "system_u:object_r:http_client_packet_t:s0"
  }
  map secmapping_in {
    type inet_service : secmark
    elements = { 80 : "http_server" }
  }
  map secmapping_out {
    type inet_service : secmark
    elements = { 80 : "http_client" }
  }
  chain input {
    type filter hook input priority 0;
    ct state new meta secmark set tcp dport map @secmapping_in
    ct state new ct secmark set meta secmark
    ct state established,related meta secmark set ct secmark
  }
  chain output {
```

```
        type filter hook output priority 0;
        ct state new meta secmark set tcp dport map @secmapping_out
        ct state new ct secmark set meta secmark
        ct state established,related meta secmark set ct secmark
    }
}
```

The syntax that nftables uses is recognizable when we compare it with iptables. The script starts with defining the SECMARK values. After that, we create a mapping between a port (80 in the example) and the value used for the SECMARK support. Of course, already established sessions also receive the appropriate SECMARK labeling.

If we define multiple entries, the elements variable uses commas to separate the various values:

```
elements = { 53 : "dns_client" , 80 : "http_client" , 443 :
"http_client" }
```

Next to nftables. A second firewall solution that is gaining traction is eBPF, which we cover next.

Assessing eBPF

eBPF (and the bpfilter command) is completely different in nature compared to iptables and nftables, so let's first see how eBPF functions before we cover the SELinux support details for it.

Understanding how eBPF works

The **extended Berkeley Packet Filter** (**eBPF**) is a framework that uses an in-kernel virtual machine that interprets and executes eBPF code, rather low-level instructions comparable to processor instruction set operations. Because of its very low-level, yet processor-agnostic language, it can be used to create very fast, highly optimized rules.

BPF was originally used for analyzing and filtering network traffic (for example, within tcpdump). Because of its high efficiency, it was soon found in other tools as well, growing beyond the plain network filtering and analysis capabilities. As BPF expanded toward other use cases, it became extended BPF, or eBPF.

The eBPF framework in the Linux kernel has been successfully used for performance monitoring, where eBPF applications hook into runtime processes and kernel subsystems to measure performance and feed back the metrics to user-space applications. It, of course, also supports filtering on (network) sockets, cgroups, process scheduling, and many more — and the list is growing rapidly.

As with the LSM framework, which uses hooks into the system calls and other security-sensitive operations in the Linux kernel, eBPF hooks into the Linux kernel as well. Occasionally it can use existing hooks (as with the Linux **kernel probes** or **kprobes** framework) and thus benefit from the stability of these interfaces. We can thus expect eBPF to grow its support further in other areas of the Linux kernel as well.

eBPF applications (**eBPF programs**) are defined in user space, and then submitted to the Linux kernel. The kernel verifies the security and consistency of the code to ensure that the virtual machine will not attempt to break out of the boundaries it works in. If approved (possibly after the code is slightly altered, as the Linux kernel has some operations that modify eBPF code to suit the environment or security rules), the eBPF program runs in the Linux kernel (within its virtual machine) and executes its purpose.

> **Note**
>
> The Linux kernel can compile the eBPF instructions into native, processor-specific instructions, rather than having the virtual machine interpret them. However, as this leads to a higher security risk, this **Just-In-Time** (**JIT**) eBPF support is sometimes disabled by Linux distributions in their Linux kernels. It can be enabled by setting `/proc/sys/net/core/bpf_jit_enable` to 1.

These programs can load and save information in memory, called maps. These **eBPF maps** can be read or written to by user-space applications, and thus offer the main interface to interact with running eBPF programs. These maps are accessed through file descriptors, allowing processes to pass along and clone these file descriptors as needed.

Various products and projects are using eBPF to create high-performance network capabilities, such as software-defined network configurations, DDoS mitigation rules, load balancers, and more. Unlike the netfilter-based firewalls, which rely on a massive code base within the kernel tuned through configuration, eBPF programs are built specifically for their purpose and nothing more, and only that code is actively running.

Securing eBPF programs and maps

The default security measures in place for eBPF programs and maps are very limited, partly because lots of trust is put in the Linux kernel verifier (which verifies the eBPF code before it passes the code on to the virtual machine), and partly because the eBPF code was only allowed to be loaded when the process involved has the CAP_SYS_ADMIN capability. And as this capability basically means full system access, additional security controls were not deemed necessary.

Since Linux kernel 4.4, some types of eBPF programs (such as socket filtering) can be loaded even by unprivileged processes (but, of course, only toward the sockets these processes have access to). The system allows loading programs to work on cgroups **socket buffers** (**skb**) if the process has the CAP_NET_ADMIN capability. Recently, the permission to load eBPF programs has been added to the CAP_BPF and CAP_TRACING capabilities, although not all Linux distributions offer a Linux kernel that supports these capabilities already. But Linux administrators that want more fine-grained control over eBPF can use SELinux to tune and tweak eBPF handling.

SELinux has a bpf class, which governs the basic eBPF operations: prog_load, prog_run, map_create, map_read, and map_write. Whenever a process creates a program or map, this program or map inherits the SELinux label of this process. If the file descriptors regarding these maps or programs are leaked, the malicious application still requires the necessary privileges toward this label before it can exploit it.

User-space operations can interact with the eBPF framework through the /sys/fs/bpf virtual filesystem, so some Linux distributions associate a specific SELinux label (bpf_t) with this location as well. This allows administrators to manage access through SELinux policy rules in relation to this type.

While eBPF is extremely extensible, the number of simplified frameworks surrounding it is small given its very early phase. We can, however, expect that more elaborate support will come soon, as a new tool called bpfilter is showing off the capabilities of eBPF-based firewalling on Linux systems.

Filtering traffic with bpfilter

The bpfilter application is an application that builds a new eBPF program to filter and process traffic. It allows administrators to build firewall capabilities without understanding the low-level eBPF instructions, and has recently started supporting iptables: administrators create rules with iptables, and bpfilter translates and converts these into eBPF programs.

> **Important note**
> While bpfilter is part of the Linux kernel tree, it should be considered a proof-of-value currently, rather than a production-ready firewall capability.

bpfilter creates eBPF programs that hook inside the Linux kernel between the network device driver and the TCP/IP stack in a layer called the **eXpress Data Path** (**XDP**). At this level, the eBPF programs have access to the full network packet information (including link layer protocols such as Ethernet).

To use `bpfilter`, the Linux kernel needs to be built with the appropriate settings, including `CONFIG_BPFILTER` and `CONFIG_BPFILTER_UMH`. The latter is the `bpfilter` user mode helper that will capture `iptables`-generated firewall rules, and translate those into eBPF applications.

Before we load the `bpfilter` user mode helper, we need to allow `execmem` permission in SELinux:

```
# setsebool allow_execmem on
```

Next, load the `bpfilter` module, which will have the user mode helper active on the system:

```
# modprobe bpfilter
# dmesg | tail
...
bpfilter: Loaded bpfilter_umh pid 2109
```

Now, load the `iptables` firewall using the commands listed previously. The instructions are translated into eBPF programs, as shown with `bpftool`:

```
# bpftool p
1: xdp   tag 8ec94a061de28c09 dev ens3
         loaded_at Apr 25/23:19  uid:0
         xlated 533B  jited 943B  memlock 4096B
```

The eBPF code itself can be displayed as well, but is hardly readable at this point for administrators.

All of the aforementioned firewall capabilities interact with the TCP/IP stack supported within the Linux kernel. There are, however, networks that do not rely on TCP/IP, such as InfiniBand. Luckily, even on those more specialized network environments, SELinux can be used to control communication flows.

Securing high-speed InfiniBand networks

The **InfiniBand** standard is a relatively recent (in network history) technology that enables very high throughput and very low latency. It accomplishes this by having a very low overhead on the network layer (protocol) and direct access from user applications to the network level. This direct access also has implications for SELinux, as the Linux kernel is no longer actively involved in the transport of data across an InfiniBand link.

Let's first look at what InfiniBand looks like, after which we can see how to still apply SELinux controls to its communication flows.

Directly accessing memory

One of the main premises of InfiniBand is to allow user applications to have direct access to the network. By itself, InfiniBand is a popular **Remote Direct Memory Access (RDMA)** implementation, which has received significant support from vendors. We find RDMA actively used in high-performance clusters.

Because of the direct access, controls are only possible while setting up the access approach. Without SELinux, all that is needed to set up and manage InfiniBand communications is to have access to the device file itself. If a process can write to the InfiniBand device, then it can use InfiniBand. By default, these devices are only accessible by the root user.

The InfiniBand devices are the network cards or **Host Channel Adapters (HCA)** and can have multiple ports. An InfiniBand **port** is the link or interface that connects to an InfiniBand subnet. The subnet is the high-speed network on which multiple machines (ports) are connected. As with regular networks, InfiniBand switches are used to facilitate communication across a subnet, and routers can be used to connect different subnets with each other.

An InfiniBand subnet is managed by a **Subnet Manager (SM)**. This is a process that coordinates the management of the different ports within the subnet, as well as the partitions. **Partitions** in InfiniBand are a way to differentiate between different communications within a subnet, like **Virtual Local Area Networks (VLANs)** in more regular networks. With partitioned communication, it is the subnet manager that tells which ports can be used for which partitions of the communication.

Protecting InfiniBand networks

Unlike regular networks, where firewalls and switch-level access controls are the norm for preventing unauthorized access, InfiniBand has few protection measures in place. InfiniBand largely assumes that the network is within a trusted environment. However, that does not exclude us from applying more rigid controls over which process can access the InfiniBand network in SELinux.

As the communication flow itself is directly mapped in-memory toward the devices, the Linux kernel does not have any hooks available to do packet-level controls like it can with regular TCP/UDP traffic (using the SECMARK capabilities), or even session-level controls with sockets. Instead, SELinux focuses on two main controls, as visualized in the following diagram:

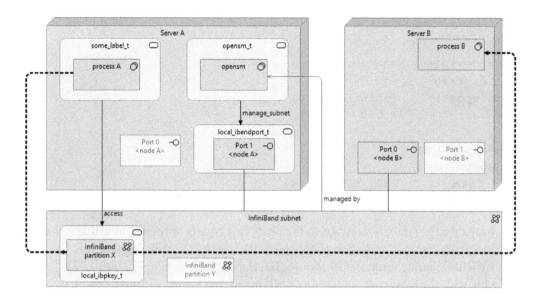

Figure 5.1 – SELinux InfiniBand controls

These two main controls are as follows:

- Controlling who can manage the InfiniBand subnet
- Controlling who can access an InfiniBand partition

To properly govern these controls, the semanage application assigns the right type to the appropriate InfiniBand resource. However, not all SELinux policies already contain the appropriate types, so we need to add those in as well.

Managing the InfiniBand subnet

Let's start with managing the InfiniBand network. With InfiniBand on Linux, this is most often accomplished using the opensm application. Many InfiniBand adapters have multiple ports, allowing a server to participate in multiple InfiniBand subnets. With SELinux, we can control which domain can manage a subnet by controlling access to the InfiniBand port on a device.

First, we need to assign a label to the InfiniBand port associated with a subnet. To accomplish that, we first need to obtain the right InfiniBand device, create the appropriate label (type), and then assign it to the port.

Let's start by querying the available InfiniBand-capable devices on the system using `ibv_devinfo`:

```
# ibv_devinfo
hca_id: rxe0
   transport:      InfiniBand (0)
   fw_ver:         0.0.0
   ...
   phys_port_cnt:
     port:  1
      state:        PORT_ACTIVE (4)
   ...
```

Next, we create a type (label) to assign to the port. This type is only used to validate the access from the `opensm` application to this port. We use the CIL language for this (which we will elaborate upon in *Chapter 16, Developing Policies with SELinux CIL*). Create a file with the following content (let's call it `infiniband_subnet.cil`):

```
(typeattribute ibendport_type)
(type local_ibendport_t)
(typeattributeset ibendport_type local_ibendport_t)
(allow opensm_t local_ibendport_t (infiniband_endport (manage_subnet)))
```

In the previous code, we enhance the SELinux policy with a new type called `local_ibendport_t`, assign it the `ibendport_type` attribute, and then grant the `opensm_t` domain the `manage_subnet` privilege within the `infiniband_endport` class.

Let's load this policy enhancement:

```
# semodule -i infiniband_subnet.cil
```

Finally, we assign this newly created type to the InfiniBand port:

```
# semanage ibendport -a -t local_ibendport_t -z rxe0 1
```

This command assigns the `local_ibendport_t` type to port number 1 of the `rxe0` device (as obtained from `ibv_devinfo`). Once this mapping is in place, we can query it using `semanage` as well:

```
# semanage ibendport -l
SELinux IB End Port Type     IB Device Name     Port Number
local_ibendport_t            rxe0               0x1
```

Without any mappings, the command does not display any output.

> **Important note**
>
> Currently, most Linux distributions have not incorporated InfiniBand support within the SELinux policy, requiring us to create our own custom labels. We can expect that distributions will add in default types for InfiniBand resources, and that SELinux support for InfiniBand will be extended with sane defaults.

If we use InfiniBand on an SELinux-enabled system without any port mappings, the initial security context for unlabeled classes will be used as the label for this port, namely, `unlabeled_t`. It is, however, not recommended to stick to this label, as it is more widely used for unlabeled resources. Granting any privilege to the `unlabeled_t` type should be limited to highly privileged processes, and its use should be carefully considered to ensure that logging interpretation and SELinux policy rules vis-à-vis InfiniBand resources are clear (through well-documented types).

Controlling access to InfiniBand partitions

While the previous section focused on allowing the management application `opensm` to manage a subnet, this section will focus on restricting access to the InfiniBand network to the right domains. As mentioned before, an InfiniBand subnet can be divided further into separate networks using InfiniBand partitions.

Originally, these partitions are used to allow **Quality of Service (QoS)** or specific bandwidth and performance requirements on flows. The SM defines the partitions and its attributes, and applications use a **Partition Key (P_Key)** to inform the InfiniBand network as regards to which partition certain communications must be done.

SELinux can govern these partitions by creating a mapping between the InfiniBand subnet plus P_Key and an SELinux type. However, as with the subnet management, we need to find the appropriate details first and create an appropriate SELinux type before we can define the mapping.

Let's start by figuring out the subnet and partition details. Both are managed by `opensm`. If you do not have access to the `opensm` configuration, then you need to ascertain these details from the (InfiniBand) network administrator.

Within the `opensm` partition configuration (`/etc/rdma/partitions.conf`), the subnet and prefix can be found as follows:

```
# grep '=0x' /etc/rdma/partitions.conf
Default=0x7fff, rate=3, mtu=4, scope=2, defmember=full;
Default=0x7fff, ipoib, rate=3, mtu=4, scope=2;
 rxe0_1=0x0610, rate=7, mtu=4, scope=2, defmember=full;
 rxe0_1=0x0610, ipoib, rate=7, mtu=4, scope=2;
```

In this example, two partitions are defined. The first one is the default partition, which needs to remain (`0x7fff`). The second partition with key `0x0610` is active on the `rxe0` device and port `1`. It is this second partition that we will protect with SELinux.

Let's create a new type to assign to this partition. We use the CIL format again to define the policy enhancement, and store these rules in a file called `infiniband_pkey.cil`:

```
(typeattribute ibpkey_type)
(type local_ibpkey_t)
(typeattributeset ibpkey_type local_ibpkey_t)
(allow unconfined_t local_ibpkey_t (infiniband_pkey (access)))
```

Within this example, we've created the `local_ibpkey_t` type, assigned it to the `ibpkey_type` attribute, and granted `unconfined_t` access privilege within the `infiniband_pkey` class.

Let's load the policy:

```
# semodule -i infiniband_pkey.cil
```

We can now create an appropriate mapping to this partition, and limit it to the `ff12::` subnet prefix:

```
# semanage ibpkey -a -t local_ibpkey_t -x ff12:: 0x0610
# semanage ibpkey -l
SELinux IB PKey Type    Subnet_Prefix       Pkey Number
local_ibpkey_t             ff12::              0x610
```

While we can create separate types for each partition, we can also use an SELinux range to use SELinux category support:

```
# semanage ibpkey -a -t local_ibpkey_t -r s0-s0:c0.c4 -x ff12::
0x0610
```

With categories, we can grant access based on the source domain category, something we benefit from with other network protection measures such as labeled networking, which we tackle next.

Understanding labeled networking

Another approach to further fine-tune access controls on the network level is to introduce labeled networking. With labeled networking, security information passes on between hosts (unlike SECMARK, which only starts when the netfilter subsystem receives the packet, and whose marking never leaves the host). This is also known as peer labeling, as the security information passes on between hosts (peers).

The advantage of labeled networking is that security information remains across the network, allowing end-to-end enforcement on mandatory access-control settings between systems as well as retaining the sensitivity level of communication flows between systems. The major downside, however, is that this requires an additional network technology (protocol) that can manage labels on network packets or flows.

SELinux currently supports two implementations as part of the labeled networking approach: NetLabel and labeled IPsec. With NetLabel, two implementations exist: fallback labeling and CIPSO. In both cases, only the sensitivity of the source domain is retained across the communication. Labeled IPsec supports transporting the entire security context with it.

> **Note**
>
> NetLabel actually supports loopback-enabled, full-label support. In that case, the full label (and not only the sensitivity and categories) is passed on. However, this only works for communications that go through the loopback interface and, as such, do not leave the current host.

Quite some time ago, support for NetLabel/CIPSO and labeled IPsec merged into a common framework, which introduces three additional privilege checks in SELinux: interface checking, node checking, and peer checking. These privilege checks are only active when labeled traffic is used; without labeled traffic, these checks are simply ignored.

Fallback labeling with NetLabel

The NetLabel project supports fallback labeling, where administrators can assign labels to traffic from or to network locations that don't use labeled networking. By using fallback labeling, the peer controls mentioned in the next few sections can be applied even without labeled IPsec or NetLabel/CIPSO being in place.

The `netlabelctl` command controls the NetLabel configurations. Let's create a fallback label assignment for all traffic originating from the `192.168.100.1` address:

```
# netlabelctl unlbl add interface:eth0 address:192.168.100.1
label:system_u:object_r:netlabel_peer_t:s0
```

To list the current definitions, use the following command:

```
# netlabelctl -p unlbl list
Accept unlabeled packets : on
Configured NetLabel address mappings (1)
  interface: eth0
    address: 192.168.100.1/32
      label: "system_u:object_r:netlabel_peer_t:s0"
```

With this rule in place, labeled networking is active. Any traffic originating from the 192.168.100.1 address will be labeled with the netlabel_peer_t:s0 label, while all other traffic will be labeled with the (default) unlabeled_t:s0 label. Of course, the SELinux policy must allow all domains to have the recv permission from either the unlabeled_t peers or the netlabel_peer_t peers.

Fallback labeling is useful for supporting a mix of labeled networking environments and non-labeled networks, which is why we list it here before documenting the various labeled networking technologies.

Limiting flows based on the network interface

The idea involving interface checking is that each packet that comes into a system passes an ingress check on an interface, whereas a packet that goes out of a system passes an egress check. ingress and egress are the SELinux permissions involved, whereas interfaces are given a security context.

Interface labels can be granted using the semanage tool and are especially useful for assigning sensitivity levels to interfaces in case of MLS, although assigning different labels to the interface is also possible (but requires more adjustments to the running SELinux policy to return with a working system):

```
# semanage interface -a -t netif_t -r s1-s1:c0.c128 eth0
```

Like the other semanage commands, we can view the current mappings as follows:

```
# semanage interface -l
SELinux Interface        Context
eth0                     system_u:object_r:netif_t:s1-s1:c0.c128
```

Keep in mind that for inbound communications, the acting domain is the peer. With labeled IPsec, this would be the client domain initiating the connection, whereas in NetLabel/CIPSO, this is the associated peer label (such as netlabel_peer_t).

By default, the interface is labeled with `netif_t` and without sensitivity constraints. This will, however, not be shown in the `semanage interface -l` output as its default output is empty.

Accepting peer communication from selected hosts

SELinux nodes represent specific hosts (or a network of hosts) that data is sent to (`sendto`) or received from (`recvfrom`) and are handled through the SELinux node class. Just like interfaces, these can be listed and defined by the `semanage` tool. In the following example, we mark the `10.0.0.0/8` network with the `node_t` type and associate a set of categories with it:

```
# semanage node -a -t node_t -p ipv4 -M 255.255.255.255 -r
s0-s0:c0.c128 192.168.100.1
```

Again, we can list the current definitions, too:

```
# semanage node -l
```

Like the network interface flow, the acting domain for incoming communications is the peer label.

By default, nodes are labeled with `node_t` and without category constraints. This will, however, not be shown in the `semanage node -l` output as its default output is empty.

Verifying peer-to-peer flow

The final check is a `peer` class check. For labeled IPsec, this is the label of the socket sending out the data (such as `mozilla_t`). For NetLabel/CIPSO, however, the peer will be static, based on the source, as CIPSO is only able to pass on sensitivity levels. A common label seen for NetLabel is `netlabel_peer_t`.

Unlike the interface and node checks, peer checks have the peer domain as the target rather than the source.

Important note

In all the labeled networking use cases, the process listed in a denial has nothing to do with the denial shown in the audit logs. This is because the denial triggers from within a kernel subsystem rather than through a call made by a user process. As a result, the kernel interrupts an unrelated process to prepare and log the denial, and this process name is used in the denial event.

To finish up, look at the following diagram, which provides an overview of these various controls and the level to which they apply:

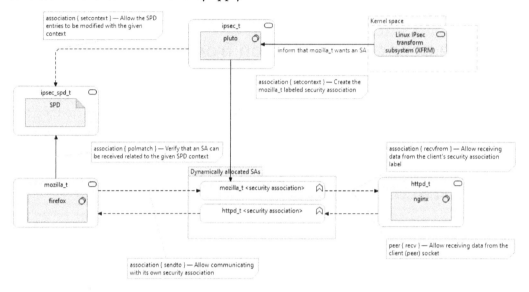

Figure 5.2 – Schematic overview of the various network-related SELinux controls

The top-level controls are handled on the domain level (such as `httpd_t`), whereas the bottom-level controls are on the peer level (such as `netlabel_peer_t`).

Using old-style controls

Most Linux distributions enable the `network_peer_control` capability. This is an enhancement within the SELinux subsystem that uses the previously mentioned peer class for verifying peer-to-peer flow.

However, SELinux policies can opt to return to the previous approach, where peer-to-peer flow is no longer controlled over the peer class, but uses the `tcp_socket` class for communication. In that case, the `tcp_socket` class will be used against the `peer` domain, and it will also use the `recvfrom` permission (on top of the existing `tcp_socket` permissions).

The current value of the `network_peer_control` capability can be queried through the SELinux filesystem:

```
# cat /sys/fs/selinux/policy_capabilities/network_peer_controls
1
```

If the value is 0, then the previously mentioned peer controls will be handled through the `tcp_socket` class instead of the peer class.

The default labeled networking controls within SELinux do not pass on any process context, and the use of fallback labeling with NetLabel is most commonly used in environments where the system participates in both labeled as well as unlabeled networks. However, there is a much more common networking implementation that not only supports labeled networking, but even passes on the domain context and does not require specialized environments: labeled IPsec.

Using labeled IPsec with SELinux

Although setting up and maintaining an IPsec setup is far beyond the scope of this book, let's look at a simple IPsec example to show how to enable labeled IPsec on a system. Remember that the labeled network controls on the interface, node, and peer levels, as mentioned earlier, are automatically enabled the moment we use labeled IPsec.

In an IPsec setup, there are three important concepts to be aware of:

- The **security policy database** (**SPD**) contains the rules and information for the kernel to know when communication should be handled by an IP policy (and, as a result, handled through a security association).

- A **security association** (**SA**) is a one-way channel between two hosts and contains all the security information about the channel. When labeled IPsec is in use, it also contains the context information of the client that caused the security association to materialize.

- The **security association database** (**SAD**) contains the individual security associations.

Security associations with a labeled IPsec setup are no longer purely indexed by the source and target address, but also the source context. As such, a Linux system that participates in a labeled IPsec setup will easily have several dozen SAs for a single communication flow between hosts, as each SA now also represents a client domain.

Labeled IPsec introduces a few additional access controls through SELinux:

- Individual entries in the SPD are given a context. Domains that want to obtain an SA need to have the `polmatch` privilege (part of the `association` class) against this context. Also, domains that initiate an SA need to have the `setcontext` privilege (also part of the `association` class) against the target domain.

- Only authorized domains can make modifications to the SPD, which is also governed through the `setcontext` privilege, but now also against the SPD context entries. This privilege is generally granted to IPsec tools, such as Libreswan's pluto (`ipsec_t`).

- Domains that participate in IPsec communication must have the `sendto` privilege with their own association and the `recvfrom` privilege with the association of the `peer` domain. The receiving domain also requires the `recv` privilege from the `peer` class associated with the `peer` domain.

So while labeled IPsec cannot govern whether `mozilla_t` can communicate with `httpd_t` (as `mozilla_t` only needs to be able to send to its own association), it can control whether `httpd_t` allows or denies incoming communication from `mozilla_t` (as it requires the `recvfrom` privilege on the `mozilla_t` association). The following diagram displays this complex game of privileges:

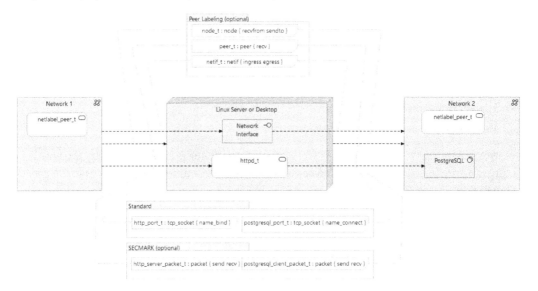

Figure 5.3 – Example SELinux controls for labeled IPsec

In the next example, we will set up a simple IPsec tunnel between two hosts using the Libreswan tool.

Setting up regular IPsec

Configuring Libreswan is a matter of configuring Libreswan's main configuration file (`ipsec.conf`). Most distributions will use an `include` directory (such as `/etc/ipsec.d`) where admins or applications can place connection-specific settings. Generally, this `include` directory is used for the actual IPsec configurations, whereas the general `ipsec.conf` file is for Libreswan behavior.

To create a host-to-host connection, we first define a shared secret on both hosts. Let's call the connection `rem1-rem2` (as those are the hostnames used for the two hosts), so the shared secret will be stored as `/etc/ipsec.d/rem1-rem2.secrets`:

```
192.168.100.4 192.168.100.5 : PSK "somesharedkey"
```

Next, we define the VPN connection in `/etc/ipsec.d/rem1-rem2.conf` as follows:

```
conn rem1-rem2
    left=192.168.100.4
    right=192.168.100.5
    auto=start
    authby=secret
    #labeled-ipsec=yes
    #policy-label=system_u:object_r:ipsec_spd_t:s0
```

The settings that enable labeled IPsec are commented out for now to first test the IPsec connection without this feature.

Launch the IPsec service on both systems:

```
# systemctl start ipsec
```

Verify whether the connection works, for instance, by checking the network traffic with `tcpdump`, or by checking the state with `ip xfrm state`.

Enabling labeled IPsec

To use labeled IPsec with Libreswan, uncomment the `labeled-ipsec` and `policy-label` directives in the `/etc/ipsec.d/rem1-rem2.conf` IPsec definition. Restart the `ipsec` service, and try the connection again.

When an application tries to communicate over IPsec with remote domains, `pluto` (or any other **Internet Key Exchange version 2 (IKEv2)** client that supports labeled IPsec) will exchange the necessary information (including context) with the other side. Both sides will then update the SPD with the necessary SAs and associate the same **security policy information (SPI)** with it. From that point onward, the sending side will add the agreed-upon SPI information to the IPsec packets so that the remote side can immediately associate the right context with it again.

The huge advantage here is that the client and server contexts, including sensitivity and categories, are synchronized (they are not actually sent over the wire with each packet, but exchanged initially when the security associations are set up).

In certain specialized or highly secure environments, labeled networking is supported within the network itself. The most common labeling technology used is CIPSO, whose SELinux support we cover next.

Supporting CIPSO with NetLabel and SELinux

NetLabel/CIPSO labels and transmits sensitivities across the network. Unlike labeled IPsec, no other context information is sent or synchronized. So, when we consider the communication flows between two points, they will have a default, common SELinux type (rather than the SELinux type associated with the source or target) but will have sensitivity labels based on the sensitivity label of the remote side.

Part of NetLabel's configuration are mapping definitions that inform the system which communication flows (from selected interfaces, or even from configured IP addresses) are for a certain **Domain of Interpretation (DOI)**. The CIPSO standard defines the DOI as a collection of systems that interpret the CIPSO label similarly, or, in our case, use the same SELinux policy and configuration of sensitivity labels.

Once these mappings have been established, NetLabel/CIPSO will pass on the sensitivity information (and categories) between hosts. The context we will see on the communication flows will be `netlabel_peer_t`, a default context assigned to NetLabel/CIPSO-originated traffic.

Through this approach, we can start daemons with a sensitivity range and thus only accept connections from users or clients that have the right security clearance, even on remote, NetLabel/CIPSO-enabled systems.

Configuring CIPSO mappings

A preliminary requirement for having a good CIPSO-enabled network is to have a common understanding of which DOI will be used and what its consequences are. Labeled networks can use different DOIs for specific purposes.

Along with the DOI, we also need to take care of how the categories and sensitivities are passed on over the CIPSO-enabled network. The CIPSO tag controls this setting, and NetLabel supports this with the following three values:

- With `tags:1`, the categories are provided in the CIPSO package in a bitmap approach. This is the most common approach, but limits the number of supported categories to 240 (from 0 to 239).

- With `tags:2`, the categories are enumerated separately. This allows a wider range of categories (up to 65,543), but only supports at most 15 enumerated categories. Try to use `tags:2` when you have many categories but for each scope, only a few categories need to be supported.

- With `tags:5`, the categories can be mentioned in a ranged approach (lowest and highest), with at most seven such low/high pairs.

Note that the CIPSO tag results are handled under the hood: system administrators only need to configure the NetLabel mapping to use a selected tag value.

Let's assume that we have two CIPSO-enabled networks, which have `10.1.0.0/16` associated with `doi:1` and `10.2.0.0/16` associated with `doi:2`. Both use the tag value 1. First, we enable CIPSO and allow it to pass CIPSO-labeled packages with the DOI set to either 1 or 2. We don't perform any translations (so the category and sensitivity set on the CIPSO package is the one used by SELinux):

```
# netlabelctl cipsov4 add pass doi:1 tags:1
# netlabelctl cipsov4 add pass doi:2 tags:1
```

If we need to translate (say that we use sensitivity `s0-s3` while the CIPSO network uses sensitivity `100-103`), a command would look like so:

```
# netlabelctl cipsov4 add std doi:1 tags:1
levels:0=100,1=101,2=102
```

Next, we implement mapping rules, telling the NetLabel configuration which network traffic is to be associated with `doi:1` or `doi:2`:

```
# netlabelctl map del default
# netlabelctl map add default address:10.1.0.0/16
protocol:cipsov4,1
# netlabelctl map add default address:10.2.0.0/16
protocol:cipsov4,2
```

To list the current mappings, use the `list` option:

```
# netlabelctl map list -p
Configured NetLabel domain mappings (2)
  domain: DEFAULT (IPv4)
    address: 10.1.0.0/16
      protocol: CIPSO, DOI = 1
  domain: DEFAULT (IPv4)
    address: 10.2.0.0/16
      protocol: CIPSO, DOI = 2
```

That's it. We removed the initial default mapping (as that would prevent the addition of new default mappings) and then configured NetLabel to tag traffic for the given networks with the right CIPSO configuration.

Adding domain-specific mappings

NetLabel can also be configured to ensure that given SELinux domains use a well-defined DOI rather than the default one configured earlier on. For instance, to have the SSH daemon (running in the `sshd_t` domain) have its network traffic labeled with CIPSO `doi:3`, we'd use this:

```
# netlabelctl cipsov4 add pass doi:3 tags:1
# netlabelctl map add domain:sshd_t protocol:cipsov4,3
```

The mapping rules can even be more selective than that. We can tell NetLabel to use `doi:2` for SSH traffic originating from one network, use `doi:3` for SSH traffic originating from another network, and even use unlabeled network traffic when it comes from any other network:

```
# netlabelctl map del domain:sshd_t protocol:cipsov4,3
# netlabelctl map add domain:sshd_t address:10.1.0.0/16
protocol:cipsov4,1
```

```
# netlabelctl map add domain:sshd_t address:10.4.0.0/16
protocol:cipsov4,3
```

```
# netlabelctl map add domain:sshd_t address:0.0.0.0/0
protocol:unlbl
```

The NetLabel framework will try to match the most specific rule first, so 0.0.0.0/0 is only matched when no other rule matches.

Using local CIPSO definitions

As mentioned before, NetLabel, by default, only passes the sensitivity and categories. However, when using local (over the loopback interface) CIPSO, it is possible to use full label controls. When enabled, peer controls will not be applied against the default netlabel_peer_t type, but will use the client or server domain.

To use local CIPSO definitions, first declare the DOI for local use:

```
# netlabelctl cipsov4 add local doi:5
```

Next, have the local communication use the defined DOI (5 in our example):

```
# netlabelctl map add default address:127.0.0.1
protocol:cipsov4,5
```

With this enabled, local communication will be associated with doi:5 and use the local mapping, passing the full label to the mandatory access control system (SELinux).

Supporting IPv6 CALIPSO

CIPSO is an IPv4 protocol, but a similar framework exists for IPv6, named **Common Architecture Label IPv6 Security Option** (**CALIPSO**). As with CIPSO, CALIPSO is supported by the NetLabel project. When we need CALIPSO support, the protocol target is calipso rather than cipsov4.

CALIPSO has a few small differences compared to CIPSO in NetLabel:

- Only one tag type is supported (unlike CIPSO's three tag types). As a result, CALIPSO administrators do not need to specify tags:# anywhere.

- CALIPSO only uses pass-through mode. Translations are not supported.

- The NetLabel CALIPSO implementation currently does not support local mode, where the full label would be passed on.

Beyond these differences, the use of CALIPSO is very similar to CIPSO.

Summary

SELinux, by default, uses access controls based on the file representation of communication primitives or the sockets used. On InfiniBand networks, access controls are limited to accessing the InfiniBand port and partitions. For TCP, UDP, and SCTP ports, administrators have some leeway in handling the controls through the `semanage` command without resorting to SELinux policy updates. Once we go into the realms of network-based communication, more advanced communication control can be accomplished through Linux netfilter support, using SECMARK labeling, and through peer labeling.

In the case of SECMARK labeling, local firewall rules are used to map contexts to packets, which are then governed through SELinux policy. With peer labeling, either the application context itself (labeled IPsec) or its sensitivity level (netfilter/CIPSO) identify the resources the access controls apply. This allows an almost application-to-application network flow control through SELinux policies.

We learned that the most common firewall frameworks (`iptables` and `nftables`) support SECMARK already, while the more recent eBPF-based `bpfilter` application has yet to receive this support.

In the next chapter, we look at how we can use common infrastructure-as-code frameworks to address the various SELinux controls in a server environment.

Questions

1. How do you map an SELinux type to a TCP port?
2. Does SECMARK labeling change the network packets as they go over the wire?
3. What `semanage` subcommands are used for InfiniBand support?
4. Is specialized equipment needed for labeled IPsec?

6
Configuring SELinux through Infrastructure-as-Code Orchestration

With the advent of large distributed application platforms, cloud services, and the high adoption of virtualized infrastructure, system administrators are actively managing their systems through **Infrastructure-as-Code** frameworks: orchestration and configuration tooling that uses source code-like information to manage the systems.

In this chapter, administrators will learn how to distribute and load custom SELinux policy modules, set file context definitions and apply those to the systems, set the permissive state of the system or SELinux domains, configure the SELinux settings on the systems, and how to customize SELinux actions if they are not supported by the tooling. We will apply this with four popular automation frameworks: Ansible, Chef, Puppet, and SaltStack.

We will cover the following topics in this chapter:

- Introducing the target settings and policies
- Using Ansible for SELinux system administration
- Utilizing SaltStack to configure SELinux
- Automating system management with Puppet
- Wielding Chef for system automation

Technical requirements

The code files for this chapter can be found in our Git repository at `https://github.com/PacktPublishing/SELinux-System-Administration-Third-Edition`.

Check out the following video to see the Code in Action: `https://bit.ly/2T4Fksv`

Introducing the target settings and policies

Before we embark on the journey of using these four automation frameworks, we need to clarify what we want to accomplish. After all, to truly compare automation frameworks, we need to test each framework with the same tests each time.

The idempotency of actions

Whenever we create a remote management environment with a central repository, we need to consider the impact of running remote management activities on the system. A very common best practice, strongly adopted by all these frameworks, is idempotency.

An **idempotent** task is a task that will not modify a system if the system's state is already how it should be. Or, differently put, repeatedly executing a task does not affect the system or the processes that run on it if nothing needs to be changed. As an example, consider loading an SELinux module: if the module is already loaded, then the module should not be reloaded. If it isn't loaded yet, then we will load the proper module.

While most actions supported by the automation frameworks are idempotent, we will need to create custom actions ourselves if the framework does not support what we want. For instance, if the framework does not support loading SELinux modules, then we need to write our own code to do so.

Most orchestration frameworks will envelope non-idempotent tasks in a definition that is more idempotent. For instance, if a change in a configuration file requires a system reboot, then the enveloped definition would be something like *reboot after file change*. The engine can check the state of the file (when it changed) and the system (when it rebooted) and deduce whether a reboot is needed or not, even though a system reboot as a task is a non-idempotent task.

Policy and state management

The first set of scenarios that we want to support through the automation frameworks is to ensure that SELinux is active (enforcing) and that the right SELinux policy is loaded, a task usually performed by the machine's package management system. While allowing the package management system to handle this is convenient, it only offers the ability to use distribution-specific default policies. Sysadmins of systems with different security requirements will be restrained when using default policies and will need to create custom policies and policy handling routines. So, we will examine how to distribute and load custom policies.

The custom policy we will use in the examples is a CIL policy, which is very new and often not directly supported by the automation frameworks. However, it gives us a nice reoccurring situation to create custom rules within the automation framework. We store the policy itself in a file called `test.cil` that has the following content:

```
(auditallow staff_sudo_t sysadm_t (process (transition)))
```

This simple policy will enable logging any transition from the `staff_sudo_t` domain to the `sysadm_t` domain and is easy to test out with `sudo`. In our example, it serves no other purpose than to quickly allow us to verify that the policy has been correctly loaded.

State-wise, we will ensure that the system is in enforcing mode, but have the `zoneminder_t` SELinux domain marked as permissive.

SELinux configuration settings

The second group of actions we want to take up is to configure the system with the various SELinux settings we've discussed in different chapters before. Most of these we've seen through the `semanage` commands, and we will learn how the various automation frameworks support these entries, and to what extent.

We will not go through every setting, but rather focus on the supported configuration sets within each automation framework. If a framework does not support a particular configuration (such as the `semanage ibpkey` one, which is fairly new), we will need to create custom actions for this. In that case, we will show how to approach this once, as it is a recurring and similar approach for the others as well.

Setting file contexts

The third and final group of actions we want to see is how the automation frameworks support applying file contexts to resources. This can be applying an `semanage fcontext` configuration, after which a restore operation is done (such as with `restorecon`), but also validating whether the framework supports applying contexts directly.

Directly applying the context allows administrators to use the frameworks directly without having to twiddle with creating and reapplying file context definitions (which can have some performance overhead). However, this should only be considered if the automation framework is the sole method through which system changes can be made. In any other case, having missing file context definitions might lead to administrators resetting contexts to an incorrect state.

Recovering from mistakes

In this chapter, we're diving into the various frameworks that allow managing SELinux across a multitude of systems. It is not the intention of this chapter to explain the frameworks themselves in detail, nor the secure configuration of the frameworks themselves. We don't recommend immediately applying this to production systems without testing first, and make sure to have backups!

That being said, many settings applied in this chapter are easily corrected if things fail. We refer to *Chapter 2, Understanding SELinux Decisions and Logging*, to selectively put SELinux in permissive mode if needed.

Furthermore, each framework can easily be suspended, allowing administrators to correct issues without being affected by the framework overwriting the changes immediately after.

Comparing frameworks

Every framework we discuss further has its own approach to infrastructure automation and configuration. It is not the intention of this book to dwell on the details of each framework, but rather to focus on its core support and how it deals with SELinux. We will also abstract away how to handle different Linux distributions and have all examples based on CentOS.

Furthermore, these frameworks are continuously improving and evolving. When we consider these frameworks in this chapter, we only explore how they are commonly used, and not how they can specialize in specific deployments. For instance, if a framework uses an agent-based architecture by default but also supports SSH-based connections, we will only consider the agent-based one in this book, as that is the default setup for these frameworks and we want to focus on the SELinux configuration support features.

But don't let this stop you from experimenting with the frameworks further and adapting them to your own liking! That said, let's dive into our first engine, Ansible.

Using Ansible for SELinux system administration

The first orchestration and automation tooling we'll consider is Ansible, a very popular open source solution for the remote management of systems. Ansible has commercial backing through Red Hat but does not limit its support to Red Hat or even Linux systems. Other environments such as Windows environments or even network setups have significant Ansible-based support.

How Ansible works

Ansible generally uses a central server that hosts the configuration and interprets the settings. The Ansible runtime then connects to the remote systems over SSH, sending the necessary data to a temporary location, and then executes the steps locally.

The use of SSH as its main connection approach has significant advantages: administrators know how this protocol works and how to configure and control it. Furthermore, Ansible does not require any additional deployments on the target machines, except for Python and libselinux's Python bindings (which are often installed on SELinux-enabled machines by default).

Ansible knows how to address the various resources through its modules. **Ansible modules** contain the logic that Ansible uses to execute tasks correctly. The module code is distributed to the target machines and is executed on the remote systems.

The definitions that administrators configure systems with are stored in Ansible playbooks. **Playbooks** define how a system should be configured, and Ansible will read and interpret playbooks to see what it must execute on each system.

To facilitate the management of Ansible playbooks in larger environments, Ansible uses **Ansible roles** to bundle coherent definitions. Administrators can then, in their playbooks, assign roles to systems to automatically uplift the state of those systems accordingly. For instance, a role can be created to create a properly configured web server, a database, and so on.

In this chapter, we will create a role called `packt_selinux` and apply it to a remote system. Within that role, we will show how to configure and execute the various SELinux tasks using Ansible.

Installing and configuring Ansible

To install and set up Ansible, most Linux distributions offer out-of-the-box support for the framework. On CentOS, the following steps can be taken. Users of other distributions can easily deduce the steps for their platform:

1. You need to enable **Extra Packages for Enterprise Linux** (**EPEL**), after which you can install Ansible easily. Execute this on the master node (from which you want to manage the other systems):

    ```
    # yum install epel-release
    # yum install ansible
    ```

2. Once installed, create an SSH key pair to use between the master system and the target systems that we will be managing with Ansible. Use the `ssh-keygen` command to create a key pair on the master system, and then copy the public key (`~/.ssh/id_rsa.pub`) to the remote systems, saving it as `~/.ssh/authorized_keys`:

    ```
    # ssh-keygen
    # scp ~/.ssh/id_rsa.pub rem1:/root/.ssh/authorized_keys
    ```

3. Test to see whether the remote connection works properly, for instance, by executing the `id` command remotely:

    ```
    # ssh rem1 id
    ```

4. If the test is successful, we can configure Ansible to see this remote system as one of the nodes it will be managing. To accomplish this, edit `/etc/ansible/hosts` and add the hostname to the list:

    ```
    # cat /etc/ansible/hosts
    rem1
    ```

5. To see whether Ansible can correctly manage the remote system, we can ask it to gather all the facts about the remote system. Facts in Ansible represent the discovered settings of the remote system and can be used to fine-tune playbooks and roles later. For instance, the Ansible facts discovered of the distribution can be used to select which package name an installation uses:

```
# ansible all -m setup
```

This instruction asks all managed hosts (all, reflecting all entries in /etc/ansible/hosts) to execute the tasks in the setup module.

The output of the last task is a large set of discovered facts, showing us that the connection succeeded and that Ansible is ready to manage the remote system.

Creating and testing the Ansible role

To allow reusable configurations across multiple systems, Ansible recommends the use of its Ansible roles. We will create a role called packt_selinux, have it create a custom directory, and then assign this role to the remote system:

1. Use ansible-galaxy to create an empty yet ready-to-use role:

```
# cd /etc/ansible/roles
# ansible-galaxy init packt_selinux --offline
- Role packt_selinux was created successfully
```

This command will create the necessary files and directories that constitute a role. The file we will use is packt_selinux/tasks/main.yml, which will host all the settings and definitions we want to apply when we assign the packt_selinux role to a system. The other directories are, for our brief introduction to Ansible, less relevant, but play an important role in making sufficiently modular roles.

2. Edit the main.yml file and have it create a custom directory. The content of the file should look like this:

```
---
- name: Create /usr/share/selinux/custom directory

  file:
      path: /usr/share/selinux/custom
      owner: root
      group: root
      mode: '0755'
      state: directory
```

In later steps, this file will be extended with more and more blocks. Each block will start with a name that identifies the block, and then the state definition. In the current block, we used Ansible's `file` module to assert that a file or directory is available with the parameters given.

3. Assign the role to the remote system and apply the playbook. We accomplish this by first creating an `/etc/ansible/site.yml` file with the following content:

```
---
- hosts: all
  roles:
        - packt_selinux
```

4. Run this playbook to apply the setting defined in our role to the remote systems:

```
# ansible-playbook /etc/ansible/site.yml
```

Ansible will display its progress, as well as for which tasks it has executed a change. In our case, a change would mean that the directory has been created.

Now that we have tested our role and assigned the role to the remote system, all we need to do is update the role gradually until it contains all the logic we need. No other configuration is needed, and after each change, we can rerun the `ansible-playbook` command from the main server.

Assigning SELinux contexts to filesystem resources with Ansible

In the current role, we create a custom directory inside `/usr/share/selinux`. This parent directory has the `usr_t` SELinux type set, so the newly created subdirectory has it as well. The SELinux user of this directory, however, will be different, as Ansible has created the directory after remotely logging in to the system. In a default CentOS configuration, this means that the target directory's context will have `unconfined_u` as its SELinux user component.

Let's update the definition in `main.yml` and explicitly set the SELinux user and type:

```
---
- name: Create /usr/share/selinux/custom directory
  file:
        path: /usr/share/selinux/custom
        owner: root
        group: root
        mode: '0755'
```

```
state: directory
setype: 'usr_t'
seuser: 'system_u'
```

After applying the change (using `ansible-playbook`), the updated definition results in a correctly set SELinux user and SELinux type for this directory.

In this case, we added two parameters to the file definition: `setype` and `seuser`. The Ansible file module supports the following SELinux-related parameters:

- `seuser` is the SELinux user of the resource. Set this to `system_u` for system resources, as used in the example.

- `serole` is the SELinux role of the resource. This is generally not used, as role inheritance on the system will generally result in the resource being labeled with the `object_r` role, which is correct most of the time.

- `setype` is the SELinux type of the resource and is the most commonly used SELinux parameter in file modules.

- `selevel` is the SELinux sensitivity level for the resource. By default, it is set to `s0`.

As we've learned from the example already, you do not need to declare the type if the inherited context is correct.

Loading custom SELinux policies with Ansible

Ansible's current release has no support for loading custom SELinux modules. While custom modules are found on Ansible galaxy (the ecosystem where contributors can add more modules), let's see how we would handle distributing a custom policy to the systems under Ansible control and loading the module, but only if it is not loaded yet.

While we could start creating custom modules ourselves, let's use a combination of tasks in the existing role to accomplish this. We will try to accomplish the following tasks in sequence:

1. Upload a custom policy called `test.cil` to the remote system.
2. Check whether this custom policy is already loaded.
3. Load the custom policy, but only if the previous check failed.

These three tasks are handled through three modules: the `copy` module, the `shell` module, and the `command` module. We will use each of these modules in separate steps:

1. Create the custom policy mentioned earlier in this chapter by placing the `test.cil` file in the `files/` folder of the `packt_selinux` role.

2. Create a new code block in the `main.yml` file of the role, with the following content:

```
- name: Upload test.cil file to /usr/share/selinux/custom
  copy:
        src: test.cil
        dest: /usr/share/selinux/custom/test.cil
        owner: root
        group: root
        mode: '0644'
```

This will ensure that the `test.cil` file, currently on the master machine, is distributed to the target nodes in the directory we've previously created.

3. Next, we check whether the policy is already loaded. For this, we use the `shell` module and use the fail or success state later. Hence, we store the return in the `test_is_loaded` variable, and explicitly tell Ansible to ignore a failure as we use this as a check rather than a state definition:

```
- name: Check if test SELinux module is loaded
  shell: /usr/sbin/semodule -l | grep -q ^test$
  register: test_is_loaded
  ignore_errors: True
```

4. The `command` module loads the policy file, and only if the previous task failed:

```
- name: Load test.cil if not loaded yet
  command: /usr/sbin/semodule -i /usr/share/selinux/
custom/test.cil
  when: test_is_loaded is failed
```

This approach shows how we can use our knowledge of SELinux to define and set states. This method can be used for other SELinux settings as well, for instance, by validating the output of listings (for example, with `semanage`) before defining or adjusting settings.

Using Ansible's out-of-the-box SELinux support

Ansible has quite a few modules available to provide native support for several SELinux-related settings, which we briefly cover here:

- The `selinux` module can be used to set or change the SELinux state (enforcing or permissive) as well as to select the appropriate SELinux policy type (such as targeted):

```
- name: Set SELinux to enforcing mode
  selinux:
        policy: targeted
        state: enforcing
```

- With the `seboolean` module, the SELinux booleans can be adjusted at will:

```
- name: Set httpd_builtin_scripting to true
  seboolean:
        name: httpd_builtin_scripting
        state: yes
```

- The `sefcontext` module allows us to change SELinux file context definitions:

```
- name: Set the context for /srv/web
  sefcontext:
        target: '/srv/web(/.*)?'
        setype: httpd_sys_content_t
        state: present
```

- With `selinux_permissive`, we can selectively mark certain SELinux policy domains as permissive:

```
- name: Set zoneminder_t as permissive domain
  selinux_permissive:
        name: zoneminder_t
        permissive: true
```

- The `selogin` module can be used to map a login to an SELinux user, as with `semanage login`:

```
- name: Map taylor's login to the unconfined_u user
  selogin:
        login: taylor
        seuser: unconfined_u
        state: present
```

- `seport` can be used to create an SELinux port mapping:

```
- name: Set port 10122 to ssh_port_t
  seport:
          ports: 10122
          proto: tcp
          setype: ssh_port_t
          state: present
```

Other SELinux settings might be supported through custom modules, but with the method presented earlier, administrators can already start configuring SELinux across all systems in their environment.

Utilizing SaltStack to configure SELinux

The second orchestration and automation framework we'll consider is SaltStack, which has commercial backing by the SaltStack company. SaltStack uses a declarative language similar to Ansible and is also written in Python. In this chapter, we will use the open source SaltStack framework, but an enterprise version of SaltStack is available as well, which adds more features on top of the open source one.

How SaltStack works

SaltStack, often also described as just Salt, is an automation framework that uses an agent/server model for its integrations. Unlike Ansible, SaltStack generally requires agent installations on the target nodes (called **minions**) and activation of the minion daemons to enable communications to the master. This communication is encrypted, and the minion authentication uses public-key validation, which needs to be approved on the master to ensure no rogue minions participate in a SaltStack environment.

While agent-less installations are possible with SaltStack as well, we will focus on agent-based deployments. In such a configuration, the minions regularly check with the master to see whether any updates need to be applied. But administrators do not need to wait until the minion pulls the latest updates: you can also trigger updates from the master, effectively pushing changes to the nodes.

The target state that a minion should be in is written down in a **Salt State file**, which uses the `.sls` suffix. These Salt State files can refer to other state files, to allow a modular design and reusability across multiple machines.

If we need more elaborate coding, SaltStack supports the creation and distribution of modules, called **Salt execution modules**. However, unlike Ansible's Galaxy, no community repositories currently exist to find more execution modules.

Installing and configuring SaltStack

The installation of SaltStack is similar across the different Linux distributions. Let's see how the installation is done on a CentOS machine:

1. We first need to enable the SaltStack repository that contains its software. The project maintains the repository definitions through RPM files that can be installed immediately:

```
# yum install https://repo.saltstack.com/py3/redhat/salt-
py3-repo-latest.el8.noarch.rpm
```

2. Once we have enabled the repository on all systems, install `salt-master` on the master, and `salt-minion` on the remote systems:

```
master ~# yum install salt-master
remote ~# yum install salt-minion
```

3. Before we start the daemons on the systems, we first update the minion configuration to point to the master. By default, the minions will attempt to connect to a host with the hostname `salt`, but this can be easily changed by editing `/etc/salt/minion` and setting the right hostname:

```
remote ~# vim /etc/salt/minion
master: ppubssa3ed
```

4. With the minion configured, we can now launch the SaltStack master (`salt-master`) and minion (`salt-minion`) daemons:

```
master ~# systemctl start salt-master
remote ~# systemctl start salt-minion
```

5. The minion will connect to the master and present its public key. To list the agents currently connected, use `salt-key -L`:

```
master ~# salt-key -L
Accepted Keys:
Denied Keys:
Unaccepted Keys:
rem1.internal.genfic.local
Rejected Keys:
```

We need to accept the keys for the remote machines:

```
master ~# salt-key -a rem1.internal.genfic.local
The following keys are going to be accepted:
Unaccepted Keys:
rem1.internal.genfic.local
Proceed? [n/Y] y
Key for minion rem1.internal.genfic.local accepted.
```

6. Once we have accepted the key, the master will know and control the minion. Let's see whether we can properly interact with the remote system:

```
master ~# salt '*' service.get_all
```

This command will list all system services on the minion.

The `salt` command is the main command used to query and interact with the remote minions from the master. If the last command is successfully returning all system services, then SaltStack is correctly configured and ready to manage the remote systems.

Creating and testing our SELinux state with SaltStack

Let's create our SELinux state called `packt_selinux`, and have it applied to the remote minion:

1. We first need to create the top file. This file is the master file for SaltStack, from which the entire environment is configured:

```
master ~# mkdir /srv/salt
master ~# vim /srv/salt/top.sls
base:
  '*':
    - packt_selinux
```

2. Next, we create the state definition for `packt_selinux`:

```
master ~# mkdir /srv/salt/packt_selinux
master ~# vim /srv/salt/packt_selinux/init.sls
/usr/share/selinux/custom/test.cil:
  file.managed:
    - source: salt://packt_selinux/test.cil
    - mode: 644
    - user: root
    - group: root
    - makedirs: True
```

The `init.sls` file is the main state file for this `packt_selinux` state. So, when SaltStack reads the `top.sls` file, it sees a reference to the `packt_selinux` state and then searches for the `init.sls` file inside this state.

3. Place the SELinux `test.cil` module, as defined earlier on in this chapter, inside `/srv/salt/packt_selinux` as we refer to it in the state definition. Once placed, we can apply this state to the environment:

```
master ~# salt '*' state.apply
```

The `state.apply` subcommand of the `salt` command is used to apply the state across the environment. Each time we modify our state definition, this command can be used to force an update to the minions. Without this, the minions will (by default) update their state every 60 minutes. These scheduled state updates are called mine updates and are configured on the agents inside `/etc/salt/minion`.

Assigning SELinux contexts to filesystem resources with SaltStack

At the time of writing, support for addressing SELinux types in resources has not yet reached the stable versions of SaltStack. SaltStack, however, supports running commands but only if a certain test has succeeded (or failed).

Update the `init.sls` file and add the following code to it:

```
{%- set path = '/usr/share/selinux/custom/test.cil' %}
{%- set context = 'system_u:object_r:usr_t:s0' %}
set {{ path }} context:
  cmd.run:
    - name: chcon {{ context}} {{ path }}
    - unless: test $(stat -c %C {{ path }}) == {{ context }}
```

In this code snippet, we declare two variables (`path` and `context`) so that we do not need to iterate the path and context multiple times, and then use these variables in a `cmd.run` call.

The `cmd.run` approach allows us to easily create custom SELinux support using the commands we've seen earlier on in this book. The `unless` check contains the test to see whether we need to execute the command or not, allowing us to create idempotent state definitions.

Loading custom SELinux policies with SaltStack

Let's load our custom SELinux module on the remote systems. SaltStack has support for loading SELinux modules through the `selinux.module` state:

```
load test.cil:
  selinux.module:
    - name: test
    - source: /usr/share/selinux/custom/test.cil
    - install: True
    - unless: "semodule -l | grep -q ^test$"
```

As in the previous section, we need to add an `unless` statement, as otherwise, SaltStack will attempt to load the SELinux module repeatedly every time the state is applied.

Using SaltStack's out-of-the-box SELinux support

SaltStack's native SELinux support is gradually expanding but still has much room for improvement:

- With `selinux.boolean`, the SELinux boolean values can be set on the target machines:

  ```
  httpd_builtin_scription:
    selinux.boolean:
      - value: True
  ```

- The file contexts, as managed with `semanage fcontext`, can be defined using the `selinux.fcontext_policy_present` state:

  ```
  "/srv/web(/.*)?":
    selinux.fcontext_policy_present:
      - sel_type: httpd_sys_content_t
  ```

- To remove the definition, use the `selinux.fcontext_policy_absent` definition.

- With `selinux.mode`, we can put the system in enforcing or permissive mode:

  ```
  enforcing:
    selinux.mode
  ```

- Port mappings are handled using the `selinux.port_policy_present` state:

```
tcp/10122:
  selinux.port_policy_present:
    - sel_type: ssh_port_t
```

With the `cmd.run` approach mentioned earlier, we can apply SELinux configuration updates to systems in a repeatable fashion for unsupported settings.

Automating system management with Puppet

Puppet is the third automation framework that we will check out. It is the oldest one in our list, with its first release in 2005, and is commonly seen as the baseline against which other automation frameworks are compared. It has commercial backing through the Puppet company, also often referred to as Puppet Labs.

How Puppet works

Like SaltStack, **Puppet** uses an agent/server-based model with public-key authentication of the agents to ensure no rogue agents are active within the environment.

The **Puppet master** has access to the **Puppet manifests**, which is the declaration of the state that Puppet wants to achieve. These manifests use a specific language inspired by Ruby and can refer to classes provided by modules to ensure reusability across the environment.

Puppet modules, hence, are the workhorse within Puppet, and Puppet has a significant community called Puppet Forge that allows you to download and install modules created by the community to more easily manage your environment.

Puppet agents will regularly connect to the master, informing the master of the current details of the remote machine. These current details are called **facts** and can be used by Puppet to dynamically handle changes in the environment. The master then compiles the target state in what it calls a **catalog** and sends that catalog over to the agent. The agent then applies this catalog and reports the results back.

Installing and configuring Puppet

The Puppet company offers integrated packages for several Linux distributions. The following instructions focus on RPM-compatible distributions, but other platforms have very similar instructions:

1. The Puppet company provides repository definitions through RPM files. After the repositories are established, you can install puppetserver and pdk (on the master) and puppet-agent (on the remote systems) so that the software is readily available to use:

    ```
    # yum install https://yum.puppet.com/puppet6-
    release-el-8.noarch.rpm
    master ~# yum install puppetserver pdk
    remote ~# yum install puppet-agent
    ```

2. Configure the master to have its certificate properly named. Edit the puppet. conf file inside /etc/puppetlabs/puppet and, within the [master] section, update or add the following settings:

    ```
    master ~# vim /etc/puppetlabs/puppet/puppet.conf
    certname = ppubssa3ed.internal.genfic.local
    server = ppubssa3ed.internal.genfic.local
    environment = production
    ```

3. Start the Puppet server so that the clients can start connecting to it:

    ```
    master ~# systemctl start puppetserver
    ```

4. On the remote systems, edit the same configuration file, and update or add the following settings in the [main] section:

    ```
    remote ~# vim /etc/puppetlabs/puppet/puppet.conf
    [main]
    certname = rem1.internal.genfic.local
    server = ppubssa3ed.internal.genfic.local
    environment = production
    runinterval = 1h
    ```

5. Next, start the Puppet agent:

    ```
    remote ~# systemctl start puppet
    ```

6. On the master node, we can now query the pending certificate requests. It should display the requests from the agents we recently started:

```
master ~# /opt/puppetlabs/bin/puppetserver ca list
Requested Certificates:
  rem1.internal.genfic.local    (SHA256) ...
```

7. We can accept this request (sign the certificate) as follows:

```
master ~# /opt/puppetlabs/bin/puppetserver ca sign
--certname rem1.internal.genfic.local
Successfully signed certificate request for rem1.
internal.genfic.local
```

8. To validate whether the connection works, log in on the remote machine and trigger the agent to apply the (currently empty) catalog:

```
remote ~# /opt/puppetlabs/bin/puppet agent --test
```

Unlike SaltStack, where we can push a change to the agents, Puppet relies on the agents to frequently poll the server. In the configuration we made earlier, we configured the agent to check every hour. With the puppet agent --test command, we can signal the agent to run the state check immediately.

Creating and testing the SELinux class with Puppet

Let's create our packt_selinux class, through which we will configure our remote machine's SELinux settings:

1. Call the **Puppet Development Kit** (**PDK**) on the master node inside the /etc/puppetlabs/code/modules directory:

```
master ~# cd /etc/puppetlabs/code/modules
master ~# pdk new module packt_selinux --skip-interview
```

The result is an empty module with lots of default files and directories. We will be mostly working with the module's manifest file.

2. Inside the packt_selinux/manifests directory, create a new file named init.pp with the following content:

```
class packt_selinux {
  file { "/usr/share/selinux/custom":
    ensure => directory,
    mode => "0755",
```

```
      }
    }
```

3. Next, inside the `/etc/puppetlabs/code/environments/production/`
    `manifests` location, create a file called `site.pp` with the following content:

    ```
    node 'rem1.internal.genfic.local' {
      include packt_selinux
    }
    ```

    The `site.pp` file provides the top-level hierarchy for Puppet to associate its
    environment with the appropriate definitions. In this example, the node with the
    hostname `rem1.internal.genfic.local` is configured through a reference to
    `packt_selinux`, the module we created previously.

    Inside the `packt_selinux` module, we've created the `packt_selinux`
    class, which currently is composed of a single directive to create `/usr/share/`
    `selinux/custom`.

4. With these definitions in place, have the remote agent update its state:

    ```
    remote ~# puppet agent -t
    ```

    In product environments, it is common to have this command either scheduled
    regularly or to run the Puppet agent continuously as a daemon.

With the class properly assigned to the node, we can expand our configuration with more
SELinux details.

Assigning SELinux contexts to filesystem resources with Puppet

Let's augment our current class definition with the following snippet:

```
file { 'selinux_custom_module_test':
  path => "/usr/share/selinux/custom/test.cil",
  ensure => file,
  owner => "root",
  group => "root",
  source => "puppet:///modules/packt_selinux/test.cil",
  require => File["/usr/share/selinux/custom"],
  seltype => "usr_t",
}
```

For this block to work properly, we need to place the `test.cil` SELinux module in the `files/` folder inside the `packt_selinux` module location. This block will have Puppet upload the file to the directory, with the dependency set that the directory must exist. The `require` statement refers to the previously defined block.

We also see that Puppet has out-of-the-box support for SELinux type definitions. The file class has several SELinux-supported parameters that can be used:

- `seluser` defines the SELinux user for the resource.
- `selrole` defines the SELinux role for the resource.
- `seltype` defines the SELinux type for the resource.
- `selrange` defines the SELinux sensitivity range for the resource.
- `selinux_ignore_defaults` tells Puppet to ignore the default SELinux context (as queried from the SELinux policy).

Our previous example is thus actually superfluous because Puppet will actively query the SELinux policy to discover what the right resource context is and apply this. With `selinux_ignore_defaults` set to `true`, Puppet will not query and adjust the context accordingly, which can be useful when testing out new setups that do not have proper context definitions set.

Loading custom SELinux policies with Puppet

Puppet does have support for loading and managing SELinux modules. However, its support is currently restricted to the more traditional SELinux policy modules, and not the CIL powered ones.

So, let's create another block in our module definition that loads the `test.cil` file, but only if no test SELinux module is already loaded:

```
exec { '/usr/sbin/semodule -i /usr/share/selinux/custom/test.
cil':
  require => File['selinux_custom_module_test'],
  unless => '/usr/sbin/semodule -l | grep -q ^test$',
}
```

This approach allows us to create custom SELinux configuration adjustments if the native Puppet support does not suffice.

Using Puppet's out-of-the-box SELinux support

Puppet has a few SELinux-related classes supported out of the box but has more support through Puppet Forge, an ecosystem of community-contributed modules. One of the modules that we can recommend is the puppet-selinux module, which Puppet (the company) maintains on Puppet Forge (and thus has a higher chance of remaining supported in later versions of Puppet).

Installing new modules is quite easy, using the puppet module command:

```
master ~# /opt/puppetlabs/bin/puppet module install puppet-
selinux
```

We can then refer to the selinux class (provided through this module) within our manifest:

- The selinux class can be directly used to set the enforcing (or permissive) state of the system:

```
class { selinux:
  mode => 'enforcing',
  type => 'targeted',
}
```

- The (native) selboolean class can be used to set SELinux booleans:

```
selboolean { 'httpd_builtin_scripting':
  value => off,
}
```

- SELinux file contexts can be defined using the selinux::fcontext class:

```
selinux::fcontext { '/srv/web(/.*)?':
  seltype => 'httpd_sys_content_t',
}
```

- Equivalence definitions for the file context are handled by selinux::fcontext::equivalence, like so:

```
selinux::fcontext::equivalence { '/srv/www':
  ensure => 'present',
  target => '/srv/web',
}
```

- Custom port mappings are handled by `selinux::port`:

```
selinux::port { 'set_ssh_custom_port':
  ensure => 'present',
  seltype => 'ssh_port_t',
  protocol => 'tcp',
  port => 10122,
}
```

- Individual SELinux domains can be made permissive using `selinux::permissive`:

```
selinux::permissive { 'zoneminder_t':
  ensure => 'present',
}
```

- If standard SELinux modules are present, the use of `selmodule` allows loading it up. In this case, it will search for the SELinux module named after the block, inside the directory referred to by `selmoduledir`:

```
selmodule { 'vlock':
  ensure => 'present',
  selmoduledir => '/usr/share/selinux/custom',
}
```

While other SELinux-supporting modules might be available on Puppet Forge, be sure to validate whether these modules are mature and sufficiently stable. If their support is uncertain, you might want to pursue the `exec` route, as used earlier on, in *Loading custom SELinux policies with Puppet*.

Wielding Chef for system automation

The last automation framework we will explore is Chef. Chef is a slightly more hands-on and development-oriented automation framework than the previous ones, but powerful nonetheless. It has commercial backing by the similarly named company Chef.

How Chef works

Chef has a slightly more extensive approach to automation and requires slightly more work to get up and running. Once set up, however, it offers a very flexible and programmable environment wherein infrastructure automation can be worked out.

There are three types of systems in the Chef architecture:

- The **Chef server** acts as the central hub on which the automation code is maintained, and which interacts with the remote systems to apply the changes.

- The **Chef workstation** is an endpoint on which administrators and engineers develop Chef recipes (code) and cookbooks and interact with the Chef server. There can be multiple Chef workstations per Chef environment.

- The **Chef client** is an agent running on the remote systems (nodes) managed by the Chef environment.

Developers create automation code in **recipes**, which are like tasks. Multiple recipes are bundled in a **cookbook** and uploaded to the Chef server before the recipes can be applied to one or more nodes. Cookbooks can be compared with modules in the previous automation frameworks.

The Chef clients and server use public key-based authentication and encryption for their interactions. It is the client that takes the initiative, connecting to the server to download the latest cookbooks and other resources, after which it calculates and applies the latest changes, sending feedback on these changes back to the server.

Installing and configuring Chef

A full Chef installation requires a few components to be installed. The Chef workstation and the Chef server need to be installed by the administrator, whereas the Chef agents will be installed by Chef later.

Installing the Chef workstation

To install and use Chef, first download the Chef workstation. All Chef software can be downloaded from `https://downloads.chef.io`. For CentOS, the Chef workstation is available as an RPM, which can be installed using `yum`.

However, unlike common packaged software, the Chef workstation dependencies are not explicitly listed as RPM dependencies, causing the software to be installed without its necessary libraries. At the end of the installation, the RPM file will execute a post-installation script that checks the dependencies and reports on the missing libraries:

```
master ~# yum install chef-workstation-0.17.5-1.el7.x86_64.rpm
```

The dependencies, currently, require the following CentOS packages to be installed:

```
master ~# yum install libX11-xcb libXcomposite libXcursor
libXdamage nss gdk-pixbuf2 gtk3 libXScrnSaver alsa-lib git
```

After the installation, run `chef  -v` (as a regular, non-root user) to verify whether all dependencies are met:

```
master ~$ chef -v
```

The command should output the versions of the included Chef components.

Installing and configuring the Chef server core

The second installation is the Chef server core. This software is again made available as RPM:

1. Install the Chef server core using `yum`:

    ```
    master ~# yum install chef-server-core-13.2.0-1.el7.
    x86_64.rpm
    ```

    After the installation finishes, we need to configure it for our environment.

2. Create a directory named `/var/opt/chef`. We will use this directory to store the cryptographic keys to authenticate against the Chef server:

    ```
    master ~# mkdir /var/opt/chef
    ```

3. Next, configure the Chef server using `chef-server-ctl`:

    ```
    master ~# chef-server-ctl reconfigure
    ```

    This will set up the Chef server on the current system. This setup can take a while to complete, but once finished, we can continue with creating a user account inside of Chef.

4. Let's create an account called `chefadmin` for the user `lisa` on this system and give it a custom password:

    ```
    master ~# chef-server-ctl user-create chefadmin Lisa
    McCarthy lisa@ppubssa3ed.internal.genfic.local pw4chef
    --filename /var/opt/chef/chefadmin.pem
    ```

5. Create an organization unit inside the Chef configuration, which we associate with the newly created user:

    ```
    master ~# chef-server-ctl org-create ppubssa3ed "Packt
    Pub SSA 3rd Edition" --association_user chefadmin
    --filename /var/opt/chef/ppubssa3ed-validator.pem
    ```

With this done, the server administration itself is all done, and we can start creating our development environment.

Preparing the development environment

As mentioned earlier on, Chef is somewhat more development-oriented than the previous automation frameworks. The user that will interact with Chef (using the Chef workstation) needs to establish a development environment first:

1. We previously created an account called `chefadmin` for the user `lisa`. Now, log in as the user `lisa` and create a development environment in the user's home directory:

   ```
   master ~$ mkdir chef
   master ~$ cd chef
   master ~$ git init
   ```

2. We create a Git-enabled environment as the Chef utilities require it. If you have no active Git configuration yet, you might need to add your email and name:

   ```
   master ~$ git config --global user.email "lisa@
   ppubssa3ed.internal.genfic.local"
   master ~$ git config --global user.name "Lisa McCarthy"
   ```

3. Next, create the Chef knife configuration as `.chef/knife.rb` within this environment (so `~/chef/.chef/knife.rb` in our example):

   ```
   master ~$ mkdir .chef
   master ~$ vim .chef/knife.rb
   current_dir = File.dirname(__FILE__)
   log_level          :info
   log_location       STDOUT
   node_name          "chefadmin"
   client_key         "/var/opt/chef/chefadmin.pem"
   chef_server_url    "https://ppubssa3ed/organizations/
   ppubssa3ed"
   cookbook_path      ["#{current_dir}/../cookbooks"]
   ```

This configuration references the key used previously as well as the organization we created. If the Chef workstation is a different system than the Chef server, don't forget to copy over the key (`chefadmin.pem` in our example) and adjust the configuration accordingly.

4. Download the certificates that the Chef server uses (these certificates are self-signed certificates) and then check the SSL connection:

```
master ~$ knife ssl fetch
master ~$ knife ssl check
```

5. If the checks are successful, we can commit the changes:

```
master ~$ git add -A
master ~$ git commit -m 'Chef configuration baseline'
```

We are now ready to start our recipe and cookbook development.

Creating the SELinux cookbook

The cookbook we are going to develop will contain the various SELinux configuration entries, which are then assigned to the remote node:

1. Let's start by creating a cookbook called `packt_selinux`:

```
master ~$ mkdir cookbooks
master ~$ cd cookbooks
master ~$ chef generate cookbook packt_selinux
master ~$ cd packt_selinux
```

This command creates the default files for the cookbook, of which we will handle `metadata.rb` and `recipes/default.rb`. The `metadata.rb` file contains information about the cookbook and, while it is not necessary for our example, it is sensible to edit and update this file immediately. Later, we will adjust this file to include dependency information toward other cookbooks.

2. The `recipes/default.rb` file contains the actual logic we want to apply to the remote systems. Let's create a definition for the `/usr/share/selinux/custom` directory:

```
master ~$ vim recipes/default.rb
directory '/usr/share/selinux/custom' do
  owner 'root'
  group 'root'
  mode '0755'
  action :create
end
```

3. Now upload the cookbook to the Chef server:

    ```
    master ~$ knife cookbook upload packt_selinux
    ```

4. We can query the available cookbooks on the Chef server with the `list` subcommand:

    ```
    master ~$ knife cookbook list
    packt_selinux    0.1.0
    ```

5. With the cookbook available, let's bootstrap the target node. Bootstrapping only needs to occur once, but must be triggered from a Chef authenticated user:

    ```
    master ~$ knife bootstrap rem1 --ssh-user root --node-
    name rem1
    ```

6. This ensures the Chef server knows the remote system. We can query the nodes using `knife node list` and get more details about a node with the `show` subcommand:

    ```
    master ~$ knife node show rem1
    ```

7. Assign the `packt_selinux` recipe to the node using the `run_list add` subcommand:

    ```
    master ~$ knife node run_list add rem1 'recipe[packt_
    selinux]'
    ```

    Adding the recipe to the node list does not automatically trigger the requested update. For this, the remote node's administrator needs to ensure that the `chef-client` binary executes either regularly (through a cron job or similar) or starts as a daemon.

8. For our purposes, we will trigger the `chef-client` command on the remote system to download and apply the latest changes:

    ```
    remote ~# chef-client
    ```

    The output of `chef-client` should show how it found and applied the changes listed in the recipe.

If this command returns successfully, then Chef is ready to manage the remote system using the cookbook we've developed.

Assigning SELinux contexts to filesystem resources with Chef

Chef has limited native support for SELinux contexts. When instructed to create or modify files on nodes, it will relabel those files according to the present file context definitions on the nodes. We can, however, subscribe to events defined in the recipe, and trigger appropriate actions when they occur. For instance, to explicitly set the context of a directory, we can create something like this:

```
execute 'set_selinux_custom_context' do
  command '/usr/bin/chcon -t usr_t /usr/share/selinux/custom'
  action :nothing
  subscribes :run, 'directory[/usr/share/selinux/custom]',
:immediately
end
```

After adding this to the `recipes/default.rb` file, we first need to upload the updated cookbook to the server:

```
master ~$ knife cookbook upload packt_selinux
```

Afterward, we can rerun `chef-client` on the remote node to apply this updated recipe. If the directory was previously already created, the recipe will not change anything as the subscription will not be triggered.

Loading custom SELinux policies with Chef

Let's update our recipe to include the logic to load a custom policy. We will use two blocks in our recipe, one to upload the `test.cil` file to the node, and another one to load it, but only if it was not loaded previously:

```
cookbook_file '/usr/share/selinux/custom/test.cil' do
  source 'test.cil'
  owner 'root'
  group 'root'
  mode '0755'
  action :create
end
bash 'load_test_cil' do
  code '/usr/sbin/semodule -i /usr/share/selinux/custom/test.
cil'
  not_if '/usr/sbin/semodule -l | grep -q ^test$'
  only_if { ::File.exists?('/usr/share/selinux/custom/test.
```

```
cil') }
end
```

Put the `test.cil` file in a folder called `files` inside the `packt_selinux` cookbook directory, before uploading the updated cookbook and reapplying the changes using `chef-client`.

Using Chef's out-of-the-box SELinux support

While Chef itself has limited out-of-the-box SELinux support, cookbooks are available online on Chef Supermarket (where the Chef community manages and distributes their custom cookbooks). Chef (the company) maintains the `selinux` cookbook itself, which allows managing the SELinux state of a system, whereas the `selinux_policy` cookbook addresses a few other SELinux settings.

Let's download and install the `selinux` and `selinux_policy` cookbooks:

```
master ~$ knife supermarket install selinux_policy
master ~$ knife supermarket install selinux
master ~$ knife cookbook upload selinux_policy
master ~$ knife cookbook upload selinux
```

Next, adjust the `metadata.rb` file of our own cookbook to include the dependency to this newly added cookbook:

```
depends 'selinux_policy'
depends 'selinux'
```

We can now use some of the predefined recipes to handle SELinux configuration settings:

- With `selinux_state`, we can place the system in an enforcing or permissive state:

    ```
    selinux_state "SELinux enforcing" do
      action :enforcing
    end
    ```

- The `selinux_policy_boolean` recipe can configure an SELinux boolean value:

    ```
    selinux_policy_boolean 'httpd_builtin_scripting' do
      value false
    end
    ```

- With `selinux_policy_port`, a custom SELinux port mapping can be defined:

```
selinux_policy_port '10122' do
  protocol 'tcp'
  secontext 'ssh_port_t'
end
```

- A file context definition can be set using `selinux_policy_fcontext`:

```
selinux_policy_fcontext '/srv/web(/.*)?' do
  secontext 'httpd_sys_content_t'
end
```

- An SELinux domain can be put in permissive mode using the `selinux_policy_permissive` recipe:

```
selinux_policy_permissive 'zoneminder_t' do
end
```

Don't forget to upload the changed cookbook before calling `chef-client` on the remote systems.

Summary

Automation frameworks such as Ansible, SaltStack, Puppet, and Chef can be easily used to manage SELinux settings on a multitude of systems. While not all frameworks can deal with SELinux settings natively, this is easily mitigated by either using community-provided modules or by creating custom rules that check and update the settings accordingly. In this chapter, we've seen how to accomplish this by installing a custom, CIL-based SELinux policy.

We learned that these frameworks all have their specific approaches. Ansible, for instance, does not use any software installations on remote systems and communicates with the target systems using SSH. The other frameworks all use an agent/server model but have their own views on configuring settings (the syntax between Puppet and SaltStack is noticeably different) or design (Chef uses a workstation where developers have their development environment). All these frameworks are easily put in place and configured and can handle most SELinux settings without any problems. All tools have a way of modularizing the definitions so they can be applied easily against a larger number of systems.

Now that we know how to apply SELinux settings consistently, let's see what other SELinux controls exist, but now through userspace application-specific support.

Questions

1. Which of the four tools have native support for setting SELinux contexts on resources?

2. How do these orchestration tools allow reusable customization beyond native support?

3. What are some obvious differences between the listed orchestration tools?

Section 2: SELinux-Aware Platforms

Some applications and platforms have explicit SELinux support to further tighten security controls. In this part, the most common platform SELinux controls are explained.

This section comprises the following chapters:

- *Chapter 7, Configuring Application-Specific SELinux Controls*
- *Chapter 8, SEPostgreSQL – Extending PostgreSQL with SELinux*
- *Chapter 9, Secure Virtualization*
- *Chapter 10, Using Xen Security Modules with FLASK*
- *Chapter 11, Enhancing the Security of Containerized Workloads*

7
Configuring Application-Specific SELinux Controls

Several Linux services and applications enable additional SELinux controls besides the kernel-enforced SELinux policy. They allow the administrator to further manipulate and enforce policy rules through the application itself—isolating users, reducing data leakage risks, and mitigating the impact of malicious behavior.

In this chapter, we will look at several SELinux-aware applications, such as systemd services and how they allow administrators to set up and specify target domains and resource labels. We'll also cover the D-Bus service, which allows SELinux policies to control the service binding and message communication within D-Bus itself. Next, we'll jump to PAM-enabled services that allow users to log in through them.

Finally, we'll end the chapter with mod_selinux, an Apache module that allows SELinux-specific tuning of the web server's behavior. This approach shows how applications that do not natively have SELinux support can still be extended to address the administrator's requirements.

We will cover the following topics in this chapter:

- Tuning systemd services, logging, and device management
- Communicating over D-Bus
- Configuring PAM services
- Using mod_selinux with Apache

Technical requirements

Check out the following video to see the Code in Action: `https://bit.ly/37jYtze`

Tuning systemd services, logging, and device management

systemd is a core component of many Linux distributions. Since its birth in 2010, many distributions have gradually adopted systemd as the core `init` system, responsible for handling services and boot-up operations.

Throughout its development phase, systemd added several other components to its portfolio:

- D-Bus, which offers a system and session bus service allowing the use of D-Bus for inter-application communication, merged with systemd.
- systemd also incorporated `udev`, which offers a flexible device-node management application.
- Login capabilities were added to systemd, enabling fine-grained control over user sessions.
- The `journald` daemon joined the systemd family to provide a new approach to system and service logging, replacing some of the functionality of standard system loggers.
- The `timerd` daemon provides support for the time-based execution of tasks, replacing some of the functionality of standard cron daemons.
- Network configurations can be managed by systemd-networkd.

This ongoing approach of absorbing several system services into a single application suite has not gone unnoticed and isn't without controversy. Some distributions even refuse to have systemd as the default `init` system.

The systemd project includes SELinux support for most of its services. Applications such as systemd, which not only include SELinux awareness but also enforce access controls on specific SELinux classes and permissions (rather than relying on the Linux kernel), are called **userspace object managers**:

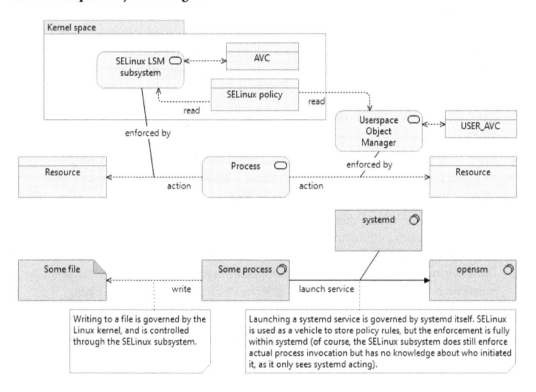

Figure 7.1 — The difference between kernel-enforced, standard SELinux, and userspace-managed SELinux

If an application enforces access controls toward certain classes and permissions, then it will also have its own AVC (see *Chapter 2, Understanding SELinux Decisions and Logging*, for more information about the AVC). Log events resulting from these applications will be identified as USER_AVC events rather than (kernel-managed) AVC events. The systemd application has support for systemd-specific classes, as we will see in the *Governing unit operation access* section. But before we dive into these specific details, let's first see what systemd is all about and what SELinux support it has.

Service support in systemd

The main capability of the system daemon that most people know about is its support for system services. Unlike traditional SysV-compatible `init` systems, systemd does not use scripts to manage services. Instead, it uses a declarative approach for the various services, documenting the wanted state and configuration parameters while using its own logic to ensure that the right set of services start at the right time and in the correct order.

Understanding unit files

systemd uses unit files to declare how a service should behave. These unit files use the INI-style syntax, supporting sections and key/value pairs within each file. A service can have multiple unit files that influence the service at large. It is important to remember that different unit files for the same service are all related:

- The `*.service` unit files define how a system service should be launched, what its dependencies are, how systemd should treat sudden failures, and so on.

- The `*.socket` unit files define which socket(s) should be created and which permissions should be assigned to it. systemd uses this for services that can be launched on request rather than directly at boot.

- The `*.timer` unit files define at what time or frequency the service should be launched. Services that do not necessarily run daemonized but need to execute a certain logic at defined intervals can use these timer files to ensure regular runs. These settings are comparable to the more classic yet still widely used crontabs, which we briefly touch upon in *PAM services*, in the subsection called *Cron*.

Other unit files exist as well, although those have more in common with generic system configurations (such as slice definitions and automount settings) and less with runtime services.

System unit files can be placed in one of three locations:

- Unit files are installed by default by the system's package manager inside `/usr/lib/systemd/system`.

- At runtime, updates can be placed inside `/run/systemd/system`, which will override the unit files in the default location. However, this location is transient and will not persist across reboots.

- System administrators can override the configurations in the two locations by placing unit files in `/etc/systemd/system`. These unit files override previous definitions, so there is no need to remove the unit files from the previous locations.

As an example, check out the default Nginx service unit file, `nginx.service`, inside `/usr/lib/systemd/system`:

```
[Unit]
Description=The nginx HTTP and reverse proxy server
After=network.target remote-fs.target nss-lookup.target

[Service]
Type=forking
PIDFile=/run/nginx.pid
ExecStartPre=/usr/bin/rm -f /run/nginx.pid
ExecStartPre=/usr/sbin/nginx -t
ExecStart=/usr/sbin/nginx
ExecReload=/bin/kill -s HUP $MAINPID
KillSignal=SIGQUIT
TimeoutStopSec=5
KillMode=mixed
PrivateTmp=true

[Install]
WantedBy=multi-user.target
```

This unit file declares the command to launch Nginx with and informs systemd that the service should be launched after successfully reaching the `network`, `remote-fs`, and `nss-lookup` targets (which is a milestone in the boot process, allowing proper dependency handling). The unit file also declares that it is a dependency of the `multi-user` target (which is the equivalent of the default run level when using SysV-style `init` services), which means the service should launch when the system boots.

Setting the SELinux context for a service

When systemd launches a service, it executes the command defined through the `ExecStart=` configuration entry in the service unit file. By default, a standard domain transition will occur as defined through the SELinux policy.

Package developers and system administrators can, however, update the service unit files to have the service launched in an explicitly mentioned SELinux domain. To accomplish this, the `[Service]` section of the unit file can be extended with the `SELinuxContext=` configuration entry.

For instance, to ensure that Nginx launches with the `httpd_t:s0:c0.c128` context, you'd use this:

```
[Service]
Type=forking
PIDFile=/run/nginx.pid
ExecStartPre=/usr/bin/rm -f /run/nginx.pid
ExecStartPre=/usr/sbin/nginx -t
ExecStart=/usr/sbin/nginx
ExecReload=/bin/kill -s HUP $MAINPID
SELinuxContext=system_u:system_r:httpd_t:s0:c0.c128
KillSignal=SIGQUIT
TimeoutStopSec=5
KillMode=mixed
PrivateTmp=true
```

Of course, it is also possible to use this to have a service running with a different context, which can be useful when developing custom policies for daemons. However, keep in mind that the SELinux policy rules still apply: you cannot ask systemd to launch Nginx, for instance, with the `dnsmasq_t` domain without updating the SELinux policy so that `httpd_exec_t` (the entry point for the `httpd_t` domain) is also made an entry point for the `dnsmasq_t` domain.

When you request systemd to explicitly use an SELinux context for a service, systemd will attempt to use this context for all execution-related tasks: `ExecStartPre`, `ExecStart`, `ExecStartPost`, `ExecStopPre`, `ExecStop`, `ExecStopPost`, and `ExecReload`. As these tasks often are not labeled with the right entry point label, these commands can fail. In that case, prefix the commands with + so that the SELinux context definition does not apply to them:

```
[Service]
Type=forking
PIDFile=/run/nginx.pid
ExecStartPre=+/usr/bin/rm -f /run/nginx.pid
ExecStartPre=/usr/sbin/nginx -t
ExecStart=/usr/sbin/nginx
ExecReload=/bin/kill -s HUP $MAINPID
SELinuxContext=system_u:system_r:httpd_t:s0:c0.c128
KillSignal=SIGQUIT
TimeoutStopSec=5
KillMode=mixed
PrivateTmp=true
```

While developing and changing unit files, the changed settings might not always be immediately applied to the system. Running `systemctl daemon-reload` after modifying unit files will ensure that the latest changes on the system are read by systemd.

Using transient services

systemd can also be used to launch applications as if they are services and have them under systemd's control. Such applications are called **transient services** as they lack the unit files that generally declare how systemd should behave.

Transient services are launched through the `systemd-run` application. To show this, let's create a simple Python script (one that calculates Pi up to 10,000 digits):

```
from decimal import Decimal, getcontext
getcontext().prec=10000
with open('/tmp/pi.out', 'w') as f:
  print(sum(1/Decimal(16)**k * (
    Decimal(4)/(8*k+1)-
    Decimal(2)/(8*k+4)-
    Decimal(1)/(8*k+5)-
    Decimal(1)/(8*k+6)) for k in range(10000)), file=f)
```

As this takes some time, we can opt to run this Python script under systemd's control:

```
# systemd-run python3.6 /tmp/pi.py
Running as unit: run-rf9ce45c...f343.service
```

As transient services do not have unit files to manage, changing the SELinux context must be accomplished through the command line as well. Of course, this is only needed if the standard domain transitions defined in the policy do not result in the wanted behavior:

```
# systemd-run -p SELinuxContext=guest_u:guest_r:guest_t:s0
python3.6 /tmp/pi.py
```

The `systemd-run` application supports this through the `--property` (or `-p`) option, through which unit file properties can be added. In the previous example, we use this option to run the script in the `guest_t` domain using the `SELinuxContext` property, similar to how we would define this in the unit file itself.

Requiring SELinux for a service

Some services should only run when SELinux is enabled or disabled. With systemd, this can be defined through its conditional parameters.

A service unit file can contain several conditions that need to be valid before systemd will consider executing the service. These conditionals can point to the system type (virtualized or not), kernel command-line parameters, files that do or don't exist, and so on. The one we are interested in is `ConditionSecurity`, which represents the state of the given security system—in our case, SELinux.

For instance, look at the `selinux-autorelabel.service` unit file inside `/usr/lib/systemd/system`:

```
[Unit]
Description=Relabel all filesystems
DefaultDependencies=no
Conflicts=shutdown.target
After=sysinit.target
Before=shutdown.target
ConditionSecurity=selinux
[Service]
ExecStart=/usr/libexec/selinux/selinux-autorelabel
Type=oneshot
TimeoutSec=0
RemainAfterExit=yes
StandardOutput=journal+console
```

Similarly, the Linux distribution provides the `selinux-autorelabel-mark.service` file. This service ensures that, if SELinux is not active when the system boots (and no `/.autorelabel` file exists yet), then systemd will create an empty `/.autorelabel` file. This file ensures that, when the system reboots with SELinux support, the relabeling operation occurs.

Relabeling files during service startup

One of the actions that many services require is the preparation of service-specific runtime directories, such as `/run/httpd` for the Apache service. systemd supports this through `tmpfiles.d`. We have briefly covered `tmpfiles` in *Chapter 4, Using File Contexts and Process Domains*. Within `tmpfiles`, we can define the files and locations requested to be provided or updated immediately (at boot time) when these are not placed in the (persisted) filesystem.

For instance, the package that provides the Apache daemon installs the following definition as `/usr/lib/tmpfiles.d/httpd.conf` on the system:

```
d /run/httpd      710 root apache
d /run/httpd/htcacheclean     700 apache
```

Like the systemd unit files, the files that contain these settings should be declared in one of the following three locations. Each location overrides the settings of the previous one:

- The default, package-provided location is /usr/lib/tmpfiles.d.
- Runtime declarations can be placed in /run/tmpfiles.d.
- Local system administrator-provided declarations are placed in /etc/tmpfiles.d.

These definitions can get much more specific than just directory creation. Through the tmpfiles.d application, definitions can be set to create files, empty directories upfront, create sub-volumes, manage special files such as symbolic links or block devices, set extended attributes, and more.

One of its features is to set the file mode and ownership, and restore the SELinux context on a file (z) or recursively against a directory (Z). This can be used to change contexts on files that have a proper context definition in the policy, but whose context is not properly assigned.

For instance, look at the definitions in the selinux-policy.conf file inside /usr/lib/tmpfiles.d:

```
z /sys/devices/system/cpu/online - - -
Z /sys/class/net - - -
z /sys/kernel/uevent_helper - - -
w /sys/fs/selinux/checkreqprot - - - - 0
```

We need to relabel files inside /sys because this location is labeled with sysfs_t by default and changing the context at runtime does not preserve its status across reboots. Yet some of its files should have a different label – the /sys/devices/system/cpu/online file, for instance, requires the cpu_online_t label:

```
# matchpathcon /sys/devices/system/cpu/online
/sys/devices/system/cpu/online  system_u:object_r:cpu_
online_t:s0
```

The definition ensures that this (pseudo) file is relabeled at boot so that all other processes that rely on the file labeled with cpu_online_t can happily continue working.

The other arguments to the definition are explicitly marked with a dash in the previous example, meaning that no other parameters need to be configured. They can be used to set the mode, **User Identifier (UID)**, **Group Identifier (GID)**, age, and argument related to the rule.

An example configuration that uses some of these other parameters with the z or Z state is the `systemd.conf` file:

```
# grep ^[zZ] /usr/lib/tmpfiles.d/systemd.conf
z /run/log/journal 2755 root systemd-journal - -
Z /run/log/journal/%m ~2750 root systemd-journal - -
z /var/log/journal 2755 root systemd-journal - -
z /var/log/journal/%m 2755 root systemd-journal - -
z /var/log/journal/%m/system.journal 0640 root systemd-journal
- -
```

For more information about the definition format, see `man tmpfiles.d`.

Using socket-based activation

The system daemon also supports socket-based activation. When configured, systemd will create the socket on which the daemon usually listens and will have the daemon launched when the socket is first used. This allows systems to boot quickly (as many daemons do not need to be launched immediately) while still ensuring that all required sockets are available.

When a client only writes information to the socket (such as with the `/dev/log` socket), the client does not even need to wait for the daemon to be activated. The data is stored in a buffer until the daemon can read it. Only when the buffer is full will the operation block until the daemon flushes the buffer.

Take a look at the `systemd-journald.socket` unit file, available inside `/usr/lib/systemd/system`:

```
[Unit]
Description=Journal socket
Documentation=man:systemd-journal.service(8) man:journald.
conf(8)
DefaultDependencies=no
Before=sockets.target
IgnoreOnIsolate=yes
[Socket]
ListenStream=/run/systemd/journal/stdout
ListenDatagram=/run/systemd/journal/socket
SocketMode=0666
PassCredentials=yes
PassSecurity=yes
ReceiveBuffer=8M
Service=systemd-journald.service
```

When a client uses one of the mentioned sockets, then systemd will launch the `systemd-journald.service` unit to accommodate the client interaction. As long as these sockets are not used, the service will not be started.

Inside the `[Socket]` section, an SELinux-specific entry can be defined: `SELinuxContextFromNet=true`. When a unit file has this entry set, systemd will obtain the MLS/MCS information from the client context (the application connecting to the socket) and append this to the context of the service. This sensitivity inheritance can be used to prevent any information leakage from taking place when communication is happening through sockets.

Governing unit operation access

Until now, we've looked at configuration settings related to systemd's SELinux support. systemd also uses SELinux to control access to services defined through unit files. When a user wants to perform an operation against a unit (such as starting a service or checking the state of a running service), systemd queries the SELinux policy to see whether it will allow this operation.

The systemd daemon uses the service class to validate the permissions of the client's domain toward the requested operation. For instance, to validate whether a user context, `sysadm_t`, can view the status of the service associated with the `sshd.service` unit file, it checks the context of this file (being `sshd_unit_file_t`) and then validates whether the status permission is granted:

```
# sesearch -s sysadm_t -t sshd_unit_file_t -c service -p status
-A
```

Other supported permissions are `disable`, `enable`, `reload`, `start`, and `stop`. When a permission is not granted, a `USER_AVC` denial message will be visible in the audit logs (rather than an `AVC` message) as the message is not generated by the Linux kernel, but by systemd. So, while the rules themselves are part of the SELinux policy, it is systemd that enforces the access.

systemd, or the client through which systemd is queried, might also provide additional error messages to reflect that the SELinux policy prevents the action. For instance, if we attempt to query systemd over D-Bus (which we cover in the *D-Bus communication* section) from an unprivileged user domain, then we get the following error:

```
Error: GDBus.Error:org.freedesktop.DBus.Error.AccessDenied:
SELinux policy denies access
```

To facilitate troubleshooting any systemd-triggered failures, systemd also has an extensive logging component, called `systemd-journald`, which we'll cover next.

Logging with systemd

systemd is not only responsible for service management: it takes up several other tasks as well. One of these tasks is log management, traditionally implemented through a system logger.

While systemd still supports running with a traditional system logger, it now suggests the use of `systemd-journald`. One of the advantages of the journal daemon is that it is not limited to textual, single-line log messages. Daemons can now use binaries as well as multiline messages as part of its logging capabilities.

The journal daemon also registers information about the sending process alongside the log messages themselves. This additional information contains ownership data (the process owner) including the SELinux context of the sending process.

Retrieving SELinux-related information

The traditional approach to receive SELinux-related information (excluding the audit events we tackled before) is to `grep` through the log information. With the journal daemon, we can accomplish this as follows:

```
# journalctl -b | grep -i selinux
```

The `-b` option passed on to the journal control application informs the journal daemon that we are only interested in the log messages that originated for a specific boot.

Querying logs given an SELinux context

A unique feature of the journal daemon is to use the information associated with the log messages as part of the query to be launched against the journal database. For instance, we can ask the journal daemon to only show those messages that originated from a daemon or application running in the `udev_t` context:

```
# journalctl _SELINUX_CONTEXT=system_u:system_r:init_t:s0
```

The available contexts can be retrieved through the Bash completion support on the system. After writing `_SELINUX_CONTEXT=`, press *Tab* twice to see the possible values.

Using setroubleshoot integration with journal

The SELinux troubleshoot daemon is also integrated with `systemd-journald`. Any alert that comes up from `setroubleshootd` is also available through the journal daemon.

This helps administrators as they will quickly find out about SELinux denials when investigating problems. For instance, when the Nginx web server is not working properly and this is due to an SELinux policy, a quick investigation of the status of the service will reveal that the SELinux policy is preventing some actions:

```
# systemctl status nginx
```

To get more information about the message, use `journalctl`:

```
# journalctl -xe
```

As you can see, `systemd-journald` has captured environment information related to the service, which can provide much-needed guidance on resolving potential problems.

A third systemd service that has SELinux configuration possibilities is the device daemon.

Handling device files

Linux has a long history of device managers. Initially, administrators needed to make sure that the device nodes were already present on the filesystem (`/dev` was part of the persisted filesystem). Gradually, Linux adopted more dynamic approaches for device management.

Nowadays, device files are managed through a combination of a pseudo filesystem (`devtmpfs`) and a userspace device manager called udev. This device manager is merged in systemd as well, becoming `systemd-udevd`.

The device manager listens on a kernel socket for kernel events. These events inform the device manager about detected or plugged-in devices (or the removal of such devices) and allow the device manager to take appropriate action. For udev, these actions are defined in udev rules.

Using udev rules

Configuring the udev subsystem is mainly done through udev rules. These rules are one-liners that contain a matching part and an action part.

The matching part contains validations, executed against the event(s) that udev receives from the Linux kernel. This validation uses key/value pairs obtained from the event, and includes the following possible keys:

- Kernel-provided device name (KERNEL)

- Device subsystem (SUBSYSTEM)

- Kernel driver (DRIVER)

- Specific attributes (ATTR)

- Active environment variables (ENV)

- The action type to inform if the device is detected or removed (ACTION)

While more match keys are possible, the preceding list is most commonly used.

The Linux kernel will also inform the device manager about the device hierarchy. This allows rules to be defined based on, for instance, the USB controller through which a USB device is plugged in. Alongside the information for the device itself, the kernel will also provide hierarchically related information through similar key/value pairs. These pairs, however, use a key definition in plural form: SUBSYSTEMS instead of SUBSYSTEM, DRIVERS instead of DRIVER, and so on.

For instance, to match a USB webcam with vendor ID 05a9 and product ID 4519, the match-related pairs could look like this:

```
KERNEL=="video[0-9]*", SUBSYSTEM=="video4linux",
SUBSYSTEMS=="usb", ATTR{idVendor}=="05a9",
ATTR{idProduct}=="4519"
```

The second part of a udev rule is the action to take. The most common action is to create a symbolic link to the created device file, ensuring that applications can always reach the same device through the same symbolic link, even when the device from the kernel point of view has a different name. We can, for instance, extend the preceding example with SYMLINK+="webcam1" to have /dev/webcam1 point to this newly detected device.

The udev application supports many more actions than just defining symbolic links, of course. It can associate ownership (OWNER) or group membership (GROUP) on the device, controlling who can access the devices. udev can also set environment variables (ENV) and even run a command (RUN) when the matched device is plugged in or detached from the system. To make sure the command is only executed when the device is added, we need to add an ACTION setting such as ACTION=="add".

> **Important note**
>
> udev can interpret ENV as both a matching key as well as an action key. The difference is the operation performed (a single equals sign = or a double ==). ENV{envvar}=="value" is a match operation (checking whether the variable matches the given value), whereas ENV{envvar}="value" is an action (setting the variable to value).

udev rules are provided by default through the /usr/lib/udev/rules.d location. Distributions and applications/drivers will store their default rules in this location. Additional rules or rule overrides can be placed in /etc/udev/rules.d.

It's important to remember that udev will continue processing rules even when it has already encountered a matching rule. This can be changed on a per-rule basis through the OPTIONS action, as with OPTIONS+="last_rule", which informs udev that it can stop processing further rules for this event.

Setting an SELinux label on a device node

One of the actions that udev supports is to assign an SELinux context on the device node. We can do this using the SECLABEL{selinux} action:

```
KERNEL=="fd0", ..., SECLABEL{selinux}="system_u:object_r:my_
device_t:s0"
```

Note that this action only sets the context on the device node. If the rule also sets a symbolic link, then the symbolic link itself will inherit the default device_t context.

Placing an SELinux label on a device node is often done together with the other security-related permissions, so the rule often receives additional actions such as setting the target owner (OWNER), group (GROUP), and permission set (MODE). After all, SELinux security controls only apply *after* the regular, discretionary access control checks have passed, so don't forget to make sure your users have access to the device nodes outside of the SELinux controls as well.

All the settings we've seen so far are about systemd service management and system support. Another component within the systemd ecosystem is D-Bus, which is less about system management and more about facilitating communication and interaction between different applications over a programmable communication bus.

Communicating over D-Bus

The D-Bus daemon provides an inter-process communication channel between applications. Unlike traditional IPC methods, D-Bus is a higher-level communication channel that offers more than simple signaling or memory sharing. Applications that want to chat over D-Bus link with one of the many D-Bus-compatible libraries, such as those provided by the libdbus, sd-bus (part of systemd), GDBus, and QtDBus applications.

The D-Bus daemon is part of the systemd application suite.

Understanding D-Bus

Linux generally supports two D-Bus types – system-wide and session-specific D-Bus instances:

- The system-wide D-Bus is the main instance used for system communication. Many services or daemons will associate themselves with the system D-Bus to allow others to communicate with them through D-Bus.

- The session-specific D-Bus is an instance running for each logged-in user. It is commonly used by graphical applications to communicate with each other within a user session.

Both D-Bus instances are provided through the dbus-daemon application. The system-wide D-Bus will run with the --system option, whereas a session-specific instance will run with the --session option.

Applications register themselves against D-Bus through a namespace. Conventionally, this namespace uses the domain name of the project. For instance, systemd declares the org.freedesktop.systemd1 namespace, whereas D-Bus is at org.freedesktop.DBus.

The currently associated applications can be queried using Python easily:

```
# python3.6
>>> import dbus
>>> for service in dbus.SystemBus().list_names():
...    print(service)
org.freedesktop.DBus
org.freedesktop.login1
org.freedesktop.systemd1
org.freedesktop.PolicyKit1
com.redhat.tuned
:1.10
:1.11
```

```
org.freedesktop.NetworkManager
...
```

Each application then provides objects on the bus that can be reached by other objects (other applications)—of course, assuming they have the privileges to do so. These objects are represented through a path-like syntax and generally also use the domain of the project as a prefix.

For instance, to list the objects currently associated with org.freedesktop. systemd1, we can use the gdbus command. To facilitate its use, we first enable auto-completion support, after which we can use the *Tab* key to easily add the appropriate values:

```
# source /usr/share/bash-completion/completions/gdbus
# gdbus call --system --dest <TAB><TAB>
# gdbus call --system --dest org.freedesktop.systemd1 --object-
path /org/freedesktop/systemd1<TAB><TAB>
Display all 220 possibilities? (y or no)
/org/freedesktop/systemd1
/org/freedesktop/systemd1/job
/org/freedesktop/systemd1/unit
...
```

Applications can trigger methods on these objects, or send messages to the applications bound to these objects through these methods.

For instance, to get the state of the sshd.service unit through D-Bus, we invoke the org.freedesktop.systemd1.Manager.GetUnitFileState method on the org.freedesktop.systemd1 object reachable through the /org/freedesktop/ systemd1 path, and with the sshd.service argument, like this:

```
# gdbus call --system \
  --dest org.freedesktop.systemd1 \
  --object-path /org/freedesktop/systemd1 \
  --method org.freedesktop.systemd1.Manager.GetUnitFileState \
  sshd.service
('enabled',)
```

These calls can also be controlled through the SELinux policy, as we will learn next.

Controlling service acquisition with SELinux

The D-Bus application, like systemd, will query the SELinux policy to verify whether to allow an operation. Again, it is the D-Bus application itself that enforces the policy and not a Linux kernel subsystem.

The first control that administrators can enable within D-Bus is to ensure that only well-established domains can acquire a specified object within D-Bus. Without this control, malicious code could register itself as `org.freedesktop.login1`, for instance, and act as a system daemon on the bus. Other applications might mistakenly send out sensitive information to the application.

Applications store this policy information in files hosted in `/usr/share/dbus-1/system.d`. The login service, for instance (stored as `org.freedesktop.login1.conf`) has the following policy snippet installed:

```
<busconfig>
  <policy user="root">
    <allow own="org.freedesktop.login1"/>
    <allow send_destination="org.freedesktop.login1"/>
    <allow receive_sender="org.freedesktop.login1"/>
  </policy>
  <policy context="default">
    <deny send_destination="org.freedesktop.login1"/>
    <allow
        send_destination="org.freedesktop.login1"
        send_interface="org.freedesktop.DBus.Introspectable"/>
    ...
  </policy>
</busconfig>
```

As the login daemon runs in the `systemd_logind_t` domain, we could enhance this configuration as follows:

```
<busconfig>
  <selinux>
    <associate
      own="org.freedesktop.login1"
      context="system_u:system_r:systemd_logind_t:s0" />
  </selinux>
  ...
</busconfig>
```

With this enhancement in place, D-Bus will check whether the application (which we presume is running in the `systemd_logind_t` context) has the `acquire_svc` permission (of the `dbus` class) against the `systemd_logind_t` context. By default, the SELinux policy does not have this permission, and as such, the registration fails:

```
# systemctl restart dbus-org.freedesktop.login1
Job for systemd-logind.service failed because a timeout was
exceeded.
See "systemctl status systemd-logind.service" and "journalctl
-xe" for details.
# ausearch -m user_avc -ts recent
```

When we add the following SELinux policy rule, the registration of `systemd-logind` will succeed, as expected:

```
(allow systemd_logind_t systemd_logind_t (dbus (acquire_svc)))
```

Load this policy (say `test.cil`) and try the `restart` operation again:

```
# semodule -i test.cil
# systemctl restart dbus-org.freedesktop.login1
```

By limiting which domains can obtain a given service, we ensure that only trusted applications are used. Non-trusted applications will generally not run within the domain of that application (end users, for instance, cannot trigger a transition to such a domain) even if they receive root privileges (which is another check that D-Bus does for the login service, as shown in the first `busconfig` snippet).

Administrators can enhance this D-Bus configuration without having to alter the existing configuration files. For instance, the previously mentioned SELinux-governing `busconfig` snippet could very well be saved as a different file.

Governing message flows

A second control that D-Bus validates is which applications can communicate with each other. This is not configurable through the service configurations but is a pure SELinux policy control.

Whenever a source application is calling a method of a target application, D-Bus validates the `send_msg` permission between the two domains associated with the source and target applications.

For instance, communication over D-Bus between a user domain (`sysadm_t`) and service domain (`systemd_logind_t`) will check the following permissions:

```
allow sysadm_t systemd_logind_t : dbus send_msg;
allow systemd_logind_t sysadm_t : dbus send_msg;
```

If these permissions are not granted, then D-Bus will not allow the communication to happen. If at any point, the application context cannot be obtained, then the bus daemon context will be used.

Failures will be logged as `USER_AVC` entries in the audit log. If the communication should be allowed, we can create a simple SELinux policy file to address this like so:

```
(allow sysadm_t systemd_logind_t (dbus (send_msg)))
(allow systemd_logind_t sysadm_t (dbus (send_msg)))
```

Store these rules in a file with the suffix `.cil` (say, `local_logind_systemd.cil`), and load it with `semodule`:

```
# semodule -i local_logind_systemd.cil
```

Let's consider a few other applications that have SELinux support, not necessarily built-in, but through the SELinux policy and PAM integration within the system.

Configuring PAM services

systemd and D-Bus are SELinux-aware applications, with explicit SELinux support built in. Several other services exist on a Linux system that play nicely together with SELinux yet are not SELinux-aware themselves. Many of these services have an affinity with SELinux through their PAM integration.

We covered PAM integration in *Chapter 3*, *Managing User Logins*. In this section, we'll cover three example services using PAM, and how SELinux can be further fine-tuned to support these services.

Cockpit

Cockpit is a simple, browser-based management application that allows administrators to easily see system resources (monitoring) as well as to interact with the system. It also allows users to log into the system through the browser.

It is this browser-based terminal that we want to configure: by tuning the target SELinux roles for the SELinux users, we can selectively put users in a specific role. This effectively defines what the users can accomplish through this browser-based session.

Installing Cockpit

The Cockpit application is readily available in the CentOS repository, so installing it is a breeze:

```
# yum install cockpit
```

While the application does not need additional configuration, if you do need tweaks, you will need to create the configuration file, /etc/cockpit/cockpit.conf, yourself as the application does not create a default configuration file. Within this configuration file, you can configure the TLS settings, or disable encrypted communication generally.

Let's disable the encrypted communication for this demonstration run (but if you intend to use Cockpit in production, you should not only keep encryption on but also ensure that only trusted hosts are connecting, possibly even requiring client certificate authentication using the ClientCertAuthentication directive):

```
[WebService]
AllowUnencrypted=true
```

With this set, we can continue with configuring SELinux for Cockpit.

Restricting user logins

Through these instructions, we will add the more restricted user_r role to the staff_u SELinux user, and then ensure that all logins mapped to the staff_u SELinux user are logged in using the user_r role when they log in through Cockpit. If they log in through other services, they will continue using the default staff_r role.

> **Note**
>
> The use of the user_r role rather than the (even more restricted) guest_r role is to allow the Cockpit application to function properly. The application will run a service under the user's privileges, which are not sufficient for Cockpit if we use the guest_t user domain.

Let's first add the user_r role so that we can put the users in the correct context later:

```
# semanage user -m -R "staff_r sysadm_r system_r user_r"
staff_u
```

Next, we want to update the SELinux configuration so that any Cockpit login by `staff_u` mapped users is going to use the `user_r` role. The Cockpit application has logins done through a service running in the `cockpit_session_t` context, which we find out by checking the context of the process first, and then logging in on Cockpit and checking the context of the processes again. There, we notice that a new process (`cockpit-session`) runs with the `cockpit_session_t` context:

```
# ps -eZ | grep cockpit
system_u:system_r:cockpit_ws_t:s0   ... cockpit-ws
system_u:system_r:cockpit_session_t:s0 ... cockpit-session
localhost
```

With this information now available, we can edit the `/etc/selinux/targeted/contexts/users/staff_u` file as follows:

```
system_r:local_login_t:s0     staff_r:staff_t:s0
sysadm_r:sysadm_t:s0
system_r:remote_login_t:s0    staff_r:staff_t:s0
system_r:sshd_t:s0            staff_r:staff_t:s0
sysadm_r:sysadm_t:s0
system_r:cockpit_session_t:s0    user_r:user_t:s0
system_r:crond_t:s0           staff_r:staff_t:s0
staff_r:cronjob_t:s0
```

By adjusting the order of the roles listed for the `cockpit_session_t` context (or limiting them to only the `user_r` role), we ensure that users allowed to run with the `user_r` role (like the `staff_u` user we configured earlier on) do so through the `user_r` role. As this role is more restricted than the default `staff_t` user domain, logins through Cockpit are thus more isolated.

This approach can be used for all PAM-enabled services, as this solely relies on the `pam_selinux.so` call in the service PAM configuration. For some services, the SELinux policy administrators add in a few more tweaks to use, such as with cron and SSH, which we'll discuss next.

Cron

Cron services on a system allow you to run tasks or commands on predefined schedules. Some cron applications are explicitly made SELinux-aware (such as fcron), allowing them to compute the target context a job should run in. Even cron systems that do not have any specific SELinux logic built in can be fine-tuned.

Switching between user-specific and generic contexts

A common setup supported through the SELinux policy is to toggle whether user tasks run in the user's default context (such as `staff_t` for staff users) or in a default, restricted cron context (`cronjob_t`). Both approaches have their pros and cons.

When we configure the system to have user jobs run in the user's default context, then users know what the privileges are of their jobs. A guest user has guest privileges, a staff user has staff privileges, and so forth. This is the most common configuration, and the default cron system on CentOS uses the context of the file containing the user's tasks (located in `/var/spool/cron`) to deduce the target runtime context.

By running user jobs in a more restricted context such as `cronjob_t`, all users' cron jobs run with the same privileges, and the administrator can easily fine-tune the privileges for all user jobs. This also allows the administrator to grant specific privileges for cron jobs while keeping the user contexts free of these rights.

Let's have a simple task executed every minute, namely a 59-second sleep. As a regular user, create a file (let's say `lisa.cron`) with the following content:

```
* * * * * sleep 59
```

This file uses the common cron syntax, where the following applies:

1. The first field covers the minute.
2. The second field covers the hour.
3. The third field covers the day of the month.
4. The fourth field covers the month.
5. The fifth field covers the day of the week.
6. The rest of the line is the command to execute.

The fields can use expressions to facilitate time definitions. For instance, to run every 15 minutes, you can use `*/15` in the first field. If you want to run only at 8 o'clock and 18 o'clock, you can use the `8,18` value in the second field. Another example is if you only want to run on workdays, for which you can use `1-5` in the fifth field (in cron, Sunday holds both 0 and 7 as valid values).

By loading it with the `crontab` command, the file is checked for errors and, if error-free, is securely placed inside `/var/spool/cron` (the `crontab` command is a `setuid` command that is able to modify `/var/spool/cron` even though this location is inaccessible by regular users):

```
$ crontab ./lisa.cron
```

From here, the cron daemon will pick up this file, and 1 minute later we will see the command active in the background:

```
$ ps -efZ | grep sleep
staff_u:staff_r:staff_t:s0 ...   sleep 59
```

As seen from the output, the command is running in the `staff_t` context. To change this to the `cronjob_t` type, rather than editing the SELinux context definition file as we did with the Cockpit application, use the `cron_userdomain_transition` SELinux boolean:

```
# setsebool cron_userdomain_transition off
```

This boolean changes the active SELinux policy behavior so that any user task executed from the cron system executes within the `cronjob_t` domain. You might need to reset the crontab definition (this depends on the cron system used), but afterward, we will see the job running in the `cronjob_t` domain:

```
$ ps -efZ | grep sleep
staff_u:staff_r:cronjob_t:s0 ...   sleep 59
```

The use of SELinux booleans to allow administrators to differentiate system behavior as needed is commonly used. For the SSH daemon, SELinux policy administrators have defined something similar.

OpenSSH

The OpenSSH daemon is the most common secure shell daemon around. It allows users to remotely access systems through a terminal, as well as to securely transfer files, tunnel application communications, and more.

When logging in through SSH, the PAM controls apply, but the SELinux policy also has specific SSH controls embedded and controllable through SELinux booleans.

Directly logging in as sysadm_t

The first change to assess is to allow directly logging in using the `sysadm_r` role. Users mapped to the `staff_u` SELinux user by default log in using the (more restricted) `staff_r` role, and then need to explicitly switch roles to obtain the more privileged `sysadm_r` role.

The first change we need to make is to edit the `/etc/selinux/targeted/contexts/users/staff_u` file and adjust the order of the roles listed for the `sshd_t` context:

```
system_r:local_login_t:s0     staff_r:staff_t:s0
sysadm_r:sysadm_t:s0
system_r:remote_login_t:s0    staff_r:staff_t:s0
system_r:sshd_t:s0            sysadm_r:sysadm_t:s0
staff_r:staff_t:s0
system_r:cockpit_session_t:s0  user_r:user_t:s0
system_r:crond_t:s0           staff_r:staff_t:s0
staff_r:cronjob_t:s0
```

However, this is not enough. The SELinux policy administrators have disabled direct logins through SSH to the `sysadm_r` role, forcing users to explicitly change roles (and thus reauthenticate). This approach is because SSH is often a publicly reachable and not otherwise easily controllable service (unlike services such as web servers, which can have reverse proxies and web application firewalls in front).

Change the SELinux `ssh_sysadm_login` boolean to `true` to enable the wanted behavior:

```
# setsebool ssh_sysadm_login true
```

This boolean changes the SELinux policy behavior to allow logins to the `sysadm_r` role from the SSH daemon.

Chrooting Linux users

Another feature that SSH supports is forcing logins from selected users to be chrooted. A **chroot** (which is a portmanteau of **change root**) is an isolation method for processes, where the process no longer sees the entire filesystem but only a part of it.

> **Informational note**
>
> Now, chroot environments are an easy way to isolate processes, but a chroot itself is still governed through Linux's discretionary access controls, and escaping chroot environments is not impossible. Using SELinux to further confine the process is recommended but is not in the scope of this section. For that, we refer to *Chapter 14, Dealing with New Applications*.

Before we configure SSH to chroot some users, we need to create a properly functioning environment: once we change the root for a process, all commands and libraries that the process wants to read or execute need to be available within this chroot environment.

Let's first create a chroot environment. A nice utility that assists in creating the right folder structure and files is Jailkit. Jailkit is not available by default through the regular repositories but can be easily installed and only requires a working compiler and Python environment.

We start off by installing the necessary dependencies:

```
# yum install gcc python36-devel
```

Next, we download the Jailkit source code and build it. As CentOS does not have a linked Python binary by default (as it requires the use of python3 as the runtime), we need to tell the build scripts how to address Python. We do this by declaring the PYTHONINTERPRETER environment variable:

```
# wget https://olivier.sessink.nl/jailkit/jailkit-2.21.tar.bz2
# tar xvf jailkit-2.21.tar.bz2
# cd jailkit-2.21
# export PYTHONINTERPRETER=/usr/bin/python3
# ./configure
# make
# make install
```

Once the installation is complete, you might need to remove a duplicate includesections call within the Jailkit configuration file (the jk_init command, which we will use next, will inform you about it if you don't). The openvpn section in /etc/jailkit/jk_init.ini should look like this:

```
[openvpn]
comment = jail for the openvpn daemon
paths = /usr/sbin/openvpn
users = root,nobody
```

```
groups = root,nobody
devices = /dev/urandom, /dev/random, /dev/net/tun
includesections = netbasics, uidbasics
need_logsocket = 1
```

With the configuration updated, we can now create the chroot environment. Let's create the /srv/chroot directory and then populate it with the necessary files, directories, device nodes, and more with the jk_init command:

```
# mkdir /srv/chroot
# jk_init -v -j /srv/chroot extshellplusnet
```

We want to make sure that the SELinux contexts for the resources inside this location are equivalent to the root location, so let's create a file context equivalency definition:

```
# semanage fcontext -a -e / /srv/chroot
# restorecon -RvF /srv/chroot
```

With the chroot environment set, we can now update the SSH configuration to chroot a user:

```
Match User lisa
  X11Forwarding no
  AllowTcpForwarding no
  ChrootDirectory /srv/chroot
```

While not applicable to all systems (as it depends on the distribution), we might need to tell the SELinux policy that the user domains for the users can chroot. This privilege (sys_chroot) is often not enabled by default for user domains:

```
# setsebool selinuxuser_use_ssh_chroot true
```

With this set, restart the SSH daemon and see whether the chroot is successful:

```
# systemctl restart ssh
```

Chroot environments are not only sensible for SSH access; other daemons might support chroot environments to further protect the resources on the system. In the past, chroot support was a common way to further harden the system. Namespace and resource isolation support has, however, largely surpassed the need for chroot jails. These new features have also jumpstarted the containerized ecosystem, which we will cover in *Chapter 11, Enhancing the Security of Containerized Workloads*.

The SELinux support for applications such as Cockpit, cron, and OpenSSH is generally provided through the SELinux policy and uses PAM integration to link SELinux controls within the application. It is, however, also possible to explicitly build in SELinux support in applications not intentionally SELinux-aware, but who support dynamic additions of logic through a modular design. As an example of this, we will look at Apache and the `mod_selinux` Apache module next.

Using mod_selinux with Apache

Applications are often web-based, exposing their interface as either a common website or a simple web service, and executing the bulk of logic either within the web server or in backend services that the web server interacts with for the user.

A web-based application has the huge advantage that end users often don't require any application or client to be installed on top of what is available by default on their device, be it a workstation, laptop, mobile, wristwatch, or smart TV.

However, unlike the services discussed earlier, Apache does not run individual user sessions through PAM logins on the system. Instead, user requests are handled by the web server threads and processes themselves, which makes easy SELinux-based controls a bit harder to accomplish.

Introducing mod_selinux

Apache has support for modules: dynamically loadable code that enhances the functionality of the web server, without having to rebuild the web server code itself. This modularity has given rise to the popularity of Apache, as we can see through its support for features such as PHP, introducing dynamic web applications to a server platform that was once meant to serve static content only.

`mod_selinux` uses the same modular support, which allows the Apache web server to become SELinux-aware. Once we enable `mod_selinux`, we can configure Apache to switch SELinux sensitivity or even SELinux domains for running code, further isolating the behavior of the web server and allowing SELinux policies to control what the web server can do. `mod_selinux` also supports user mappings, allowing the Apache web server to run specific user sessions in different domains.

Before building the `mod_selinux` module, let's first install the necessary dependencies on the system:

```
# yum install gcc git httpd httpd-devel redhat-rpm-config
libselinux-devel
```

Once the dependencies are installed, we can download and build the `mod_selinux` code. The code is available on GitHub in Kaigai's `mod_selinux` repository:

```
# git clone https://github.com/kaigai/mod_selinux
# cd mod_selinux
# apxs -c -i mod_selinux.c
```

The `apxs` command is the **Apache Extension Tool**, which facilitates building and installing Apache modules. The command both compiles (`-c`) and installs (`-i`) the mod_selinux module. We have yet to activate it in the Apache configuration though, which we accomplish by creating a new module configuration file in `/etc/httpd/conf.modules.d` called `99-selinux.conf` (you can pick whatever name you want, but make sure it ends with the `.conf` suffix):

```
 LoadModule selinux_module modules/mod_selinux.so
```

Now, while we have now installed the module, it is not ready for consumption yet, as we have not loaded the SELinux policy for it.

The `mod_selinux` repository contains the necessary SELinux policy code. However, it is not fully compatible with the more recent SELinux policy used by Linux distributions. We need to edit the `mod_selinux.if` file and remove all references to `httpd_user_script_ro_t`, `httpd_user_script_rw_t`, and `httpd_user_script_ra_t`, as those types are no longer present in current SELinux policies:

```
# sed -i '/script_r/d' mod_selinux.if
```

A second change – cosmetic for now – is to rename the calls from `miscfiles_read_certs` to `miscfiles_read_generic_certs`. These are functions used in the reference policy, a different – and still the most common way – of writing SELinux policies (which we cover in *Chapter 15, Using the Reference Policy*), and while both functions are supported at the time of writing, the `miscfiles_read_certs` function is no longer recommended for use and will disappear soon:

```
# sed -i 's/miscfiles_read_certs/miscfiles_read_generic_
 certs/g' mod_selinux.if
```

Once we have adjusted the policy, we can build and load it. As this policy is developed using the reference policy style, the installation first requires building the module before we load it (unlike the directly loadable CIL examples we've used so far):

```
# make -f /usr/share/selinux/devel/Makefile mod_selinux.pp
# semodule -i mod_selinux.pp
```

With the SELinux module loaded and the `mod_selinux` Apache module installed, we can start configuring the Apache daemon with SELinux-specific controls.

Configuring the general Apache SELinux sensitivity

The simplest configuration setting that `mod_selinux` supports is to configure Apache to run with a specific SELinux sensitivity. Suppose we want Apache to run with the `s0-s0:c0.c100` sensitivity, then we need to adjust the Apache configuration and use the `selinuxServerDomain` directive.

Assuming we want to adjust the sensitivity for the default welcome site, edit `/etc/httpd/conf.d/welcome.conf` and add in the following code snippet:

```
<IfModule mod_selinux.c>
  selinuxServerDomain *:s0-s0:c0.c100
</IfModule>
```

If the Apache web server uses virtual host definitions (allowing a single web server definition to manage multiple websites, based on the hostname that the client is using to access the web content), the `selinuxDomainVal` directive needs to be used instead of the `selinuxServerDomain` one.

For instance, suppose the web server manages two virtual hosts, one for the `apps.genfic.local` domain, and the other for `intranet.genfic.local`, then we can assign each virtual host with its own sensitivity set like so:

```
<VirtualHost *:80>
  DocumentRoot /srv/web/apps/htdocs
  ServerName apps.genfic.local
  selinuxDomainVal *:s0:c1,c2
</VirtualHost>
<VirtualHost *:80>
  DocumentRoot /srv/web/intranet/htdocs
  ServerName intranet.genfic.local
  selinuxDomainVal *:s0:c3,c4
</VirtualHost>
```

Restart the Apache web server and validate that the setting is active:

```
# systemctl restart httpd
# ps -efZ | grep httpd_t
system_u:system_r:httpd_t:s0-s0:c0.c100 ... /usr/sbin/httpd
```

As you can see, the web server is now running with the given sensitivity. An important caveat though: the `mod_selinux` code does not support `mcstransd`, the translation daemon we covered in *Chapter 3*, *Managing User Logins*, so you cannot use human-readable sensitivity definitions such as `SystemLow-SystemHigh`.

Mapping end users to specific domains

To map users, when logged in to a web application, to a specific domain, we need to create a user mapping file. This mapping file is then referred to using the `selinuxDomainMap` directive in the web server configuration.

Let's first create the mapping file inside `/etc/httpd/conf.d`, naming it `mod_selinux.map`, with the following content:

```
test user_webapp_t:s0:c0.c100
*     user_webapp_t:s0:c0,c1
__anonymous__    anon_webapp_t:s0
```

This mapping file contains three mappings:

- The first one is for a user called `test` and is mapped to the `user_webapp_t` domain and `s0:c0.c100` sensitivity.

- The second one is for any successfully authenticated user and is mapped to the `user_webapp_t` domain and `s0:c0,c1` sensitivity.

- The third one is for unauthenticated users and is mapped to the `anon_webapp_t` domain.

We can then refer to this map by adjusting the previously created snippet like so:

```
<IfModule mod_selinux.c>
  selinuxServerDomain *:s0-s0:c0.c100
  selinuxDomainMap /etc/httpd/conf.d/mod_selinux.map
</IfModule>
```

Restart the web server to apply the changes.

Changing domains based on source

The `mod_selinux` module also supports setting the server domain value based on environment variables that we have defined elsewhere in the configuration. For instance, we can first declare the value in an environment variable when a certain condition triggers, and then tell `mod_selinux` that this environment variable's value is to be used for the server domain setting.

Let's make this a bit more tangible with an example. Suppose the website manages web applications for both local (internal) people, as well as for people that work from remote locations. Assuming these users enter the web server through different source IP addresses, we can use the source IP address to differentiate between the two and assign a different SELinux sensitivity value.

We can do this in the Apache configuration with the `SetEnvIf` directive, which declares an environment variable but only if a request matches a particular condition. The condition we use is then the `Remote_Addr` directive, which checks the source IP address against the expression that follows.

Suppose local users come from `10.10.0.0/16` and remote users from a load balancer or reverse proxy with the IP address `10.121.12.15`, then we can differentiate this as follows:

```
SetEnvIf Remote_Addr "10.10.[0-9]+.[0-9]+$"
SENSITIVITY=*:s0:c0.c80
SetEnvIf Remote_Addr "10.121.12.15" SENSITIVITY=*:s0:c90
selinuxDomainEnv SENSITIVITY
```

It is possible to mix and match multiple `mod_selinux` directives. The module will use the first successful declaration, so you could use a user mapping first, and if that user mapping does not result in a hit (because the user is not declared in the map), use the environment variable, and if that fails, fall back to a default setting.

All we have to do to accomplish this fallback definition is to sequentially declare the `mod_selinux` directives, like so:

```
selinuxDomainMap /etc/httpd/conf.d/mod_selinux.map
selinuxDomainEnv SENSITIVITY
selinuxDomainVal *:s0:c0,c1
```

Through these declarations, you can fine-tune the web server security using SELinux domains and sensitivities. While this should never replace the security approach within the application itself, it provides additional isolation in case an unauthorized or malicious user exploits an error within the application.

Summary

In this chapter, we started out with an introduction to systemd and a strong focus on the service management capabilities that systemd offers. We learned how to start a service with a custom SELinux context as well as how additional files can be properly labeled upon boot. Alongside the service management, through systemd's unit files, this chapter also covered transient services and how to immediately associate the right SELinux context.

Other systemd capabilities and services were touched upon as well. We saw how SELinux contexts are registered as part of the systemd journal and how to query for events using this context. We took a brief look at udev and how its rules can be used to support administrators in managing devices. One of its actions is to set the SELinux context of the device node.

We then looked at D-Bus, how SELinux can be used to control the association of applications with services, and how D-Bus uses the `send_msg` permission to validate communications across its channels.

After D-Bus, we looked at several services that use PAM to launch user contexts, and we dived into specific examples such as SSH, learning how SELinux policy developers have further fine-tuned support for these services.

We finished with a look at `mod_selinux`, a dynamic module for Apache that enables SELinux support within Apache's configuration even though Apache itself does not have any SELinux specifics in it.

In the next chapter, we will look at another SELinux-aware application, SEPostgreSQL, which extends the popular and robust PostgreSQL database with mandatory access control support through SELinux.

Questions

1. Why should you not update unit files in `/usr/lib/systemd/system` directly?
2. What application allows resetting the SELinux context of files during boot?
3. How can we get all log events in journald associated with a given SELinux context?
4. How can you set the SELinux label for a device node created by udev?
5. Are SELinux controls always applicable to D-Bus associations?
6. How is it possible for Apache to be SELinux-aware without Apache having any SELinux code in it?

8
SEPostgreSQL – Extending PostgreSQL with SELinux

In the previous chapter, we covered a few example SELinux-aware applications: applications that know and interact with the SELinux subsystem to further enhance security within the application context. Some of these use existing policy constructs, such as Apache's mod_selinux, whereas others enhance the policy with custom classes to further fine-tune their behavior (as with D-Bus and the acquire_svc permission).

With **Security-Enhanced PostgreSQL** (**SEPostgreSQL**), we get a more elaborate example of an SELinux-aware application, which uses multiple additional classes within SELinux, as well as labeling its internal database objects to further enforce security rules. In this chapter, we will learn how to apply labels within PostgreSQL, debug its enforcement rules, associate the right labels with the PostgreSQL resources, and show how this label-based security method can be used to augment specific security practices within a relational database.

In this chapter, we're going to cover the following main topics:

- Introducing PostgreSQL and `sepgsql`
- Understanding SELinux's database-specific object classes and permissions
- Using MCS and MLS
- Integrating SEPostgreSQL into a network

Technical requirements

Check out the following video to see the Code in Action: `https://bit.ly/3dDcg4Z`

Introducing PostgreSQL and sepgsql

PostgreSQL is a popular, featureful, and mature relational database management system. Like Apache, it also enables a modular extension of its functionalities through loadable modules. The module we will investigate is called **sepgsql**, shorthand for **Security Enhanced PostgreSQL** or **SEPostgreSQL**. Through `sepgsql`, PostgreSQL enhances itself with SELinux support for additional access controls, offering fine-grained data flow controls based on SELinux policy rules.

Please be aware though that `sepgsql` does not implement a full mandatory access control system within PostgreSQL, as not all PostgreSQL statements will result in a policy check. While it augments the security posture of the PostgreSQL database, the module has a few limitations listed in its online documentation, available at `https://www.postgresql.org/docs/10/sepgsql.html` (adjust the version number in the URL as needed; the referenced document at this URL is for PostgreSQL 10, which is the version currently used within CentOS 8 and used throughout this chapter).

Reconfiguring PostgreSQL with sepgsql

Before we can install `sepgsql`, we need to have a working PostgreSQL system at our disposal. Most Linux distributions have readily available tutorials on how to deploy PostgreSQL, which often involves creating the databases associated with it.

In this chapter, we will assume that the database itself is available inside `/var/lib/pgsql/data`, the default location for a CentOS-based PostgreSQL installation. The PostgreSQL configuration files are also located inside this location.

To install `sepgsql`, the following steps should be executed:

1. Let's first see whether the database is functioning properly by logging in as the (default) `postgres` superuser, and listing the currently available databases:

```
# su postgres -
$ psql postgres
psql (10.6)
Type "help" for help.

postgres=# \l
                 List of databases
    Name     |   Owner    |  Encoding    | ...
-------------+------------+--------------+ ...
  postgres   |  postgres  |  UTF8        | ...
  template0  |  postgres  |  UTF8        | ...
  template1  |  postgres  |  UTF8        | ...
```

    If at any point a failure occurs, check the log file inside `/var/lib/pgsql/data/log` to get more information. This log file is the default log file for all PostgreSQL-related activities, as we will see when troubleshooting its SELinux support in the *Troubleshooting sepgsql* section.

2. Assuming PostgreSQL is working properly, let's configure it to use the `sepgsql` module. This module is part of the contributed modules within PostgreSQL, and is maintained by the PostgreSQL community. In CentOS, the `sepgsql` module is part of the `postgresql-contrib` package, which can be easily added to the system using `yum install postgresql-contrib` if it is not present yet.

3. Edit the `postgresql.conf` file inside `/var/lib/pgsql/data` and search for the `shared_preload_libraries` statement. By default, it will be commented out, so uncomment it and add `sepgsql` inside:

```
shared_preload_libraries = 'sepgsql' # (change requires
restart)
```

4. As mentioned, changing this parameter requires restarting the database. We will do that later, but first, we will shut down the database as our next steps will require an offline database:

```
# systemctl stop postgresql
```

5. Next, we need to reconfigure all databases and enable the `sepgsql`-related functions. We will cover these functions in the *Using sepgsql specific functions* section. To enable the functions, we have to become the `postgres` superuser again, and for each database available, we load a specific SQL file:

```
# su postgres -
$ export PGDATA=/var/lib/pgsql/data
$ for DBNAME in template0 template1 postgres; do
    postgres --single -F -c exit_on_error=true $DBNAME <
/usr/share/pgsql/contrib/sepgsql.sql > /dev/null;
  done
```

The databases listed in the example are the three default databases available in a brand-new installation. You can obtain the actual list of databases on the system through PostgreSQL's shorthand \l command, which we used earlier to check whether the database is functioning properly.

6. Let's validate whether `sepgsql` is working by starting the PostgreSQL database, logging in to PostgreSQL, and asking for our current context:

```
# systemctl start postgresql
# su postgres -
$ psql postgres
...
postgres# SELECT sepgsql_getcon();
        sepgsql_getcon()
----------------------------------------------------------
unconfined_u:unconfined_r:unconfined_t:s0-s0:c0.c1023
```

What we did here was to execute the freshly installed `sepgsql` function `sepgsql_getcon()`, which retrieves the current context for the session.

Let's further configure the database with a test account that we can use to validate the `sepgsql` controls.

Creating a test account

To validate whether the `sepgsql` controls are working, we should have a test account outside of the `postgres` superuser, and a local user that we can map to different SELinux contexts. As the SELinux context will heavily decide which privileges are associated with a session, we want to be able to show the impact of one context compared to the others.

First, inside PostgreSQL (with the `postgres` superuser), create a test account called `testuser`, and allow the account to authenticate with a given password:

```
postgres=# CREATE USER testuser PASSWORD 'somepassword';
```

We also need to configure the database to allow password-based authentication (as the default PostgreSQL setup will use system trust or another means of authentication). To accomplish that, edit the `pg_hba.conf` file inside `/var/lib/pgsql/data` with the following settings:

```
local           all    postgres                            peer
local           all    testuser                            md5
host     all    testuser        127.0.0.1/32       md5
host     all    testuser        192.168.100.0/24   md5
```

The `pg_hba.conf` file manages the host-based authentication rules for PostgreSQL. We update it to allow password-based authentication for the `testuser` account (which uses `md5` as an identifier) while allowing the `postgres` superuser to continue to authenticate using peer trust.

With these changes in place, PostgreSQL allows password-based authentication of the `testuser` account both when the user initiates the communication over a local, socket-based interaction, as well as when a network-based communication is used.

We also need to tell the SELinux policy that regular users will be allowed to connect to the PostgreSQL service:

```
# setsebool -P selinuxuser_postgresql_connect_enabled on
```

While this would be sufficient for accessing the PostgreSQL service, it is not adequate to allow the regular user domain (`user_t`) to interact with `sepgsql`. To accomplish that, we need to adjust the SELinux policy so that the `user_t` domain is also associated with the `sepgsql_client_type` attribute, and that the `user_r` role can have the `sepgsql`-related types active.

We do this through a small CIL policy, as follows:

```
(typeattributeset cil_gen_require sepgsql_client_type)
(typeattributeset cil_gen_require user_t)
(typeattributeset cil_gen_require sepgsql_trusted_proc_t)
(typeattributeset cil_gen_require sepgsql_ranged_proc_t)
(typeattributeset sepgsql_client_type (user_t))
(roleattributeset cil_gen_require user_r)
(roletype user_r sepgsql_trusted_proc_t)
(roletype user_r sepgsql_ranged_proc_t)
```

It is also possible to accomplish this with a reference policy style module, as follows:

```
policy_module(local_sepgsql, 1.0)
gen_require(`
    role user_r;
    type user_t;
')
postgresql_role(user_r, user_t)
```

Assuming we stick with the CIL-based policy, let's load the file (that is, `local_sepgsql.cil`) as an SELinux policy module:

```
# semodule -i local_sepgsql.cil
```

Don't forget to restart the PostgreSQL service after changing the `pg_hba.conf` file.

Tuning sepgsql inside PostgreSQL

The `sepgsql` module introduces two configuration parameters that can be used to tweak `sepgsql` inside PostgreSQL:

- The `sepgsql.permissive` parameter tells PostgreSQL not to enforce the SELinux policy rules inside PostgreSQL. This is similar to the permissive state of SELinux on the system, but covers the `sepgsql`-related functionality inside PostgreSQL alone.

- The `sepgsql.debug_audit` parameter tells PostgreSQL to always log the SELinux-related decisions, even when they are to allow a statement to be processed. This is similar to the `auditallow` statements for SELinux on the system.

It is very important however to understand that `sepgsql` is a user-space object manager, as explained in *Chapter 7, Configuring Application-Specific SELinux Controls*: the SELinux subsystem in the Linux kernel is not used for enforcing the access controls, only `sepgsql` is. The only purpose that the SELinux subsystem has is to allow PostgreSQL to query the active SELinux policy or obtain current SELinux context information.

Hence, the previous configuration parameters work mostly independently of the configuration of the system. While SELinux must be active on the system, it does not need to be in enforcing mode to have `sepgsql` enforce the rules inside PostgreSQL, nor does a permissive SELinux system make the enforcement of `sepgsql` permissive as well.

The `sepgsql.debug_audit` parameter does have some relationship with the system policy. We can add `auditallow` statements to the SELinux policy to force the logging of events even when they are allowed. What the `sepgsql.debug_audit` parameter does is force all events to be logged, something useful for troubleshooting `sepgsql`, as we will see next.

Troubleshooting sepgsql

Let's enable the debug statements for an individual session and reinvoke the `sepgsql_getcon` function again:

```
# su postgres -c "/usr/bin/psql postgres"
postgres=# SET sepgsql.debug_audit = true;
SET
postgres=# SELECT sepgsql_getcon();
...
```

If you want to enable the configuration for the entire system, you can place the configuration inside the `postgresql.conf` file:

```
sepgsql.debug_audit = true
```

Inside the PostgreSQL logs, we will notice the following information:

```
STATEMENT:   SET sepgsql.debug_audit = true
STATEMENT:   SELECT sepgsql_getcon();
LOG:  SELinux: allowed { execute } \
  scontext=unconfined_u:unconfined_r:unconfined_t:s0-s0:c0.
c1023 \
  tcontext=system_u:object_r:sepgsql_proc_exec_t:s0 \
  tclass=db_procedure name="pg_catalog.sepgsql_getcon()"
```

The first two lines log the statements that we have executed within the session, whereas the third line is the SELinux log event related to the execution of `sepgsql_getcon`.

The event tells us that the `unconfined_t` domain (source context) has attempted (and succeeded) to execute the database procedure (as indicated by the `db_procedure` class) labeled with the `sepgsql_proc_exec_t` type. The in-database function is the `sepgsql_getcon` function within the `pg_catalog` schema.

If a denial occurs, this will result in a similar event in the logs, but will also be made visible to the end user that triggered the denial, as PostgreSQL will show an error message like so:

```
ERROR:  SELinux: security policy violation
```

Unlike the audit logging executed by, for instance, D-Bus (which results in USER_AVC events in the regular audit log), sepgsql will follow the log configuration of the PostgreSQL database itself, so keep a close eye out on this log file (or other log targets configured in PostgreSQL) when trying to troubleshoot sepgsql.

In this simple example, you might already have noticed that the event references a database-specific class (db_procedure). In the next section, we will look into the various classes, permissions, and types associated with sepgsql and thus supported by the SELinux policy.

Understanding SELinux's database-specific object classes and permissions

The sepgsql module uses several database-specific SELinux classes to fine-tune the policies and access controls. The supported classes can be listed through /sys/fs/selinux/class or the seinfo command:

```
# seinfo --class | grep db_
db_blob
db_column
db_database
db_language
db_procedure
db_schema
db_sequence
db_table
db_tuple
db_view
```

These classes have an obvious relational database meaning: db_database is for database-related permissions, db_table for table permissions, db_procedure for database procedures, and so on. While not all classes are still supported by sepgsql (the db_database class has no immediate support anymore), most do have their usual mapping within the PostgreSQL database.

Let's see what permissions are supported by `sepgsql` and how this can be used to fine-tune access controls within the database.

Understanding sepgsql permissions

The access controls that `sepgsql` enforces are on top of the discretionary access controls already supported by PostgreSQL. Rather than using the privileges of the role or user currently acting within the database, the `sepgsql` module will use the context associated with the session.

As we can use different SELinux contexts for sessions that are authenticated using the same database role, we can create distinct access controls within the database without associating this with the user account itself. We can, for instance, differentiate based on the initialization of the database session: a remote session might have a separate context compared to a locally launched session, or the authorizations might be unique across different Linux users even when they share the same account within the database.

> **Important note**
>
> As remote connections require the peer context to be accessible, `sepgsql` requires either the use of labeled IPSec, or we need to introduce fallback labeling using NetLabel and CIPSO, as seen in *Chapter 5, Controlling Network Communications*. We will establish such a mapping in the *Integrating SEPostgreSQL in the network* section, after explaining the various permission mappings.

Once logged in, a query on a table will trigger a few checks against the SELinux policy:

- Any `SELECT`, `INSERT`, `UPDATE`, or `DELETE` statement on a table results in a permission check against the `select`, `insert`, `update`, or `delete` permissions within the `db_table` class.

- When the `WHERE` clause lists one or more different tables, then the `select` privilege for those different tables is checked as well.

- Furthermore, column-level permissions are checked for each referenced column, and this is checked against the permissions within the `db_column` class. Again, permission checks against the `select` permission validate the read access, whereas the `update` or `insert` permissions reflect the controls to check when the values are changed.

A more elaborate overview of the supported permissions is available in the PostgreSQL `sepgsql` documentation.

Using the default supported types

The default SELinux policy has several types readily available for use within a `sepgsql` setup. Most of the SEPostgreSQL configurations will not deviate from these default types, and instead rely on the category- and sensitivity-oriented controls that we touched upon in *Chapter 3, Managing User Logins*.

To see what these default types are, what they are used for, and how to assign these labels within PostgreSQL, let's start with creating a new database called `db_test`:

```
# su postgres -c "/usr/bin/psql postgres"
postgres=# CREATE DATABASE db_test;
CREATE DATABASE
```

Next, we connect to this newly created database and create a simple table, called `tb_users`, which has the following columns:

- The user's ID, named `uid`

- The user's name, named `name`

- The user's email address, named `mail`

- The user's mailing address, named `address`

- The user's password salt and hash, named `salt` and `phash`

> **Important note**
>
> The example used is merely an example, meant to show how to approach SELinux labels and `sepgsql`. Proper database design and best practices for addressing password hashes and other sensitive data are well beyond the scope of this book!

As you can imagine, we will be securing some of these columns further: while the password hash should obviously be considered very sensitive, we should also make sure to properly protect the mail and address fields as this is **Personally Identifiable Information** (**PII**), which in many areas of the world is governed by specific privacy laws:

```
postgres=# \c db_test;
db_test=# CREATE TABLE tb_users(uid int primary key, name text,
mail text, address text, salt text, phash text);
```

What is now the label associated with this table? For that, we need to query the PostgreSQL internal tables/views, more specifically the `pg_seclabels` one:

```
db_test=# SELECT objname,provider,label FROM pg_seclabels WHERE
objname='tb_users';
  objname  | provider |                       label
-----------+----------+---------------------------------------------------
 tb_users  | selinux  | unconfined_u:object_r:sepgsql_table_t:s0
```

As you can see, the table has received the `sepgsql_table_t` type and default sensitivity (`s0`).

`sepgsql_table_t` is the default type for tables. We usually find this type used for general table support and columns. Alongside the `sepgsql_table_t` type, the policy has a few other table- and column-oriented types that administrators can use to differentiate the controls that `sepgsql` enforces:

- The `sepgsql_fixed_table_t` type can be used for tables or columns that can only be appended to (inserted into) but not updated. This could be for log-related tables or audit events where we want to use the `sepgsql` controls to further enforce this (beyond the in-database controls that could be used for this as well).

- The `sepgsql_ro_table_t` type can be used for tables or columns that should only be read from (read-only).

- The `sepgsql_secret_table_t` type can be used for tables or columns that cannot be accessed by regular users or sessions, and only by administrative ones. This is generally used for tables or columns that are only used through protected and/or privileged procedures.

- The `unpriv_sepgsql_table_t` type is like the `sepgsql_table_t` type, but specific to tables or columns managed by admins or unconfined users that cannot be accessed by confined users.

- The `user_sepgsql_table_t` type on the other hand is specifically constructed for tables or columns managed by confined users. This allows administrators to differentiate between user-specific tables and general tables.

Let's grant the `testuser` account (full) access to this table and database, and add some data to the table:

```
db_test=# GRANT ALL PRIVILEGES ON ALL TABLES IN SCHEMA public
TO testuser;
db_test=# INSERT INTO tb_users VALUES (1, 'Sven Vermeulen',
'some@example.com', 'Some Place 10001, Somewhere', 'abc123',
```

```
 'f5ba94...3');
 db_test=# INSERT INTO tb_users VALUES (2, 'Lisa McCarthy',
 'lisa@example.com', 'Lisa Place 15, Someplace', 'def456',
 'ba53f2...0');
```

If we query the data through our test user, we can see all data added to the table:

```
 db_test=> SELECT * FROM tb_users;
```

Let's change the type of the phash column to sepgsql_secret_table_t:

```
 db_test# SECURITY LABEL ON COLUMN tb_users.phash IS
 'system_u:object_r:sepgsql_secret_table_t:s0';
```

This alone however will not prevent the testuser user from accessing the data. It will depend on how the testuser logs in to the database—from which context the session will be initiated. If we launch the session from an unconfined domain, then the session will still allow access to the data. Let's instead log in from a regular user session (user_t), and try to access the data again:

```
 db_test=> SELECT * FROM tb_users;
 ERROR:  SELinux: security policy violation
```

Even though the user has all the privileges within the database, we notice that the policy has prevented access. We can, however, query the columns not marked as sepgsql_secret_table_t:

```
 db_test=> SELECT uid, name, mail, address, salt from tb_users;
```

As the phash column is now marked as sepgsql_secret_table_t, we would still want the regular database user to be able to query if a hash matches the hash in the database, or set a new hash. This allows the database user to manage the accounts without easily leaking the password hashes. We do this through functions, which we will describe next.

Creating trusted procedures

PostgreSQL supports functions and procedures to facilitate isolating or combining actions within the database or on the data in a more structured and managed way. Procedures are allowed to do transactional updates in the database, but do not return a value by themselves. Functions return a value, but are not allowed to do transactional updates. In our example, we will create two functions, one to compare a hash with the stored hash (but without showing the stored hash to the database user) and another to update the stored hash.

> **Informational note**
>
> While we should be using procedures for the second function, not all PostgreSQL versions in use today support them. Support for procedures has only been included from PostgreSQL version 11 onward, whereas our examples use PostgreSQL 10.6, as that is the current version supported by CentOS 8.

Let's first create the two functions:

```
postgres=# CREATE FUNCTION compare_hash(fuid int, fphash text)
RETURNS boolean AS 'SELECT phash = regexp_replace(fphash,
''[^a-f0-9]*'', '''', ''g'') FROM tb_users WHERE uid = fuid'
LANGUAGE sql;
postgres=# CREATE FUNCTION set_hash(fuid int, fphash
text) RETURNS int AS 'UPDATE tb_users SET phash = regexp_
replace(fphash, ''[^a-f0-9]*'', '''', ''g'') WHERE uid = fuid
RETURNING uid' LANGUAGE sql;
```

We introduce a regular expression in the function to sanitize the input as we will be marking these functions as trusted later, and we do not want the functions to be a jumping ground for activities such as SQL injection.

Once the functions are defined, authorized users can use them to access the more protected data. Of course, we need to properly label these functions. In the default SELinux policy, the following types are available to deal with procedures and functions:

- `sepgsql_proc_exec_t` is the type to assign to regular functions or procedures. Once executed, the procedure will run within the current context of the user, so no transition will occur.

- `sepgsql_trusted_proc_exec_t` is the type to assign to trusted procedures or functions. Once executed, these functions will run in the `sepgsql_trusted_proc_t` domain, which has access to more privileged types such as `sepgsql_secret_table_t`.

- `sepgsql_ranged_proc_exec_t` is the type to assign to a trusted procedure or function, but with an additional privilege: ranged procedures are allowed to change the current sensitivity. Ranged procedure privileges are useful to assign to a function or procedure that can access columns labeled with a category that the current context would not be able to access otherwise. Once executed, these functions and procedures will run in the `sepgsql_ranged_proc_t` domain.

- User-managed procedures can be labeled with `unpriv_sepgsql_proc_exec_t` (for unconfined users) and `user_sepgsql_proc_t` (for confined users). These procedures and functions will continue to run in the user domain itself.

To get the currently assigned label for the function, use the `LIKE` statement as the functions are defined (in the `objname` column) with variables in their name. As such, they are not always that obvious to immediately select:

```
db_test=# SELECT objname,provider,label FROM pb_seclabels WHERE
objname LIKE 'compare_hash%';
```

Let's mark these functions as trusted:

```
db_test=# SECURITY LABEL ON FUNCTION compare_hash(fuid integer,
fphash text) IS 'system_u:object_r:sepgsql_trusted_proc_
exec_t:s0';
db_test=# SECURITY LABEL ON FUNCTION set_hash(fuid integer,
fphash text) IS 'system_u:object_r:sepgsql_trusted_proc_
exec_t:s0';
```

With these labels in place, the database user can execute the appropriate checks and changes even though the user has no access to the `phash` column itself:

```
db_test=> SELECT compare_hash(1, 'abc123');
 f
```

```
db_test=> SELECT set_hash(1, 'abc123');
1
db_test=> SELECT compare_hash(1, 'abc123');
t
```

Of course, preventing unauthorized users from accessing sensitive data is not something that PostgreSQL cannot do without `sepgsql`. PostgreSQL can have procedures and functions marked as running with the privileges of the owner of the function or procedure, rather than the executing session. What `sepgsql` provides is another means to accomplish this, or offer data protection through other security models.

For instance, in our example, the in-database permissions of the `testuser` account are still applicable, we are not granting the `testuser` account other privileges or escalating its privileges to a higher set – instead, we are using the SELinux labels and context information to additionally filter privileges.

Using sepgsql-specific functions

The `sepgsql` PostgreSQL module adds a handful of functions that we can use to interact with the labeling within the database:

- With `sepgsql_getcon()`, we can obtain the current context for the session.

- With `sepgsql_setcon()`, we can change the context of the current session, provided that the current context has the permissions to do so, of course.

- With `sepgsql_restorecon()`, all objects within the current database are relabeled back to the default setup. The function supports a single argument, which can be NULL, or be a reference to a file that defines the new defaults.

- With `sepgsql_mcstrans_in()` and `sepgsql_mcstrans_out()`, we can interact with the `mcstrans` daemon (if it is running), translating from a human-readable sensitivity range to raw (`_in()`) or vice versa (`_out()`).

These functions are useful when maintaining labels or defining functions that have logic included that depends on the context information.

Using MCS and MLS

The most common use case for enabling the `sepgsql` module is to use **Multi-Category Support** (**MCS**) and **Multi-Level Security** (**MLS**) support within SELinux to fine-tune access to resources.

Limiting access to columns based on categories

Suppose we use the range of category numbers from `c900` to `c909` to address specific PII datasets, and grant users access to these categories either by granting them direct access, or by using specific SELinux contexts to consult this data.

Within the database, we could mark the PII-sensitive data with a category number within that range:

```
db_test=# SECURITY LABEL ON COLUMN tb_users.mail IS
'system_u:object_r:sepgsql_table_t:s0:c903';
db_test=# SECURITY LABEL ON COLUMN tb_users.address IS
'system_u:object_r:sepgsql_table_t:s0:c903';
```

With the labels applied, a user that does not have access to this category will not be able to access the data:

```
db_test=> SELECT sepgsql_getcon();
user_u:user_r:user_t:s0-s0:c0.c100
db_test=> SELECT uid,name,mail,address FROM tb_users;
ERROR:  SELinux: security policy violation;
```

With the category range for the user set correctly, access to the data is granted:

```
db_test=> SELECT sepgsql_getcon();
user_u:user_r:user_t:s0-s0:c0.c100,c900.c904
db_test=> SELECT uid,name,mail,address FROM tb_users;
```

It is important to understand though that most domains will be allowed to switch their category set, as long as it remains within the allowed range:

```
# semanage login -l
Login Name      SELinux User      MLS/MCS Range      ...
...
taylor          user_u            s0-s0:c0.c100,c900.c903 ...
```

This means that, even when a user session for this user launches with a more limited category set (for instance, using the `runcon` command), the user will still be able to call `runcon` again to extend the category range, or use the `sepgsql_setcon()` function:

```
db_test=> SELECT sepgsql_getcon();
user_u:user_r:user_t:s0-s0:c0.c100;
db_test=> SELECT sepgsql_setcon('user_u:user_r:user_t:s0-s0:c0.
c100,c900.c903');
```

```
db_test=> SELECT sepgsql_getcon();
user_u:user_r:user_t:s0-s0:c0.c100,c900.c903
```

To remediate this, we need to have the target domain be MCS-constrained.

Constraining the user domain for sensitivity range manipulation

The SELinux policy always allows reducing the category range, so a range that initially includes the c900 category can always switch to a category range that excludes this category. The rules within SELinux that grant domains the privilege to reduce their category range use dominance rules, which are basically algorithms running mathematical set expressions on the source and target set: if the target set is fully enclosed within the source set, then SELinux will allow the range transition to occur.

The policy however also allows for extending the category range (if the range remains within the allowed range as defined by the SELinux configuration for the user), unless the domain itself is marked as **MCS-constrained**. The default MCS-constrained domains are generally those domains used for sandbox usage or virtualization, as we will see in *Chapter 9, Secure Virtualization*.

However, we can easily add more domains. For instance, to mark the user domain as MCS-constrained, load the following CIL policy:

```
(typeattributeset cil_gen_require mcs_constrained_type)
(typeattributeset cil_gen_require user_t)
(typeattributeset mcs_constrained_type (user_t))
```

This will prevent the user_t domain from growing its category range again.

Integrating SEPostgreSQL into the network

When we use the sepgsql module in PostgreSQL, all database sessions need to have a security context associated with them. While for local communications (which use Unix domain sockets) this context is readily available, networked sessions (which are the most common) do not automatically have a context set.

If the system does not participate in a labeled networking setup, as we saw in *Chapter 5, Controlling Network Communications*, interaction with the database will fail:

```
$ psql -U testuser -h ppubssa3ed db_test
psql: FATAL:  SELinux: unable to get peer label: Protocol not
available
```

To resolve this, the recommended approach is to start using labeled IPSec. However, we can also use NetLabel to introduce fallback labeling where needed.

Creating a fallback label for remote sessions

With Linux's NetLabel and CIPSO support (as seen in *Chapter 5*, *Controlling Network Communications*) we can introduce both fallback labeling (associating a label based on the source address), as well as use full labeling for localhost communication.

With full, local label support, NetLabel can pass the source context to the target if all this communication solely traverses over the loopback device (as such communication does not leave the system, allowing NetLabel to trace and support the flow from end to end and provide context information to the receiving service).

Let's create the CIPSO definition for local labeling:

```
# netlabelctl cipsov4 add local doi:2
```

We now create a default context for communication coming from the network (over the eth0 interface and the 192.168.100.1/24 network). It is this context that we will see when connecting to the PostgreSQL server over the network:

```
# netlabelctl unlbl add interface:eth0 address:192.168.100.0/24
label:user_u:user_r:user_t:s0
```

We can now remove the default mapping rules, and add mapping rules for the different communication types:

```
# netlabelctl map del default
# netlabelctl map add default address:0.0.0.0/0 protocol:unlbl
# netlabelctl map add default address:::/0 protocol:unlbl
# netlabelctl map add default address:127.0.0.1
protocol:cipsov4,2
```

The mappings we created will allow unlabeled communication for everything (but keep in mind that we have a specific label defined for communication coming from 192.168.100.0/24) and loopback-based full labeling on the localhost.

Tuning the SELinux policy

Next to the labeling configuration, we might also need to further fine-tune the SELinux policy for PostgreSQL. A couple of SELinux booleans are worth mentioning here:

- The `postgresql_selinux_transmit_client_label` SELinux boolean (disabled by default) allows the `postgresql_t` domain to set its own session contexts. The PostgreSQL server might want to set its own session context when the server itself has database connections to other, remote databases (for instance, using PostgreSQL's **Foreign Data Wrapper** (**FDW**) support). When enabled, the client context will be passed on to the remote databases as well.

- The `postgresql_selinux_unconfined_dbadm` SELinux boolean (enabled by default) grants administrative database privileges in `sepgsql` to any unconfined user domain.

- The `postgresql_selinux_users_ddl` SELinux boolean (enabled by default) allows unprivileged users to run **Data Definition Language** (**DDL**) statements. There are database statements that create new tables, views, and so on, and will result in user-oriented types such as `user_sepgsql_table_t` being used.

- The `selinuxuser_postgresql_connect_enabled` SELinux boolean (disabled by default) allows user domains to connect to the PostgreSQL daemon over the Unix domain sockets.

Don't forget to persist the boolean changes (using `setsebool -P`) as otherwise, a system reboot will revert the settings back to their default values.

Summary

The PostgreSQL database can be extended with SELinux support using the `sepgsql` module. The module adds label support to the various objects within a database, and checks access permissions between the session context and the target label. To obtain the session context, `sepgsql` relies either on purely socket-based communication, or labeled networking.

In this chapter, we learned how to enable the `sepgsql` module and how to troubleshoot possible policy issues. We then used the various default types within an example database and used these types to show how the access controls in `sepgsql` work. We then used SELinux's MCS support to further handle category-based access controls. Finally, we integrated PostgreSQL in a network using fallback labeling support.

In the next chapter, we will examine secure virtualization within Linux and see how SELinux contributes to the isolation of virtual guests.

Questions

1. Is SEPostgreSQL part of the default PostgreSQL technology?

2. What else needs to be additionally enabled before `sepgsql` can be used properly?

3. How do you set or query the labels on database objects?

4. Why are the `sepgsql` decision events not available in the system audit log?

9
Secure Virtualization

More and more system tools have built-in support for SELinux or use SELinux's features to further harden their own service offering. When we look at virtualization, libvirt is the reigning champion as a virtualization management tool, using the **QEMU** and **Kernel-Based Virtual Machine** (**KVM**) hypervisors.

In this chapter, administrators will learn what **secure Virtualization** (**sVirt**) is and how it is applied by the libvirt tool suite, which SELinux domains are put in place, and how sVirt uses SELinux categories to isolate guests from each other. We will study how SELinux can help reduce the risks of virtualization and understand how the SELinux policy is tuned to support virtualization services.

In this chapter, we're going to cover the following main topics:

- Understanding SELinux-secured virtualization
- Enhancing libvirt with SELinux support
- Using Vagrant with libvirt

Technical requirements

Check out the following video to see the Code in Action: `https://bit.ly/2T805Ug`

While it is possible to run the examples in this chapter on an older system, we recommend using a more modern system that has hardware support for virtualization. This will ensure higher performance during the exercises, as full emulation can severely hamper the progress, especially on older systems.

To verify whether your system has hardware support for virtualization (and can therefore use the Linux KVM-based virtualization), the following command should have output:

```
# grep -E 'svm|vmx' /proc/cpuinfo
flags    : fpu vme de ... vmx ...
```

If no output is shown, then the system does not support hardware-assisted virtualization.

Understanding SELinux-secured virtualization

Virtualization is a core concept that plays a part in many infrastructural service designs. Ever since its inception in the early 1970s as a means of isolating workloads and abstracting hardware dependencies, virtualization implementations have grown tremendously. When we look at infrastructure service offerings today, we quickly realize that many cloud providers would be out of service if they could not rely on the benefits and virtues of virtualization.

One of the properties that virtualization offers is isolation, which SELinux can support and augment quite nicely.

Introducing virtualization

When we look at virtualization, we look at the abstraction layers it provides to hide certain resource views (such as hardware or processing power). Virtualization contributes to the development of more efficient hardware usage (which results in better cost control), centralized views on resources and systems, more flexibility in the number of operating systems that the company can deal with, standardization of resource allocation, and even improved security services.

There are several virtualization types around:

- **Full-system emulation**: Where hardware is completely emulated through software. QEMU is an open source emulation software capable of handling full-system emulation, allowing administrators and developers to run virtual platforms with different processor architectures not otherwise compatible with their own systems.

- **Native virtualization**: Where main parts of the hardware are shared across instances, and guests can run unmodified on them. Linux's **KVM**, which is also supported through QEMU, is an example of this type of virtualization.

- **Paravirtualization**: Where the guest operating system uses specific APIs offered by the virtualization layer (on which unmodified operating systems cannot be hosted). Initial releases of Xen only supported paravirtualization. Using KVM with VirtIO drivers is another, more modular example.

- **OS-level virtualization or containerization**: Where the guest uses the host operating system (kernel) but does not see the processes and other resources running on the host. Docker containers or LXC containers are examples of OS-level virtualization.

- **Application virtualization**: Where the application runs under a specialized software runtime. A popular example here is the support for Java applications, running on the **Java Virtual Machine (JVM)**.

Many virtualization platforms support a few virtualization types. QEMU can range from full emulation to paravirtualization, depending on its configuration.

When we work with virtualization layers, the following terms come up frequently:

- The **host** is the (native) operating system or server on which the virtualization software is running.

- The **guest** is the virtualized service (generally an operating system or container) that runs on the host.

- The **hypervisor** is the specialized virtualization software that manages the hardware abstraction and resource-sharing capabilities of the virtualization platform. It is responsible for creating and running the virtual machines.

- An **image** is a file or set of files that represents the filesystem, disk, or other medium assigned to a guest.

- A **virtual machine** is the abstracted hardware or resource set in which the guest runs.

We will be using these terms in this chapter, as well as in *Chapter 10, Using Xen Security Modules with FLASK*, and *Chapter 11, Enhancing the Security of Containerized Workloads*, as those chapters also cover specific virtualization implementations and how SELinux actively provides additional security controls in them.

Before we embark on configuring and tuning virtualization services, let's first see what SELinux has to offer for virtualized environments.

Reviewing the risks of virtualization

Virtualization comes with a number of risks though. If we ask architects or other risk-conscious people about the risks of virtualization, they will talk about virtual machine sprawl, challenges related to secure or insecure APIs, the higher complexity of virtualized services, and whatnot.

Going over the challenges of virtualization itself is beyond the scope of this chapter, but there are a few notable risks that play directly into SELinux's field of interest. If we can integrate SELinux with a virtualization layer, then we can mitigate these risks more proactively:

- The first risk is **data sensitivity** within a virtual machine. Whenever multiple virtual machines are hosted together, you could have the risk that one guest is able (be it through a flaw in the virtualization software, the hypervisor's networking capabilities, or through side-channel attacks) to access sensitive data on another virtual machine.

  With SELinux, data sensitivity can be controlled using sensitivity ranges. Guests can run with different sensitivity ranges, guaranteeing the data sensitivity even on the virtualization layer.

- Another risk is the **security of offline guest images**. Here, either administrators or misconfigured virtual machines might gain access to another guest image. SELinux can prevent this through properly labeled guest images and ensuring that images of offline virtual machines are typed differently from online virtual machines.

- Virtual machines can also **exhaust the resources** on a system. On Linux systems, many resources can be controlled through the **control groups** (**cgroups**) subsystem. As this subsystem is governed through system calls and regular file APIs, SELinux can be used to further control access to this facility, ensuring that the cgroups maintained by libvirt, for instance, remain solely under the control of libvirt.

- **Break-out attacks**, where vulnerabilities within the hypervisor are exploited to try to reach the host operating system, can be mitigated through SELinux's type enforcement as even a hypervisor does not require full administrative access to everything on the host.

- SELinux can also be used to **authorize access to the hypervisor**, ensuring that only the right teams (through the role-based access controls) are able to control the hypervisor and its definitions.

- Finally, SELinux also offers improved **guest isolation**, which goes beyond just the guest image accesses. Thanks to SELinux's MCS implementation, guests can be separated from each other in a mandatory approach. With type enforcement, the allowed behavior of guests can be defined and controlled. This is a key capability used by hosting providers as they allow running (for them) untrusted guest virtual machines.

SELinux, however, is not a full security solution for virtualization providers. One main design constraint with SELinux is that it is not dynamic if the system itself is not SELinux-aware. When we assign a type to a virtual machine, this type is generally rigid and set in stone. Virtual machines will have different behavior characteristics depending on the software running on them.

A virtual machine running a web server has different behavior characteristics than one running a database or an email gateway. Although SELinux policy administrators would be capable of creating new domains for each virtual machine, this is not efficient. As a result, most SELinux policies will only offer a few domains usable by the virtual machine with broad characteristics.

With libvirt, these domains are part of the sVirt solution.

Reusing existing virtualization domains

When Red Hat introduced its virtualization solution, it also added SELinux support, calling the resulting technology **sVirt**, derived from *secure virtualization*. As secure virtualization as a term is hardly unique in the market, we use the term sVirt predominantly to refer to the SELinux integration within virtualization management solutions such as libvirt.

With sVirt, the open source community has a reusable approach for augmenting the security posture of virtualization and containerization through SELinux. It does this through the following domains and types, which can be used regardless of the underlying virtualization platform:

- The hypervisor software itself, such as `libvirtd`, uses the `virtd_t` domain.
- Guests (virtual machines) that do not require any interaction with the host system and resources beyond those associated with a generic virtual machine generally use the `svirt_t` domain. This domain is the most isolated guest domain for full virtualization solutions.
- Guests that require more interaction with the host, such as using the QEMU networking capabilities and sharing services, will use the `svirt_qemu_net_t` domain.

- Guests that use the KVM networking capabilities and sharing services will use the `svirt_kvm_net_t` domain. It is very similar in permissions to `svirt_qemu_net_t` but optimized for KVM.

- Containerized guests, as we will see in *Chapter 11, Enhancing the Security of Containerized Workloads*, will use the `svirt_lxc_net_t` domain, whose privileges are optimized for OS-level virtualization.

- Guests that require more flexible memory accesses (such as executing writable memory segments and memory stacks) will use the `svirt_tcg_t` domain. This flexible memory access is common for full virtualization guests whose emulation/virtualization requires the use of a **Tiny Code Generator** (**TCG**), hence the name.

- Image files that contain a guest's data will be labeled with the `svirt_image_t` type.

- Image files that are not in use at the moment will use the default `virt_image_t` type.

- Image files used in a read-only fashion will have the `virt_content_t` type assigned to them.

To enable some flexibility in what the domains are allowed to do, additional SELinux booleans are put in effect, which we'll cover next.

Fine-tuning virtualization-supporting SELinux policy

Use caution when toggling SELinux booleans to control the confinement of virtualization domains. Such booleans influence the SELinux policy on the host level, and cannot be used to change the access controls or privileges of individual guests. As such, when we change the value of an SELinux boolean, the change affects the permissions of all guests on that host.

Let's see what the various SELinux booleans are for virtualized environments:

- The `staff_use_svirt` boolean, if enabled, allows the `staff_t` user domain to interact with and manage virtual machines, as by default this is only allowed for unconfined users.

- The `unprivuser_use_svirt` boolean, if enabled, allows unprivileged user domains (such as `user_t`) to interact with and manage virtual machines.

- With the `virt_read_qemu_ga_data` and `virt_rw_qemu_ga_data` booleans, the QEMU guest agent (which is an optional agent running inside the guests, facilitating operations such as freezing filesystems during backup routines) can read or even manage data labeled with the `virt_qemu_ga_data_t` type. This type, however, is not in use by default, and these SELinux booleans are disabled by default.

- The `virt_sandbox_share_apache_content` boolean allows the guest domains to share web content. This is most commonly used for containers but is possible on guests as well if the hypervisor supports mapping host filesystems into the guest.

- With `virt_sandbox_use_audit` enabled, this boolean allows the guest domains to send audit messages to the host's audit service.

- The `virt_sandbox_use_fusefs` boolean grants the guest domains the privilege to mount and interact with **Filesystem in Userspace** (**FUSE**) filesystems. The `virt_use_fusefs` boolean allows the guests to read files on these filesystems.

- If the `virt_sandbox_use_netlink` boolean is active, then guest domains can use Netlink system calls to manipulate the networking stack within the host.

- With `virt_transition_userdomain`, containers can transition to a user domain (including the unconfined user domain `unconfined_t`).

- When we enable `virt_use_execmem`, guests can use executable memory.

- The `virt_use_glusterd`, `virt_use_nfs`, and `virt_use_samba` booleans allow guests to use network filesystems mounted on the host, offered through GlusterFS, NFS, and Samba respectively. Note that this does not involve mounts inside the guest itself, such as a guest that connects to an NFS server. The booleans handle interaction through filesystem mounts on the host.

- Device access is also governed through some SELinux booleans, such as the `virt_use_comm` boolean to interact with serial and parallel communication ports, `virt_use_pcscd` to allow guests to access smartcards, and `virt_use_usb` to grant access to USB devices.

- The `virt_use_rawip` boolean allows guests to use and interact with raw IP sockets, allowing network interaction that circumvents some of the processing logic within the regular network stack.

- With `virt_use_sanlock`, guests can interact with the sanlock service, a lock manager for shared storage.

- When `virt_use_xserver` is set to true, guests can use the X server on the host.

If security-sensitive operations need to be allowed for a single guest or a small set of guests, it is advisable to run those guests on an isolated host where these operations are then allowed while running the other guests on hosts where the policy does not allow these particular actions.

Administrators can also use different SELinux domains for specific guests, fine-tuning the access controls for an individual virtual machine. How we can assign specific domains depends on the underlying technology of course. In the *Enhancing libvirt with SELinux support* section, we will introduce this for libvirt-based virtualization.

Understanding sVirt's use of MCS

The SELinux domains and the mentioned types are not enough to implement proper confinement and isolation between guests. sVirt adds another layer of security by using SELinux's **Multi-Category Security** (**MCS**) extensively.

Within SELinux, some domains are marked as an MCS-constrained type. When this is the case, the domain will not be able to access resources that do not have the same set of categories (or more) assigned as the current context, as it will not be able to extend their own active category set—something we saw in *Chapter 8*, *SEPostgreSQL – Extending PostgreSQL with SELinux*.

The sVirt implementation ensures that the virtualization domains mentioned earlier are all marked as MCS-constrained types. This can be confirmed by asking the system which types have the `mcs_constrained_type` attribute set:

```
# seinfo -amcs_constrained_type -x
Type Attributes: 1
  attribute mcs_constrained_type
    container_t
    netlabel_peer_t
    openshift_app_t
    openshift_t
    sandbox_min_t
    sandbox_net_t
    sandbox_t
    sandbox_web_t
    sandbox_x_t
    svirt_kvm_net_t
    svirt_qemu_net_t
```

```
svirt_t
svirt_tcg_t
```

Through the MCS constraints, sVirt enables proper isolation between guests. Every running virtual machine (generally running as `svirt_t`) will be assigned two (random) SELinux categories. The images that virtual machine needs to use are assigned the same two SELinux categories.

Whenever a virtual machine wants to access the wrong image, the difference in MCS categories will result in SELinux denying the access. Similarly, if one virtual machine is trying to connect to or attack another virtual machine, the MCS protections will once again prevent these actions from happening.

sVirt selects two categories to allow a large number of guests to run even when there are only a few categories available. Assume that the hypervisor is running with the `c10 . c99` category range. That means that the hypervisor can only select 90 categories. If each guest only receives a single category, then the hypervisor can support 90 guests before allowing multiple guests to interact with each other (assuming a malicious actor found a vulnerability that allows that, of course, the hypervisor software will generally disallow such accesses as well). With two categories, however, the number of supported simultaneously running guests becomes 4,005 (the number of unique pairs in a set of 90, obtained through the formula $n*(n-1)/2$).

Let's see what libvirt's SELinux support looks like.

Enhancing libvirt with SELinux support

The libvirt project offers a virtualization abstraction layer, through which administrators can manage virtual machines without direct knowledge of or expertise in the underlying virtualization platform. As such, administrators can use the libvirt-offered tools to manage virtual machines running on QEMU, QEMU/KVM, Xen, and so on.

To use the sVirt approach, libvirt can be built with SELinux support. When this is the case and the guests are governed (security-wise) through SELinux, then the sVirt domains and types are used/enforced by libvirt. The libvirt code will also perform the category selection to enforce guest isolation and will ensure that the image files are assigned the right label (image files that are in use should get a different label than inactive images files).

Differentiating between shared and dedicated resources

The different labels for images allow for different use cases. The image used to host the main operating system (of the guest) will generally receive the `svirt_image_t` label and will be recategorized with the same pair of categories as the guest runtime itself (running as `svirt_t`). This image is writable by the guest.

When we consider an image that needs to be readable or writable by multiple guests, then libvirt can opt not to assign any categories to the file. Without categories, MCS constraints don't apply (well, they still apply, but any set of categories dominates an empty set, and as such, actions against those properly labeled files are allowed).

Images that need to be mounted read-only for a guest (such as bootable media) are assigned the `virt_content_t` type. If they are dedicated, then categories can be assigned as well. For shared read access, no categories need to be assigned.

Note that these label differences apply mainly to virtualization technologies and not container technologies.

Assessing the libvirt architecture

The libvirt project has several clients that interact with the `libvirtd` daemon. This daemon is responsible for managing the local hypervisor software (be it QEMU/KVM, Xen, or any other virtualization software) and is even able to manage remote hypervisors. This latter functionality is often used for proprietary hypervisors that offer the necessary APIs to manage the virtual resources on the host:

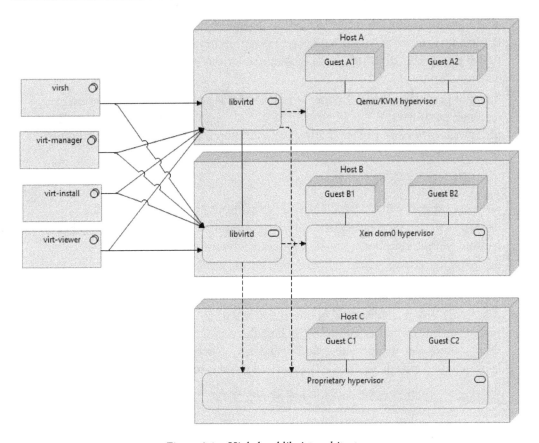

Figure 9.1 – High-level libvirt architecture

Due to the cross-platform and cross-hypervisor nature of the libvirt project, sVirt is a good match. Instead of hypervisor-specific domains, generic (yet confined) domains are used to ensure the security of the environment.

Configuring libvirt for sVirt

Most systems that support libvirt on SELinux systems will have SELinux support automatically enabled. If this is not the case, but SELinux support is possible, then all it takes is to configure libvirt to allow the SELinux security model. We map the SELinux security model in libvirt on a per-hypervisor basis.

The configuration parameters related to sVirt are generally defined on a per-hypervisor basis. For instance, for the QEMU-based virtualization driver, we need to edit the `/etc/libvirt/qemu.conf` file. Let's look at the various parameters related to secure virtualization:

- The first parameter, which defines whether sVirt is active or not, is the `security_driver` parameter. While libvirt will by default enable SELinux once it detects SELinux is active, we can explicitly mark sVirt support as enabled by setting the `selinux` value:

```
security_driver = "selinux"
```

  SELinux support will by default be enabled without explicitly marking the `security_driver` variable in the configuration file. If you want to use libvirt without SELinux support (and consequently without sVirt), then you need to explicitly mark the `security_driver` setting as none:

```
security_driver = "none"
```

- A second sVirt-related setting in libvirt is `security_default_confined`. This variable defines whether guests are by default confined (and thus associated with the sVirt protections) or not. The default value is `1`, which means that the confinement is by default enabled. To disable it, you need to set it to `0`:

```
security_default_confined = 0
```

- Users of the libvirt software can also ask to create an unconfined guest (and libvirt allows this by default). If we set `security_require_confined` to `1`, then no unconfined guests can be created:

```
security_require_confined = 1
```

We can confirm that sVirt is running when we have a guest active on the platform, as we can then consult the label for its processes to verify that it indeed received two random categories.

Let's create such a guest, using the regular QEMU hypervisor. We use an Alpine Linux ISO to boot the guest with, but that is merely an example—you can substitute it with any ISO you want:

```
# virt-install --virt-type=qemu --name test \
  --ram 128 --vcpus=1 --graphics none \
  --os-variant=alpinelinux3.8 \
  --cdrom=/var/lib/libvirt/boot/alpine-extended-x86_64.iso \
  --disk path=/var/lib/libvirt/images/test.
qcow2,size=1,format=qcow2
```

The locations mentioned are important, as they will ensure that the files are properly labeled:

- In `/var/lib/libvirt/boot` (and `/var/lib/libvirt/isos`), read-only content should be placed, which will result in the files automatically being labeled with `virt_content_t`.

- In `/var/lib/libvirt/images`, we create the actual guest images. When the guests are shut down, the images will be labeled with `virt_image_t`, but once started, the labels will be adjusted to match the categories associated with the domain.

The command will create a guest called `test`, with 128 MB of memory and 1 vCPU. No specific graphics support will be enabled, meaning that the standard console or screen of the virtual machine will not be associated with any graphical service such as **Virtual Network Computing** (**VNC**) but will rely on a serial console definition inside the guest. Furthermore, we have the guest use a small, 1 GB disk that uses the **QEMU copy-on-write** (**QCOW2**) format.

Once we have created the guest and launched it, we can check its label easily:

```
# ps -efZ | grep test
system_u:system_r:svirt_tcg_t:s0:c533,c565 /usr/bin/qemu-
system-x86_64 -name guest=test,...
```

To list the currently defined guests, use the `virsh` command:

```
# virsh list --all
 Id    Name        State
----------------------------
 1     test        running
```

The `--all` argument will ensure that even guests that are defined but are not running currently are listed as well.

> **Important note**
> Within libvirt, guests are actually called **domains**. As SELinux (and thus this book) also uses the term *domain* frequently when referring to the context of a process, we will be using *guest* as terminology when referring to libvirt's domains to keep possible confusion to a minimum.

The `virsh` command is the main entry point for interacting with libvirt. For instance, to send a shutdown signal to a guest, you would use the `shutdown` argument, whereas the `destroy` argument will force the shutdown of the guest. Finally, to remove a definition, you would use `undefine`.

As shown in the previous example, the guest we defined is running with the `svirt_tcg_t` domain. Let's see how we can adjust the labels used by libvirt for guests.

Changing a guest's SELinux labels

Once a guest has been defined, libvirt allows administrators to modify its parameters by editing an XML file representing the guest. Within this XML file, the SELinux labeling has a place as well.

To view the current definition, you can use the `dumpxml` argument to `virsh`:

```
# virsh dumpxml test
```

At the end of the XML, the security labels are shown. For SELinux, this could look like so:

```
<seclabel type='dynamic' model='selinux' relabel='yes'>
   <label>system_u:system_r:svirt_tcg_t:s0:c533,c565</label>
   <imagelabel>system_u:object_r:svirt_image_t:s0:c533,c565</
imagelabel>
</seclabel>
```

If we want to modify these settings, we can use the `edit` argument to `virsh`:

```
# virsh edit test
```

This will open the XML file in the local editor. However, once we accomplish that, we'll notice that the `seclabel` entries are nowhere to be found. That is because the default behavior is to use dynamic labels (hence `type='dynamic'`) with default labels, which does not require any default definition.

Let's instead use a static definition, and have the guest run with the c123,c124 category pair. In the displayed XML, at the end (but still within the <domain>...</domain> definition), place the following XML snippet:

```
<seclabel type='static' model='selinux' relabel='yes'>
  <label>system_u:system_r:svirt_tcg_t:s0:c123,c124</label>
</seclabel>
```

To run a guest with a different type is of course done in a similar fashion, changing svirt_tcg_t to a different type. However, keep in mind that not all types can be used regardless. For instance, the default svirt_t domain cannot be used with QEMU's full-system virtualization (as QEMU uses TCG if it cannot use KVM).

> **Important note**
>
> The default types that libvirt uses are declared inside /etc/selinux/targeted/contexts, in the virtual_domain_context and virtual_image_context files. However, it is not recommended to change these files as they will be overwritten when SELinux policy updates are released by the distribution.

The relabel statement requests libvirt to relabel all resources for the guest according to the guest's current assigned label (relabel='yes') or not (relabel='no'). With dynamic category assignment, this will always be yes, while with static definitions both values are possible.

Of course, if we want to, we can use dynamic category assignment with custom type definitions as well. For that, we declare type='dynamic' but explicitly define a label within a <baselabel> entity, like so:

```
<seclabel type='dynamic' model='selinux'>
  <baselabel>system_u:system_r:svirt_t:s0</baselabel>
</seclabel>
```

This will have the guest run with a dynamically associated category pair, while using a custom label rather than the default selected one.

Customizing resource labels

If the guest definition has relabeling active (either because it uses dynamic category assignment or on explicit request of the administrator), then the resources that the guest uses will be relabeled accordingly.

Administrators can customize the labeling behavior of libvirt through the same interface we used previously: guest definition files. For instance, if we would not want libvirt to relabel the `test.qcow2` file that represents the guest's disk, we could add to the XML like so:

```
<disk type='file' device='disk'>
  <driver name='qemu' type='qcow2'/>
  <source file='/var/lib/libvirt/images/test.qcow2'>
    <seclabel relabel='no'/>
  </source>
  <target dev='hda' bus='ide'/>
  <address type='drive' controller='0' bus='0'
           target='0' unit='0'/>
</disk>
```

This is useful when you want to allow the sharing of some resources across different guests, without making them readable by all guests. In such a situation, we could label the file itself with (say) `svirt_image_t:s0:c123` and have the guests with category pairs always contain the category `c123`.

Controlling available categories

When libvirt selects random categories, it does so based on its own category range. By default, MCS systems will have this range set to `c0.c1023`. To change the category range, we need to ensure that we launch the libvirt daemon (`libvirtd`) in the proper context.

With systemd, we saw in *Chapter 7, Configuring Application-Specific SELinux Controls*, that this can be accomplished by editing the service unit file and defining the right `SELinuxContext` variable. Let's apply this to `libvirtd` as well:

1. First, copy over the system-provided `libvirtd.service` file to `/etc/systemd/system`:

    ```
    # cp /usr/lib/systemd/system/libvirtd.service /etc/
    systemd/system
    ```

2. Edit the `libvirtd.service` file and add the following definition:

```
SELinuxContext=system_u:system_r:virtd_t:s0-s0:c800.c899
```

3. Reload the daemon definitions for systemd so that it picks up the new `libvirtd.service` file:

```
# systemctl daemon-reload
```

4. Restart the `libvirtd` daemon:

```
# systemctl stop libvirtd
# systemctl start libvirtd
```

5. We can now start our guests again and verify that each guest is now running with a category pair within the range defined for the `libvirtd` daemon:

```
# virsh start test
# ps -efZ | grep virt
system_u:system_r:virtd_t:s0-s0:c800.c899 /usr/sbin/
libvirtd
system_u:system_r:svirt_t:s0:c846,c891 /usr/bin/qemu-
system-x86_64 -name guest=test...
```

As we can see, the categories selected by libvirt are now within the defined range.

Systems that do not use systemd can edit the SysV-style `init` script and use `runcon`:

```
runcon -l s0-s0:c800.c899 /usr/sbin/libvirtd \
  --config /etc/libvirt/libvirtd.conf --listen
```

Every time we launch a new guest, the libvirt code will randomly select two categories. The service will then check whether these categories are part of its own range and whether the category pair is already used or not. If any of these checks fail, libvirt will randomly select a new pair of categories until a free pair matches the requirements.

Changing the storage pool locations

A very common configuration change with libvirt is to reconfigure it to use a different storage pool location. This has a slight impact on SELinux as well, as we do not have proper file context definitions for the new location.

Let's see how to create a new pool location and change the SELinux configuration for it:

1. List the current storage pools to make sure the new pool name is not already taken:

    ```
    # virsh pool-list --all
     Name                           State      Autostart
    -------------------------------------------------------
     boot                           active     yes
     images                         active     yes
     root                           active     yes
    ```

2. Create the target location:

    ```
    # mkdir /srv/images
    ```

3. Create the new storage pool with `pool-define-as`. In the following command, we name the pool `large_images`:

    ```
    # virsh pool-define-as large_images dir - - - - "/srv/
    images"
    Pool large_images defined
    ```

4. Configure SELinux to label the pool properly:

    ```
    # semanage fcontext -a -t virt_image_t "/srv/
    images(/.*)?"
    ```

5. Relabel the directory structure:

    ```
    # restorecon -R /srv/images
    ```

6. Have libvirt populate the directory structure:

    ```
    # virsh pool-build large_images
    ```

7. Start the storage pool:

    ```
    # virsh pool-start large_images
    ```

8. Turn on auto-start so that, when `libvirtd` starts, the pool is immediately usable as well:

    ```
    # virsh pool-autostart large_images
    ```

9. We can verify that everything is functioning properly with the `pool-info` command:

```
# virsh pool-info large_images
```

The output will show the current and available capacity for the new location.

If we host the storage pool on an NFS-mounted location, then we need to enable the `virt_use_nfs` SELinux boolean as well.

Now that we've fully grasped how to configure libvirt and SELinux for it, let's see how we can use the popular Vagrant tool with libvirt.

Using Vagrant with libvirt

Vagrant is a framework to quickly spin up and manage virtual machines and is very popular within development communities. While Vagrant uses Oracle VirtualBox as the hypervisor by default, we can install a libvirt plugin to use Vagrant with libvirt, benefiting from the sVirt security offered by SELinux.

Deploying Vagrant and the libvirt plugin

The Vagrant application can be installed from a single RPM file. Find the latest version at `https://www.vagrantup.com/downloads.html` and install it. For instance, for CentOS systems, you can use yum directly:

```
# yum install https://releases.hashicorp.com/vagrant/2.2.9/
vagrant_2.2.9_x86_64.rpm
```

To install the libvirt plugin, we first need to make sure that the dependencies are installed as well. The documentation, online at `https://github.com/vagrant-libvirt/vagrant-libvirt`, gives a good overview of which packages need to be installed. Do not forget this step, as dependency failures during the plugin installation are not always obvious.

Once the dependencies are installed, use vagrant itself to download and install the plugin:

```
# vagrant plugin install vagrant-libvirt
```

After installing the plugin, we can go forward with setting up a Vagrant box.

Installing a libvirt-compatible box

Vagrant uses **boxes**: images prepared for quick installation using Vagrant. Not all Vagrant boxes are compatible with the libvirt provider. Luckily, the Vagrant Cloud website at `https://app.vagrantup.com/boxes/search?provider=libvirt` allows you to quickly find compatible boxes.

Suppose we want to use a Fedora image called `fedora/32-cloud-base`, then we can configure it as follows:

1. Create a new directory, which we will define the box configuration in, and enter this location:

   ```
   # mkdir vagrant
   # cd vagrant
   ```

2. Initialize the Vagrant box, using the `fedora/32-cloud-base` box definition:

   ```
   # vagrant init fedora/32-cloud-base
   ```

   This will create an empty `Vagrantfile` that can be used to further configure the box.

3. Edit the `Vagrantfile`, and add the following code:

   ```
   config.vm.provider :libvirt do |libvirt|
     libvirt.storage_pool_name = "images"
     libvirt.driver = "qemu" # or kvm
   end
   ```

   This will configure the libvirt provider to use the `images` directory as the default storage pool, and use the QEMU driver within libvirt.

4. Still inside the `Vagrantfile`, add the following code to give the box a proper name:

   ```
   config.vm.define :test do |test|
     test.vm.box = "fedora/32-cloud-base"
   end
   ```

   The name chosen here is `test`, and will result in a virtual guest named `vagrant_test`.

5. To launch the test guest, run the `vagrant up` command like so:

   ```
   # vagrant up --provider=libvirt
   ```

   Depending on the speed of the system, this step can take a while to complete.

> **Tip**
>
> Rather than calling `vagrant` up every time with the
> `--provider=libvirt` parameter, we can also declare the `VAGRANT_`
> `DEFAULT_PROVIDER="libvirt"` environment variable and drop the
> command-line argument, as the environment variable will then be used.

Once the guest is up and running, you can connect to it using `vagrant ssh`. While you can manipulate the guest with the `virsh` commands, you can also use `vagrant halt` to shut down, or `vagrant destroy` followed by `vagrant box remove` to remove the box from the system completely.

Configuring Vagrant boxes

Once a box is deployed, it is available through libvirt as a standard guest. That means that the operations we've seen before to modify its labels or tweak SELinux controls using the SELinux booleans still apply.

Let's first verify that Vagrant is indeed using libvirt to launch its own boxes:

```
# virsh list --all
 Id    Name             State
-----------------------------
 1     vagrant_test     running
```

Sure enough, the guest is available and titled `vagrant_test`. We can modify its configuration with `virsh edit` as well:

```
# virsh edit vagrant_test
```

As long as the Vagrant box is not destroyed, the settings in libvirt will persist.

Summary

Virtualization is a powerful technology whose security posture can be augmented thanks to SELinux. With sVirt, the open source community has a powerful approach to isolate guests and ensure virtual machines are only able to access the resources they should.

In this chapter, we looked at virtualization and the risks associated with it. We discussed how some of these risks can be mitigated through the same set of controls that SELinux offers, such as type enforcement (limiting what guests can do) and MCS confinement (isolating guests from each other).

We then covered how libvirt supports several virtualization technologies on Linux platforms and how it includes a technology called sVirt that enables SELinux integration, offering guest isolation and access controls. We saw how administrators can manipulate the sVirt logic within libvirt, such as through different domain labels or category sets. We finished the chapter with information on how to use Vagrant with libvirt.

In the next chapter, we'll look at another virtualization solution, called Xen, which has adopted an SELinux-based technology for its hardening.

Questions

1. What is unique about sVirt that cannot be done with regular SELinux configuration?

2. What are the two main risks that SELinux tackles with virtualization?

3. What is the difference between `virt_image_t`, `svirt_image_t`, and `virt_content_t`?

4. How do you change guest labels with libvirt?

5. How can we use Vagrant yet still benefit from sVirt?

10
Using Xen Security Modules with FLASK

In *Chapter 9, Secure Virtualization*, we saw that libvirt is able to apply sVirt protection measures, based upon SELinux domains and category assignation, to several supported hypervisors. Xen, another popular open source hypervisor, is also supported by libvirt, but it is much more common to use Xen on its own, independent from libvirt.

Xen itself has a security framework called **Xen Security Modules (XSM)**, similar to **Linux Security Modules (LSM)**, and an access control system called XSM-FLASK, which is their SELinux-based security framework. We'll see how Xen uses XSM, how to build Xen with XSM support, and finally, how we can apply policies to Xen domains.

In this chapter, we're going to cover the following main topics:

- Understanding Xen and XSM
- Running XSM-enabled Xen
- Applying custom XSM policies

Technical requirements

Check out the following video to see the Code in Action: `https://bit.ly/3kcCePl`

Understanding Xen and XSM

The Xen Project is a Linux Foundation project that maintains the Xen hypervisor. While the Xen Project manages multiple security and virtualized-related software titles, our focus is on the Xen hypervisor.

Introducing the Xen hypervisor

The Xen hypervisor runs directly on top of hardware and sits in between the various virtual machines and the hardware itself. Unlike QEMU or KVM, which run as a process within Linux to offer the virtualization functionality, Xen works more independently. As a result, administrators will not see the running instances as separate processes. Instead, they need to rely on Xen commands and APIs to get more information and to interact with the Xen hypervisor.

> **Important note**
>
> As with libvirt, the Xen hypervisor uses the term *domain* to point to its guests. As we use the term *domain* frequently in SELinux to mean the SELinux type of a running process, and thus also the SELinux type of a running guest, we will use *guest* wherever possible. However, there will be some terminology associated with Xen where we will have to keep the *domain* terminology in place.

Xen always has at least one virtual guest defined, called **Domain 0 (dom0)**. This guest manages the system and runs the Xen daemon (`xend`). It is through dom0 that administrators will create and operate virtual guests running within Xen. These regular guests are unprivileged, and therefore abbreviated as **domU—unprivileged domains**.

When administrators boot a Xen host, they boot into Xen's *dom0* instance, through which they then further interact with Xen. The Linux kernel has included support for running both within *dom0* as well as *domU* for quite some time now (with complete support, including backend drivers, since Linux kernel 3.0).

Let's use an existing Linux deployment to install Xen, and use this existing deployment as Xen's dom0 guest.

Installing Xen

While many Linux distributions offer Xen out of the box, it is very likely that these deployments do not support XSM (which we will enable in the *Running XSM-enabled Xen* section). So, rather than fiddling with prebuilt Xen environments first, we want to build it from source as released by the Xen Project immediately.

Before we start using Xen, let alone its XSM support, we first need to make sure that we are running with a Xen-enabled Linux kernel.

Running with a Xen-enabled Linux kernel

The Linux kernel on the system must have support for running (at least) inside a dom0 guest. Without this support, not only will the dom0 guest not be able to interact with the Xen hypervisor, it will also not be able to boot the Xen hypervisor itself (the Xen-enabled kernel needs to bootstrap the Xen hypervisor before launching itself as the dom0 guest).

If you build your own Linux kernel, you need to configure the kernel with the settings as documented at `https://wiki.xenproject.org/wiki/Mainline_Linux_Kernel_Configs`. Some Linux distributions provide more in-depth build instructions (such as Gentoo at `https://wiki.gentoo.org/wiki/Xen`). On CentOS, however, out-of-the-box Xen support is currently missing from the last release (as CentOS focuses more on libvirt and related technologies for its virtualization support).

Luckily, the community offers well-maintained Linux kernel builds that do include Xen support, through the `kernel-ml` package. Let's install this kernel package:

1. Enable the **Enterprise Linux Repository** (**ELRepo**), which introduces several other, community-driven repositories:

    ```
    # yum install elrepo-release
    ```

2. Install the `kernel-ml` package, which will install the most recent Linux kernel, with a configuration that includes Xen support. We simultaneously enable the `elrepo-kernel` repository, through which this package is made available:

    ```
    # yum install --enablerepo=elrepo-kernel kernel-ml
    ```

3. Generally, the Linux boot loader will be reconfigured to include these new kernels. If not, or you want to make sure that the kernel is properly detected, the following command can be used to regenerate the **Grand Unified Bootloader** (**GRUB2**) configuration file:

    ```
    # grub2-mkconfig -o /boot/grub2/grub.cfg
    ```

Of course, if your system uses a different boot loader, different instructions apply. Consult your Linux distribution's documentation for more information on how to configure the boot loader.

4. Reboot the system using the newly installed kernel:

    ```
    # reboot
    ```

If all goes well, you will now be running with a Xen-compatible kernel. That, of course, does not mean that Xen is active, but merely that the kernel can support Xen if it is needed. Let's now move forward with building the Xen hypervisor and related tooling.

Building Xen from source

The Xen hypervisor and tools have dependencies on various programs and libraries, and not all tools and libraries are properly detected as dependencies while building Xen from source.

Let's first install these dependencies:

1. Enable the `PowerTools` repository:

    ```
    # dnf config-manger --set-enabled PowerTools
    ```

2. Install the dependencies supported by the CentOS repositories:

    ```
    # yum install gcc xz-devel python36-devel acpica-tools
    uuid-devel ncurses-devel glib2-devel pixman-devel yajl
    yajl-devel zlib-devel transfig pandoc perl-Pod-Html git
    glibc-devel.i686 patch libuuid-devel
    ```

3. Install the `dev86` package. At the time of writing, this package is not yet available for CentOS 8 so we deploy the version from CentOS 7 instead:

    ```
    # yum install https://download-ib01.fedoraproject.org/
    pub/epel/7/x86_64/Packages/d/dev86-0.16.21-2.el7.x86_64.
    rpm
    ```

With the dependencies now installed, let's download the latest Xen and build it:

1. Go to `https://xenproject.org/downloads/` and go to the last Xen Project release.

2. At the bottom of the page, download the latest archive.

3. Unpack the downloaded archive on the system:

    ```
    $ tar xvf xen-4.13.1.tar.gz
    ```

4. Enter the directory the archive is unpacked in:

    ```
    $ cd xen-4.13.1
    ```

5. Configure the sources for the local system. At this point, no specific arguments need to be passed on:

    ```
    $ ./configure
    ```

6. Build the Xen hypervisor and associated tools:

    ```
    $ make world
    ```

7. Install the Xen hypervisor and tools on the system:

    ```
    # make install
    ```

8. Reconfigure the boot loader. This should automatically detect the Xen binaries and add the necessary boot loader entries:

    ```
    # grub2-mkconfig -o /boot/grub2/grub.cfg
    ```

9. Configure the system to support libraries installed in /usr/local/lib:

    ```
    # echo "/usr/local/lib" > /etc/ld.so.conf.d/local-xen.
    conf
    # ldconfig
    ```

10. Create equivalence rules for the subdirectories in /usr/local so that SELinux file contexts are correctly applied:

    ```
    # semanage fcontext -a -e /usr/local/bin /usr/bin
    # semanage fcontext -a -e /usr/local/sbin /usr/sbin
    ```

11. Relabel the files inside /usr/local:

    ```
    # restorecon -RvF /usr/local
    ```

12. The result of these steps is that Xen is ready to be booted on the system. The boot loader will not use the Xen-enabled kernel by default though, so during reboot, it is important to select the right entry. Its title will contain *with Xen hypervisor*:

```
# reboot
```

13. After rebooting into the Xen-enabled system, all we need to do is to start the Xen daemons:

```
# systemctl start xencommons
# systemctl start xendomains
# systemctl start xendriverdomain
# systemctl start xen-watchdog
```

14. To verify that everything is working as expected, list the currently running guests:

```
# xl list
Name              ID      Mem    VCPUs    State      Time(s)
Domain-0          0       7836     4      r-----       46.2
```

The listing should contain a single guest, named `Domain-0`, which is the guest you just executed the `xl list` command in.

15. Finalize the installation by ensuring that the previously started daemons are started at boot:

```
# systemctl enable xencommons
# systemctl enable xendomains
# systemctl enable xendriverdomain
# systemctl enable xen-watchdog
```

Before we move on to XSM, let's also create a guest inside Xen (as a domU) so that we can associate policies with it later, in the *Using XSM labels* section.

Creating an unprivileged guest

When the Xen hypervisor is active, the operating system through which we interact with Xen is called dom0 and is the (only) privileged guest that Xen supports. The other guests are unprivileged, and it is the interaction between these guests and the actions taken by these guests that we want to isolate and protect further with XSM.

Let's first create a simple, unprivileged guest to run alongside the privileged dom0 one. We use Alpine Linux in this example, but you can easily substitute this with other distributions or operating systems. This example will use the **ParaVirtualized** (PV) guest approach, but Xen also supports **Hardware Virtual Machine (HVM)** guests:

1. Download the ISO for the Alpine Linux distribution, as this distribution is more optimized for low memory consumption and lower (virtual) disk size requirements. Of course, you are free to pick other distributions as well if your system can handle it. We pick the release optimized for virtual systems from `https://www.` `alpinelinux.org/downloads/` and store the ISO on the system in `/srv/` `data`.

2. Mount the ISO on the system so that we can use its bootable kernel when creating an unprivileged guest in our next steps:

```
# mount -o loop -t iso9660 /srv/data/alpine-virt-
3.8.0-x86_64.iso /media/cdrom
```

3. Create an image file, which will be used as the boot disk for the virtual guest:

```
# dd if=/dev/zero of=/srv/data/a1.img bs=1M count=3000
```

4. Next, create a configuration file for the virtual guest. We call the file `a1.cfg` and place it in `/etc/xen`:

```
# Alpine Linux PV DomU

# Kernel paths for install
kernel = "/media/cdrom/boot/vmlinuz-virt"
ramdisk = "/media/cdrom/boot/initramfs-virt"
extra = "modules=loop,squashfs console=hvc0"

# Path to HDD and ISO file
disk = [
   'format=raw, vdev=xvda, access=w, target=/srv/data/
a1.img',
   'format=raw, vdev=xvdc, access=r, devtype=cdrom,
target=/srv/data/alpine-virt-3.8.0-x86_64.iso'
]

# DomU settings
memory = 512
name = "alpine-a1"
```

```
vcpus = 1
maxvcpus = 1
```

5. Boot the virtual guest using the xl create command:

    ```
    # xl create -f /etc/xen/a1.cfg -c
    ```

    The -c option will immediately show the console to interact with, allowing you to initiate and complete the installation of the operating system in the guest.

6. When the guest needs to reboot, use shutdown instead, and edit the configuration file. Remove the line referring to the ISO to prevent the guest from booting into the installation environment again.

7. To launch the guest again, use the xl create command again. If the guest installation finishes and you no longer need to have access to the console, drop the -c option:

    ```
    # xl create -f /etc/xen/xa1.cfg
    ```

8. We can confirm that the virtual guest is running with xl list:

    ```
    # xl list
    Name                ID    Mem VCPUs        State      Time(s)
    Domain-0            0    7836    4       r-----         99.4
    alpina-a1           1     128    1       -b----          2.5
    ```

With Xen, guests are launched with the create subcommand and shut down with the shutdown (graceful) or destroy subcommands.

With these steps behind us, we now have a working Xen installation and a running guest. It's time to learn what Xen has to offer us from a security perspective.

Understanding Xen Security Modules

In *Chapter 1, Fundamental SELinux Concepts*, we learned that SELinux is implemented through a Linux subsystem called **Linux Security Modules (LSM)**. Xen has borrowed this idea and has a similar approach to its own security measures.

With **Xen Security Modules** (**XSM**), Xen makes it possible to define and control actions between Xen guests, and between a Xen guest and the Xen hypervisor. Unlike the Linux kernel though, where several mandatory access control frameworks exist that can plug into the LSM subsystem, Xen currently only has a single module available for XSM, called **XSM-FLASK**.

FLASK stands for **Flux Advanced Security Kernel** and is the security architecture and approach that SELinux also uses for its own access control expressions. With XSM-FLASK, developers and administrators can do the following:

- Define permissions and fine-grained access controls between guests

- Define limited privilege escalation for otherwise unprivileged guests

- Control direct hardware and device access from guests on a policy level

- Restrict and audit activities executed by privileged guests

While XSM-FLASK uses SELinux-like naming conventions (and even SELinux build tools to build the policy), the XSM-FLASK-related settings are independent of SELinux. If dom0 is running with SELinux enabled (and there is no reason why it shouldn't), its policy has nothing to do with the XSM-FLASK policy.

The labels that XSM-FLASK uses will also not be visible for regular Linux commands running inside the guests (and thus also dom0). As the running guests are not shown as processes within the system, they do not have an SELinux label at all, only an XSM-FLASK label (if enabled). Hence, Xen cannot benefit from the sVirt approach, as documented in *Chapter 9, Secure Virtualization*.

Running XSM-enabled Xen

Switching from a regular Xen deployment to an XSM-enabled Xen deployment is a matter of rebuilding Xen with XSM support and rebooting the system. Xen comes with an out-of-the-box policy that can be readily applied, which we will use as part of our XSM endeavor.

Rebuilding Xen with XSM support

Let's rebuild the Xen hypervisor and tools on the system with XSM support:

1. Clean up the previous build by running the `make clean` command inside the `build` directory (`xen-4.13.1` in our example):

    ```
    $ make clean
    ```

2. Inside the `build` directory, go to the `xen` directory:

    ```
    $ cd xen
    ```

3. Launch the Xen configuration using `make menuconfig`:

    ```
    $ make menuconfig
    ```

4. Navigate to the XSM setting and enable the XSM-related parameters:

    ```
    Common Features --->
      [*] Xen Security Modules support
      [*]    FLux Advanced Security Kernel support
      [*]       Compile Xen with a built-in FLAS security
                policy
      [*]    SILO support
               Default XSM implementation (FLux Advanced
               Security Kernel)
    ```

5. Go back to the main build directory (`xen-4.13.1` in our example):

    ```
    $ cd ..
    ```

6. Rebuild the Xen hypervisor and tools:

    ```
    $ ./configure
    $ make world
    ```

7. Install the updated Xen build on the system:

    ```
    # make install
    ```

    This will not only update the tools but will also provide an updated Xen kernel and an XSM policy inside `/boot` (named `xenpolicy-4.13.1`).

8. Reconfigure the boot loader with the new Xen build, ensuring that the XSM policy is also loaded with it:

    ```
    # grub2-mkconfig -o /boot/grub2/grub.cfg
    ```

9. Reboot the system:

    ```
    # reboot
    ```

10. Once rebooted, we can verify that the XSM policy is loaded and used by querying Xen for the labels associated with the running guests:

```
# xl list -Z
Name                    ID   ...      Security Label
Domain-0                 0   ...      system_u:system_r:dom0_t
alpina-a1                1   ...      system_u:system_r:domU_t
```

If the xl list command, given the -Z argument, lists the security labels, then Xen is running with an XSM policy active. Let's see where these labels are used.

Using XSM labels

When Xen boots with XSM support and has its default policy active, the following types can be used by guests:

- The dom0_t type is reserved for the privileged guest.

- The domU_t type is the default type to use for unprivileged guests.

- The isolated_domU_t type is the type to assign to unprivileged guests that should not be able to interact with other unprivileged guests, only with the privileged dom0 one.

- The prot_domU_t type is meant for guests that will be prevented from starting if the XSM policy boolean prot_doms_locked is set.

- The nomigrate_t type is applied to guests that are not allowed to be migrated from one Xen host to another. Internally, this prevents the dom0 guest from accessing the guest's memory once booted.

There are a few other types also available inside the XSM policy that are not meant for regular guests themselves:

- The dm_dom_t type is assigned to the device model guest. This is a special, privileged guest that represents the hardware virtualized for an HVM-type guest, without jeopardizing dom0.

- The xenstore_t type is assigned to the xenstore stub guest. This is a special, privileged guest that provides support for unprivileged guests to access their virtualized resources, without jeopardizing dom0.

- The nic_dev_t type is assigned to hardware devices that can be used in passthrough mode (meaning domU guests can directly interact with these hardware devices rather than going through the privileged guests).

These stub guests (**stub domains** or **stubdoms** as they are called in Xen) are a way for Xen to further increase its security posture, as privileged operations that cannot be prevented are more isolated from dom0. If at any point a security vulnerability can be exploited in these privileged services, they do not necessarily affect dom0 and, with a proper XSM policy, can even be mitigated fully.

Assigning one of these labels to a guest is a matter of editing the guest's configuration file inside /etc/xen and adding in the seclabel configuration parameter:

```
seclabel = 'system_u:system_r:isolated_domU_t'
```

Once configured and rebooted (using xl create), the new label will be visible when querying the running guests:

```
# xl list -Z
Name                    ID   ...     Security Label
Domain-0                 0   ...  system_u:system_r:dom0_t
alpina-a1                1   ...  system_u:system_r:isolated_domU_t
```

Applying the right label to the guest is the most common use case (as it effectively handles the access control and protection measures we seek from the XSM implementation), but other operations are supported as well.

Manipulating XSM

As with SELinux, several activities can be executed to further manipulate the XSM subsystem or the active policy.

Defining the state, ranging from disabled to enforcing

When Xen boots, we can add a kernel parameter called flask, which can be set to one of the following values:

- With flask=enforcing, we ensure that XSM is active, enforcing the policy between its guests and resources, and that the enforcement is immediate (no delayed activation).

- With flask=permissive, XSM will load the policy, but XSM will not enforce the rules set in the policy. This is obviously meant for development purposes and behaves similarly to SELinux's permissive mode.

- With `flask=late`, XSM will not enforce any access controls until a policy is loaded, after which the policy is enforced. This allows administrators to boot with XSM active, but only to load and apply a policy when the administrator deems it ready.

- With `flask=disabled`, XSM will not enforce any access controls nor load the policy.

This parameter can be set either directly when booting (from the boot loader) or through the boot loader configuration on the system. For instance, with GRUB2, we can edit `/etc/default/grub` and add or modify the following parameter:

```
GRUB_CMDLINE_XEN_DEFAULT="flask=enforcing"
```

Don't forget to regenerate the GRUB2 configuration file:

```
# grub2-mkconfig -o /boot/grub2/grub.cfg
```

As with SELinux, we can also manipulate the state of XSM through the command line. With `xl getenforce`, we can query the current state:

```
# xl getenforce
Enforcing
```

The `xl setenforce` command can be used to switch to another state:

```
# xl setenforce permissive
```

These commands have nothing to do with the SELinux configuration within dom0: switching Xen from permissive mode to enforcing or vice versa is specific to Xen and has no impact on the SELinux settings inside dom0.

Querying XSM logs

Like SELinux, XSM also uses AVC logging to provide feedback to the administrator about the decisions it has taken. With `xl dmesg`, we can query this log information (alongside the other Xen output logging):

```
# xl dmesg
...
(XEN) avc: granted { setenforce } for
domid=0 scontext=system_u:system_r:dom0_t
tcontext=system_u:system_r:security_t tclass=security
```

Not all granted operations will be logged, but denied operations will always result in an AVC entry. The AVC entries themselves are fully formatted like SELinux AVC entries, allowing administrators to use SELinux tools such as `audit2allow` to generate XSM policies.

Using XSM booleans

The default policy enabled by Xen has two booleans that can be toggled:

- The `guest_writeconsole` boolean, which defaults to 1 (on), allows guests to access and write to the Xen console.

- The `prot_doms_locked` boolean, which defaults to 0 (off), will disallow `prot_domU_t` guests from launching if enabled.

While no subcommand is available for the `xl` command to query and set XSM booleans, two other commands are installed on the system to accomplish this – `flask-get-bool` and `flask-set-bool`:

- With `flask-get-bool`, we can query the current state of a boolean, or list all booleans with their current value:

```
# flask-get-bool -a
guest_writeconsole: 1
prot_doms_locked: 0
```

- The `flask-set-bool` command is used to toggle booleans:

```
# flask-set-bool prot_doms_locked 1
```

This is very similar to SELinux's `getsebool` and `setsebool` commands.

Querying the XSM policy

The XSM policy file (`xenpolicy-4.13.1`) is quite similar to an SELinux policy file. As a result, we can use the SELinux tools to query this file and learn more about the policy:

- With `seinfo`, we can query statistics about the policy, view which classes are supported, the constraints that are enabled within, and more. The only query that fails is listing the types supported within the policy:

```
$ seinfo --all ./xenpolicy-4.13.1
```

- With `sesearch`, we can query the XSM policy rules themselves, for instance, to list all allow rules:

```
$ sesearch -A ./xenpolicy-4.13.1
```

When we discuss analyzing SELinux policies in *Chapter 13, Analyzing Policy Behavior*, we will get familiar with other tools that can also be used to analyze XSM policy files.

Labeling hardware resources

With the `flask-label-pci` command, administrators can label specified PCI devices with a given type. This approach allows administrators to mark certain devices for passthrough access by unprivileged guests.

For instance, to label the PCI device with address `3:2:0` with the `nic_dev_t` type, use the following

```
# flask-label-pci 0000:03:02.0 system_u:object_r:nic_dev_t
```

As you might guess from the name, this type is initially defined for passthrough access to network devices but can be used for other PCI hardware as well.

Applying custom XSM policies

Xen also allows administrators to build and use their own, custom policy.

The default policy for Xen is available inside the `tools/flask/policy` directory within the Xen build directory. For instance, the policy rules for the dom0 guest are available inside `modules/dom0.te`.

> **Important note**
>
> Adjusting the Xen XSM policy is beyond the scope of this chapter. You will find instructions on how to create SELinux policies using the reference policy-style method in *Chapter 15, Using the Reference Policy*. The Xen XSM policy is based upon this style.

Building a custom policy is a matter of updating these files (make a backup before you do) and then rebuilding the policy itself:

```
$ make
```

The result of the policy build is a new `xenpolicy-4.13.1` file. This file can be loaded directly using the `xl loadpolicy` command:

```
# xl loadpolicy /path/to/xenpolicy-4.13.1
```

This command is similar to the `flask-loadpolicy` command:

```
# flask-loadpolicy /path/to/xenpolicy-4.13.1
```

If, after testing, the policy is deemed ready to be used continuously, copy it over to `/boot` so that it is automatically picked up at the next boot as well.

Summary

The Xen hypervisor is quite different from the QEMU and KVM hypervisors, which are more readily used in libvirt. SELinux support for Xen is also different than sVirt as the SELinux subsystem can only be active inside Xen guests, and SELinux does not see other guests.

Xen has resolved that by implementing its own SELinux copy as XSM-FLASK and has integrated the appropriate support for the XSM-FLASK labels in its own tooling. In this chapter, we've learned how to apply our own types to Xen guests, toggle the XSM state, toggle XSM booleans, and even how we can build and load our own XSM-FLASK policy.

In the next chapter, we'll look at container workloads and how SELinux can help administrators to further harden and secure their container runtimes. We will see how sVirt can be applied to container runtimes, and how the tooling deals with SELinux support.

Questions

1. Why doesn't the regular SELinux subsystem govern Xen guests?
2. How are labels assigned to Xen guests?
3. What are the common Xen commands that deal with XSM labels?
4. How can administrators load a custom policy for testing purposes?

11
Enhancing the Security of Containerized Workloads

Container platforms and management frameworks provide application-level abstraction to administrators and developers. Lightweight container frameworks allow for rapid development and deployment of new applications, whereas heavier container platforms allow for optimal resource consumption and highly resilient hosting platforms.

SELinux plays a vital role in many of these frameworks and platforms, ensuring that untrusted containers cannot escape or interact with resources they are not supported to interact with. In this chapter, we look at how SELinux is supported, ranging from systemd-nspawn to podman (and Docker), and finally in larger environments with Kubernetes. We also learn how to create custom SELinux domains for containers using the udica utility.

In this chapter, we're going to cover the following main topics:

- Using SELinux with systemd's container support

- Configuring podman

- Leveraging Kubernetes' SELinux support

Technical requirements

Check out the following video to see the Code in Action: `https://bit.ly/34aHOfl`

Using SELinux with systemd's container support

In *Chapter 7, Configuring Application-Specific SELinux Controls*, we introduced systemd as an SELinux-aware application suite, capable of launching different services with configurable SELinux contexts. Besides service support, systemd has quite a few other features up its sleeve. One of these features is `systemd-nspawn`.

With `systemd-nspawn`, systemd provides container capabilities, allowing administrators to interact with systemd-managed containers in an integrated way, almost as if these containers were services themselves. It uses the same primitives as LXC from the Linux Containers project (which was the predecessor of the modern container frameworks) and Docker, based upon namespaces (hence the n in `nspawn`).

> Informational note
>
> **The Linux Containers project** has a product called **LXC** that combines several isolation and resource management services within the Linux kernel, such as **control groups** (**cgroups**) and namespace isolation. cgroups allow for capping or throttling resource consumption in the CPU, memory, and I/O, whereas namespaces allow for hiding information and limiting the view on system resources. Early versions of Docker were built upon LXC, although Docker has since embraced the Linux services itself directly without using LXC.

SELinux-wise, the software running inside the container might not have a correct view on the SELinux state (depending on the container configuration) as the container is isolated from the host itself. SELinux does not yet have namespace support to allow containers or other isolated processes to have their own SELinux view, so if a container has a view on the SELinux state, it should never be allowed to modify it.

Now, unlike Docker, podman, and Kubernetes, which can use the sVirt approach we saw in *Chapter 9, Secure Virtualization*, the systemd-nspawn approach does not support this technology.

> **Informational note**
>
> The systemd-nspawn command might not be installed by default. On CentOS, Debian, and related distributions, the package that provides this tool is called systemd-container. Other distributions such as Gentoo and Arch Linux have it installed as part of the default systemd installation.

Let's see how systemd-nspawn works and what its SELinux support looks like.

Initializing a systemd container

To create a systemd container, we need to create a place on the filesystem where its files will be stored, and then call systemd-nspawn with the correct arguments. To prepare the filesystem, we can download prebuilt container images, or create one ourselves. Let's use the Jailkit software, as used in *Chapter 7, Configuring Application-Specific SELinux Controls*, and build a container from it:

1. First, create the directory the container runtimes will be hosted in:

   ```
   # mkdir /srv/ctr
   ```

2. Edit the /etc/jailkit/jk_init.ini file and include the following section:

   ```
   [nginx]
   comment = nginx runtime
   paths = /usr/sbin/nginx, /etc/nginx, /var/log/nginx, /
   var/lib/nginx, /usr/share/nginx, /usr/lib64/nginx, /usr/
   lib64/perl5/vendor_perl
   users = root,nginx
   groups = root,nginx
   includesections = netbasics, uidbasics, perl
   ```

   This section tells Jailkit what it should copy into the directory, and which users to support.

3. Execute the `jk_init` command to populate the directory:

    ```
    # jk_init -v -j /srv/ctr/nginx nginx
    ```

4. Finally, start the container using `systemd-nspawn`:

    ```
    # systemd-nspawn -D /srv/ctr/nginx /usr/sbin/nginx \
      -g "daemon off;"
    ```

As Nginx will by default attempt to run as a daemon, the container would immediately stop as it no longer has an active process. By launching with the `daemon off` option, `nginx` will remain in the foreground, and the container can continue to work.

Using a specific SELinux context

When we launch a container directly, this container will run with the SELinux context of the user. We can, however, pass on the target context for the container using command-line arguments:

*   The `--selinux-context=` option (`-Z` for short) allows the administrator to define the SELinux context for the runtime processes of the container.

*   The `--selinux-apifs-context=` option (`-L` for short) allows the administrator to define the SELinux context for the files and filesystem of the container.

The SELinux types that can be used here, however, need to be carefully selected. The processes running inside a container cannot perform any type of transitions, so regular SELinux domains are often not feasible to use. Taking our Nginx example again, the `httpd_t` domain cannot be used for this container.

We can use the SELinux types that the distribution provides for container workloads. Recent CentOS versions will use a domain such as `container_t` (which was previously known as `svirt_lxc_net_t`) and a file-oriented SELinux type, `container_file_t`. While this domain does not hold all possible privileges needed for any container, it provides a good baseline for containers.

Let's use this type for our container:

1. First, we need to extend the `container_t` privileges with some additional rights for the `nginx` daemon. Create a CIL policy file with the following content:

    ```
    (typeattributeset cil_gen_require container_t)
    (typeattributeset cil_gen_require container_file_t)
    (typeattributeset cil_gen_require http_port_t)
    ```

```
(typeattributeset cil_gen_require node_t)
(allow container_t container_file_t (chr_file (read open
getattr ioctl write)))
(allow container_t self (tcp_socket (create setopt bind
listen accept read write)))
(allow container_t http_port_t (tcp_socket (name_bind)))
(allow container_t node_t (tcp_socket (node_bind)))
(allow container_t self (capability (net_bind_service
setgid setuid)))
```

2. Load this file as a new SELinux module:

    ```
    # semodule -i custom_container.cil
    ```

3. Relabel the files of the container with the `container_file_t` SELinux type:

    ```
    # chcon -R -t container_file_t /srv/ctr/nginx
    ```

4. Launch the container with the appropriate labels:

    ```
    # systemd-nspawn -D /srv/ctr/nginx \
    -Z system_u:system_r:container_t:s0 \
    -L system_u:object_r:container_file_t:s0 \
    /usr/sbin/nginx -g "daemon off;"
    ```

Whenever a container is launched, it remains attached to the current session. We can of course create service files that launch the containers in the background, or use session management services such as `screen` or `tmux`. A more user-friendly approach, however, is to use `machinectl`.

Facilitating container management with machinectl

The `machinectl` command allows administrators to manage containers or even virtual machines more easily through systemd. For containers, `machinectl` will use `systemd-nspawn`.

Let's use this `machinectl` command to download, start, and stop a container:

1. First, download a ready-to-go container image with the `pull-tar` argument and prepare it on the system:

    ```
    # machinectl pull-tar https://nspawn.org/storage/
    archlinux/archlinux/tar/image.tar.xz archlinux
    ```

We can also download the archive manually, and then import it using `machinectl import-tar`:

```
# machinectl import-tar archlinux.tar.xz
```

2. List the available images with the `list-images` argument:

```
# machinectl list-images
```

3. We can now clone this image and launch the container:

```
# machinectl clone archlinux test
# machinectl start test
```

4. To access the container environment, use the `shell` argument:

```
# machinectl shell test
```

5. We can shut down the container using the `poweroff` argument:

```
# machinectl poweroff test
```

When we use `machinectl`, the containers will run in the `unconfined_service_t` SELinux domain. There is currently no way to override this. Luckily, we have other tools available to facilitate container management that do have more significant built-in SELinux support, such as Docker and `podman`.

Configuring podman

The `podman` utility is the default container management utility on CentOS 8 and other distributions derived from Red Hat Enterprise Linux. Other distributions such as Gentoo can also easily get access to `podman` by installing `libpod`.

Selecting podman over Docker

When we compare `podman` with Docker, we might not see a big difference when we are simply using it for basic container management operations. The commands are very similar, and `podman` even has a Docker compatibility layer that facilitates the usage of `podman` for administrators who are used to working with Docker.

Under the hood though, there are quite a few differences. For one, podman is a daemon-less container management system, which allows end users to easily run containers within their confined space. The libpod project also uses different design principles and supports a different container runtime, which supports the **Open Container Initiative (OCI)**-based definitions, called the **Container Runtime Interface for OCI (CRI-O)**.

Let's use podman to deploy a PostgreSQL container on the system:

1. First, we need to find the appropriate container. We can use the podman search command for this:

   ```
   # podman search postgresql
   ```

2. Of the various PostgreSQL containers listed, we pick the Bitnami one:

   ```
   # podman pull docker.io/bitnami/postgresql
   ```

   This command will download the container base image to the system, storing the files in /var/lib/containers/storage.

3. We can now launch a container, assign a password to the PostgreSQL superuser (postgres), and make sure that the PostgreSQL port (5432) is made available to the system:

   ```
   # podman run -dit --name postgresql-test \
     -e POSTGRESQL_PASSWORD="pgsqlpass" \
     -p 5432:5432 postgresql
   ```

   This command will create a container definition, based on the container base we've just downloaded, and start it on the system.

4. We can use psql to validate that the database runs:

   ```
   # psql -U postgres -h localhost
   ```

5. When we're done with the container, we can stop it (using podman stop), which keeps the current container information, allowing us to revive it again later (using podman start) or remove the container from the system completely:

   ```
   # podman rm postgresql-test
   ```

6. Removing the container removes the container runtime, but the base container image remains on the system:

    ```
    # podman images
    ```

    This allows us to quickly start another container without having to download the files again.

Using containers is a fast and effective way to quickly install and deploy software on the system. Additionally, SELinux provides some additional protections to make sure that these containers do not misbehave.

Using containers with SELinux

When we look at the active runtime, we will notice that SELinux is already confining these containers in a way we understand:

```
# ps -efZ | grep postgres
system_u:system_r:container_t:s0:c182,c609 ... /opt/bitnami/
postgres -D ...
```

The running processes have two categories assigned and are executing in the container_t SELinux domain. This is the sVirt approach we saw in *Chapter 9*, *Secure Virtualization*. Unlike virtual machines though, containers are often used in a more transient way: when a new version of the container base is released, the containers are scrapped, and new ones are started. Virtual machines often undergo in-system upgrades, and thus have a longer lifespan.

The transient approach with containers also means that we need to provide data persistence in a different way. The approach that most containers use is to allow mapping locations from the host into the container environment.

Let's use podman to map a location outside the container to the /bitnami/ postgresql location inside the container, as needed by the PostgreSQL container:

1. First, create the location where we want to store the PostgreSQL data(base) on the host:

    ```
    # mkdir -p /srv/db/postgresql-test
    ```

2. Next, change the ownership of this location to the user with user ID 1001 (the user ID that the container uses internally):

    ```
    # chown -R 1001:1001 /srv/db/postgresql-test
    ```

3. Now start the container, creating a mapping from this location to the container:

```
# podman run -dit --name postgresql-test \
  -e POSTGRESQL_PASSWORD="pgsqlpass" \
  -v /srv/db/postgresql-test:/bitnami/postgresql:Z \
  -p 5432:5432 postgresql
```

This will have the PostgreSQL data stored in `/srv/db/postgresql-test`. If we later delete the container and create a new one (for instance, because an update for the container base has been made available), the database itself is not affected.

The mapping itself contains an SELinux-specific variable, namely the trailing `:Z`. If we were to omit this from the mapping, then the location would still be made accessible inside the container. However, the PostgreSQL runtime would not be able to use it.

> **Important note**
>
> The use of `:Z` in directory mappings (or **volume mounts** as they are also often called) is the most frequently forgotten option that system administrators are confronted with. Whenever SELinux is active on the system and the container runtime uses sVirt, you are more likely to need `:Z` (or `:z`, as we will see shortly) than not!

Containers are still part of the host operating system. When we create the `/srv/db/postgresql-test` location, it will receive the `var_t` SELinux type by default. Containers that want to use this location would require write privileges to `var_t`. However, this privilege is not one we want to provide. After all, the containers should be isolated as much as possible from the host—this isolation is what the sVirt technology is about after all.

Hence, we need to relabel this location accordingly. The SELinux type to use for generic containers is `container_file_t`. Moreover, we want to make sure that only the right container can access this location. Restricting and isolating access is what the `:Z` (with a capitalized Z) does in the command: labeling the directory with the `container_file_t` type and associating the right categories with it.

If we want to have a location accessible by *multiple containers*, we can tell `podman` to *share* the location, yet still be labeled with the `container_file_t` SELinux type. To accomplish that, we would use the `:z` argument (with a lowercase z), like so:

```
# podman run -dit --name postgresql-test \
  -e POSTGRESQL_PASSWORD="pgsqlpass" \
  -v /srv/db/postgresql-test:/bitnami/postgresql:z \
  -p 5432:5432 postgresql
```

Creating appropriate mappings is not the only approach where SELinux configuration comes into play. If we want, we can also tell `podman` to use different SELinux domains for the container as well.

Changing a container's SELinux domain

To control the SELinux context under which a container is launched, we use the `--security-opt` argument to the `podman` command. For instance, to run an Nginx container with the `container_logreader_t` SELinux domain, we use the following:

```
# podman run -dit --name nginx-test -p 80:80 \
  --security-opt label=type:container_logreader_t nginx
```

This domain is slightly more privileged than the default `container_t` domain, as it also has read privileges on log files. We could use this to have a web server expose the log files, for instance.

Other labeling options that we can pass on are as follows:

- The SELinux user, with the `label=user:<SELinux user>` argument.
- The SELinux role, with the `label=role:<SELinux role>` argument.
- The SELinux sensitivity level, with the `label=level:<SELinux level>` argument.
- The SELinux type for the files, with the `label=filetype:<SELinux type>` argument. This sets the SELinux context for the location mappings that have the `:Z` and `:z` suffixes set. The selected type must be an entry point for the container's SELinux domain.

There is also another option that we can use, namely `label=disable`. With this argument set, a container will run without any SELinux isolation. Now, it does not disable SELinux for the container, but associates an unconfined domain called `spc_t` with the container:

```
# podman run -dit --name nginx-test -p 80:80 \
  --security-opt label=disable \
  -v /srv/web/localhost:/usr/share/nginx/html nginx
# ps -efZ | grep nginx
unconfined_u:system_r:spc_t:s0 ... nginx: worker process
```

While for most use cases, the default `container_t` domain is sufficiently privileged, it might be too privileged for some. Luckily, we can easily create new SELinux domains specific to our use case.

Creating custom domains with udica

The `container_t` domain is configured to be widely reusable, which implies that it has many privileges for common use cases, which you might not want to give to each container. Furthermore, if we would launch a container but need to associate more privileges with it, then we would have to extend `container_t` with more privileges, resulting in all containers receiving this privilege extension.

To quickly build up new policies, a tool called `udica` can be used. The `udica` tool reads the container definition and creates a custom SELinux policy from it. We can then use this custom policy for this particular container, allowing other containers to remain untouched.

Let's use this for a Jupyter Notebook, which we want to grant read/write privileges to a (shared) user home directory location:

1. First, we create the definition of the container:

   ```
   # podman run -dit --name notebook-test -p 8888:8888 \
     -v /home/lisa/work:/home/jovyan/shared scipy-notebook
   ```

2. Next, inspect this container using `podman inspect` and store the results in a file:

   ```
   # podman inspect notebook-test > notebook-test.json
   ```

3. Use `udica` to generate an SELinux policy for it:

   ```
   # udica -j notebook-test.json custom-notebook-test
   Policy custom-notebook-test created!
   Please load these modules using:
   # semodule -i custom-notebook-test.cil /usr/share/udica/
   templates/{base_container.cil,net_container.cil}
   Restart the container with: "--security-opt
   label=type:custom-notebook-test.process" parameter
   ```

4. Load the custom policy as mentioned by the `udica` output:

   ```
   # semodule -i custom-notebook-test.cil \
       /usr/share/udica/templates/base_container.cil \
       /usr/share/udica/templates/net_container.cil
   ```

5. Stop and remove the container, and then recreate it with the parameter as mentioned in the `udica` output:

   ```
   # podman stop notebook-test
   # podman rm notebook-test
   ```

```
# podman run -dit --name notebook-test -p 8888:8888 \
-v /home/lisa/work:/home/jovyan/shared \
--security-opt \
label=type:custom-notebook-test.process scipy-notebook
```

The custom SELinux policy has the privileges to write to the home directory, as the container had a mapping from /home/lisa/work, and udica automatically created the permissions for it. If we wanted the container to only have read-only privileges, we could use a mapping with a trailing :ro (rather than :Z or :z for SELinux-specific changes). This would map the location inside the container with read-only access, and udica would only create read privileges for the associated SELinux type.

If creating custom policies is a bit too specific, we can also fine-tune the privileges of the container_t domain with the appropriate SELinux booleans.

Toggling container_t privileges with SELinux booleans

The container_t SELinux domain is associated with the svirt_sandbox_domain attribute, and through that association, will automatically be managed by several of the virt_* SELinux booleans that we saw in *Chapter 9, Secure Virtualization.*

There are a few container-specific SELinux booleans as well:

- With container_use_cephfs, containers can use CephFS-based storage. This is predominantly used when the containers are managed by larger container-cluster software such as Kubernetes.

- With container_manage_cgroup, containers can manage cgroups. This is needed when the container hosts systemd inside, which is often the case for full-blown container runtimes (rather than process-specific containers). Such containers host almost complete Linux systems.

- With container_connect_any, the container_t SELinux domain can connect to any TCP port.

Keep in mind though that these booleans influence the privileges of the container_t domain, and thus are in effect for all containers.

Tuning the container hosting environment

The podman utility will by default store its container volumes and base images in /var/lib/containers. Administrators can add more locations through the storage.conf configuration file available in /etc/containers. However, you need to adjust the SELinux configuration accordingly as well.

Suppose that the `/srv/containers` location will be used, then we need to create an equivalence rule to make sure that this location is labeled appropriately:

```
# semanage fcontext -a -e /var/lib/containers \
  /srv/containers
# restorecon -R -v /srv/containers
```

If the location is a network mount, you might need to change the appropriate SELinux booleans as well.

Leveraging Kubernetes' SELinux support

When containers are used in a larger environment, they are often managed through container orchestration frameworks that allow scaling container deployment and management across multiple systems. Kubernetes is a popular container orchestration framework with a good community, as well as commercial support.

Kubernetes uses the container software found on the machines under the hood. When, for instance, we install Kubernetes on Fedora's CoreOS, it will detect that Docker is available and use the Docker engine for managing the containers.

Configuring Kubernetes with SELinux support

Installing Kubernetes can be a daunting task, and several methods exist, ranging from single-node playground deployments up to commercially supported installations. One of the well-documented installation methods on the Kubernetes website is to use `kubeadm` for bootstrapping Kubernetes clusters.

> **Important note**
> The installation of Kubernetes is documented on the Kubernetes website at `https://kubernetes.io/docs/setup/production-environment/tools/kubeadm`. In this section, we will not go through the individual steps to set up a working Kubernetes instance, but give pointers as to which changes are needed for having proper SELinux support.

The `kubeadm` command, when initializing the Kubernetes cluster, will download and run the various Kubernetes services as containers. Unfortunately, Kubernetes' services use several mappings from the host system into the container to facilitate their operations. These mappings are not done using the `:Z` or `:z` options—it would even be wrong to do so, as the locations are system-wide locations that should retain their current SELinux labels.

As a result, Kubernetes' services will be running with the default `container_t` SELinux domain (as Docker will happily apply the sVirt protections), which does not have access to these locations. The most obvious change we can apply is to have the services run with the highly privileged `spc_t` domain for now. Applying this change however during the installation is hard, as we would need to change the domain sufficiently quickly before the installation fails.

While we can create deployment configuration information for Kubernetes that immediately configures the services with `spc_t`, another method can be pursued:

1. Mark the `container_t` type as a permissive domain before the installation starts. While this will prevent any SELinux controls on the container, we can argue that the installation of Kubernetes is done in a contained and supervised manner:

    ```
    # semanage permissive -a container_t
    ```

2. Run `kubeadm init`, which will install the services on the system:

    ```
    # kubeadm init
    ```

3. When the services are installed, go to `/etc/kubernetes/manifests`. Inside this directory, you will find four manifests, each one representing a Kubernetes service:

    ```
    # cd /etc/kubernetes/manifests
    ```

4. Edit each manifest file (`etcd.yaml`, `kube-apiserver.yml`, `kube-controller-manager.yml`, and `kube-scheduler.yml`) and add a security context definition that configures the service to run with the `spc_t` domain. This is done as a configuration directive under the `containers` section:

    ```
    apiVersion: v1
    kind: Pod
    metadata:
      name: etcd
    spec:
      containers:
      - command: ...
        securityContext:
          seLinuxOptions:
            type: spc_t
        image: k8s.gcr.io/etcd:3.4.3-0
      ...
    ```

5. During the Kubernetes installation, the `kubelet` service will be installed, which will detect that these files have been changed, and will automatically restart the containers. If not, you can shut down and remove the container definitions within Docker, and `kubelet` will automatically recreate them:

```
# docker ps
CONTAINER ID        ...        NAMES
548f0c3ed18e                   k8s_POD_etcd-ppubssa3ed_kube…
b7b1df2d0027                   k8s_POD_kube-apiserver-…
eecd4d4ad108                   k8s_POD_kube-scheduler-…
76da4910b927                   k8s_POD_kube-controller-…
# for n in 548f0c3ed18e b7b1df2d0027 eecd4d4ad108
76da4910b927; do docker stop $n; docker rm $n; done
```

6. Verify that the services are now running with the privileged `spc_t` domain:

```
# ps -ef | grep spc_t
```

7. Remove the permissive state of `container_t` so that it is back to enforcing mode:

```
# semanage permissive -d container_t
```

With these slight adjustments during the installation, Kubernetes is now running fine with SELinux support enabled.

Setting SELinux contexts for pods

Within Kubernetes, containers are part of pods. A **pod** is a group of containers that all see the same resources and can interact with each other seamlessly. Previously, in the *Configuring podman* section, we worked on the container level. The `podman` utility is also able to use the pods concept (hence the name). For instance, we could put the Nginx container in a pod called `webserver` like so:

```
# podman pod create -p 80:80 --name webserver
# podman pull docker.io/library/nginx
# podman run -dit --pod webserver --name nginx-test nginx
```

Unlike `podman`, Kubernetes does not rely on command-line interaction to create and manage resources such as pods. Instead, it uses manifest files (as we've briefly touched upon in the *Configuring Kubernetes with SELinux support* section). Kubernetes administrators or DevOps teams will create manifest files and apply those to the environment.

For instance, to have the Nginx containers run on Kubernetes, the following manifest could be used:

```
apiVersion: apps/v1
kind: Deployment
metadata:
  name: nginx-test-deployment
spec:
  selector:
    matchLabels:
        app: nginx-test
  replicas: 2
  template:
    metadata:
      labels:
          app: nginx-test
    spec:
      containers:
      - name: nginx-test
        image: nginx:latest
        ports:
        - containerPort: 80
```

This manifest is a Kubernetes deployment, and tells Kubernetes that we want to run two Nginx containers. To apply this to the environment, use `kubectl apply`:

```
$ kubectl apply -f simple-nginx.yml
```

As with the manifests for the Kubernetes services, we can tell Kubernetes to use a specific SELinux type:

```
...
spec:
  containers: ...
  securityContext:
    seLinuxOptions:
      type: "container_logreader_t"
```

The `seLinuxOptions` block can contain `user`, `role`, `type`, and `level` to define the SELinux user, SELinux role, SELinux type and SELinux sensitivity level.

Unlike the regular container management services (such as Docker or CRI-O), Kubernetes does not allow changing SELinux labels on mapped volumes (except on single-node deployments): when we map volumes into containers, they retain their current SELinux label on the system. Hence, if you want to make sure that the resources are accessible from a regular `container_t` domain, you need to make sure these locations are labeled with `container_file_t`.

Kubernetes does offer advanced access controls itself. Enabling volumes within the containers is also handled by a plugin architecture, with several plugins already available. When the plugin enables SELinux labeling, then Kubernetes will attempt to relabel the resource and assign the categories (as with sVirt). However, this support is currently only made available on single-node deployments (using the local host storage plugin)—and for such deployments, using `podman` is much simpler.

Summary

Containerized workloads allow administrators to add capabilities quickly and easily to a system, while retaining possible dependencies within a container. Each container hosts its own dependencies, allowing containers to be removed and added from the system without affecting others. With SELinux, this workload is further isolated from the host and, in case of sVirt protections, also from each other.

We've seen how systemd has container support but lacks sVirt-based protections, and how `podman` can apply sVirt protections on its own container environments. We learned that Docker and `podman` are very similar in usage, yet different under the hood. Both frameworks allow us to apply different SELinux types to the containers and resources, and with `udica` we've learned how to create custom policies without much development effort. Finally, we've seen how Kubernetes can be configured to use SELinux labeling as well.

With all these SELinux-capable technologies behind us, we are ready to tackle the SELinux policy development itself. In the next chapter, we'll learn to work with SELinux policies in depth and tune the policies to our needs.

Questions

1. Why is Docker or `podman` preferred over `machinectl` for SELinux?

2. How do we ensure host data is properly mapped within a container?

3. How can we create a custom policy from a container definition?

4. Where in Kubernetes' manifests can we place SELinux settings?

Section 3: Policy Management

SELinux behavior is defined by the policy. In this part, we cover policy changes and development, including the creation of custom policies.

This section comprises the following chapters:

- *Chapter 12, Tuning SELinux Policies*
- *Chapter 13, Analyzing Policy Behavior*
- *Chapter 14, Dealing with New Applications*
- *Chapter 15, Using the Reference Policy*
- *Chapter 16, Developing Policies with SELinux CIL*

12
Tuning SELinux Policies

Until now, we have been working with an existing SELinux policy by tuning our system to deal with the proper SELinux contexts and assigning the right labels to files, directories, and even network ports. We've learned that the behavior that SELinux enforces is defined within the policies. To fine-tune the policy enforcement rules, we have already briefly covered SELinux booleans.

It's time we look into SELinux booleans in more detail, learning how to look up the impact booleans have. Within this chapter, we then consider SELinux policy modules themselves and what options administrators have when dealing with these modules. Finally, we will look at how to update or even replace existing policies.

In this chapter, we're going to cover the following main topics:

- Working with SELinux booleans
- Handling policy modules
- Replacing and updating existing policies

Technical requirements

Check out the following video to see the Code in Action: `https://bit.ly/2T7MkVK`

Working with SELinux booleans

One of the methods of manipulating SELinux policies is by toggling SELinux booleans. Ever since *Chapter 2, Understanding SELinux Decisions and Logging,* where we used the `secure_mode_policyload` boolean, these tunable settings have been popping up over the course of this book. With their simple ON/OFF state, they enable or disable parts of the SELinux policy. Policy developers and administrators use SELinux booleans to toggle parts of the policy that not all deployments always need to be active, but some still do.

These booleans are added to the policy based on feedback from, and with the help of, the community at large. By establishing which policy rules are necessary against those that are optional, SELinux developers can provide an SELinux policy that works for a majority of systems, even when the uses of these systems differ.

Listing SELinux booleans

An overview of SELinux booleans can be obtained by using the `semanage` command with the `boolean` option. On a regular system, we can easily find over a hundred SELinux booleans, so it is necessary to filter them out for the description of the boolean we need:

```
# semanage boolean -l | grep policyload
secure_mode_policyload (off, off)
   Boolean to determine whether the system permits loading
   policy, setting enforcing mode, and changing boolean values.
   Set this to true and you have to reboot to set it back.
```

The output not only gives us a brief description of the boolean, but also the current value (actually, it gives us the current value and then the value pending a policy change, but this will almost always be the same).

Another method for getting the current value of a boolean is through the `getsebool` command, as follows:

```
# getsebool secure_mode_policyload
secure_mode_policyload --> off
```

If the name of the boolean is not exactly known, we can ask for an overview of all booleans (and their values) and filter for the one we need:

```
# getsebool -a | grep policy
secure_mode_policyload --> off
```

Another utility that can be used to view SELinux boolean descriptions is the `sepolicy booleans` command:

```
# sepolicy booleans -b secure_mode_policyload
secure_mode_policyload=_ ("Boolean to ...")
```

However, this command does not show the current value of the boolean.

Finally, booleans are also represented through the `/sys/fs/selinux` filesystem:

```
# cat /sys/fs/selinux/booleans/secure_mode_policyload
0 0
```

Here, booleans can be read as if they were regular files, and they return two values:

- The first value is the current state of the boolean, where `0` means OFF and `1` means ON.
- The second value is the pending state of the boolean.

A pending state allows administrators to change multiple boolean values simultaneously, but only when manipulating booleans through the `/sys/fs/selinux` filesystem, as we will see next.

Changing boolean values

We can change the value of a boolean using the `setsebool` command. For instance, to toggle the `httpd_can_sendmail` SELinux boolean, we can use the following command:

```
# setsebool httpd_can_sendmail on
```

Some Linux distributions might also have the `togglesebool` command available. This command will flip the value of the boolean, so ON becomes OFF, and OFF becomes ON:

```
# togglesebool httpd_can_sendmail
```

SELinux booleans have a default state defined by the policy administrator (and thus the default SELinux policy active on the system). Changing the value using `setsebool` updates the current active access controls, but this does not persist across reboots (if we toggle the boolean, then after rebooting, the old value will be used again).

In order to keep the changes permanently, add the `-P` option to the `setsebool` command as follows:

```
# setsebool -P httpd_can_sendmail off
```

In the background, the updated SELinux boolean value is included in the policy store. Then, the current policy file is rebuilt and loaded. As a result, the policy file (called `policy.##` with ## representing an integer value) residing in `/etc/selinux/targeted/policy` will be regenerated. This regeneration takes time, which is why switching a boolean value persistently (using `-P`) takes more time to complete than when we change a value without persisting it (using `setsebool` without `-P` or `toggleseboo1`) to the policy store.

Another way to change and persist the boolean settings is to use the `semanage boolean` command as follows:

```
# semanage boolean -m --on httpd_can_sendmail
```

In this case, we modify (`-m`) the boolean value and set it to ON (`--on`).

Booleans can also be changed through their `/sys/fs/selinux/booleans` representation. When this happens, the boolean value is not immediately activated – the change of the value is pending. This allows administrators to modify multiple booleans through `/sys/fs/selinux/booleans` first:

```
# echo 0 > /sys/fs/selinux/booleans/httpd_can_sendmail
# getsebool httpd_can_sendmail
httpd_can_sendmail --> on pending: off
```

To commit the changes, write the value 1 into `/sys/fs/selinux/commit_pending_bools`:

```
# echo 1 > /sys/fs/selinux/commit_pending_bools
```

As long as you modify booleans through the `semanage` or `setsebool` commands though, the changes will immediately be committed. Only operations through the `/sys/fs/selinux` structure allow pending boolean changes.

Inspecting the impact of a boolean

To discover which policy rules a boolean manipulates, the description usually suffices. Sometimes though, we might want to know which SELinux rules change when we alter a boolean value. With the `sesearch` application, we can query the SELinux policy, displaying the rules affected by a given boolean. To show this information in detail, we use the `-b` option (for the boolean) and `-A` option (to show all `allow` rules):

```
# sesearch -b httpd_can_sendmail -A
allow httpd_suexec_t bin_t:dir { getattr open search }; [
httpd_can_sendmail ]:True
...
allow system_mail_t httpd_t:process sigchld; [ httpd_can_
sendmail ]:True
```

When we query the SELinux policy directly, conditional rules can be shown as part of the output:

```
# sesearch -s system_mail_t -t httpd_t -A
allow domain domain:key { link search };
allow system_mail_t httpd_t:fd use; [ httpd_can_sendmail ]:True
...
```

When `allow` rules are suffixed with an SELinux boolean between square brackets followed by `:True`, then these rules are only applied if the boolean is active. If the boolean is followed by `:False`, then the rule is applied if the boolean is not active.

Not all situations can be perfectly defined by policy writers though. Sometimes we will need to create our own SELinux policy modules and load those. Let's see how we can handle SELinux policy modules specifically.

Handling policy modules

When the system loads the SELinux policy in memory, it uses the `policy.##` file, with `##` representing the policy version, as explained at the end of *Chapter 1, Fundamental SELinux Concepts*. This file, which resides in `/etc/selinux/targeted/policy`, is generated every time the policy is modified. This can be when booleans are changed (and persisted), or when SELinux policy modules are added or removed.

Listing policy modules

SELinux policy modules are sets of SELinux rules that can be loaded and unloaded. These modules, with .pp or .cil suffixes, can be loaded and unloaded as needed by the administrator. Once loaded, the policy module is made part of the SELinux policy store, and will be loaded even after a system reboot. Unlike SELinux boolean changes, SELinux policy module loads are always persisted.

To list the currently loaded SELinux policy modules, we recommend using the semodule command. By default, semodule will show all loaded SELinux policy modules without any details:

```
# semodule -l
abrt
accountsd
...
zosremote
```

SELinux policy modules can, however, be loaded at a specified priority. This allows administrators to load a policy that overrules an already loaded policy: SELinux policy modules with a higher **policy module priority** take precedence over similarly named SELinux policy modules with lower priorities. To see the current priorities, use the --list-modules=full argument:

```
# semodule --list-modules=full
100 abrt        pp
100 accountsd   pp
...
400 test        cil
...
100 zosremote   pp
```

Alongside the priority, the listing also shows whether the policy module is based upon the binary module format (pp) or the more modern **Common Intermediate Language** (**CIL**) format (cil).

The SELinux utilities will copy the active policy modules into a policy-specific location. This allows administrators to list the currently active modules through regular filesystem queries as well:

```
# ls /var/lib/selinux/targeted/active/modules/*
/var/lib/selinux/targeted/active/modules/100:
abrt
accountsd
```

```
. . .
/var/lib/selinux/targeted/active/modules/400:
test
```

The use of the filesystem location for querying active policies is, however, not recommended, as we have no guarantee that the loaded policies match the filesystem: non-SELinux utilities can add or remove files from these locations without adjusting the SELinux policy state.

Loading and removing policy modules

In the *Replacing and updating existing policies* section, we will learn how to generate new policy modules. Once created, they need to be loaded and/or removed. We load policy modules with semodule as well, regardless of the policy format (.pp or .cil):

```
# semodule -i screen.pp
```

By default, SELinux policy modules are loaded at the 400 priority when invoked by the administrator, whereas SELinux policy modules loaded as part of the default system policy will be loaded at the 100 priority. When loading policies, the priority can be adjusted using the -X option. For instance, to load the test.cil policy with a priority of 500 we use the -X option as follows:

```
# semodule -X 500 -i test.cil
libsemanage.semanage_direct_install_info: Overriding test
module at lower priority 400 with module at priority 500.
```

To remove a policy module with semodule, use the --remove or -r option. In this case, we are not referring to an SELinux policy module *file*, but to the *name* of the module itself as displayed by semodule. Hence, we do not need to pass on a suffix:

```
# semodule -r test
```

To remove an SELinux policy module from a specified priority, use the -X option:

```
# semodule -X 500 -r test
libsemanage.semanage_direct_remove_key: test module at priority
400 is now active.
```

The order of the arguments is important: the -X option will set the priority for the actions that follow it, not those that precede it. If it is not set, then a priority value of 400 will be used.

Finally, it is possible to keep an SELinux policy module but disable it. This keeps the module in the policy store, but disables all the SELinux policy rules inside of it. We use the `--disable` (or `-d`) option to accomplish this:

```
# semodule -d screen
```

To re-enable the policy, use the `--enable` (or `-e`) option:

```
# semodule -e screen
```

The disabled and enabled states of SELinux policy modules persist through reboots as well. Furthermore, if you are disabling an SELinux module, all instances of that module (including lower priority ones) will be disabled.

Disabling policies is strongly recommended when the policy module is part of the distribution's SELinux policy, as the modules themselves are not always available on the system and might require a reinstallation of the policy package just to get it back.

With loading and unloading policies explained, let's see how we can generate updates on the current SELinux policy.

Replacing and updating existing policies

When we replace or update existing policies, we need to load them using the `semodule` commands, as shown in the *Handling policy modules* section. But how do we create or update the policies, exactly? Let's consider a few use cases where SELinux policy adjustments are triggered.

Creating policies using audit2allow

When SELinux prevents certain actions, we know it will log the appropriate denial (assuming no `dontaudit` statements are defined) in the audit logs. This denial can be used as the source to generate a custom SELinux policy that allows the activity.

Consider the following denial, which occurred when a confined user called `su` to switch to the root user:

```
type=AVC msg=audit(...): avc: denied { write }
for pid=58002 comm="su" name="btmp" dev="vda1"
ino=4213650 scontext=staff_u:staff_r:staff_t:s0
tcontext=system_u:object_r:faillog_t:s0 tclass=file
permissive=0
```

If we are certain that these operations need to be granted, then we can use the `audit2allow` command to generate a policy module for us that allows these activities. The **audit2allow** application transforms a denial (or set of denials) into SELinux `allow` rules. These rules can then be saved in a file, ready to be built into an SELinux policy module, which can then be loaded.

To generate SELinux policy `allow` rules, pipe the denials through the `audit2allow` application:

```
# grep btmp /var/log/audit/audit.log | audit2allow
#============ staff_t ============
allow staff_t faillog_t:file write;
```

Based on the denials, `audit2allow` prepared an `allow` rule. We can also ask `audit2allow` to immediately create an SELinux policy module:

```
# grep btmp /var/log/audit/audit.log | audit2allow -M
localpolicy
************ IMPORTANT ************
To make this policy package active, execute:
semodule -i localpolicy.pp
```

A file called `localpolicy.pp` will be available in the current directory, which we can load using the `semodule` command. The source file will also be present, named `localpolicy.te`.

If the denials that occurred are considered cosmetic in nature (meaning that the system functions as expected and the denials should not cause any updates on the policy), you can use `audit2allow` to generate `dontaudit` rules rather than `allow` rules. In that case, the denials will no longer be visible in the audit logs, while still preventing the actions from taking place:

```
# grep btmp /var/log/audit/audit.log | audit2allow -D -M
localpolicy
```

It is likely, after including the necessary rules, that the action will result in more denials that were not previously triggered. As long as the previous AVC denials are still available in the audit logs, it is sufficient to regenerate the policy and continue. After all, `audit2allow` will consider all AVC denials that it encountered, regardless of the current SELinux policy state.

Another popular approach is to put the system (or the application domain) in permissive mode to generate and fill up the audit logs with all the AVC denials related to the action. Although this generates more AVC denials to work with, it could also result in wrong decisions by the `audit2allow` command. Hence, always verify the denials before generating new policy constructs, and review the generated policy to make sure that it will enforce the right set of access controls and not grant more privileges than needed.

When the previous AVC denials are no longer available inside the audit log, a new policy module will need to be generated, as otherwise the previously fixed accesses will be denied again: the newly generated policy will no longer contain the `allow` rules from before, and when we load the new policy, the old policy is no longer active.

Using sensible module names

In the previous section, we used the `audit2allow` command to generate a policy module named `localpolicy`. However, this name does not reveal what the purpose of the module is.

Once we create a (binary) policy (such as the `localpolicy.pp` file) and load it, it is not always clear to the administrators and users at first glance what this module is meant to accomplish. Although it is possible to unpack the `.pp` file (using `semodule_unpackage`) and then disassemble the resulting `.mod` file into a `.te` file, it requires software not available on most distributions (the `dismod` application, for instance, part of the `checkpolicy` software, is often not included). Considering that we just want to get insights into the rules that are part of a module, this is a very elaborate and time-intensive approach.

The content of a module can also be somewhat deduced from its CIL code. For instance, an active `screen` module will have its code available at `/var/lib/selinux/targeted/active/modules/100/screen`, in a file called `cil`. On some distributions, this file will be a compressed file, so you might need to unzip it before viewing:

```
# file screen/cil
cil: bzip2 compressed data, block size = 500k
# bzcat screen/cil
(typealias secadm_screen_home_t
...
```

Still, having to dive into the rules to know what `localpolicy` is about is not only very cumbersome, but also requires sufficient privileges to be able to read these files.

Instead, it is a best practice to name the generated modules for their intended purposes. An SELinux policy that fixes a few AVC denials that come up when `su` executes from within the `staff_t` domain would be best named `custom_staff_su_faillog`, for instance.

It is also recommended to prefix (or suffix) the custom policies, so they can be more easily found:

```
# semodule -l | grep ^custom_
custom_staff_su_faillog
```

This identifies that the policy module has been added by the administrator (or organization) and is not sourced from the default Linux distribution's policy.

Generating reference policy style modules with audit2allow

The reference policy project provides distributions and policy writers with a set of functions that simplify the development of SELinux policies. As an example, let's see what the reference policy functions (called **macros**) can do with the `su` situation:

```
# grep btmp /var/log/audit/audit.log | audit2allow -R
require {
   type staff_t;
}
#============= staff_t =============
auth_rw_faillog(staff_t)
```

The rule in the example is `auth_rw_faillog(staff_t)`. This is a reference policy macro that explains an SELinux rule (or set of rules) in a more human-readable way. In this case, it allows the `staff_t` domain to read/write on `faillog_t` labeled resources. The `faillog_t` type is part of the system authentication SELinux policy (as suggested by the `auth_` prefix, which identifies the source SELinux policy module).

> **Important note**
>
> As `audit2allow -R` uses an automated approach for finding potential functions, we need to review the results carefully. Sometimes it selects a method that creates far more privileges for a domain than needed.

All major distributions base their SELinux policies upon the macros and content provided by the reference policy. The list of methods we can call while building SELinux policies is available on the local filesystem, at `/usr/share/doc/selinux-policy/html`.

These named methods bundle a set of rules related to the functionality that SELinux policy administrators want to enable. For instance, the `storage_read_tape()` method allows us to enhance an SELinux policy, providing a given domain with read access to tape storage devices.

Building reference policy - style modules

If we generate an SELinux policy using reference policy macros but do not have access to the binary policy module anymore, then we need to build the policy before loading it. CIL-based policies can be loaded directly, which is why this book uses CIL as much as possible. However, given the wide use of the reference policy, knowing how to build these modules is important as well.

Suppose that the *reference policy*-based SELinux policy code resides in a file called `custom_staff_su_faillog.te`, then we can build it into a `.pp` file as follows:

```
# make -f /usr/share/selinux/devel/Makefile custom_staff_su_
faillog.pp
Compiling targeted custom_staff_su_faillog.pp policy package
rm tmp/custom_staff_su_faillog.mod tmp/custom_staff_su_faillog.
mod.fc
```

Once built, we can load it using `semodule`. Every time we change the policy code (in the `.te` file) or other policy information (such as file context definitions in the `.fc` file), we need to rebuild the `.pp` file before we can load it.

Building legacy-style modules

If we ask `audit2allow` to generate the policy rules without using reference policy style macros (which we call a *legacy-style* SELinux policy), then building the `.pp` file from it requires a different approach.

Suppose we have the `.te` file as generated by `audit2allow -M`, but not the `.pp` file, then we can generate it as follows:

1. First, create the `.mod` file using `checkmodule`:

    ```
    # checkmodule -M -m -o custom_nonrefpol.mod \
      custom_nonrefpol.te
    ```

2. Next, generate the `.pp` file using `semodule_package`:

```
# semodule_package -o custom_nonrefpol.pp \
  -m custom_nonrefpol.mod
```

If an `.fc` file (which contains file context definitions) is present, use the `-f` option:

```
# semodule_package -o custom_nonrefpol.pp \
  -m custom_nonrefpol.mod -f custom_nonrefpol.fc
```

The `audit2allow` command will automatically execute these commands, so this is only needed if the `.pp` file is no longer present, or when these more legacy-style SELinux policies are shared with you and you need to build and load them manually.

Replacing the default distribution policy

When adding custom SELinux policies, all that users can do is to add more `allow` rules. SELinux does not have a deny rule that can be used to remove currently allowed access rules from the active policy.

If the current policy is too permissive for the administrator's liking, then the administrator will need to update the policy rather than just enhance it. That implies that the administrator has access to the current SELinux policy rules in use.

To replace an active SELinux policy, most Linux distributions allow you to get the source code of the policy. For instance, for RPM-based Linux distributions, the source RPM of the SELinux policy package can be downloaded and unpacked to gain access to the policy as follows:

1. First, find out what the current version of the SELinux policy is:

```
$ rpm -qi selinux-policy
Name        : selinux-policy
Version     : 3.14.3
...
Source RPM : selinux-policy-3.14.3-20.el8.src.rpm
...
```

2. Next, try to obtain the source RPM shown in the output. Source RPMs can also be downloaded from third-party repositories. If the package is difficult to find, you can try to find it through `https://rpmfind.net`.

3. Next, use the `rpmbuild` utility to extract the source RPM:

```
$ rpmbuild --rebuild --nobuild \
  selinux-policy-3.14.3-20.el8.src.rpm
```

This will unpack the source RPM in the ~/rpmbuild directory.

4. When finished, the SELinux policy source code can be found inside ~/rpmbuild/ SOURCES and is probably named selinux-policy-9c02e99.tar.gz or similar, which you can extract further:

```
$ tar xvf selinux-policy-9c92e99.tar.gz
$ tar xvf selinux-policy-contrib-c8ebb9f.tar.gz
```

The SELinux policy can then be found in the created subdirectories. For instance, the screen.te file can be found in the ./selinux-policy-contrib-c8ebb*/policy/modules/contrib subdirectory.

The policy files can now be safely copied over, manipulated at will, and built to replace the existing policy. If we load the updated SELinux policy module with the same (or higher) priority as the already loaded policy, it will take precedence in the policy.

Most distributions will also have their active SELinux policy available through an online source-controlled repository. For instance, the current SELinux policy for CentOS is available at https://github.com/fedora-selinux/selinux-policy.

Summary

The SELinux policy can be adjusted by administrators, either through SELinux booleans as provided by the SELinux policy itself, or by loading new SELinux policy modules. These modules can be generated automatically, or built manually by the policy developers.

In this chapter, we've learned how to use SELinux booleans and how to query the active policy for the effects that the booleans will have on the system. We then learned how to use semodule to load and unload policies, or enable/disable modules on the system. We ended the chapter with information on how to generate and replace policies.

In the next chapter, we will extend our query of the SELinux policy beyond just booleans, and learn how to analyze policy behavior in detail using specialized tools.

Questions

1. How can we mark a boolean change as pending but not commit it yet?

2. Which command can be used to query the impact of a boolean?

3. Why can SELinux policy modules be loaded with different priorities?

4. How can denials be transformed into new SELinux policy modules?

13
Analyzing Policy Behavior

Although SELinux policies enforce the mandatory access controls and application behavior on a system, knowing how a policy will act upfront is useful for administrators to perform assessments and root cause analysis activities.

Throughout this chapter, we will learn how to query the SELinux policy in depth, using a multitude of tools to query process transitions, analyze information flows, and compare policies. We will consider the `apol` tool, a graphical interface with which we can perform several analyses on a policy, as well as command-line tools such as `sesearch`, `sedta`, `seinfoflow`, and `sepolicy`. Finally, we will use `sediff` to compare policies.

In this chapter, we're going to cover the following main topics:

- Performing single-step analysis
- Investigating domain transitions
- Analyzing information flow
- Comparing policies

Technical requirements

Check out the following video to see the Code in Action: `https://bit.ly/31Y56LB`

Performing single-step analysis

Until now, we've covered a few methods of analyzing SELinux policies through command-line utilities such as `seinfo` and `sesearch`. These utilities can assist users in performing single-step analyses: they either provide immediate information about an SELinux object (which is mainly what `seinfo` is about) or are capable of querying direct SELinux rules (which is the scope of `sesearch`).

Not all capabilities of the `seinfo` and `sesearch` utilities have been discussed yet though, so let's see what other tricks these commands have up their sleeves.

Using different SELinux policy files

Many SELinux analysis tools, including `seinfo` and `sesearch`, can access both the currently loaded SELinux policy and a specified SELinux policy file. The latter allows developers to query SELinux policies of systems they do not have direct access to, for which direct access is cumbersome (such as mobile devices), or that have been used in previous situations (backups) and are no longer active.

For instance, to analyze a policy file called `policy.sepolicy-2`, the following `seinfo` command can be used:

```
$ seinfo ./policy.sepolicy-2
Statistics for policy file: ./policy.sepolicy-2
Policy Version:            30 (MLS enabled)
Target Policy:             selinux
Handle unknown classes:    deny
   Classes:            63    Permissions:        286
   Sensitivities:       1    Categories:        1024
   Types:            1858    Attributes:          28
   Users:               1    Roles:                2
   Booleans:            0    Cond. Expr.:          0
   Allow:          108120    Neverallow:           0
   Auditallow:         24    Dontaudit:          553
   Type_trans:        639    Type_change:          0
   Type_member:         0    Range_trans:          0
   Role allow:          0    Role_trans:           0
   Constraints:         0    Validatetrans:        0
   MLS Constrain:      59    MLS Val. Tran:        0
```

Permissives:	0	Polcap:	2
Defaults:	0	Typebounds:	0
Allowxperm:	185	Neverallowxperm:	0
Auditallowxperm:	0	Dontauditxperm:	0
Initial SIDs:	27	Fs_use:	16
Genfscon:	83	Portcon:	0
Netifcon:	0	Nodecon:	0

When the command is not explicitly told to parse a given policy file, it will try to query the current active policy through the `/sys/fs/selinux/policy` pseudo-file.

Displaying policy object information

The main purpose of the `seinfo` application is to display SELinux object information. This information is presented on a per-object basis. Various SELinux object types are supported, ranging from the well-known types, attributes, roles, and users, to the more specialized `fs_use_*` declarations or `genfscon` statements.

A complete list of supported object types (and their resulting `seinfo` options) can be found on the `seinfo` manual page, or through the direct help:

```
$ seinfo --help
```

Regardless of the object type that the user is interested in, `seinfo` has three main modus operandi:

- In the first mode, it lists the objects of a given type. For this, only the option has to be passed on, without additional information. For instance, to list all object classes available in the policy, use the following command:

```
$ seinfo --class
```

- In the second mode, it can confirm (or deny) the presence of an object instance. To accomplish this, add the instance name to the command. For instance, to validate if the `memprotect` class is available in the policy, use the following command:

```
$ seinfo --class memprotect
Classes: 1
  memprotect
```

Sadly, regardless of whether the instance is available or not, the return code of the application is the same, so scripts cannot use this without additional statements to verify whether the instance exists. Instead, they will need to check the output of the command (which will state that zero instances exist that match the name).

- The third mode displays expanded information about a selected instance. Although not all information objects support an expanded set, most of the common ones do. The expanded information generally shows a list of (different) instances related to the initial query:

```
$ seinfo --class memprotect -x
Classes: 1
    class memprotect
  {
      mmap_zero
  }
```

The supported types that `seinfo` can query are the following:

- With `--attribute` (`-a`), `seinfo` shows all currently known SELinux attributes in the policy. When expanded, it shows the types associated with a given attribute.

- With `--bool` (`-b`), `seinfo` shows all currently known SELinux booleans in the policy. When expanded, it shows the current value of the boolean.

- With `--class` (`-c`), `seinfo` shows the supported SELinux classes. When expanded, it shows the permissions supported by that class.

- With `--role` (`-r`), `seinfo` shows the SELinux roles supported in the policy. When expanded, it shows the domains allowed for that role.

- With `--type` (`-t`), `seinfo` shows the SELinux types in the policy. When expanded, it shows the aliases that the type has, as well as the attributes.

- With `--user` (`-u`), `seinfo` shows the SELinux users (not the Linux users or logins) known by the policy. When expanded, it shows the roles and sensitivity range associated with the SELinux user.

- With `--category`, `seinfo` shows the currently supported categories. When expanded, it shows the sensitivities for which the category is associated (only in MLS policies).

- With `--common`, `seinfo` shows the common permission sets. These are sets inherited by different classes. When expanded, it shows the permissions part of that set.

- With `--constrain`, `seinfo` shows the current constraints. There is no expanded information for this query.

- With `--default`, `seinfo` shows the `default_*` rules within the policy. One of these rules, for instance, is the default sensitivity range for a class (`default_range`). There is no expanded information for this query.

- With `--fs_use`, `seinfo` shows the `fs_use_*` rules within the SELinux policy. One of these rules is to allocate a security context for filesystems that support extended attributes (`fs_use_xattr`). There is no expanded information for this query.

- With `--genfscon`, `seinfo` shows the context allocations for filesystems that do not support extended attributes. There is no expanded information for this query.

- With `--initialsid`, `seinfo` shows all the initial **Security Identifiers** (**SID**). These are all the classes that have predefined contexts set. When expanded, it shows the context associated with the SID.

- With `--netifcon`, `seinfo` shows the contexts currently associated with the network interfaces. This is only applicable when labeled networking is active. There is no expanded information for this query.

- With `--nodecon`, `seinfo` shows the contexts currently associated with the node definitions (hosts). This is only applicable when labeled networking is active. There is no expanded information for this query.

- With `--permissive`, `seinfo` shows which types are currently marked as permissive domains. There is no expanded information for this query.

- With `--polcap`, `seinfo` shows the policy capabilities (that is, in-policy settings that define the SELinux subsystem behavior, such as support for SCTP through the `extended_socket_class` policy capability that we saw in *Chapter 5, Controlling Network Communications*). When expanded, it shows the actual policy capability statements in the policy.

- With `--portcon`, `seinfo` shows the current port mappings and their associated contexts (which is also interpreted by `semanage port -l`). There is no expanded information for this query.

- With `--sensitivity`, `seinfo` shows the currently supported sensitivity levels. When expanded, it shows the actual policy statements to declare the sensitivities.

- With `--typebounds`, `seinfo` shows the type bounds (SELinux types or domains bounded by a parent domain). There is no expanded information for this query.

- With `--validatetrans`, `seinfo` shows the transition constraints active in the policy (these are constraints that limit when a file transition is allowed). This is not used in most Linux distributions. There is no expanded information for this query.

The `seinfo` command also has an `--all` option that shows all possible information it can get from a policy file. However, this does not include the expanded information.

Understanding sesearch

Where `seinfo` displays information about SELinux objects, `sesearch` is used to query SELinux rules and behavior information between a source and a target resource.

We have been using `sesearch` to query standard `allow` rules (type enforcement-related access controls) as well as the impact of SELinux booleans on these `allow` rules. The `sesearch` application allows us to not just query rules based on the rule type, but also filter based on additional parameters. Let's see which parameters can be used for `sesearch` filters:

- The most common queries are to filter out the rules that match a given source expression using `--source` (`-s`) and/or target expression using `--target` (`-t`):

  ```
  $ sesearch -A -s mount_t -t unconfined_t
  ```

  The `sesearch` application can also deal with indirect source or target information. For instance, when querying information related to the `svirt_sandbox_domain` attribute, it will also display rules of all types that have this attribute assigned. We can selectively disable this behavior using `-ds` (for source) and `-dt` (for target):

  ```
  $ sesearch -A -s svirt_sandbox_domain -ds
  ```

- With the `--class` (`-c`) argument, we can search for only those rules affecting a specified resource class (such as `file`, `dir`, `tcp_socket`, and so forth—the list of all possible classes can be obtained using `seinfo --class`):

  ```
  $ sesearch -A -s svirt_sandbox_domain -c file
  ```

- If we are interested in only a particular action (or permission), we can use the `--perm` (`-p`) argument. This is particularly useful when we encounter a denial for a certain action (say, `write`) and want to see which domains are allowed to perform this action, as it might indicate that we are examining the wrong source domain. We can list multiple permissions, in which case `sesearch` will display the rules that have at least one permission in them:

  ```
  $ sesearch -A -s staff_t -c file -p write
  ```

  With the `-ep` option, `sesearch` will only list the rules that have all permissions in them, rather than at least one.

- We can also query only those rules influenced by an SELinux boolean using the `--bool` (`-b`) argument, as we saw in *Chapter 12, Tuning SELinux Policies*.

  If we use the `-eb` option, then all booleans listed on the command line must be matched, rather than at least one.

- The `sesearch` application can also use regular expressions rather than actual values. This is not the default behavior, but can be activated with `-rs` (for the source type or role), `-rt` (for the target type or role), `-rc` (for the class), `-rd` (for the default type or role), and `-rb` (for the boolean):

```
$ sesearch -A -s staff_.*_t -c process -p transition -rs
```

As this provides insights into the most common SELinux behavior and access controls, let's go through the various rules and the impact they have on the system.

Querying allow rules

The first set of rules are the `allow` rules, of which many subtypes exist. The standard `allow` rule defines which actions a source domain can successfully trigger toward or against a target type:

```
$ sesearch --allow -s guest_t -t cgroup_t -c dir
allow guest_usertype cgroup_t:dir { getattr ioctl lock open
read search };
allow guest_usertype filesystem_type:dir { getattr open search
};
```

There are a few similar rules that SELinux policies can define, and these can be queried similarly with `sesearch` as follows:

- Using `--auditallow`, we can query which actions are allowed by SELinux but will still result in an audit event.

- Using `--dontaudit`, we can query which actions will not trigger an audit event, even when the action is denied.

- Using `--neverallow`, we can query which actions are forbidden from being declared within the policy. Such actions, when defined, will cause the system to refuse to load new SELinux policies if they violate the rule. It cannot be used to negate existing rules though, and `neverallow` rules that you attempt to add to the policy afterward will fail if the current policy already has deviations against this rule.

SELinux also supports **extended permission rules**. These rules are similar to regular `allow` rules but take an additional (number) parameter that further limits the applicability of the rule, and are used to provide fine-grained access control for device queries. These queries are generally handled by the `ioctl()` system call, but until its support for extended permissions, SELinux could only control whether a domain was allowed to use the `ioctl()` system call or not, rather than filtering on the explicit query through `ioctl()`.

With extended permission rules, SELinux policy developers can specify which `ioctl()` queries are allowed and which ones aren't. For instance, we can grant a domain the ability to get a hardware address (known as `SIOCGIFHWADDR`, which is defined with number `0x8927`) as follows:

```
allowxperm <domain> <resource> : tcp_socket ioctl 0x8927;
```

Within `sesearch`, we can query these rules using `--allowxperm`. Like regular `allow` rules, we also have the `--auditallowxperm`, `--dontauditxperm`, and `--neverallowxperm` options to cover the extended-permission-equivalent rules. These have the same impact on the query and also on the extended permission rules.

Querying type transition rules

A second set of rules are the type transition rules. Rather than informing the system which actions are allowed or not, **type transitions** influence the SELinux context of objects and resources through actions taken by the processes on the system. Type transition rules, for instance, define what context a newly written file receives when it is written by a particular domain within a directory that has a given SELinux type, or what domain a newly created process receives when it is executed from a given source domain:

```
$ sesearch -T -s guest_t -c process
type_transition guest_t abrt_helper_exec_t:process abrt_
helper_t;
type_transition guest_t chfn_exec_t:process chfn_t;
...
```

In this output, we can see that when the guest domain successfully executes a binary labeled with `abrt_helper_exec_t`, its resulting process will be assigned the `abrt_helper_t` context.

These rules are queried and interpreted by various tools in the *Investigating domain transitions* section.

Querying other type rules

Alongside the `allow` rules and type transition rules, `sesearch` can also query two other type-related rules: `type_change` and `type_member`. These rules are meant for SELinux-aware applications and are not enforced by the in-kernel SELinux subsystem:

- With `type_change` statements (which can be filtered in `sesearch` using the `--type_change` option), developers inform the SELinux-aware application that a target resource should be relabeled with a given type on behalf of the source domain.

  For instance, when systemd assigns a terminal to a user, it queries the SELinux policy for `type_change` statements for the user domain, given the current terminal's SELinux type, and will return the following `type_change` statement:

  ```
  type_change guest_t tty_device_t:chr_file user_tty_
  device_t;
  ```

  As the device file itself already exists and is only reassigned to a user, no type transition itself is done. Instead, the `type_change` rule is interpreted by the SELinux-aware application that relabels the device file accordingly.

- The `type_member` rule (which can be filtered in `sesearch` using the `--type_member` option) informs SELinux-aware applications that participate in setting up polyinstantiated locations (as we saw in *Chapter 3*, *Managing User Logins*) about the target SELinux type of such directories. For instance, when the `/tmp` location (which is labeled with `tmp_t`) is polyinstantiated for a user, then the following rule is used to understand that the `/tmp` view for this user is to be labeled with `user_tmp_t`:

  ```
  type_member guest_t tmp_t:dir user_tmp_t;
  ```

  The PAM module responsible for addressing the polyinstantiation is SELinux-aware, and will use these rules to deduce what the target types must be for the created locations.

Alongside the type-related statements, `sesearch` can also handle role-related queries.

Querying role-related rules

SELinux also has rules related to role activities and transitions. With the `sesearch` application, we can query which SELinux roles are allowed to be accessed from other roles, and when a role transition (such as switching from a user role to the system role) is performed:

```
$ sesearch --role_allow -s dbadm_r;
allow dbadm_r sysadm_r;
$ sesearch --role_trans -s dbadm_r;
role_transition dbadm_r mysqld_initrc_exec_t:process system_r;
role_transition dbadm_r postgresql_initrc_exec_t:process
system_r;
```

The distinction between the two is that the allowed access (using `--role_allow`) shows which roles can be accessed from a given role, but they do not dictate when the change is done. The role transitions (using `--role_trans`) show when the system attempts to automatically change a role (and to what role it would be changed) when executing a script or binary. Hence, they can be compared with the `allow` rules (which specify what is allowed) and type transitions (defining SELinux behavior).

Analyzing role transitions and role `allow` rules helps administrators deduce which roles are too powerful or could result in potential security issues. For instance, allowing the dbadm_r role to switch to the system_r role through the `postgresql_initrc_exec_t` type might allow that role to invoke actions outside its scope if it also has the rights to modify `postgresql_initrc_exec_t` resources:

```
$ sesearch -A -s dbadm_t -t postgresql_initrc_exec_t -c file;
allow dbadm_t postgresql_initrc_exec_t:file { execute execute_
no_trans getattr ioctl map open read };
```

While directly modifying `postgresql_initrc_exec_t` files is thus not allowed, it is not enough to only look at the main user type. A decent analysis needs to include all types reachable by the dbadm_r role, which we will cover in the *Investigating domain transitions* and *Analyzing information flow* sections. These sections will use `apol`, so let's first see what this application is all about.

Browsing with apol

An advanced tool to perform policy analysis is apol, which can be launched by just executing the command without any arguments. The tool is graphical in nature and allows analysts and administrators to perform a wide range of analytical actions against the SELinux policy.

Once started, the first action to take with apol is to load a target policy (either the currently active policy or a file copied over from a different system). This can be accomplished through the **Open Policy** button, or by navigating to **File | Open Policy**.

The tool will then display a generic overview of the loaded policy:

Figure 13.1 – The apol application after loading a policy file

Once it has been loaded, select **New Analysis** to initiate the policy analysis functions:

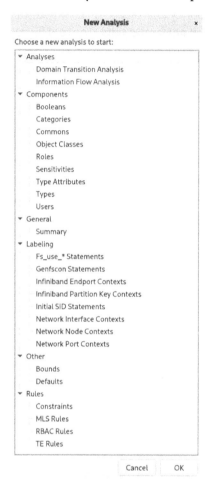

Figure 13.2 – apol's overview of supported analysis methods

A decent number of analysis methods are provided. Let's select **Types** to browse through the available types, or select an attribute to find out which SELinux types are assigned to that attribute:

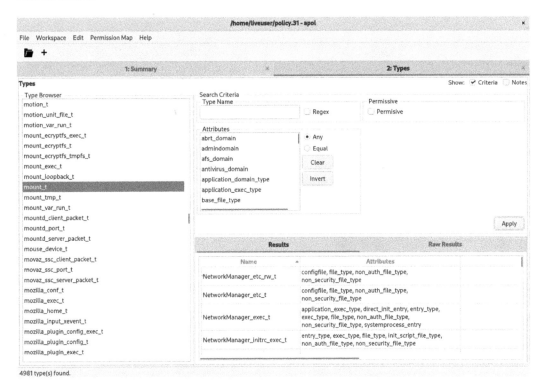

Figure 13.3 – Type browsing with apol

Similarly, with the **TE Rules** analysis, we can perform the same analysis as we did with the `sesearch` application:

Figure 13.4 – Querying type enforcement rules with apol

The more advanced analysis methods are covered in the *Investigating domain transitions* and *Analyzing information flow* sections.

Using apol workspaces

Analyzing SELinux policies can take a while, especially when this involves multiple phases of analysis and fine-tuning. The `apol` tool allows you to save your current workspace to disk, so that you can later get back to the analysis from the point at which you saved it:

Figure 13.5 – Workspace management in apol

Workspaces not only retain the settings of the queries so far, but also the notes you might add. Notes are an important feature within `apol` where you can write down thoughts and observations from the queries you've made. The notes are associated with the tabs you have open, allowing you to switch between different queries as needed.

Now that we know how the `apol` application works, let's see how we can use it (and other tools) for more in-depth analyses.

Investigating domain transitions

An important analytical approach when dealing with SELinux policies is to perform a **domain transition analysis**. Domains are bounded by the access controls in place for a given domain, but users or processes can transition to other domains by executing the right set of applications.

Analyzing whether and how a transition can occur between two SELinux domains allows administrators to validate the secure state of the policy. Given the mandatory nature of SELinux, adversaries will find it difficult to be able to execute target applications if a domain transition analysis shows that the source domain cannot execute said application, either directly or indirectly.

Administrators should use domain transition analysis to confirm a domain is correctly confined, and that vulnerabilities within the applications running inside a domain cannot lead to privilege escalations.

Using apol for domain transition analysis

After starting `apol`, select **New Analysis** followed by **Domain Transition Analysis**. The analysis screen itself will show several possible analytical approaches:

Figure 13.6 – Querying possible transition paths between staff_t and unconfined_t

This analysis will attempt to find a path between a given source domain and target domain, and display the execution trail that could lead to the transition. Administrators can then verify whether the applications associated with these domain transitions can be trusted or not. Such analysis is sensible when we need to assert that certain domains cannot break out of their confinement, or when we are developing new policies and want to ensure that the confinement is within the boundaries we want.

The transition analysis can be fine-tuned through the following settings:

- With **Shortest paths**, `apol` will show domain transitions between the source domain and the target domain, seeking the shortest transitions possible. For instance, a transition from `staff_t` to `staff_sudo_t` to `unconfined_t` is a two-step path. When a path is found, `apol` will not search for longer paths.

- When we select **All paths up to**, `apol` will perform the analysis up to a certain number of steps. When we use up to one step, then this is similar to doing direct queries with `seinfo` or `sesearch`.

- Using **Transitions out of the source domain** and **Transitions into the target domain** will show all transitions that can occur from a given source domain or to the target domain. This is used for a more interactive session, where users can click through the domains to see the next set of domains that can be transitioned to.

To further fine-tune the analysis, a few options can be selected. For instance, we can exclude certain types from being used in the domain transition analysis. This allows us to mark certain domains as trusted (such as the `*_sudo_t` domains), which will make `apol` ignore those domains to find more appropriate transition chains to analyze.

Using sedta for domain transition analysis

The path analysis done by `apol` can also be executed from a command-line application called `sedta`. It has the same capabilities as the domain transition analysis functionality within `apol`.

The type of analysis is selected through command-line arguments: `-S` is used for shortest path analysis, whereas `-A` (followed by a number) runs the equivalent of **All paths up to**.

For instance, to check for a domain transition path between the `staff_t` domain and the `unconfined_t` domain, excluding the `staff_sudo_t`, `newrole_t`, and `init_t` domains, use the following command:

```
$ sedta -S -s staff_t -t unconfined_t staff_sudo_t newrole_t
Domain transition path 1:
Step 1: staff_t -> oddjob_t
```

```
Domain transition rule(s):
allow staff_t oddjob_t:process transition;

Set execution context rule(s):
allow staff_t staff_t:process { dyntransition fork getattr
getcap getpgid getrlimit getsched getsession noatsecure
rlimitinh setcap setcurrent setexec setfscreate setkeycreate
setpgid setrlimit setsched setsockcreate share sigchld siginh
sigkill signal signull sigstop transition };

Entrypoint oddjob_exec_t:
        Domain entrypoint rule(s):
        allow oddjob_t oddjob_exec_t:file { entrypoint execute
getattr ioctl lock map open read };

        File execute rule(s):
        allow staff_t oddjob_exec_t:file { execute execute_no_
trans getattr ioctl map open read };

        Type transition rule(s):
        type_transition staff_t oddjob_exec_t:process oddjob_t;

Step 2: oddjob_t -> openshift_initrc_t
...
```

We can analyze a different policy than the current system policy using the `-p` option.

Using sepolicy for domain transition analysis

The `sepolicy` tool has a built-in domain transition analysis capability using the `transition` argument. It is, however, not as flexible as `sedta` or `apol`, as no tuning can be done to the command. It also does not seem to cover all possible paths, often displaying extensive and elaborate routes that could be much simpler:

```
$ sepolicy transition -s mount_t -t unconfined_t
mount_t ... glusterd_t ... ipsec_t ... ipsec_mgmt_t
   ... initrc_t ... condor_schedd_t ... condor_startd_t
   ... openshift_initrc_t ... stunnel_t ... telnetd_t
   ... remote_login_t @ shell_exec_t --> unconfined_t
   -- Allowed True [ unconfined_login=1 ]
mount_t ... glusterd_t ... ipsec_t ... ipsec_mgmt_t
   ... initrc_t ... condor_schedd_t ... condor_startd_t
   ... openshift_initrc_t ... kmscon_t ...
```

```
   local_login_t @ shell_exec_t --> unconfined_t
   -- Allowed True [ unconfined_login=1 ]
mount_t ... glusterd_t ... ipsec_t ... ipsec_mgmt_t
   ... initrc_t ... condor_schedd_t ... condor_startd_t
   ... openshift_initrc_t ... kdumpgui_t ... kdumpctl_t
   ... sge_execd_t ... sge_shepherd_t ...
   sshd_t @ shell_exec_t --> unconfined_t
   -- Allowed True [ ssh_sysadm_login=0 || unconfined_login=1 ]
mount_t ... glusterd_t ... ipsec_t ... ipsec_mgmt_t
   ... initrc_t ... condor_schedd_t ... condor_startd_t
   ... openshift_initrc_t ... kdumpgui_t ... kdumpctl_t ...
   sulogin_t @ shell_exec_t --> unconfined_t
   -- Allowed True [ unconfined_login=1 ]
mount_t ... glusterd_t ... ipsec_t ... ipsec_mgmt_t
   ... initrc_t ... condor_schedd_t ... condor_startd_t
   ... openshift_initrc_t ... kdumpgui_t ... kdumpctl_t
   ... inetd_t ...
   rshd_t @ shell_exec_t --> unconfined_t
   -- Allowed True [ unconfined_login=1 ]
mount_t ... glusterd_t ... ipsec_t ... ipsec_mgmt_t
   ... initrc_t ... condor_schedd_t ... condor_startd_t

   ... openshift_initrc_t ... kdumpgui_t ... kdumpctl_t
   ... piranha_pulse_t ...
   crond_t @ shell_exec_t --> unconfined_t
   -- Allowed True [ cron_userdomain_transition=1 || unconfined_
login=1 ]
mount_t ... glusterd_t ... ipsec_t ... ipsec_mgmt_t
   ... initrc_t ... condor_schedd_t ... condor_startd_t
   ... openshift_initrc_t ... kdumpgui_t ... kdumpctl_t
   ... piranha_pulse_t ... cockpit_ws_t ...
   cockpit_session_t @ unconfined_exec_t --> unconfined_t
```

Let's compare this with `sedta`, which we use against the same policy and for the same domain transition:

```
$ sedta -S -s mount_t -t unconfined_t | \
  grep -E '(transition path|Step)'
Domain transition path 1:
Step 1: mount_t -> glusterd_t
Step 2: glusterd_t -> sulogin_t
Step 3: sulogin_t -> unconfined_t
Domain transition path 2:
```

```
Step 1: mount_t -> glusterd_t
Step 2: glusterd_t -> virtd_lxc_t
Step 3: virtd_lxc_t -> unconfined_t
Domain transition path 3:
Step 1: mount_t -> glusterd_t
Step 2: glusterd_t -> xdm_t
Step 3: xdm_t -> unconfined_t
Domain transition path 4:
Step 1: mount_t -> glusterd_t
Step 2: glusterd_t -> crond_t
Step 3: crond_t -> unconfined_t
Domain transition path 5:
Step 1: mount_t -> glusterd_t
Step 2: glusterd_t -> sshd_t
Step 3: sshd_t -> unconfined_t
Domain transition path 6:
Step 1: mount_t -> glusterd_t
Step 2: glusterd_t -> virtd_t
Step 3: virtd_t -> unconfined_t
6 domain transition path(s) found.
```

When comparing the transition paths with the ones generated by sedta, you will notice that sedta often finds shorter domain transitions, which sepolicy transition does not. Hence it is not recommended to rely solely on sepolicy transition for domain transition analysis.

Analyzing information flow

Another analytical investigation that can be carried out on SELinux policies is information flow analysis. Unlike domain transitions, which look at how one domain can gain a certain set of permissions through transitions to another domain, **information flow analysis** looks at how a domain could leak (purposefully or not) information to another domain.

Information flow analysis is performed by looking at all operations that occur between two types. A source type can be read by a domain, which subsequently can write information to another type that can then be accessed by another domain. While this can still be analyzed in a step-wise fashion, it quickly becomes very challenging because we cannot limit ourselves to the read and write operations.

Information can be leaked through filenames, file descriptors, and more. Information flow analysis must take all these methods into account.

Using apol for information flow analysis

After loading an SELinux policy, select **Information Flow Analysis**. The interface
we receive is similar to the domain transition analysis, but now has a few toggles
to fine-tune the path analysis specific to information flows:

Figure 13.7 – Analyzing information flow between two domains

Unlike domain transitions, the number of paths through which information can flow is
exponentially bigger. To perform a decent information flow analysis, we need to fine-tune
the search criteria:

- The **Minimum permission weight** option allows users to only look at permissions
  or actions that have a particular weight. Each action is given a weight in the tool,
  from a low priority (such as the `lock` operation, which has weight 1) to a high
  priority one (such as the `write` operation, which has weight 10). The purpose
  of these weights is to define which actions are plausible for information flow and
  which ones are much harder (but not impossible) to use for deliberate information
  exchange.

- With **Excluded Permissions**, we can selectively enable or disable certain permissions from the analysis.

The other options are similar to those in domain transition analysis.

The most important area for information flow analysis is the permission map, which we can fine-tune partially while enabling or disabling permissions in the analysis. However, we might not be happy with the weights that the current permission map uses.

To edit the permission map, select **Permission Map | Edit Permission Map** from the apol menu:

Figure 13.8 – Editing the permission map and permission weights

Within this editor, we can fine-tune the weights of the permissions to our liking, as well as the *directionality* of the action:

- None (no information flow)
- Write (information flows to the resource)

- `Read` (information is retrieved from the resource)
- `Both` (information can both flow to and from the resource)

Once we are satisfied with the results, we can (and probably should) save the permission map for later reuse (if not, the changes are only applicable to the current session and will be forgotten when `apol` is closed).

Using seinfoflow for information flow analysis

Like the `sedta` application for domain transition analysis, there is also a command-line application that offers information flow analysis capabilities similar to `apol`, that is, `seinfoflow`. Every invocation of the `seinfoflow` command requires the permission map to be passed on for its analysis. If you don't have a permission map created and saved yourself, you can use the default one available at `/var/lib/sepolgen/perm_map`.

Let's analyze the information flow possibilities between the `staff_t` and `guest_t` domains, using the default permission map, and only considering the permissions of weight `10`:

```
$ seinfoflow -S -m /var/lib/sepolgen/perm_map \
  -s staff_t -t guest_t -w 10
```

The more elaborate a permission map is, the more time it takes for the analysis to complete.

Using sepolicy communicate for simple information flow analysis

The `sepolicy` command can perform a simple flow analysis using the `communicate` option. Given a source and target domain, `sepolicy` will check through which intermediate types information can flow between the domains:

```
$ sepolicy communicate -s postgresql_t -t staff_t
krb5_host_rcache_t
cluster_conf_t
security_t
postgresql_t
postgresql_tmp_t
hugetlbfs_t
```

The preceding flow analysis is basically checking what types can be written to by the source domain, and read by the target domain.

Comparing policies

Until now, we've analyzed a single policy set, finding the domain transitions and information flow paths. The commands and applications we've used all focus on this single-policy analysis. Another important analysis is to compare two policies. Policy developers can use this to compare a new policy with an old one, or to compare two system policies to see what additional rules have been added by the administrator.

Using sediff to compare policies

The `sediff` tool looks at the differences between two policy files and reports those to the user. It is often not sensible to use this against completely different policies, but is powerful for finding slight differences between policies, which can assist in troubleshooting issues across different systems.

A common use case for `sediff` is to validate that a source-built policy file is the same as the distribution-provided binary policy file. Administrators can then be certain that the source code they've used to build a policy file is the same as that used by the distribution, even when the binary files themselves (the `policy.##` file) have different checksums:

```
$ sediff policy.31 /sys/fs/selinux/policy
Policy Properties (0 Modified)

Classes (1 Added, 0 Removed, 4 Modified)
   Added Classes: 1
      + xdp_socket
   Modified Classes: 4
      * capability2 (1 Removed permissions)
         - compromise_kernel
      * process (1 Added permissions, 1 Removed permissions)
         + getrlimit
...
```

It is possible to direct `sediff` to only show differences for a specified area or part of the SELinux policy (such as the available types, roles, booleans, or type enforcement rules).

Summary

SELinux has quite a few analysis tools that we can use to analyze policies. We've seen how to use `sesearch` to do in-depth assessments of the current policy, but noticed that it fails to validate the more dynamic analysis requirements.

With `apol`, we have seen a graphical application that is able to do more dynamic analysis, including the domain transitions (examining which domains can be reached from a current point) and information flow analysis (investigating how information can flow from one domain to another). From this experience, we've learned that such analysis is intensive and requires lots of interpretation to be done correctly.

Next to `apol`, we also learned that command-line utilities exist with similar capabilities: `sedta` for domain transition analysis, `seinfoflow` for information flow analysis, and `sepolicy`, which has a few out-of-the-box functionalities, but not as extensive or flexible as the other options we looked at.

In the end, we learned how to compare policies using `sediff`. This is useful for when new policies are being developed, which is something we'll do in the remaining chapters. We first start with aligning and extending existing policies for new applications in the next chapter, and move on to full application policy development in the last two.

Questions

1. What is the difference between `seinfo` and `sesearch`?
2. How do you check whether you can reach a domain?
3. Why does analyzing information flows take so long?
4. Can we generate a delta between policies and load it?

14
Dealing with New Applications

New applications are often not yet supported through an application-specific SELinux policy, as most application projects do not develop the SELinux policies themselves, but rely on the community in general (or Linux distributions more specifically) to create and maintain them. Some Linux distributions have implemented fallbacks to allow these applications to run, even though they might not be isolated properly. Administrators might not like the sound of having untrusted new applications running without any SELinux enforcements active though.

Hence, this chapter covers how administrators can run new applications in a number of isolated environments, ranging from the (often default) unprotected domains, to sandbox systems, and eventually by reusing existing SELinux domains without having to develop completely new ones.

In this chapter, we're going to cover the following main topics:

- Running applications without restrictions
- Using sandboxed applications
- Assigning common policies to new applications
- Extending generated policies

Technical requirements

Check out the following video to see the Code in Action: `https://bit.ly/3dGG5Bu`

Running applications without restrictions

The default behavior in many Linux distributions is to run new applications through unconfined domains. These are specially crafted domains that, while still being controlled by SELinux, are designed to have very, very broad permissions granted. You can compare such unconfined domains with a firewall that allows any possible flow: while the firewall is running, it is hardly doing any enforcement.

There is, however, another approach possible as well, namely, running an application as a permissive domain. Unlike unconfined domains, permissive domains are not enforced through SELinux: everything the domain does is allowed, even though SELinux might log every violation. We briefly touched upon permissive domains in *Chapter 3*, *Understanding SELinux Decisions and Logging*.

Let's first look at unconfined domains and how administrators can modify system configuration to apply unconfined domains to other applications, or remove applications from being unconfined.

Understanding how unconfined domains work

An **unconfined domain** is an SELinux domain that has broad permissions, restricting only a very small amount of actions that a domain can do. Unconfined domains are not really a concept that SELinux, as technology, supports. Instead, it is used by SELinux policy developers who created a set of permissions they consider as being unconfined.

End users on many Linux distributions will have noticed that their own context is `unconfined_t`. While this is indeed a reference to being an unconfined domain, there are more domains that are unconfined than `unconfined_t`.

SELinux policy developers have aggregated most of the permissions related to unconfined domains either in the domains themselves (as is the case for the reference policy) or in SELinux attributes, such as `unconfined_domain_type` and `unconfined_user_type` (as is the case for CentOS and related Linux distributions). In the case of attributes, these attributes are then assigned to one or more domains to effectively make them unconfined in nature:

```
$ seinfo -a | grep unconfined
$ seinfo -a unconfined_domain_type -x
```

Once a process is running as an unconfined domain, that does not imply that every action of that domain remains unconfined. When an unconfined domain executes a process that has a proper SELinux policy assigned, it is possible for this execution to still invoke a domain transition, effectively running the executed command in a (possibly confined) SELinux domain.

As the decision whether a domain transition is allowed or not falls within the SELinux policy, it is recommended that administrators query which domain transitions are allowed and which ones aren't. We saw how to analyze domain transitions in *Chapter 13, Analyzing Policy Behavior*. Given that we are mostly interested in single-step analysis, we can use the sesearch utility to have a quick overview of supported domain transitions:

```
$ sesearch -A -s unconfined_service_t -c process -p transition
allow unconfined_service_t chronyc_t:process transition;
allow unconfined_service_t rpm_script_t:process transition;
allow unconfined_service_t unconfined_service_t:process {
transition ...};
allow unconfined_service_t virt_domain:process { transition
...};
```

We can see the (many) permissions related to an unconfined domain by either checking them for a single domain, or for the attribute that represents unconfined domains directly:

```
$ sesearch -A -s unconfined_domain_type -ds
```

Using unconfined domains is preferred over making domains permissive, so let's see how we can mark a new application to run as an unconfined domain.

Making new applications run as an unconfined domain

When applications are executed, there are a number of checks that need to pass before this results in a domain transition:

- The source SELinux domain must be able to execute the application (implying execute rights on the SELinux type associated with the application's binary or script).
- The source SELinux domain must be able to transition to the target domain.
- The target domain must have its application binary or script labeled with an SELinux type that is marked as an entrypoint for that domain.
- The target domain must be allowed for the SELinux role that the source domain is running with (or a role transition has to be allowed, but that is a corner case).

All these checks are related to the SELinux policy and the labels. It comes as no surprise then that, in order for us to enable applications to run in an unconfined domain, we need to associate the right labels.

Let's consider two examples in the following sections, one being a user-triggered application, while the other is a daemonized service.

Running applications in an explicit unconfined domain

For applications that users execute, let's take the example of Jailkit, which we introduced in *Chapter 7, Configuring Application-Specific SELinux Controls*. By default, this application is not associated with any domain, so it runs within the same domain as the parent process. If we are logged in to the system through the unconfined_u user (in the unconfined_t SELinux domain), then we have nothing to do. But suppose that our staff user is confined, yet we want to have the command run in the unconfined_t domain.

> **Important note**
> This is used as an example that shows how to have applications run in a target domain – in our case, an unconfined domain. Allowing confined users to run unconfined applications always has a risk associated with it, because they might use this to break out of their confinement. Make sure that this is only done for applications or users where you have confidence that they will not breach security.

To allow the application to run in the unconfined_t domain, we will use sudo and its SELinux support. While we could also extend the SELinux policy to allow it transparently, this is not recommended. Updating the SELinux policy to allow confined users to run unconfined commands implies that several principles listed in the policy are overturned. You would need to allow the confined user to switch to the unconfined_r role (which is often not allowed for security reasons) transparently, for instance. It would require significant analysis to make sure that it cannot be used to break out of the confined role.

Using sudo allows us to limit the methods through which such more privileged commands are executed. SELinux-wise, the appropriate controls are put on the staff_sudo_t domain, for instance, which is only assigned when executing the sudo command, rather than the staff_t domain, which is where most of the user's interactions are executed.

Let's allow the `lisa` user to run the `jk_init` command as an unconfined process:

1. First, check whether the SELinux user for which we want to execute the command is allowed to do anything with the `unconfined_r` SELinux role (and if not, add the role to the SELinux user configuration):

    ```
    # semanage user -l
    ```

    Allowing a role does not imply that the user domain automatically switches role when needed though, but rather that it is an allowed role for the user.

2. Next, update the `/etc/sudoers` file to include a transition when executing the following command:

    ```
    # visudo
    lisa  ALL=(root) ROLE=unconfined_r TYPE=unconfined_r
    NOPASSWD: /usr/sbin/jk_init
    ```

    In this case, we not only use a ROLE and TYPE transition, but we also allow the command to be executed as the `root` user, as that is a requirement for the `jk_init` command. Of course, this can be adjusted as needed.

3. Our user can now run the command, prefixed by `sudo`, to have it execute in the right domain and using the right role:

    ```
    $ sudo /usr/sbin/jk_init -v -j /srv/chroot \
       extshellplusnet
    ```

Using `sudo` for end user applications is common when the privileges of the user also have to switch (from the user privilege to the root privilege). It is less common to use it when staying within the Linux user context though.

Running daemons in an explicit unconfined domain

The second use case, and perhaps a more common one than for end user applications, is to run daemonized services in an unconfined domain. Most Linux distributions that use unconfined domains (such as CentOS) will by default have newly installed software run as an unconfined domain as well. For instance, any service that is enabled and activated through systemd (which runs as the `init_t` SELinux domain) and that does not have an explicit labeling set (meaning the executable commands are labeled as `bin_t`) will run in the `unconfined_service_t` domain.

But what if we have a confined application that we want to run in an unconfined domain? Let's take PostgreSQL as an example. Suppose this is an isolated database that has certain extensions active that are incompatible with the existing PostgreSQL SELinux domain (postgresql_t). Administrators might not have the time to extend the current SELinux policy using methods such as audit2allow, as seen in *Chapter 12, Tuning SELinux Policies.*

Luckily, we can easily move PostgreSQL to work and run in an unconfined domain. There are two ways to approach this:

- We can remove the existing labels on its executable files (postgresql_exec_t) and set it to bin_t instead. This will then trigger the default transition when starting the PostgreSQL binary to the unconfined_service_t domain.

- We can update the SELinux policy for postgresql_t to become an unconfined domain itself.

Switching the labels is easy, but is the least recommended method. It is, however, a quick and dirty way to see whether running the service in the unconfined_service_t domain is sufficient to resolve the issue immediately:

```
# chcon -t bin_t /usr/bin/postgres
```

If agreeable, make sure that the label change remains, even after a relabel operation occurs:

```
# semanage fcontext -a -t bin_t /usr/bin/postgres
```

Updating the SELinux policy for the PostgreSQL daemon is recommended though, as it retains the existing support within the policy (including the file transitions and other integrations that the postgresql_t domain has with other domains and resources). It also allows administrators to update the policy as needed later on, when there is more time available.

To make the postgresql_t domain unconfined, we need to assign the unconfined_domain_type attribute to the postgresql_t domain. This can be accomplished by loading in the following CIL-based SELinux policy:

```
(typeattributeset cil_gen_require postgresql_t)
(typeattributeset cil_gen_require unconfined_domain_type)
(typeattributeset unconfined_domain_type (postgresql_t))
```

Save this in a file and load it using `semodule -i`, and from that point onward the `postgresql_t` domain will be augmented with the privileges associated with the `unconfined_domain_type` attribute.

Extending unconfined domains

As unconfined domains are still enforced, it might be possible that SELinux is still preventing some actions from occurring. We can adjust the SELinux policy to extend unconfined domains with more privileges though. While the default `unconfined_service_t` domain has almost all possible permissions set, more specifically, identified domains might not be as expansive.

The trick to adding more privileges to the domains is to assign the appropriate attribute to them. The method is the same as seen in *Running daemons in an explicit unconfined domain*, adding more attributes as needed. The list of attributes that we can add is very significant (as you can see from `seinfo -a`), but the most important ones, especially for the CentOS-based SELinux policy, are the following:

- `files_unconfined_type` allows the domain to manage any possible file- or filesystem-based resource.

- `devices_unconfined_type` allows the domain to interact and manage any device resource.

- `filesystem_unconfined_type` allows the domain to interact and manage all filesystems.

- `selinux_unconfined_type` allows the domain to interact with and manage the SELinux subsystem and configuration.

- `storage_unconfined_type` allows the domain to interact with storage systems and removable devices.

- `dbusd_unconfined` allows the domain to interact with all possible D-Bus services.

- `xserver_unconfined_type` allows the domain to interact with and manage all X server resources.

Furthermore, there are several `can_*` attributes that fine-tune very specific, security-sensitive actions. The names of these attributes nicely explain what they allow. For instance, `can_write_shadow_passwords` allows the domain to write to `/etc/shadow`, whereas `can_change_object_identity` means that the domain can change the SELinux user of an object.

Not all attributes have their privileges reflected in regular `allow` rules or transitions that can be queried using `sesearch`. For instance, `can_change_object_identity` is used in SELinux constraints instead:

```
# seinfo --constrain | grep can_change_object_identity
```

Querying the constraints is an often forgotten method to see what or why a certain privilege is or isn't assigned to a domain.

Suppose now that an application still fails to run correctly within an unconfined domain, then we can use permissive domains to allow this application to run unprotected, while having the rest of the system remain in enforcing mode.

Marking domains as permissive

As we saw in *Chapter 2, Understanding SELinux Decisions and Logging*, we can mark a domain as permissive using `semanage permissive`:

```
# semanage permissive -a postgresql_t
```

The same command can be used to query (`-l`) or remove (`-d`) permissive states. However, administrators should take special care before marking domains as permissive:

- First of all, if you mark a domain as permissive, then all processes running with that SELinux domain will run without any active SELinux enforcements. As an administrator, you really want to limit the number of processes that are running through permissive domains, so do not mark broadly used SELinux domains as permissive.

  A daemon that runs in an unconfined domain, yet still has problems, should not result in the unconfined domain being marked as permissive. Instead, have the daemon run as a different domain, and mark that domain as permissive.

- Secondly, permissive domains will still trigger SELinux behavior by the SELinux subsystem. Transition rules, including process transitions and file transitions, are still executed. This is of course by design, as permissive domains are meant to be short-lived, allowing administrators and developers to capture information and adapt the policy as needed before they can remove the permissive flag again.

This also implies that, if the domain does not have proper transition rules set, it might result in files being created on the system that have the wrong SELinux types set. Because of this, using permissive domains should not be considered for applications or daemons that have a wide impact on the system, but rather for more isolated situations where you, as an administrator, feel confident that you can easily fine-tune the policy if needed.

Consider the situation where we deploy pgpool-II, a load balancer for PostgreSQL databases, and find that the application does not run properly in an unconfined domain, even though it already runs in the `unconfined_service_t` SELinux domain. While we can put this domain in permissive mode, this would also apply to various other services running inside the `unconfined_service_t` domain.

What we can do is relabel its resources (executables mostly) so that the application is run through a different SELinux domain, and then mark that domain as permissive. We can either reuse an existing, unused domain or generate one, as we will see in the *Generating policies with sepolicy generate* section.

When we want to run an application in a (strictly) confined manner though, we need to take a completely different route and seek out how to put such applications in sandbox-like domains.

Using sandboxed applications

New applications that should only have very limited privileges, and that are untrusted by nature, should be confined completely. While we could look at custom SELinux policies for these applications, this is hardly possible for each and every application out there.

Instead, we can consider sandboxing the applications, isolating their access from the system. With the help of some other Linux primitives such as namespace support, a utility has been created called the SELinux sandbox, which launches applications in a tightly confined domain. This is mostly meant for end user applications.

Important note

The SELinux sandbox, its SELinux policy, and the command associated with it, is specific to Linux distributions that use or follow Red Hat packages, such as CentOS. It might not be available for your Linux distribution.

For service-oriented domains, using the container runtime and protection measures are more suited. For more information about using container protections, see *Chapter 11, Enhancing the Security of Containerized Workloads*.

Understanding the SELinux sandbox

The **SELinux sandbox** is a combination of a number of technologies and protection measures. While the SELinux policy plays an important part, other isolation measures are taken as well to really create a sandbox experience for applications and users.

The purpose of the sandbox is to create a low-privilege environment that blocks anything that could jeopardize the security of the system or the user's data. This also means that network interaction is blocked by default (no data exfiltration), and many system resources are hidden away from the sandboxed process.

Many of the access controls themselves are handled by the SELinux policy. The sandbox SELinux domains, `sandbox_t`, and derivatives such as `sandbox_xserver_t`, do not have many privileges for other resources. The sandbox utility will also apply sVirt-like categories to differentiate one sandboxed process from another.

The isolation, however, is done using different means. **Namespaces** are used to give the sandboxed process a different view of the filesystem (similar to polyinstantiation), whereas runtime capabilities are dropped before executing the process. The `seunshare` application is responsible for doing these isolation tasks.

Let's see how the SELinux sandbox works in practice.

Using the sandbox command

The SELinux sandbox uses the `sandbox` command. Now, before we can use it, we need to make sure that our SELinux user has multiple categories set as, otherwise, the SELinux sandbox cannot randomly allocate two categories for isolation:

```
# semanage login -l
# semanage login -m -r "s0-s0:c0.c100" lisa
```

Once assigned, we can prepare for running an untrusted application in a sandbox. For instance, we can download one of the International Obfuscated C Code Contest applications from `https://www.ioccc.org`, compile it, and then only run it in a sandbox mode just in case the code behaves maliciously:

1. Assuming we use the 2019 entry from `adamovsky`, we should have the `prog` binary and the `advent.unl` file ready to use. Create a location in which to store these files, and copy them over:

    ```
    $ mkdir sandbox
    $ cp 2019/adamovsky/* sandbox
    ```

2. Next, run the `prog` command from within the sandbox:

```
$ sandbox -H sandbox/ prog advent.unl
Welcome to Adventure!! Would you like instructions?
**
```

3. While the application runs, we can check its current context with `ps`:

```
# ps -efZ | grep prog
```

Alongside the `prog` command itself, which will be running in the `sandbox_t` SELinux domain and with a certain category pair set, you will notice that a `seunshare` command will run alongside it. This command provides the isolation for the process, not only by triggering the SELinux context change, but also removing unnecessary mount and filesystem views from the process's viewpoint.

4. If we exit the application, we can see that the sandbox location has been labeled with an sVirt-like MCS pair:

```
$ ls -Z sandbox/
staff_u:object_r:sandbox_file_t:s0:c29,c94 advent.unl
staff_u:object_r:sandbox_file_t:s0:c29,c94 prog
```

The method we used here was to explicitly tell the sandbox to create an isolated home directory based upon the `sandbox/` folder and run the `prog` binary from within this location (and with `advent.unl` as an argument to the `prog` command). However, this is not the sole approach.

If no explicit home directory is provided, then the sandbox will create a temporary one (and clean it up afterward). However, in that case, we cannot execute commands that are not already installed on the system, unless we allow the sandbox domain to execute `user_home_t`-labeled resources:

```
(typeattributeset cil_gen_require sandbox_t)
(allow sandbox_t user_home_t (file (execute map)))
```

With this policy loaded, we can use the sandbox with the least number of options. For instance, with the Burton contest submission (also from IOCCC's 2019 contest), we have the following:

```
$ cat prog.c | sandbox ./prog
    1       1    127
```

The use of a more known location, however, allows more flexibility, as well as allowing the sandbox to keep data across multiple sessions (as the directory pointed toward will not be cleaned up).

The SELinux sandbox also supports running graphical applications in the sandbox. To accomplish this, add the `-X` option to the `sandbox` command. The resulting process will run in the `sandbox_xserver_t` domain rather than the `sandbox_t` domain, as more privileges are needed to allow graphical applications to run. Keep in mind though that the sandbox domain has very few privileges; connecting to networked resources is not allowed, so it is not possible to use the sandbox (without additional modifications and SELinux policy adjustments) to run a sandboxed browser to interact with unsafe websites.

Assigning common policies to new applications

In between the strong isolation of an SELinux sandbox and the broad permissions of unconfined domains (or even permissive domains) sits the sufficiently privileged application domain. For most administrators, having a proper SELinux domain for applications is the best way forward, as it allows all the common behaviors and restricts unwanted ones.

When we start looking at application domains, however, we notice that there is differentiation in complexity, and as an administrator, we need to understand what the complexity is about before we can make the right choice.

Understanding domain complexity

SELinux is able to provide full system confinement: each and every application runs in its own restricted environment that it cannot break out of. But that requires fine-grained policies that are developed as quickly as the new releases of all the applications they confine.

Developing fine-grained policies at this speed is not possible, so a balance has to be struck between the maintainability of a policy and the security of the domain. This balance is the policy design complexity or domain complexity, which can be roughly categorized as follows:

- **Fine-grained policies** have separate, individual domains for each sub component of an application or service. Such policies have the advantage that they really attempt to restrict applications as much as possible. Through fine-grained policies, roles developed with users and administrators in mind become fine-grained as well, for instance, by differentiating sub-roles in the application.

The disadvantage of such policies is that they are hard to maintain, requiring frequent updates as the application itself evolves. The policies also need to take into account the impact of the various configuration options that the application supports.

Such fine-grained policies are not frequently found. An example is the policy set provided for the Postfix mail infrastructure. Each sub-service of the Postfix infrastructure has its own SELinux domain.

- **Application-level policies** use a single domain for an application, regardless of its sub-components. This balances the requirement for application confinement versus the maintainability of the application and its SELinux policy.

Such application-level policies are the most common in SELinux policies. They do still suffer from regular maintenance as applications expand their functionality, but the complexity of this is limited and SELinux policy developers should not have too many problems maintaining these policies.

- **Category-wide policies** use a single domain definition for a set of applications that implement the same functionality. This is popular for services that act very similarly and whose user-role definitions can be described without really considering the application-specific nature.

A good example of a category-wide policy is the policy for web servers. While this policy was initially written for the Apache HTTP daemon, the policy has become reusable for a number of web servers, such as the Cherokee, Hiawatha, Nginx, and Lighttpd projects.

While such policies are easier to maintain, the downside of category-wide policies is that they often have more broad privileges than really needed. As more applications are joined in the category-wide policy, additional rules and privileges are added to support those specific functions.

- **Coarse-grained policies** are used for applications or services whose behavior is hard to define. End user domains are examples of coarse-grained policies, as are unconfined domains.

When we are dealing with a new application, and we want to quickly assign a decent-enough policy, the most common method is to see whether a category-wide policy exists that we can reuse for the application.

Running applications in a specific policy

Let's consider the situation for the pgpool-II application. When we install it without any additional changes, it will run with the unconfined_service_t domain, as mentioned in the *Marking domains as permissive* section. But perhaps we can find a suitable policy to run the pgpool-II application with, through which it is more confined.

As the pgpool-II solution is a load balance-like application for PostgreSQL databases, it is likely we can run it in the PostgreSQL domain. If there are no PostgreSQL databases running on the same system, then lending this domain for the pgpool-II application might not do much harm. Let's see how well this goes:

1. The PostgreSQL policy uses the postgresql_exec_t SELinux type for its executables, so let's assign that one to the pgpool binary:

    ```
    # chcon -t postgresql_exec_t /usr/bin/pgpool
    ```

2. If we try to start the pgpool system service, we might get one or more failures:

    ```
    # systemctl start pgpool
    # systemctl status pgpool
    ...
    WARNING: Failed to open status file at: "/var/log/pgpool/
    pgpool_status"
    FATAL: could not read pid file
    ```

3. One of the failures mentioned is that the daemon cannot access its logs (in /var/log/pgpool) while another complains about the process ID file (in /var/run/pgpool) being unreachable. As these were previously created by an unconfined domain, it is indeed likely that their context is wrong as well. Let's apply the PostgreSQL-specific types to these locations:

    ```
    # chcon -R -t postgresql_log_t /var/log/pgpool
    # chcon -R -t postgresql_var_run_t /var/run/pgpool
    ```

4. After restarting pgpool, we notice it has a new failure:

    ```
    # systemctl start pgpool
    # systemctl status pgpool
    ...
    LOG: Setting up socket for ::1.9999
    FATAL: failed to create INET domain socket
    DETAIL: bind on socket failed with error "Permission
    denied"
    ```

This time, we get a permission failure, which most of the time implies that the SELinux policy is refusing a certain action:

```
# ausearch -i -m avc -ts recent
... avc: denied { name_bind } for pid=20065 comm=pgpool
src=9999 scontext=system_u:system_r:postgresql_t:s0
tcontext=system_u:object_r:jboss_management_port_t:s0
tclass=tcp_socket
```

The denial seems to reflect the information displayed earlier: pgpool wants to listen on port 9999, but SELinux is refusing this.

5. Let's create a small policy enhancement to allow postgresql_t to bind to this port:

```
(typeattributeset cil_gen_require jboss_management_
port_t)
(typeattributeset cil_gen_require postgresql_t)
(allow postgresql_t jboss_management_port_t (tcp_socket
(name_bind)))
```

6. Load this policy and restart pgpool. With this in place, pgpool starts up fine.

   Of course, having the daemon launch without problems does not mean that it will work without problems, so it is recommended to continue testing, using the service as intended.

Finding out which policy can be reused for a process requires a bit of practice and searching. For instance, you can query the policy for which domains are able to bind to the port that the daemon needs. Or you can search for a domain that has a behavior very similar to the application involved. In our example, we only had to allow the domain to bind to port 9999. We could also use this information point to seek a different policy—one that is allowed to bind to this port (such as the httpd_t domain) and see whether that one fits better.

While this approach is trial and error, it could allow running the service in a more confined domain than the unconfined domain would. A much better approach, however, is to generate a new, custom policy and work from there.

Extending generated policies

When we assign a different policy to a new application, we are reusing and possibly extending existing policies. We can go a step further and generate new policies, after which we can further extend those policies, effectively moving into the realm of developing new policies ourselves.

In *Chapter 15*, *Using the Reference Policy*, and *Chapter 16*, *Developing Policies with SELinux CIL*, we will expand further into the policy development aspects for more fine-grained control. By using policy generation tools, however, we can quickly create a first-draft policy and adapt as needed.

An important caveat is that policy generation tools often limit themselves to a single-policy format, either being reference policy style or CIL style. Administrators and organizations should try to focus on a single style and stick with that so that the learning curve for new developers and administrators isn't too high.

Understanding the limitations of generated policies

Policy generators, such as the `udica` tool we saw in *Chapter 11*, *Enhancing the Security of Containerized Workloads*, often have a very specific purpose. For instance, the `udica` tool focuses on generating new container SELinux domains and is only useful for those containers. Generators will always have a specific target in mind for what their policies should look like.

The generated policies are often application-level policies. Creating fine-grained policies with generators is hard, and defining category-wide policies requires multiple steps and occurrences, whereas generators often use single-step generations.

Furthermore, most generated policies only generally support role-based access controls within SELinux: either a user is allowed the target SELinux domain and interacting with it, or the user isn't allowed. Differentiating roles (such as application administrator versus application user) are not often included in generated policies.

Administrators should be aware that generators also have to make assumptions about how applications work. While this allows generators to be used for the majority of simple services and applications, they are definitely not ready yet to substitute a knowledgeable team of SELinux policy developers.

Introducing sepolicy generate

The `sepolicy` command is able to generate initial SELinux policy modules, which administrators and developers can then fine-tune further. This generator will use some resources on the system (such as the package database of the distribution) to better understand which resources to include, and generates a number of SELinux policy files.

As there are different types of applications around, the `sepolicy generate` command also requires the user to inform it about the application type. The following types are currently supported:

- User applications are identified with the `--application` option. Such applications are meant for end users to launch and interact with.

- System service applications are identified with the `--init` option. Applications that run in daemon mode or with their own user are most often system service applications.

- D-Bus system service applications are identified with the `--dbus` option. This type of service is invoked by D-Bus.

- **Common Gateway Interface (CGI)** scripts or applications are supported through the `--cgi` option. Using CGI-specific domains allows having CGI applications run in their own domain, rather than extending the privileges of the web server domain itself.

- **Internet services daemon (inetd)** applications are supported through the `--inetd` option.

- Sandbox applications are like user applications but much more confined, and are supported through the `--sandbox` option.

Next to application-level policy generation, `sepolicy generate` also supports generating user domains and roles:

- Standard users with support for the graphical desktop can be generated using the `--desktop_user` option. This is a common, non-administration-oriented user role.

- A more lightweight, minimal user role that still supports the graphical desktop can be generated using the `--x_user` option. This domain focuses on minimal permissions and thus requires further extensions before they can be better put to use.

- If no graphical user interface needs to be supported, then you can use the `--term_user` option. This generates a confined user domain without desktop support.

- Administration-oriented user domains can be generated using the `--admin_user` option. This is meant for broad administrative privileges.

- More confined administration domains can be generated using the `--confined_admin` option. This allows you to generate user domains that have administrative roles for a limited number of application domains, not to the system as a whole.

The generator also supports customizing existing domains further (using `--customize`) or generating specific types (using `--newtype`).

Let's use `sepolicy generate` to generate a policy for the pgpool-II application.

Generating policies with sepolicy generate

The `sepolicy generate` command will create a skeleton SELinux policy, using the reference policy code style. This policy can then be gradually extended with the privileges the application needs.

Let's create and adapt the policy for `pgool`:

1. First, we tell `sepolicy` to generate a new policy, named pgpool, which is intended for the `/usr/bin/pgpool` binary:

    ```
    # sepolicy generate -n pgpool --init /usr/bin/pgpool
    ```

2. Next, build the generated SELinux policy:

    ```
    # make -f /usr/share/selinux/devel/Makefile pgpool.pp
    ```

3. Load the policy in memory:

    ```
    # semodule -i pgpool.pp
    ```

4. Relabel the filesystem, or at least the locations mentioned in the generated `pgpool.fc` file:

    ```
    # restorecon -RvF /usr/bin/pgpool /var/log/pgpool \
      /var/run/pgpool
    ```

5. Start the pgpool service:

    ```
    # systemctl start pgpool
    ```

    After starting, be amazed that pgpool is running flawlessly.

Now, you might have the impression that this was too easy. Yes, it was. The default SELinux policy that `sepolicy generate` provides is permissive, as you can see from within the `pgpool.te` file:

```
permissive pgpool_t;
```

If we remove this statement, rebuild, and reload the policy, then we will notice the failures coming up again, such as the process not being allowed to bind to the selected ports. We can now use `audit2allow`, for instance, to help us extend the policy as needed:

```
# cat /var/log/audit/audit.log | audit2allow -R
```

Gradually extend, rebuild, and reload the policy until the application works without problems.

Summary

Linux administrators can use SELinux controls to prevent or confine access to applications, but this is not always the requirement at hand. Being able to run the application with the *right* set of permissions is, and what the right set is depends on the user's intentions and the environment.

Within this chapter, we've learned how to apply the appropriate confinement to application domains, ranging from very isolated container environments over regular application domains, category-wide permission sets, and up to unconfined domains and even permissive domains. We learned that this is done by first finding the appropriate domain, understanding which labels the domain uses, and then assigning the right labels to the files so that the application is executed in the right domain.

We also learned how to generate new policies (using `sepolicy generate`) ourselves without immediately having to dive into a full SELinux policy development approach, which is what we will consider in the final two chapters.

Questions

1. What is the difference between an unconfined domain and a permissive domain?
2. How can we run applications in a very restricted domain?
3. How can we easily switch the domain in which a service will run?
4. Why do policies generated by `sepolicy` seemingly run without problems?

15
Using the Reference Policy

Up until now, we've covered how to interact with the SELinux subsystem and gradually adjusted the SELinux policy to our liking. As we add more applications and users, we notice that developing custom SELinux policies might help us tune the system more to our liking. There are two main approaches to develop SELinux policies, and using reference policy style development is one of them. The other is discussed in *Chapter 16, SELinux Common Intermediate Language*.

To properly develop an SELinux policy, we'll learn how to use and understand the macros that the reference policy provides, and apply the main coding and development style patterns that the project requires to ensure consistency across SELinux policy modules. We then apply this to two main types of modules: application policies and user policies.

In this chapter, we're going to cover the following main topics:

- Introducing the reference policy
- Using and understanding the policy macros
- Creating application-level policies
- Getting help with supporting tools

Technical requirements

The code files for this chapter can be found in our Git repository at `https://github.com/PacktPublishing/SELinux-System-Administration-Third-Edition`.

Check out the following video to see the Code in Action: `https://bit.ly/3jcBDvI`

Introducing the reference policy

The reference policy, available through `https://github.com/SELinuxProject/refpolicy`, is the source SELinux policy for most, if not all, Linux distributions out there. While it is possible that the plain reference policy will not work out of the box for any Linux distribution (as many Linux distributions add their own touch to the policy, or adjust it so it fits the applications and support tooling installed), the development methodology, structure, and approach used by the reference policy are applicable to all major distribution policies.

We recommend checking out the SELinux policy of your distribution to see and easily modify SELinux policies for the system. In this chapter, we'll use a checkout of the reference policy:

```
$ git clone https://github.com/SELinuxProject/refpolicy.git
```

The SELinux policy repositories for the Linux distributions should be documented by the distributions themselves. A few example repositories are listed next:

- For CentOS, the policy repository can be found at `https://github.com/fedora-selinux/selinux-policy`.

- For Gentoo Linux, the policy repository can be found at `https://gitweb.gentoo.org/proj/hardened-refpolicy.git/`.

- For Debian, the policy repository can be found at `https://salsa.debian.org/cgzones/selinux-policy-debian`.

- For Arch Linux, the policy repository can be found at `https://github.com/archlinuxhardened/selinux-policy-arch/`.

If the Linux distribution does not have a publicly reachable repository for its SELinux policy, we can often still obtain it through the packages themselves, as used in *Chapter 12, Working with SELinux Policies*.

While it is not the intention to do full policy rebuilds, we can easily copy over the necessary policy files to our own development environment and fine-tune or extend the policy as needed.

Navigating the policy

At its base directory, the reference policy hosts all the common files for building the policies, explaining how to install them, and so forth. The policy itself is in the `policy` folder, which contains three directories:

- `flask` contains the initial definitions used to jumpstart SELinux, such as listing the supported classes, creating initial security identifiers, and more. We will not touch this location further.

- `modules` contains the SELinux policy code and is the main location for all policy rules.

- `support` contains macros and definitions that are reused across the policy and are not associated with a single policy module.

If we enter the `modules` directory further, we get directories that represent the type of modules or policies contained. This representation by itself is merely to have some structure across the hundreds of modules that are developed:

- `admin` contains system administration related policy modules.

- `apps` contains general application policy modules.

- `kernel` contains core system policy modules (not just kernel related ones).

- `roles` contains SELinux role definitions and default user domain policy modules.

- `services` contains general service policy modules (and is by far the largest set of policy modules).

- `system` contains common system related policy modules.

The interpretation of which folder a policy is placed in is left to the reference policy project itself, and discussed on its mailing list when it is not obvious. As policy files are required to have a unique name, we can find the appropriate location easily. For instance, to see where the `ipsec` policy module is stored:

```
$ ls policy/modules/*/ipsec.te
policy/modules/system/ipsec.te
```

While browsing, you'll notice that the policy modules are always represented by three files, which we describe next.

Structuring policy modules

If we analyze an SELinux policy module's code, such as for the dhcp module in the services folder, we'll notice that it has three files associated with it:

- dhcp.te, which contains the type enforcement rules, and is the main area of attention for most changes

- dhcp.fc, which contains the file context definitions, informing the policy which files or resources need to be labeled with dhcp related SELinux types

- dhcp.if, which contains interface definitions, which are reusable functions or macros that can be used in the dhcp SELinux policy code as well as elsewhere

Let's quickly see how each of these files is structured.

Understanding type enforcement files

The type enforcement file, dhcp.te in our example, has the following structure:

```
policy_module(dhcp, 1.18.2)

## Declarations
# SELinux booleans
# SELinux types

## Local policy
# Internal SELinux rules
# Core interfaced SELinux rules
# SELinux boolean controlled SELinux rules
# Non-blocking interfaced SELinux rules
```

Let's look at each of these areas with an example.

Declaring SELinux objects

The Declarations section in a policy tells us what SELinux types, or other SELinux objects such as SELinux booleans and SELinux roles, are defined within this module.

The following declarations are common in SELinux policies:

- The first declaration in the dhcp SELinux policy declares an SELinux boolean for this module. It is best practice to start the boolean with the SELinux policy module name, although in this case the choice is made to explicitly use dhcpd rather than dhcp to make it obvious for administrators it is about the DHCP daemon and not possible clients or other use cases:

```
## <desc>
##    <p>Determine whether DHCP daemon can use LDAP
##    backends</p>
## </desc>
gen_tunable(dhcpd_use_ldap, false)
```

  The SELinux boolean is accompanied by a specifically structured comment. Comments within the reference policy that use a double hash prefix (##) will be parsed by the build code and used to update information outside of the SELinux policy. In this case, the description of the SELinux boolean is created, which will be made visible later on through commands such as semanage boolean.

  Once a module is loaded that defines an SELinux policy, other modules can use this boolean as well.

- Some domains might also declare a role attribute, which allows easy management of which roles are allowed to use the domain:

```
attribute_role dhcpd_roles;
```

- The rest of the declarations in the dhcp SELinux policy declare the SELinux types that the policy owns:

```
type dhcpd_t;       # The SELinux domain for the daemon
type dhcpd_exec_t; # The executable label for the daemon
init_daemon_domain(dhcpd_t, dhcpd_exec_t)
                    # Linking the executable to the domain
```

  SELinux policy modules in the reference policy only declare the types and other objects that they own, not those they use. The objects used but defined by other modules should always be hidden away and interacted with through the interface calls.

While other definitions can be added to the section as well, these are the most common. Next up are the local policy rules.

Adding the domain's local rules

The local policy within the type enforcement defines the allowed behavior of the domains owned by the SELinux policy module. For the dhcp SELinux policy module, this is only focusing on the dhcpd_t SELinux domain. Other SELinux policy modules, especially if they offer a more fine-grained policy structure, will do this for several of its own SELinux domains, or even SELinux user roles.

Let's go through the SELinux policy rules for the dhcp.te example we are looking at:

- The policy starts with the internal SELinux rules, which are interactions between the SELinux types owned by the SELinux policy module itself:

```
allow dhcpcd_t self:process { getcap signal_perms };
manage_files_pattern(dhcpd_t, dhcpd_tmp_t, dhcpd_tmp_t)
```

The most simple rules are the standard allow rules, similar to those that audit2allow would recommend. These allow rules can refer to support macros (such as signal_perms), which we'll discuss in the *Using and understanding the policy macros* section. The second line, which is a call to manage_files_pattern, is also a support macro.

- The second set of local policy definitions are the core interfaced SELinux rules:

```
kernel_read_system_state(dhcpd_t)
```

These calls use the code that another SELinux policy module has defined in its interface file. In the case of the kernel_read_system_state interface, this will grant the dhcpd_t SELinux domain the rights to read proc_t labeled resources. As proc_t is not defined by the dhcp SELinux policy module, an interface call has to be used.

Core interfaced SELinux rules are rules that should at all times be available to the system. Unlike application related SELinux policy modules, which can be disabled or unloaded, these core rules are associated with type definitions that cannot be removed from the system or disabled at will.

- The third set of local policy definitions are the SELinux boolean controlled calls:

```
tunable_policy(`dhcpd_use_ldap',`
  # If boolean is true
  sysnet_use_ldap(dhcpd_t)
',`
  # If boolean is false
')
```

Here, the SELinux interface calls (which can also be standard rules such as `allow` rules) are surrounded by a `tunable_policy()` call, which identifies the SELinux boolean (in our case `dhcpd_use_ldap`) that will influence the SELinux policy rules. Most policy modules will only have a single block (for the rules that are activated if the SELinux boolean is true) but it is possible to have two blocks, where the second one defines the rules in case the SELinux boolean is false.

- The final set of local policy definitions are the non-blocking interfaced SELinux rules:

```
optional_policy(`
  bind_read_dnssec_keys(dhcpd_t)
')
```

These are the calls that use definitions provided by other SELinux policy modules, but where these SELinux policy modules might not be loaded on the system.

In our example, the `bind_read_dnssec_keys()` call allows the `dhcpd_t` SELinux domain to read `dnssec_t` labeled resources, as defined by the bind SELinux policy module. However, BIND might not be installed on the system, and the Linux distribution might thus not have its policy loaded. So this call is optional and only active if the bind SELinux policy module is loaded.

The type enforcement file is the file that will change most often. The file context definition file, which we discuss next, is a close second.

Declaring file contexts

The file context definition file, with the `.fc` suffix, tells the SELinux subsystem what SELinux types have to be associated with the file resources on the system. This information is used by tools such as `restorecon` to reset the context appropriately.

The rules inside the file are generally grouped based on the directory for which the rules apply. Each rule is structured like so:

```
<path expression>    [<type/class>]    <context>
```

Let's see what these entries imply:

- The *path expressions* are the same ones we saw in *Chapter 4, Using File Contexts and Process Domains*. Keep in mind that characters such as dot (.) have a specific meaning (in this case, it reflects any possible character) so that paths that really require a dot inside must escape the dot.

- The *type/class* is an optional setting. If omitted, then it means any possible class is used. The most common values to use are regular files (--), directories (-d), sockets (-s), and symbolic links (-l).

- The *context* is a reference to the target SELinux type for this resource. In the reference policy, these context references always need to be encased by the gen_context() macro, which will add or remove the sensitivity depending on the MLS or MCS support built inside the policy.

Let's look at a simple example from the dhcp SELinux policy module:

```
/var/named/data(/.*)?  gen_context(system_u:object_r:named_
cache_t,s0)
```

In this example, the /var/named/data directory, and any resource below it, will be labeled with the named_cache_t SELinux type.

The last file that is associated with an SELinux policy module is the interface definition file.

Exposing SELinux rules through interfaces

Interfaces within an SELinux policy module are meant to support a more flexible, modular development of SELinux policies across different modules. Whenever a domain or SELinux role needs to interact with resources that are defined in a different SELinux policy module, that module should create a properly named interface for the interaction.

Interfaces should be accompanied by a minimal amount of documentation, although this documentation is only used when building the documentation of the entire policy. When this is done, the resulting documentation is made available on the system, for instance in /usr/share/doc/selinux-policy/html.

Let's look at the definition for the dhcpd_domtrans() interface:

```
########################################
## <summary>
##    Execute a domain transition to run dhcpd.
## </summary>
## <param name="domain">
##    <summary>
##    Domain allowed to transition.
##    </summary>
## </param>
#
interface(`dhcpd_domtrans',`
  gen_require(`
```

```
      type dhcpd_t, dhcpd_exec_t;
   ')


   corecmd_search_bin($1)
   domtrans_pattern($1, dhcpd_exec_t, dhcpd_t)
')
```

As is best practice, the interface name starts with the SELinux policy name and is followed by the action that is allowed. Sometimes, this action is suffixed with the target resource. The interface itself can reference the arguments passed along to the interface using $1 (first argument), $2 (second argument), and so on. So a call such as dhcpd_domtrans(init_t) will have the interface called, where $1 is substituted with init_t.

Let's look at a few examples with common actions:

- **Domain transitions** allow a domain to transition to another domain. If the SELinux policy module only manages a single domain, then there is no target resource defined (as with dhcpd_domtrans()). If there are multiple domains, then the target resource will define which domain (as with bind_domtrans_ndc()) to allow a domain transition to the ndc_t SELinux domain.

- **Permission interactions** generally refer to the permission at hand and, if it is possible to misinterpret to which resource the permission refers, the target resource is listed. So dhcpd_setattr_state_files() allows the domain to set the attributes of the dhcpd_state_t labeled resources, whereas bind_signal() allows the domain to send signals to the named_t labeled processes. Most of the interface definitions will be permission interactions.

- **Role-oriented interfaces** will grant the associated SELinux role and SELinux domain all the privileges needed to perform a functional role for the SELinux domain. For instance, the dhcpd_admin() role will allow managing the dhcpd related resources, starting and stopping the dhcpd service, and so on.

  Suppose you want to grant this to the web administration role, then the call within the web administration SELinux policy module could look like so:

  ```
  optional_policy(`
    dhcpd_admin(webadm_r, webadm_t)
  ')
  ```

While developing SELinux policies, it is recommended to look into the interface definitions of the SELinux policy modules to see which ones exist and what they provide. Policy developers will put often requested permissions in such interfaces, so the available interfaces give a good view of what you will most likely need for your own SELinux policy module.

The interface definitions are also made available on the system at `/usr/share/selinux/devel/include` so that you can create and modify SELinux policy modules even without checking out the main source repository. Whenever we build a reference policy style module, we use a command like the following:

```
$ make -f /usr/share/selinux/devel/Makefile <name>.pp
```

This will cause the build process to look for the interfaces inside the `/usr/share/selinux/devel/include` location, as well as inside the current working directory.

Using and understanding the policy macros

Across the various SELinux policy definitions, we have come across macros that are not tied to a specific SELinux policy module. These are support macros, available inside the `policy/support/*.spt` files.

The most common macros are those declared inside the `obj_perm_sets.spt` file (which group common permissions for the same class in a single definition) and the `*_patterns.spt` files (which group permissions across different classes in a single definition).

Making use of single-class permission groups

Single-class permission groups allow developers to ignore possible extensions of the SELinux supported permissions as time goes by. For instance, if you want to allow a domain to execute a certain resource, it is most often not enough to allow the `execute` permission. You also need the `open` and `read` permissions (as otherwise, the domain cannot read the executable) and the `map` permission (to allow mapping the file in memory).

If you were to put all these permissions in your own SELinux policy module, then the rule could look like so:

```
allow dhcpd_t dhcpd_exec_t:file { getattr open map read execute
ioctl execute_no_trans };
```

If, later on, the SELinux policy is extended with an additional permission that is associated with executing resources, then you will need to look for and update these permissions all over the different SELinux policy modules.

So the reference policy moves all these permissions in a macro called `exec_file_perms`, defined as follows:

```
define(`exec_file_perms',`{ getattr open map read execute ioctl
execute_no_trans }')
```

With this macro defined, our policy line can be simplified as follows:

```
allow dhcpd_t dhcpd_exec_t:file { exec_file_perms };
```

If at any point the permissions need to be extended, all that has to happen is to extend the macro definition itself, and the SELinux policy modules can be left untouched.

Calling permission groups

While single-class permission groups are a good use for simplifying policy development, **permission groups** that cover multiple classes are even more common.

For instance, if a domain needs full management privileges (implying `read`, `write`, as well as creating and removing resources) on resources inside `/var/lib/dhcpd`, then not only are these privileges needed on the files inside that directory (which are labeled with the `dhcpd_state_t` SELinux type), but you also need read/write permissions on the directory itself.

Such a privilege definition would result in something like so:

```
allow $1 dhcpd_state_t:dir { rw_dir_perms };
allow $1 dhcpd_state_t:file { manage_file_perms };
```

Rather than declaring these as separate calls, they can be put into a single one that groups the two:

```
manage_files_pattern($1, dhcpd_state_t, dhcpd_state_t)
```

SELinux policy developers best get acquainted with the various macros available to allow for rapid and efficient SELinux policy development.

Creating application-level policies

Application-level policies provide confinement for applications or services. There are a number of different types of application-level policies around:

- End user application policies, which focus on accessing end user data, and will often call various `userdom_*` interfaces (which are provided through the `system/userdomain.if` file). Most of these applications are inside the `apps/` directory).

- Administration applications, which are still user-facing, are more likely to enable interacting with system services and resources.

- Services, which are generally daemonized applications, often interact mostly with their own resources and have a simpler structure.

When we covered the `sepolicy generate` command in *Chapter 14, Dealing with New Applications*, we could select these types (and more) to generate a simple skeleton for those applications.

Let's look into some example policies and identify useful calls that you might need when developing your own policies.

Constructing network-facing service policies

Services that are network-facing (meaning they can be interacted with from outside the system itself) are the first set of services that need to be confined. Hence, building SELinux policy modules for network-facing services should be a primary focus of any Linux administrator that needs to ensure the confinement of applications that do not have a working policy yet.

If we look at the OpenVPN service, then we find that there is an SELinux policy under `services/openvpn.te` that we can look into.

Identifying the resources that the service interacts with

As a policy starts with identifying the types and other SELinux objects, we need to consider the resources on the system that the service interacts with. When comparing service policies with each other, you'll notice that the definitions are often very similar:

- The main domain type and its entry point executable are declared first. Depending on the type of service, it contains a call as to how it would be started: as a system service (using `init_daemon_domain()`) or through the D-Bus system bus (using `dbus_system_domain()`).

- The configuration files for the service (such as `openvpn_etc_t`), which could also differentiate between read-only files and read-write (such as `openvpn_etc_rw_t`).
- Runtime files (which are generally stored in `/var/run`) such as `openvpn_runtime_t`.
- Temporary files (which are generally stored in `/tmp` or `/var/tmp`) such as `openvpn_tmp_t`.
- Log files (which are generally stored in `/var/log`) such as `openvpn_var_log_t`.

Each of the type declarations is followed by a call that marks the type appropriately. For instance, the `logging_log_file()` call will associate the type with the logfile SELinux attribute. This allows general logfile management domains to deal with the newly created resource through this attribute.

Handling the internal SELinux rules

With the resources declared, we have to define the internal SELinux rules within the SELinux policy. These rules tell SELinux what the domain can do with its own resources, and how SELinux should behave when the resources are interacted with.

We will generally have two sets of internal rules declared. One is the fine-grained permissions of the domain itself, such as if the domain is allowed to have any capabilities, creating sockets, and so on. The development of these rules is trial-and-error based: start with close to no permissions, see what AVC denials come up, extend the policy, and repeat.

The other set of internal rules focuses on the interaction with the types declared earlier on. This not only includes which permissions the domain has (such as through the `manage_files_pattern()` calls) but also whether transitions have to occur.

Setting the right set of transitions is one of the more important first steps to take while developing application policies because `audit2allow` and AVC denials generally do not consider the fact that a target resource has the wrong type assigned. So when we have a service that creates files in `/tmp` (which is labeled as `tmp_t`), we really want the target files to be labeled correctly (such as `openvpn_tmp_t`) and not inherit the `tmp_t` label from the directory:

```
allow openvpn_t openvpn_tmp_t:file manage_file_perms;
files_tmp_filetrans(openvpn_t, openvpn_tmp_t, file)
```

File transitions should be declared for all the resources involved. If a transition has to occur for both files and directories, you can mix the classes in a single call like so:

```
files_tmp_filetrans(openvpn_t, openvpn_tmp_t, { file dir })
```

We can also tell SELinux that a transition should only occur if a specific filename is used:

```
logging_log_filetrans(openvpn_t, openvpn_status_t, file,
"openvpn-status.log")
```

It is really recommended to first consider the file transitions (and other resource transitions) before expanding the actual permissions for the domain to make sure that we are not tempted to allow the domain privileges to general types when that is not necessary.

Adding network related permissions

While developing and expanding the policy, several core functions will be added, such as the `kernel_*` calls to allow processes to interact with the `proc_t` resources, system control settings, and more. Tools such as `audit2allow` will reasonably be able to deduce the right interfaces to call, although it does not hurt to review the interfaces to make sure not too many privileges are assigned.

Network related permissions on the other hand might require some more attention. As we saw in *Chapter 5*, *Controlling Network Communications*, SELinux can dynamically address certain network flows based on the system configuration.

It is likely that systems who do not have specific controls in place, such as labelled networking or SECMARK, will find that three interface calls could allow the application to work as intended:

```
corenet_tcp_bind_generic_node(openvpn_t)
corenet_tcp_bind_openvpn_port(openvpn_t)
corenet_tcp_connect_http_port(openvpn_t)
```

These three interface calls allow the domain to be network-oriented (`corenet_tcp_bind_generic_node`), listen to the OpenVPN port (`corenet_tcp_bind_openvpn_port`), as well as connecting, as a client, to HTTP ports (`corenet_tcp_connect_http_port`).

But other calls exist that you might need to add, even though they are currently not detected. They might become necessary when the system is tuned further, such as adding support for labeled networking or introducing SECMARK filtering.

The first set is to allow sending and receiving packets on generic nodes (hosts) and interfaces:

```
corenet_tcp_sendrecv_generic_node(openvpn_t)
corenet_tcp_sendrecv_generic_if(openvpn_t)
```

For NetLabel support, you might need to add support to receive labeled network packets:

```
corenet_all_recvfrom_netlabel(openvpn_t)
```

For SECMARK support, you need to add support for sending and receiving SECMARK labeled packets:

```
corenet_sendrecv_openvpn_server_packets(openvpn_t)
corenet_sendrecv_http_client_packets(openvpn_t)
```

These calls might not show up in early tests, but could be needed later on, and it is recommended to consider the impact of labeled networking and SECMARK on your policy from the beginning.

Building the service interface methods

We next focus our efforts on the interface methods. These are used to facilitate other SELinux policy modules to interact with the domain we're developing, although they can also be used to simplify policy development for your own policy.

The three most common interfaces to define, and which other policy developers will assume exist, are the following:

- A **domain transition interface**, such as openvpn_domtrans, allowing the given SELinux domain to execute the appropriate binaries or scripts and have the executed commands or applications run in our domain (and as such transition from the source domain to ours).

- A **run interface**, such as openvpn_run, which is like the domain transition interface (and in fact will call it) but also allows our domain for the role. Without this interface, some roles might not be able to transition even if they call the domain transition interface.

- An **administration interface**, such as openvpn_admin, which will be assigned to user roles/domains to allow them to administer our service. This will allow the user to interact with the processes of our domain (including killing the processes, tracing their actions, and so on) as well as to administer the files and resources used.

Within the interfaces, we need to declare the SELinux objects that we are going to explicitly reference. This allows the SELinux subsystem to validate whether the code is applicable or not: if the objects are not present in the current policy, then this interface is not valid and will not be used. Declaring objects is done with the `gen_require()` macro:

```
interface(`openvpn_run',`
  gen_require(`
    attribute_role openvpn_roles;
  ')
  openvpn_domtrans($1)
  roleattribute $2 openvpn_roles;
')
```

Other interfaces can be added as needed. While you can add interfaces already just in case, be aware that once you define an interface it can be used by other policies, and you might not be made aware of this if you are not developing all policies yourself. If you, later on, want to change the behavior of interfaces or remove them, you might break other policies.

Addressing user applications

If we develop end user applications, their structure will be very similar to those for more service-oriented applications. Content-wise, however, there are a few areas of attention to consider. Let's use the `apps/thunderbird.te` policy as an example:

- The first thing we notice is that many resource defining interfaces are prefixed with `userdom_`. For instance, a temporary file is not `files_tmp_file()` but `userdom_user_tmp_file()`. This will ensure that the resources are known as **user-managed** temporary files and not regular system temporary files.

- Another important addition is the support for the **X Desktop Group** (**XDG**) locations. The XDG locations, defined in the XDG Base Directory specification at `https://specifications.freedesktop.org/basedir-spec/basedir-spec-latest.html`, standardize which end user locations are used for what purpose. For instance, inside `~/.cache`, application cache data is stored, whereas configuration data is in `~/.config`.

The use of the XDG locations is supported through the `xdg` SELinux policy module, which enables support for types of user content as well: regular documents, downloads, music, pictures, and videos. This distinction allows developing SELinux policies that are only able to interact with that specific end user content and not all the user's data.

For instance, the thunderbird application is able to manage download data (which by default is located in `~/Downloads`) through the following:

```
xdg_manage_downloads(thunderbird_t)
```

- To easily establish user content access, user applications should also call the `userdom_user_content_access_template()` template. This will automatically create booleans as well, which administrators can toggle. For instance, for the thunderbird SELinux policy, this will create `thunderbird_manage_generic_user_content`. If set, then thunderbird can not only access the downloads-related resources but all user resources.

- Another template that user application policies will need if they are graphical in nature, is `xserver_user_x_domain_template()`. This template will generate X server related SELinux objects for the application, and allow the application to use the graphical environment on the server.

> **Important note**
> The reference policy makes a distinction between regular interfaces and templates. Interfaces grant privileges to the domains and roles that are passed to it. Templates on the other hand will generate new objects, such as SELinux booleans, types, attributes, and more. Code-wise, templates cannot be part of boolean-triggered statements (as they do not just add type enforcement rules).

When the baseline of a user application policy is drafted, including the preceding templates, then expanding the policy through trial and error should suffice. Do make sure, however, that all resources on the user location for which you are testing the application are correctly labeled, as otherwise, the denials might trick you into granting more privileges to the domain than necessary.

Adding user-level policies

If we want to create custom user and role policies, then the most confusing choice is the choice of user template to pick. This template creates a role and user domain with a specific purpose in mind, and grants a number of permissions by default:

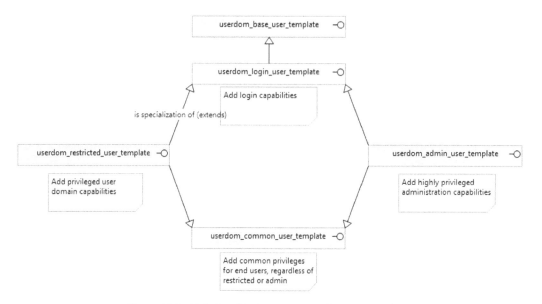

Figure 15.1 – Relationship between user domain templates

The most common templates to pick for user/role policies are the following:

- `userdom_restricted_user_template()` for (by default) unprivileged end user roles.

- `userdom_admin_user_template()` for (by default) highly privileged end user roles.

The other templates can be used as well, especially if more fine-grained controls over the roles and user domains are needed. Note, however, that the privileges assigned by the templates are mentioned as *by default*. If we want to create a role and user domain for administrating a specific service, then we do not want to use `userdom_admin_user_template()`, as this will grant many more privileges than needed.

As an example, consider the `roles/dbadm.te` SELinux policy for the database administration role. This role is based upon the `userdom_base_user_template()` interface to ensure minimal permissions are granted. The role is not meant to be used in a direct fashion (login), but rather transitioned toward (for instance, through the `newrole` command, or through well-defined role transitions within the policy).

Getting help with supporting tools

There are tools out there that help in developing SELinux policies, and if needed we can build our own support tools as well. Let's see what support environments we can use.

Verifying code with selint

While SELinux policies can be functionally working, validating whether the code itself is proper and follows best practices is important to ensure that the code is maintainable in the long run.

One of the tools that support validating SELinux policy code is `selint`, as offered from `https://github.com/TresysTechnology/selint`. Once built and installed, `selint` offers insights into four main areas:

- Convention checks validate whether the SELinux policy follows the reference policy convention on how code should be structured and documented.

- Style checks give hints for code style that might be wrong, and where the developer might have intended a different behavior.

- Warnings are triggered when the code has bad calls that might trigger runtime issues or security issues.

- Errors catch construction faults that will result in compile issues or runtime issues.

This allows the use of `selint` in automated build processes, as well as facilitating the development of policies.

Calling `selint` is simple:

```
$ selint minecraft.te
minecraft.te:  31: (C): Permissions in av rule not ordered
                         (signull before execmem) (C-005)
minecraft.te: 118: (C): Require block used in te file (use an
                         interface call instead) (S-001)
```

In this case, two convention malpractices were detected. One is in the ordering of permissions, while another has an explicit require block mentioned for a domain that is not part of that policy module.

Querying the interfaces and macros locally

To help in finding the right interface or macro, we also want to quickly be able to show interface and macro information. With some shell scripting, we can create a few functions that help us along.

The functions are provided as code together with this book. You might want to change the path that the POLICY_LOCATION variable points to at the beginning of the script. By default, it points to the system-installed interface and macros, but you can point it to repository checkouts as well:

```
POLICY_LOCATION="/usr/share/selinux/devel"
```

Source the file to have access to the helper functions:

```
$ source ./localfuncs
```

The helper functions you can use are the following:

- With sefindif you can search for an SELinux interface that has a specific SELinux rule inside. You can use regular expressions to find the appropriate one.

  For instance, to find the interface that grants a domain the privileges to manage certificate files (for readability, we only show the interface code; it will be prefixed with the location where it found it):

  ```
  $ sefindif "manage.* cert_t"
  interface(`miscfiles_manage_all_certs',`
    manage_files_pattern($1, cert_type, cert_type)
    manage_lnk_files_pattern($1, cert_type, cert_type)
  interface(`miscfiles_manage_generic_cert_dirs',`
    manage_dirs_pattern($1, cert_t, cert_t)
  interface(`miscfiles_manage_generic_cert_files',`
    manage_files_pattern($1, cert_t, cert_t)
    manage_lnk_files_pattern($1, cert_t, cert_t)
  ```

- With `seshowif` the interface in its entirety (excluding the comment) is displayed.

  For instance, to show the `miscfiles_manage_all_certs()` interface, use the following code:

```
$ seshowif miscfiles_manage_all_certs
interface(`miscfiles_manage_all_certs',`
  gen_require(`
    attribute cert_type;
  ')
  allow $1 cert_type:dir list_dir_perms;
  manage_files_pattern($1, cert_type, cert_type)
  manage_lnk_files_pattern($1, cert_type, cert_type)
')
```

- With `sefinddef` and `seshowdef`, the same is possible but for the supporting macros.

  For instance, to see the content of the `admin_pattern()` helper macro, use the following code:

```
$ seshowdef admin_pattern
define(`admin_pattern',`
  manage_dirs_pattern($1,$2,$2)
  manage_files_pattern($1,$2,$2)
  manage_lnk_files_pattern($1,$2,$2)
  manage_fifo_files_pattern($1,$2,$2)
  manage_sock_files_pattern($1,$2,$2)
  relabel_dirs_pattern($1,$2,$2)
  relabel_files_pattern($1,$2,$2)
  relabel_lnk_files_pattern($1,$2,$2)
  relabel_fifo_files_pattern($1,$2,$2)
  relabel_sock_files_pattern($1,$2,$2)
')
```

While such functions do not offer the same versatility as a full-fledged policy editor suite would, they can help in quickly finding the right interface or macro.

Summary

The reference policy is the most common source for SELinux policy development, and with years of development effort and maintenance, it has grown to be a full policy set with a vivid development community, and active support by various tools (including `audit2allow`, as well as the `selint` application).

We've learned how policies are generally structured, and how to start building SELinux policy modules for the most common use cases: application services, end user applications, and user roles. To help us in developing these policies, we've seen that `selint` can do code-style analysis, whereas some shell scripts can help us parse the interface files for quick help.

In our final chapter, we will look into CIL style SELinux development.

Questions

1. Why don't Linux distributions use the reference policy natively?

2. What are the three main policy files needed for an SELinux module, and what is their purpose?

3. Why is a permission set such as `exec_file_perms` preferred over explicitly listing the permissions?

4. What is the difference between interfaces and templates?

5. Why is the database administration role defined in `dbadm.te` not using `userdom_admin_user_template`?

16
Developing Policies with SELinux CIL

While the reference policy is the most frequently used language and development style for SELinux policies, the **Common Intermediate Language** (**CIL**) is a powerful, but more low-level language construct to use to develop SELinux policies. Low-level as it might be though, it is still very much readable and well supported, as SELinux tools will use CIL under the hood when using other languages.

Since CIL is the main language used, we know it can be used to build entire policies. Sadly, there are no supporting constructs available for developers to use, unlike the reference policy. However, we can still learn how to customize the current policy, creating specific definitions that are not possible with the more common reference policy, and even build a complete application policy if we choose.

In this chapter, we're going to cover the following main topics:

- Introducing CIL
- Creating fine-grained definitions
- Building complete application policies

Technical requirements

Check out the following video to see the Code in Action: `https://bit.ly/3dLYP2Q`

Introducing CIL

CIL has been designed to be the main language to have policies built in, and is the lowest readable format. After CIL, the SELinux code is transformed in binary to send off to the Linux kernel (and SELinux subsystem) for loading in memory.

Administrators might be inclined to think that the binary files, generated when building a SELinux policy module using the reference policy method, are the final binaries. However, as we've seen in *Chapter 1, Fundamental SELinux Concepts*, the `semodule` command converts and translates this into CIL before building the final format.

Let's see how these translations work and what we can learn from them.

Translating .pp files to CIL

When a non-CIL SELinux policy module is loaded, the `semodule` command is designed to first consider the module as an unknown format, and extract the **High Level Language (HLL)** information from it. HLL is an abstract term that the SELinux utilities use to define any SELinux source format that it knows how to convert to CIL later on. Currently, only .pp files are supported as an HLL.

As the HLL format of the SELinux policy modules built by reference policy (or the other classic SELinux development) is the same as the module generated, this phase often just involves creating a copy. We can see this when we compare an HLL file with the original:

```
$ cp /var/lib/selinux/targeted/active/modules/400/pgpool/hll
pgpool.hll.bz2
$ bunzip2 pgpool.hll.bz2
$ sha512sum pgpool.pp pgpool.hll
b81ba4ac...c0db pgpool.pp
b81ba4ac...c0db pgpool.hll
```

Once it has converted or extracted the data, `semodule` will convert it to CIL code. For each supported HLL, a convertor is available in `/usr/libexec/selinux/hll`. Currently, only the `pp` command is available, which is used to convert this older style into CIL.

Let's see this in action:

```
$ /usr/libexec/selinux/hll/pp pgpool.pp
(type pgpool_t)
(roletype object_r pgpool_t)
(type pgpool_exec_t)
...
(filecon "/var/run/pgpool(/.*)?" any (system_u object_r pgpool_
var_run_t ((s0) (s0))))
```

So, in essence, when we are developing reference policy style modules, they will be converted into CIL anyway. The resulting CIL code, however, does not have any facilitating constructions inside. For instance, all permissions are expanded, and all interactions with other resources or types outside of the SELinux policy module are listed as well. There are no longer any supporting macros or interfaces. In the *Building complete application policies* section, we'll see that CIL does support abstractions, so the current observation is only due to the translation that the pp command performs.

Understanding CIL syntax

When we develop CIL, the most obvious observation is that it likes brackets. CIL uses S-expression syntax, popularized by Lisp, which results in tree-structured data. The first identifier in an expression that tells CIL what the construction is about.

Let's take a look at the last statement we received when converting the pgpool.pp binary into CIL, now formatted for convenience:

```
(filecon
  "/var/run/pgpool(/.*)?"
  any
  (
    system_u
    object_r
    pgpool_var_run_t
    (
      (s0)
      (s0)
    )
  )
)
```

If we look at this statement in detail, we can deduce the following:

- We have a `filecon` statement, which takes three arguments: the path expression, the type of resources to which it applies, and the SELinux context to associate with it.

- The SELinux context has four fields associated with it: the SELinux user, the SELinux role, the SELinux type, and the SELinux sensitivity range.

- The SELinux sensitivity range has two values, a low-end and a high-end value.

This statement is equivalent to what the reference policy would define in the file context part of the policy module (the file with the `.fc` suffix) like so:

```
/var/run/pgpool(/.*)?  gen_context(system_u:object_r:pgpool_
var_run_t,s0)
```

Luckily, we do not need to seek and interpret the code just to understand and see what is going on. The SELinux project has extensive CIL documentation available, explaining how the language works and what it all supports. The information is available at `https://github.com/SELinuxProject/selinux/tree/master/secilc/docs`. Keep in mind though that CIL policy development is still in its infancy, so coverage of the CIL constructs that are not used by the HLL conversion mechanics is very low.

Let's now see what we can do with CIL.

Creating fine-grained definitions

Throughout this book, most small SELinux policy adjustments have been made using CIL. These are small, fine-grained definitions that require little development effort, and have the benefit of being directly loadable.

Depending on roles or types

The CIL language requires some order in how types or roles are linked in the policy. Sometimes, when we develop CIL policies, the order of the types might not be addressed properly.

To work around this issue, a default attribute called `cil_gen_require` is used. When types or roles are assigned to the `cil_gen_require` attribute, they are automatically linked correctly in the policy. This is not a CIL requirement though, but a convention that the SELinux utilities use.

The attribute actually exists twice, once as a type attribute and once as a role attribute.

They might have the same name, but are two different attributes:

```
(roleattributeset cil_gen_require system_r)
(typeattributeset cil_gen_require direct_run_init)
```

The functions used, `roleattributeset` and `typeattributeset`, assign the second argument (which is the attribute name) to the third argument (which is the role or type). Roles or types can be attributes themselves, as shown for the `direct_run_init` attribute.

For developers, it is recommended to always have the types or roles that you are going to use made part of the `cil_gen_require` attribute, and to use attributes as much as possible to simplify development activities. Rather than granting all possible `allow` rules to each and every domain that can interact with your policy resources, grant them to an attribute, and then assign this attribute to the domains. This creates a much smaller policy and is easier to maintain.

Defining a new port type

When more intricate SELinux policies are developed, there are a few settings that we cannot add in a SELinux module—at least not when using the traditional or reference policy style coding. When we want to use these, we need to rebuild the entire policy and make the adjustments in the so-called base policy; the main and first policy loaded before the modules are added. This, however, requires access to the full SELinux policy sources and a process to use them (as you will overwrite the Linux distribution's SELinux policy and should make sure that any system update does not overwrite your policy again).

One way to establish whether a statement is supported in a SELinux module, besides just testing it out, is to look at the online documentation. As an example, let's take the port declaration statement `portcon`, which is part of the network-oriented statements. This statement is documented on `https://selinuxproject.org/page/ NetworkStatements`, where we can see that `portcon` is not valid in a module policy, nor can it be toggled through a SELinux Boolean.

Luckily, this is not the case when using CIL. Let's create a custom port type, for example, `pgpool_port_t`, and map it to a free port, say, TCP port `50123`:

```
; Port type
(type pgpool_port_t)
; Some attributes to match the current SELinux policy
requirements
(typeattributeset defined_port_type pgpool_port_t)
(typeattributeset reserved_port_type pgpool_port_t)
```

```
(typeattributeset port_type pgpool_port_t)
; Our dependency mappings
(roleattributeset cil_gen_require object_r)
(typeattributeset cil_gen_require pgpool_port_t)
; Make sure object_r is allowed for pgpool_port_t
(roletype object_r pgpool_port_t)
; The port mapping itself
(portcon tcp 50123 (system_u object_r pgpool_port_t ((s0)
(s0))))
```

Before we load the policy, we can clearly see that this port is not an assigned one:

```
# seinfo --port 50123 | grep tcp
 portcon tcp 32768-60999 system_u:object_r:ephemeral_port_t:s0
```

As we've seen throughout this book, we can load this policy file immediately, without having to build or compile it:

```
# semodule -i pgpool_port.cil
```

After loading, the type is assigned to the port, and we can use it to fine-tune our SELinux policies:

```
# seinfo --port 50123 | grep tcp
 portcon tcp 50123 system_u:object_r:pgpool_port_t:s0
 portcon tcp 32768-60999 system_u:object_r:ephemeral_port_t:s0
# semanage port -l | grep 50123
pgpool_port_t      tcp      50123
```

Many of the constraints that policy developers had when using the traditional SELinux style development no longer apply to CIL. As the SELinux utilities convert all high-level constructs to CIL, it is possible that SELinux developers might remove these constraints altogether, although this has to be carefully assessed to make sure no unwanted side effects arise.

Adding constraints to the policy

Another area that was not accessible for regular policy developers was to add constraints to the policy. Constraints limit actions based on the entire SELinux context (and not just types), and they are the closest thing we can find to negating existing rules.

> **Important note**
>
> We do not recommend adding constraints to an existing policy just to work around rules that we don't like. Constraints are not visible in regular policy queries, as with `sesearch`. Administrators might be very confused when `sesearch` indicates that an action is allowed while the system is refusing to allow it.

With CIL, we can add constraints to a live policy to do exactly that. Keep in mind though that constraints don't actually allow anything – they merely put limits on what the SELinux subsystem will see as a valid action. A constraint statement that supports reading any possible type does not actually allow this, as there still need to be type enforcement rules in place to actually allow these actions.

For instance, if we want to remove the `staff_t` domain's ability to read the `/etc/passwd` file (which has the SELinux type, `passwd_file_t`), then we can add in a constraint that supports the reading of all possible types, unless the source domain is `staff_t`, in which case we support the reading of all possible types except `passwd_file_t`:

```
(constrain (file (read))
  (or
    (and
      (eq t1 staff_t)
      (not (eq t2 passwd_file_t))
    )
    (not (eq t1 staff_t))
  )
)
```

Once loaded, we can confirm that the constraint is active:

```
# seinfo --constrain | grep passwd_file_t
constrain file read (t1 == staff_t and not ( ( t2 == passwd_
file_t ) ) or not ( t1 == staff_t ) ));
```

And indeed, trying to read the `passwd` file is prohibited:

```
$ cat /etc/passwd
cat: /etc/passwd: Permission denied
```

To show how the use of constraints is confusing for administrators, let's see what `sesearch` has to say on this:

```
# sesearch -A -s staff_t -t passwd_file_t -c file -p read;
allow nsswitch_domain passwd_file_t:file { ... read };
allow staff_t passwd_file_t:file { ... read };
```

So, while the policy has two rules that would allow it (one for the `nsswitch_domain` attribute, and one explicitly for the `staff_t` domain), the constraint has limited this action, but this is not obvious from the `sesearch` output.

Building complete application policies

We can build complete application policies with CIL as well. However, keep in mind that there are no interfaces or support macros out there that we can use to rapidly develop policies. Furthermore, there are no templates or suchlike available to jumpstart such initiatives.

But that shouldn't stop us, and it will allow us to show a few more details of the CIL language. We will also see that the CIL language does support interface constructs (they are even recommended), but the community has not yet fully embraced it through a reference policy-like project.

Using namespaces

The CIL language supports namespaces, which allows for a higher flexibility in developing policies. The generated CIL policies always use the main, global namespace, so we will not find examples of namespaces in the generated policies.

We can, however, show how this works easily. Let's create a skeleton file that will contain our CIL-developed `pgpool` policy:

```
; Dependencies

; Pgpool support
(block pgpool
  ; Declarations
  (type domain)

  ; Local policy

  ; Behavior
```

```
; File contexts
)
```

The namespace created in the preceding code is the pgpool namespace, identified through the block statement. Namespaces in CIL are hierarchical. If we want, we could create a namespace within pgpool by nesting another block statement within.

When we encounter namespaces in general constructions, we need to use the dot separator. In the example, we have defined a type called domain inside the pgpool namespace. If we would want to query it later through sesearch, the full name would be pgpool.domain (which would have the same purpose as the pgpool_t name in a more classically developed policy).

> **Informational note**
>
> In subsequent code listings of the policy, we will only show the added and most relevant statements rather than including all previously added statements. Without supporting interfaces (which CIL calls macros), the policy file will quickly become quite large, which does not aid readability. By focusing on the relevant and added statements, the development pattern for CIL policies is easier to explain.

As the main policy has all objects within the global namespace, we will need to refer explicitly to this global namespace. This is done by prefixing the name with a dot. For instance, if we want to assign the pgpool.domain type to the system_r role, our policy needs to be adjusted with the following:

```
(roleattributeset cil_gen_require system_r)
(block pgpool
  (type domain)
  (roletype .system_r domain)
)
```

Here, the roletype statement is used to assign the domain type (defined in the pgpool namespace) to the system_r role (defined in the global namespace).

Extending the policy with attribute assignments

When we develop a policy, it is recommended to use attributes as much as possible. Many attributes will automatically grant the necessary privileges to jumpstart a policy development, reducing the number of allow statements that need to take part of the policy.

The main reference policy, which is still in use on the system as a whole, defines quite a few attributes, as seen in all previous chapters. So, let's assign the `daemon` attribute to our domain:

```
(typeattributeset cil_gen_require daemon)
(block pgpool
    (type domain)
    (typeattributeset .daemon domain)
)
```

By assigning the `daemon` attribute, all existing policy rules for daemons are automatically applied to the `pgpool.domain` SELinux domain.

To find out which attributes are sensible to add, we can take a peek at existing daemon domains:

```
# seinfo -t postgresql_t -x
Types: 1
   type postgresql_t, nsswitch_domain, can_change_object_
identity, corenet_unlabeled_type, domain, kernel_system_state_
reader, netlabel_peer_type, daemon, syslog_client_type, pcmcia_
typeattr_1;
```

Now, we do not need to blindly take up all attributes, starting instead with those we feel confident with.

Adding entry point information

Our next step is to add entry point information to the policy. This is a necessary step before we can start testing out, because we want the domain to become active. For that to happen, it has to be executable by the init system (or systemd) and transition to the domain we've just declared.

Let's start by defining our `entrypoint` type (`pgpool.exec`) and associate it with the right attributes:

```
(roleattributeset cil_gen_require object_r)
(typeattributeset cil_gen_require file_type)
(typeattributeset cil_gen_require direct_init_entry)
(block pgpool
    (type exec)
    (roletype .object_r exec)
    (typeattributeset .file_type exec)
    (typeattributeset .direct_init_entry exec)
```

```
    (allow domain exec (file (entrypoint ioctl read getattr lock
map execute open)))

    (typetransition .initrc_domain exec process domain)
)
```

In this code block, we've performed several steps to ensure that a transition will occur:

- We've associated the pgpool.exec type with the file_type attribute (which is a generic attribute for files) and the direct_init_entry attribute (which is for file types that are used to launch system services).
- We've marked the pgpool.exec type as entrypoint for the pgpool.domain type, as well as granted this domain the necessary privileges to read, open, and execute the pgpool.exec labeled resources (as needed for a starting process).
- We've declared a type transition so that any initrc_domain labeled process that executes the pgpool.exec labeled resource will result in a domain transition toward pgpool.domain.

We can now finish this step by adding a file context definition:

```
(block pgpool
  (filecon "/usr/bin/pgpool" file
    (.system_u .object_r exec ((s0) (s0))))
  )
)
```

With these changes made, we can load the policy and relabel the file:

```
# restorecon -v /usr/bin/pgpool
Relabeled /usr/bin/pgpool from system_u:object_r:bin_t:s0 to
system_u:object_r:pgpool.exec:s0
```

We can now attempt to start the pgpool service, and hope that it fails (as that will show that the transition was successful, given that the pgpool.domain SELinux domain hardly has sufficient privileges to successfully start the entire service).

Gradually extending the policy further

Once the domain transitions are successful, we can gradually extend the policy further through trial and error, just like we would do when developing SELinux policies using the reference policy style. However, rather than using audit2allow to guide us, we will need to interpret the denials ourselves and see how to better approach it.

Consider the failures that appear after starting the service:

```
# ausearch -i -m avc -ts recent
(Output reformatted for readability)
avc: denied { map } for scontext=pgpool.domain
                         tcontext=ld_so_t
                         tclass=file
avc: denied { read write open } for scontext=pgpool.domain
                                     tcontext=null_device_t
                                     tclass=chr_file
```

Now, rather than immediately adding `allow` rules for these types, let's see how this is accomplished for other daemons on the system:

```
# sesearch -A -s postgresql_t -t ld_so_t -c file -p map
allow domain file_type:file map; [ domain_can_mmap_files ]:True
allow domain ld_so_t:file { execute getattr ioctl map open read
};
```

So, this permission is based on the `domain` attribute, which we indeed forgot to add to the policy. Let's rectify this and retry:

```
(typeattributeset cil_gen_require domain)
(block pgpool
  (type domain)
  (typeattributeset .domain domain)
)
```

In this example, we can also see clearly what the impact is of the namespaces within CIL. We assigned the (global namespace-hosted) `domain` attribute to the (`pgpool` namespace-hosted) `domain` type. They are both named `domain`, but have a different namespace. This also shows how important attributes are.

Of course, not all privileges can be granted through attributes. By adding the target types as a dependency, we can directly include `allow` statements in our policy, like we did with the `entrypoint` declaration.

For instance, if we would want to explicitly allow our domain to signal the `postgresql_t` domain, execute the following command:

```
(typeattributeset cil_gen_require postgresql_t)
(block pgpool
  (allow domain .postgresql_t (process (signal)))
)
```

As we are adding more and more privileges to the policy, we might want to optimize some of the definitions. There are two optimizations supported by CIL, and they are, not unsurprisingly, aligned with the reference policy's simplifications as CIL was developed by the same community.

Introducing permission sets

The first simplification we can do is to simplify the permission sets we use. Remember the allow rule we added to allow our domain to execute its entrypoint file:

```
(allow domain exec
  (file
    (entrypoint ioctl read getattr lock map execute open)
  )
)
```

Were we to use a reference policy-style approach, we would combine many of these permissions through the exec_file_perms macro. Well, CIL supports something similar, through a statement called classpermissionset.

If we want to simulate the reference policy-style approach completely, we would define classpermissionset in the global namespace, and use it, as follows:

```
(classpermission exec_file_perms)
(classpermissionset exec_file_perms (file (ioctl read getattr
lock map execute open)))
(block pgpool
  (allow domain exec (file (entrypoint)))
  (allow domain exec exec_file_perms)
)
```

In this example, we've defined classpermissionset in the global namespace, and then referred to it. Unlike the reference policy, however, we cannot just add exec_file_perms inside the permissions together with entrypoint. The classpermissionset statement has an explicit reference to the class associated with it. The allow statement in CIL is therefore a separate one that does not contain a class reference itself.

Furthermore, in the example, you will also notice that we did not prefix the exec_file_perms name with a dot, to refer to the global namespace. While we can prefix it perfectly to be consistent with the rest of the policy, using a dot prefix is not mandatory if there is no possible collision. If no local definition for a name exists within the current namespace, the policy will then check whether the parent namespace (and, hence, also the global namespace) has the name defined.

So, while the preceding policy will work just fine, we do recommend to prefix the global namespace-oriented names with a dot to make sure no local override would confuse the policy later on.

Adding macros

The final simplification we can introduce is to add **macros**. CIL has an explicit support for macros, which allows them to be part of the loaded policy, and not just be referred to on the filesystem. With CIL macros, the code is part of the policy itself. There is no need to refer to the CIL code while building policies.

While this is a best practice that is aligned with object-oriented programming (as we can add macros to our namespaces so that they remain within the same object), the downside is that the current SELinux utilities are not able to quickly show which macros (and which interface they require) are available in the policy.

Now, let's enhance our pgpool policy with a domain transition macro, similar to the pgpool_domtrans() interface that would be created through a reference policy-style development:

```
(block pgpool
  (macro domtrans ((type SOURCEDOMAIN))
    (allow SOURCEDOMAIN exec exec_file_perms)
    (allow SOURCEDOMAIN domain (process (transition)))
    (typetransition SOURCEDOMAIN exec process domain)
  )
)
```

The macro definition itself starts with a name (in our case, domtrans) followed by the interface. This interface defines how many arguments are passed to the macro, and which type they have. In our example, only one argument is passed, and it is a SELinux type.

The macro is then followed by the code that is applied. The argument itself is referenced in the code (SOURCEDOMAIN) and will be substituted with the argument that is given later on, when the macro is explicitly called. While our example uses a capitalized variable name, this is not mandatory, and only serves as a visual statement of what will be substituted.

In another CIL policy, we can refer to this macro through the `call` statement. For instance, to allow the `postgresql_t` domain to transition to the `pgpool.domain` SELinux domain, we would add the following `call` statement to our policy:

```
; Equivalent to "pgpool_domtrans(postgresql_t)" in refpolicy
(typeattributeset cil_gen_require postgresql_t)
(call pgpool.domtrans (postgresql_t))
```

CIL macros provide all that is needed to generate the same simplicity in developing SELinux policies as we have within the reference policy, and even more as there are many constraints not applicable to CIL policies.

While it is possible that this will happen in the future, it is not planned at this moment for a number of reasons:

- The current reference policy has a significant amount of code in it, which would all need to be reworked. Furthermore, Linux distributions have extended this policy with many of their own additions, so the work needed to rewrite the SELinux policy code into CIL is significant. Not impossible, but not a feat to accomplish in a few weeks.

- Almost all of the information and documentation online that helps developers in writing SELinux policies is based upon the current reference policy. This major source of information would become stale the moment a switch occurs, and the amount of documentation available online for CIL-based policy development is still pretty slim.

- The CIL policy, while very powerful, is also a bit more complex due to its S-expressions. The design intention of CIL was not to replace SELinux policy development with CIL, but to allow higher level languages to be developed that translate and convert into CIL easily. Hence, if a rework is going to be done anyway, it is much more likely that a user- and development-friendly language will be designed that can be easily converted into CIL.

As the SELinux development progresses, both on the policy level as well as in terms of user space and kernel support, we can expect more additions to be added to CIL and to its supporting tools.

Summary

CIL for SELinux is a powerful, lower-level syntax and language that is used to express all possible SELinux policy code. The SELinux userspace utilities will automatically convert existing policies into CIL code, but through this conversion, a lot of CIL constructs are not used: the conversion only uses a smaller set of CIL capabilities to establish a valid translation.

The more advanced CIL capabilities, such as namespace support, macros, and the permission sets through the `classpermissionset` statement, are useful when developing our own, CIL-based SELinux policies. In this chapter, we've learned how to use CIL to build complete application policies. Because there is no reference policy-like framework to simplify development, we had to write all of the necessary code constructs ourselves.

While this means that developing CIL-based policies is more resource intensive, we did also see that CIL has a few benefits that reference policy-style development cannot deal with, such as the ability to declare ports or add SELinux constraints to an active policy.

We ended the chapter with a brief overview of why CIL-based development is not more widely used, but we will notice continuous improvements within SELinux on this matter in the foreseeable future.

This concludes our book and the information we have to offer to you. However, it is only the start of a journey, not the end. SELinux is a widely used technology, and we hope that this book provides you with the right material and knowledge to understand, grow, and contribute to the ecosystem. Thank you for your interest and your dedication.

Questions

1. How do we know CIL is here to stay?

2. Is the `cil_gen_require` attribute mandatory for CIL development?

3. What are examples of declarations that developers can do with CIL but not with other SELinux language styles?

4. How can we create similar support constructions such as interfaces in CIL?

Assessments

Chapter 1

1. The most important difference is that, with a DAC system, the user has full control over who gets which kind of access to the user's data. It is left to the discretion of the user, hence the name. With MAC systems, the system administrator (or security administrator) defines how accesses are handled and enforced. Access is mandated by a policy, and users cannot work around this if the administrator does not allow it.

2. Linux has introduced hooks inside its kernel code, which developers can subscribe to with their own code. These hooks are part of the **Linux Security Module** (**LSM**) framework, an extensible framework that is natively part of the Linux kernel.

   SELinux is one of the MAC technologies that use this LSM framework (and the hooks it offers) to provide mandatory access control capabilities to the Linux kernel and its applications. Other technologies also exist, including AppArmor.

   The SELinux subsystem code itself is also made part of the main Linux kernel, as are the main other LSM implementations, although this is not a mandatory requirement for LSM-capable technologies. It does, however, support the notion that SELinux is a well-established, open source technology.

3. The four fields of an SELinux context are as follows: the SELinux user, the SELinux role, the SELinux type, and the sensitivity level (or the sensitivity range). The sensitivity level might not always be present: Linux distributions might opt to disable support for sensitivities in their policies. In that case, the SELinux context will only have the first three fields.

4. SELinux has the concept of a role, which SELinux types can be associated with. As SELinux mostly focuses on the types to handle its enforcement (SELinux is mostly a type enforcement system), the role-based access control is implemented by limiting the types that a role can be associated with.

A user that has a DBA-related role will only be able to interact with the system from within DBA-associated types. As that role does not have any associations with other types, the user cannot acquire the privileges of these other types either.

5. While there is a project called the reference policy, most Linux distributions will deviate from this policy for several reasons. The main reason why no single SELinux policy exists is because SELinux is a fine-grained system, and thus can be tweaked and adjusted to fit the design and usage principles of a Linux distribution.

    Asking why no single SELinux policy exists for all Linux distributions is almost the same as asking why there are multiple Linux distributions. Each distribution has its own focus, design, principles, and decisions behind it, and the SELinux policy needs to be aligned with these in order to be successful.

Chapter 2

1. Administrators should first analyze the situation to see why a problem is being triggered. Perhaps the problem is due to an incorrectly assigned context, or the process has not been started using the correct methods.

    If the denial itself were to be allowed, administrators should create an update to the SELinux policy (just like they would update firewall rules as required).

    If this is not feasible, then administrators should consider putting SELinux in permissive mode, but only for that particular application that is causing problems.

    If that is also not feasible, then administrators should put the system in permissive mode, but making sure that this is accepted by the organization and security principles of the environment.

    Only if even this is not feasible or solves the problem should an administrator shake their head, curse the higher powers, and disable SELinux.

2. If the system has the audit daemon running, then SELinux logging will be part of the audit logs. They can be displayed using tools such as `ausearch`, or read directly from the system at `/var/log/audit`.

    If no audit daemon is running, then the SELinux log events will be picked up by the system logger or be available through the kernel ring buffer. The kernel ring buffer can be read using the `dmesg` command. If the system logger is picking up the events, they will most likely reside in `/var/log/messages`.

3. Applications that actively query the SELinux policy or SELinux system will link with the `libselinux` library. If that is the case, then this can be seen using `readelf`, `ldd`, or `objdump`, showing that `/lib64/libselinux.so.1` (or similar) is used:

```
$ ldd /bin/ls | grep selinux
libselinux.so.1 => /lib64/libselinux.so.1
(0x00005d415f3f03f0)
```

While applications could build statically (meaning they include the necessary code in their final build and will not show any dynamic linking with the `libselinux` library), this is more the exception than the rule for most Linux systems.

4. The AVC, or Access Vector Cache, is a cache that contains the recent and most frequently used enforcement checks, allowing the SELinux subsystem to query more rapidly whether an action can be granted. Without the AVC, the SELinux subsystem would need to go through the entire policy over and over again for each action that is taken on the system.

    Suffice to say that this would slow down the system tremendously.

5. No, there are a couple of other log events that administrators should look out for when specifically dealing with SELinux. One is `USER_AVC`, which is used for AVC-like events, but triggered from an application that uses the SELinux policy, and does the enforcements itself (rather than through the Linux kernel). The other one is `SELINUX_ERR`, which is used when an internal error or violation is triggered that is not related to regular type enforcement.

    Other event types that are closely related, but are not exclusive to SELinux, exist as well. For instance, `MAC_POLICY_LOAD`, `MAC_POLICY_CHANGE`, and `MAC_STATUS` are events that are triggered whenever a MAC system state or policy is changed.

Chapter 3

1. There is an intermediate step needed to associate a role with a Linux account, and that is the SELinux user. A Linux account (or login) is mapped to an SELinux user. The SELinux user is then mapped to one or more SELinux roles that that SELinux user can be in.

   If we want to assign an additional role to a Linux user, we need to add it to the SELinux role that that Linux account is mapped to. However, if more Linux accounts are mapped to the same SELinux user, then we first need to make sure that all these accounts are indeed allowed to use this role. If not, a dedicated SELinux user has to be created for the Linux account.

2. Yes, the mappings are considered when a user logs in through a particular service. It is possible for administrators to tune the mappings to be dependent on the service, as seen in the *Customizing logins toward services* section.

3. Most SELinux domains do not allow the SELinux user of a context to be changed. This allows the tracking of activities based on the SELinux user, even when the regular Linux user has changed their user ID. Note that this is not exclusive to SELinux, however. Linux does support a distinction between the real user ID (which stays static as much as possible) and the effective user ID (which can change, for instance, when executing a setuid application).

   SELinux users also allow granularity as regards the SELinux policy, for instance, when using user-based access control. In that case, SELinux users cannot access resources that are owned by a different SELinux user.

4. PAM is a flexible, modular system that Linux uses to authenticate users. Rather than having all the different technologies and services on a system implement authentication over and over again, they use PAM to handle the authentication flow. Administrators only then need to focus on PAM or PAM-related configurations to ensure that their systems are properly accessed.

   For SELinux, PAM is needed to allow the authentication to check the mappings (between Linux users and SELinux users), which is supported through `pam_selinux.so`.

Chapter 4

1. The most common option is -Z, and is supported by tools such as ls, mv, and ps. The same character is also used by systemd's tmpfiles application to explicitly set SELinux contexts on resources. However, while this is the most commonly used option, not all tools follow this convention, so we recommend to always consult the tool's help or manual page.

2. In most cases, the context is stored as an extended attribute of the file or directory within the filesystem. This extended attribute is the `security.selinux` attribute, and can be queried with tools such as `getfattr` or `stat`.

   However, not all filesystems support extended attributes. In that case, the SELinux context is obtained through the mount options of that filesystem, and all resources on the filesystem then use the same context.

3. The `chcon` application directly alters the SELinux context for a file, but does not adjust the system's file context definitions. If, at any point in time, the system or an administrator relabels the file or the entire filesystem (which is a common remediation for SELinux issues), then the SELinux context of the file is changed back.

   Hence, `chcon` is only recommended for transient SELinux context changes or to validate whether a context change solves an issue. Once confident that the new context is needed, it should be registered in the system's file context definition through `semanage fcontext`.

4. Yes. While SELinux's tools have the concept of *most specific rule wins* for the context definitions provided by the Linux distribution, this concept does not apply to file context definitions that are local to the system (in other words, executed by the system administrator).

   For locally defined file context definitions, the first rule that matches a patch will be used, regardless of the context definitions that follow.

5. If you only want to relabel a selected set of files, such as recursive applications to a given directory, the `restorecon` command should be used. If the entire filesystem needs to be relabeled, either use `fixfiles` (CentOS and related distributions) or `rlpkg` (Gentoo).

   Another method is to create an empty file called `/.autorelabel` and reboot the system. The system will detect this file, relabel the entire filesystem, remove this file, and then reboot again.

6.   The source domain needs the transition privilege vis-à-vis the target domain.
     It also requires the execute privilege on the executable file. This executable file has
     to be marked as an entry point for the target domain. Finally, the role for which
     a transition is to occur has to have the target domain as an allowed type.

7.   Multiple SELinux types can be assigned an SELinux attribute, and the SELinux
     policy can then use this attribute as a source or target for its rules. Such
     attribute-based rules then automatically apply to all types assigned from
     this attribute.

Chapter 5

1.   The command to apply a type to a TCP port is created with `semanage`. For
     instance, to apply the `ssh_port_t` type to TCP port `10122`, execute the following
     command:

     ```
     # semanage port -a -t ssh_port_t -p tcp 10122
     ```

     However, this only works as long as the port itself is not already explicitly mapped
     to an SELinux type. You can query whether this is the case with `sepolicy`, for
     example:

     ```
     # sepolicy network -p 10122
     ```

     If the port is part of an unreserved range, then it can be altered.

2.   No, SECMARK is local to the system. Once a network packet is received by the
     Linux host, the SECMARK rules will associate a label with that network packet, but
     this label is only retained in memory on the system itself. Once a packet leaves the
     Linux system, it will not show any trace of SECMARK labeling.

3.   The subcommands used by `semanage` are `ibendport` (to apply a label or
     sensitivity to an InfiniBand network port) and `ibpkey` (to apply a label or
     sensitivity to a partition key).

4.   While labeled IPsec itself does not require specialized equipment, it does require
     all participating hosts to have the same view on what each label implies. This means
     that all hosts, in the case of SELinux-based labeling, need to have SELinux active,
     and preferably with exactly the same SELinux policy.

Chapter 6

1. Ansible (using `setype` within the file module) and Puppet (using `seltype` in its file module) are the only two tools that have native support for explicitly setting SELinux contexts on resources. However, Chef will automatically relabel resources according to the defined file context rules, but you cannot natively override this behavior.

2. Except for SaltStack, all orchestration tools have support for community-built and community-supported modules that extend native support of the tools. Ansible's Galaxy, Puppet's Forge, and Chef's Supermarket are the main communities for these customizations.

    All orchestration tools (including SaltStack) are flexible enough to use commands and simple checks to check state and make changes, effectively allowing administrators to customize the definitions to their liking.

3. All tools have their own view and design on how they approach things. Ansible, for instance, pushes its changes to the remote nodes, whereas the others generally use remote agents to connect to the central system to obtain the latest changes. SaltStack even supports both approaches.

    While all tools have some SELinux support included, some have many more SELinux features enabled out of the box than others. Luckily, through the use of the community-supported additions (modules), the SELinux support for almost all of the orchestration tools can easily be augmented.

Chapter 7

1. The unit files in `/usr/lib/systemd/system` are managed by the Linux distribution itself. Whenever a new update to the software is deployed on the system, these files are overwritten.

    Modifications to unit files should be placed in `/etc/systemd/system` instead, as they overrule the settings in `/usr/lib/systemd`, and software deployments should not place any of their unit files in that location.

2. The application is tmpfiles, and is part of the systemd suite. To have it reset a context, a configuration file has to be created (in `/etc/tmpfiles.d` for locally defined changes) and use the z directive (to reset the context of a single file) or the Z directive (to recursively set the context of an entire directory).

3. The `journalctl` command allows filtering on variables that it obtained from the event itself. One of these variables is the SELinux context of the service that generated the event.

To filter on a particular value, you use the variable name as an argument to the `journalctl` command like so:

```
# journalctl _SELINUX_CONTEXT=system_u:system_r:init_t:s0
```

If you do not know what SELinux context to use, then the Bash completion might be of assistance. Just declare `_SELINUX_CONTEXT=` in the preceding command, and then press *Tab* twice to see all the valid values.

4. If the SELinux policy itself does not have a proper named file transition rule in place (which would automatically have the node created with the correct SELinux context), then you can tell udev to do this for you.

Find the udev rule that would create the device node for the device, and copy this rule into `/etc/udev/rules.d`. Then, update the rule by adding a `SECLABEL{selinux}=` action, like so:

```
KERNEL=="fd0", ...,
SECLABEL{selinux}="system_u:object_r:my_device_t:s0"
```

Such rules have to be placed in `/etc/udev/rules.d` rather than `/usr/lib/udev/rules.d` as the latter location is managed by the distribution, and new installations or updates will overwrite the files located therein.

5. No. The SELinux policy is only checked by D-Bus if the D-Bus policy file itself refers to an SELinux context (using the `busconfig` > `selinux` > `associate` XML entities). If no SELinux mapping is defined in the policy, then D-Bus cannot know which association to validate.

This is unlike the message flows, however, which are immediately governed by D-Bus through the SELinux policy.

6. Apache can be made SELinux-aware because it has a modular design, and allows third-party modules to be applied to its own environment. While no SELinux support is enabled within the core Apache code, additional modules (such as `mod_selinux`) can be added that do enable SELinux support.

Chapter 8

1. It is, although it is not natively enabled. SEPostgreSQL is offered through one of the additionally supplied modules within PostgreSQL called `sepgsql`. As such, it is part of the default technology, but not enabled by default.

2. As the `sepgsql` module requires a session context, the PostgreSQL database needs to either only be accessed from the local system (using the Unix domain sockets), or labeled networking needs to be enabled and set up in the network.

    Without labeled networking, any remote connection to the database will fail to provide any context information, and `sepgsql` will refuse the connection.

3. When a database object is created in PostgreSQL, it will automatically receive an SELinux label. Administrators or database owners can change the labels using the `SECURITY LABEL` statement in PostgreSQL:

    ```
    db_test=# SECURITY LABEL ON COLUMN tb_users.phash IS
    'system_u:object_r:sepgsql_secret_table_t:s0';
    ```

    To query the current label, consult the `pg_seclabels` table in PostgreSQL:

    ```
    db_test=# SELECT objname,provider,label FROM pg_seclabels
    WHERE objname='tb_users.phash';
    ```

    If you do not know the object name by heart, use `LIKE` and use `%` as a glob character.

4. The `sepgsql` module does not interact with the Linux audit subsystem, relying instead on the logging capabilities and interface used by PostgreSQL. As a result, any decision logging that `sepgsql` does will be found in the PostgreSQL system logs.

Chapter 9

1. The unique idea that sVirt has that differentiates it from a more standard SELinux configuration is to use SELinux's MCS support to the next level. By randomly assigning two categories to a guest, sVirt can deal with isolating thousands of guests even when far fewer categories are available to use.

2. The two main security measures that SELinux implements on top of the virtualization layer are as follows:

   - Intra-guest isolation, ensuring that guests cannot attack one another, or leak information between guests

   - Guest/host isolation, ensuring that guests can only access and interact with the resources on the host that are needed

   While both are, of course, also implemented within the hypervisor code, any design flaw could lead to high-impact problems. By implementing these isolations within SELinux, we use the strength of the SELinux subsystem as an independent (and much more flexible) access control system.

3. The `virt_image_t` label is used for guest images when the guest is not running. Once it is running, the image is relabeled to `svirt_image_t` and assigned the correct set of categories. The `virt_content_t` label, on the other hand, is used for read-only media, such as CD images.

4. The labels can be changed by editing the guest's XML information:

   ```
   # virsh edit myGuestName
   ```

   At the end of the XML file presented, the appropriate `seclabel` tags can be added to define target labels.

5. Vagrant, by default, does not have support for sVirt, but thanks to its plugin model, we can install the libvirt plugin for Vagrant. Once installed, Vagrant will use libvirt as its virtualization layer, automatically allowing us to use sVirt with Vagrant.

Chapter 10

1. SELinux works within the Linux kernel. Xen, however, is a hypervisor that sits between the hardware and the operating systems and does not use a full operating system as its base (unlike, for instance, QEMU and KVM).

   When we interact with Xen through Linux, we are actually interacting with Xen through the dom0 guest. Within this guest, SELinux can be running (and we even recommend it), but SELinux will remain within the virtualized guest.

   Xen, however, copied the SELinux approach and implemented it in its Xen Security Module framework.

2. You can assign a label to a Xen guest by editing its configuration file (inside /etc/ xen) and adding the seclabel parameter, like so:

    ```
    seclabel = 'system_u:system_r:prot_domU_t'
    ```

    You will need to relaunch the guest for the changes to take effect. Once the guest is booted again (using xl create), you can see its active label using xl list -Z.

    What are the common Xen commands that deal with XSM labels?

    The common commands to use are the following:

    - With xl list -Z, we can list the guests and their currently assigned labels.

    - With xl getenforce, we can query the current enforcement state of XSM.

    - With xl setenforce, we can set the new enforcement state of XSM.

    - With xl dmesg, we can see the Xen logging, including the XSM AVC log entries.

    - With flask-get-bool, we can query the current XSM-FLASK Booleans and their values.

    - With flask-set-bool, we can set a new value for an XSM-FLASK Boolean.

    - With flask-label-pci, we can assign a new XSM-FLASK type to a PCI device.

    We can also use SELinux tools that can analyze a policy file, such as seinfo or sesearch.

3. The command to load a custom policy is xl loadpolicy, or flask-loadpolicy. As long as the new policy file is not put in /boot to be automatically picked up, this loaded policy will only be active until a reboot is done, or until a new policy is loaded.

Chapter 11

1. The machinectl command does not allow administrators to change the SELinux type of the running containers. This results in all containers running by default under an unconfined domain, whereas we want confined domains to be used—preferably even with sVirt support so that containers cannot influence one another either.

2. When a container is launched with a location mapping, we should use the `:Z` option (in case of a private mapping) or the `:z` option (in case of a shared mapping) to ensure that the resources are relabeled with a container-accessible SELinux type:

    ```
    # podman run -dit --name postgresql-test -v /srv/db/
    postgresql-test:/bitnami/postgresql:Z -p 5432:5432
    postgresql
    ```

    Without this option, the label of the resource remains untouched, which generally means that the container runtime cannot access the resource at all.

3. We can use the `udica` application to generate a custom policy. The application uses the information that is provided from a `podman inspect` (or `docker inspect`) command, which shows the current container definition, and builds a custom policy specific to that container.

    The policy, once loaded, can then be used by the container through the `--security-opt` argument.

4. The main place for SELinux settings is inside the manifest under the `spec` configuration parameter. There, we can create the `securityContext` definition, which supports SELinux options through the `seLinuxOptions` object.

Chapter 12

1. When SELinux Booleans are changed through the `/sys/fs/selinux/booleans` filesystem, the changes are not automatically committed. For that to occur, you also need to write the value `1` into `/sys/fs/selinux/commit_pending_bools`.

2. The `sesearch` command is used to query the active policy, and can be used to query the impact of SELinux Booleans as well. Add the `-b <boolean>` argument to limit the query to rules that are influenced by the SELinux Boolean.

3. When an SELinux policy module is loaded, it is assigned a priority that tells the system whether it should be the active module. Administrators can load new modules at a higher priority to test them out, and remove them again, without risking that no proper SELinux rules are active on the system at all.

    Likewise, administrators can load a policy at a lower priority, ensuring that it is not yet active, and later on remove the module at the higher priority so that the newly loaded policy becomes active.

    This is unlike enabling or disabling modules, which affects all priorities.

4. The SELinux utility `audit2allow` transforms all SELinux-related audit events into SELinux policy code. The code can use both the legacy style (using `-M`) or the reference policy style (using `-R  -M`). Regardless of the style chosen, a loadable SELinux policy module (with the suffix `.pp`) will be created:

```
# grep btmp /var/log/audit/audit.log | audit2allow -R \
    -M custom_staff_su_faillog
```

The resulting file (`custom_staff_su_faillog.pp`) can be loaded using `semodule -i`.

Chapter 13

1. The `seinfo` application is used to query the policy for its type content, but not for its rules. For instance, you list the types within the policy with `seinfo`, but you don't query what these types can do.

    The `sesearch` application, on the other hand, is used to query the rules within the policy, but does not reveal anything about the various definitions inside the policy that are not really rules (such as attribute definitions and supported classes).

    Hence, the main difference is that `seinfo` focuses on the structure of the policy, whereas `sesearch` focuses on the enforcements defined within the policy.

2. Reaching a domain implies domain transitions. Hence, what we are looking for is how you can transition from your current domain (say `staff_t`) to the target domain (say `unconfined_t`) and through which means—generally, this is done by executing a binary or script that triggers a type transition.

    Analyzing domain transitions can be done using `apol` (the graphical user interface), `sedta`, or `sepolicy transition`. However, the latter might not reveal the correct paths, so it is recommended to use `sedta` or `apol` for this.

3. Information flow analysis has to take up considerably more paths than a domain transition. Domain transitions are between process domains, and only a small number of actions can trigger a transition. Information flow, on the other hand, can be effected over many, many actions.

    Such analysis not only needs to consider read and write statements, but also file descriptor usage, socket usage, signaling, the locking and unlocking of resources, and more besides. As a result, information flow analysis uses permission maps to identify the various permissions to check, and how important (weight) a permission is for an information flow analysis session.

4. Not using the tools currently at hand. The tool that compares policies, `sediff`, shows the differences between the policies, but is not, by itself, capable of generating SELinux policies that contain the differences between policies.

    Furthermore, SELinux policy modules can only add additional rules to the active policy, not remove them. Hence, even if `sediff` generated compatible output, it would still not be able to generate any statements that would remove existing rules from the active policy.

Chapter 14

1. An unconfined domain is still fully controlled and enforced by SELinux. It is called unconfined because such domains are granted extensive privileges by the SELinux policy. However, unlike what the name implies, they are still somewhat confined.

    Permissive domains, on the contrary, are not confined. SELinux will only log violations against the policy, but it will not enforce them.

2. The SELinux sandbox utility can be used to run applications in a very restricted domain. The utility will both force the application to run in a very restricted domain (`sandbox_t` for regular, non-graphical end user applications, or `sandbox_xserver_t` for graphical applications), as well as isolate or hide access to other system resources through the use of Linux's namespaces.

3. When the init system (such as systemd) launches a daemon, it will execute a specific binary or script for it. The label of this binary or script will generally define the target domain. For instance, if the resource is labeled with `bin_t`, then systemd will make sure that the target service runs as `unconfined_service_t`. If it is labeled with `postgresql_exec_t`, then the target service will run with the `postgresql_t` type.

    While other permissions are also involved (such as the source context requiring transition permissions to the target), unless we are building a new policy from scratch, switching domains will be as simple as changing the label for its executable resource, and relabeling its main locations on the filesystem (such as log locations and runtime information).

4. The default skeleton application that `sepolicy generate` builds contains the `permissive` statement, which implies that the policy will run in a permissive mode. Since this means SELinux will not enforce any controls, it is very likely that the application will work flawlessly with this policy enabled.

That is, however, not the target state, and administrators will need to remove the `permissive` setting from the policy and adjust as needed.

Chapter 15

1. Many Linux distributions add services and tools that fit the distribution's purpose and principles, yet which might be contradictory to what the reference policy is about. For instance, Red Hat Enterprise Linux and its derived Linux distributions will enable unconfined domains for many applications, whereas the reference policy will strive toward confinement of all applications.

    As a result, many Linux distributions base their policy on the reference policy, but augment and adjust it for their specific purpose.

2. The three main policy files are the following:

    - A type enforcement file, with the suffix `.te`, which contains the rules for the SELinux policy module, focusing on its owned domains.

    - An interface file, with the suffix `.if`, which exposes the interaction patterns and privileges vis-à-vis the domains and resources owned by this SELinux policy module. These interfaces are then used by other SELinux policy modules.

    - A context file, with the suffix `.fc`, which contains the file contexts for the various paths related to this SELinux policy module.

    Policy modules can be created with only a single file. In that case, the build system will assume that the other files are empty.

3. The use of a permission set allows policy developers to easily adjust and extend the permission set when needed, without having to change all possible SELinux policy module code entries.

    This is especially critical when a new permission is added by Linux (and the SELinux subsystem). For instance, suppose that the memory map system call (`map`) was not present yet, and is introduced later. We would need to add the map privilege to all execute calls. By using permission sets, we can add this to the appropriate permission set only.

4. Interfaces will grant privileges to domains or roles. They do not add or remove SELinux objects to the policy. Templates, on the other hand, will generate new SELinux types, roles, Booleans, or other objects. As a consequence, templates are not allowed to be called from within any Boolean-triggered block.

5. The database administration role does not use `userdom_admin_user_template` because it is not a system-wide administration role, but very specific to databases. `userdom_admin_user_template` would grant the role many more privileges than are needed to administer databases.

Chapter 16

1. The SELinux **Common Intermediate Language (CIL)** is not an extension to SELinux that can be easily removed. It is at the heart of SELinux policy development and support, although mainly under the hood: all SELinux policy modules that are loaded on the system are first converted into CIL before actually being loaded in memory.

   The CIL format is the only format used to interact with the Linux kernel and the SELinux subsystem. Because it is used as part of the SELinux user space utilities, it is not always as obvious to administrators or developers, but it is definitely a core component within SELinux.

2. No, it is not mandatory, but is recommended. The attribute is used to refer to types and roles in a modular fashion, and to ensure that these references are valid. CIL internally requires types and roles to be defined before they are used, and without using an attribute to force such declarations, the order of loading modules might result in failures.

   While other attributes could be declared for this purpose, or other means introduced, the use of the `cil_gen_require` attribute is supported through the SELinux user space utilities. As such, aligning with this practice is recommended.

3. With CIL, developers can create additional port mappings, declaring a new type and assigning it to an available port. With other SELinux language styles, this is only possible when rebuilding the entire policy rather than through the modules.

   Another example is to introduce constraints. SELinux constraints are not supported to be loaded in SELinux modules using other language styles. However, while constraints are a powerful construct within SELinux, they can be confusing for administrators as constraint-related failures do not result in obvious messages, and administrators who query the current policy for allow rules may notice that allow rules exist even though things still fail.

4. CIL supports macros, which are made part of the SELinux module (and the namespace), and which can be called using the `call` statement from elsewhere in the SELinux policy. We can create macros as part of a module to be similar to interfaces in reference policy, while creating macros as part of the global namespace to be similar to the support macros in reference policy.

Other Books You May Enjoy

If you enjoyed this book, you may be interested in these other books by Packt:

Mastering Linux Security and Hardening

Donald Tevault

ISBN: 978-1-83898-177-8

- Create locked-down user accounts with strong passwords
- Configure firewalls with iptables, UFW, nftables, and firewalld
- Protect your data with different encryption technologies
- Harden the secure shell service to prevent security break-ins
- Use mandatory access control to protect against system exploits
- Harden kernel parameters and set up a kernel-level auditing system
- Apply OpenSCAP security profiles and set up intrusion detection
- Configure securely the GRUB 2 bootloader and BIOS/UEFI

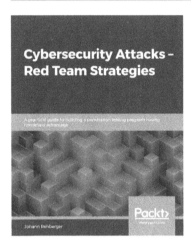

Cybersecurity Attacks – Red Team Strategies

Johann Rehberger

ISBN: 978-1-83882-886-8

- Understand the risks associated with security breaches
- Implement strategies for building an effective penetration testing team
- Map out the homefield using knowledge graphs
- Hunt credentials using indexing and other practical techniques
- Gain blue team tooling insights to enhance your red team skills
- Communicate results and influence decision makers with appropriate data

Leave a review - let other readers know what you think

Please share your thoughts on this book with others by leaving a review on the site that you bought it from. If you purchased the book from Amazon, please leave us an honest review on this book's Amazon page. This is vital so that other potential readers can see and use your unbiased opinion to make purchasing decisions, we can understand what our customers think about our products, and our authors can see your feedback on the title that they have worked with Packt to create. It will only take a few minutes of your time, but is valuable to other potential customers, our authors, and Packt. Thank you!

Index

www.ingramcontent.com/pod-product-compliance
Lightning Source LLC
Chambersburg PA
CBHW081458050326
40690CB00015B/2841